D0915447

Topics in Phonological Theory

Topics in
Phonological Theory

MICHAEL KENSTOWICZ
CHARLES KISSEBERTH

Department of Linguistics
University of Illinois
Urbana, Illinois

ACADEMIC PRESS New York San Francisco London
A Subsidiary of Harcourt Brace Jovanovich, Publishers

ACADEMIC PRESS, INC.
111 Fifth Avenue, New York, New York 10003

United Kingdom Edition published by
ACADEMIC PRESS, INC. (LONDON) LTD.
24/28 Oval Road, London NW1

Library of Congress Cataloging in Publication Data

Kenstowicz, Michael J
    Topics in phonological theory.

    Bibliography: p.
    1.   Grammar, Comparative and general—Phonology.
I.   Kisseberth, Charles W., joint author.   II.   Ti-
tle.
P217.K44   414   76-58347
ISBN 0–12–405150–2

To Braj B. Kachru

Contents

Preface

Our goal in writing this book has been to provide an up-to-date explication of some of the most important problems in current phonological theory. Although only a few, necessarily tentative, solutions are proposed, we nevertheless believe that the book contributes a much needed clarification and perspective on the issues involved.

The book is divided into six chapters. The first three deal with essentially independent topics, whereas the final three concern problems arising from the interaction between applications of phonological rules. However, the chapters should be read in order, since discussion later in the book is often based upon analyses presented in earlier chapters.

The first chapter deals with the problem of abstractness in terms of a series of successively weaker constraints that might be placed on the relationship between the underlying and phonetic representations of a morpheme. Although it is shown that none of these constraints may function as an absolute condition on underlying representations, they nevertheless serve to gauge the relative abstractness of phonological analyses in what we believe to be a new and interesting way that will contribute to further research on this fundamental problem. The second chapter begins with a discussion of the various ways in which the phonetic basis of a rule may be lost in the course of historical change, which lays the groundwork for a lengthy survey of the types of grammatical and lexical conditions that may control the application of a phonological rule. Constraints and conditions on phonological representations form the subject of the third chapter. Discussion is focused on the domain of these constraints, the level at which they hold, and their duplication of phonological rules. In the fourth chapter we take up the problem of natural rule interactions, focusing on Kiparsky's theories of maximal utilization and opacity–transparency and their deficiencies. The fifth chapter deals with Chomsky and Halle's simultaneous application principle as well as with more recent proposals concerning the multiple application problem. The similarity of the multiple application problem to the problem of rule interaction is stressed. The final chapter compares in detail the relative merits of global rules versus rule ordering for the description of opaque rule interactions. After showing that rules must be permitted to have global power, we take up the question of whether access to global information is predictable.

In the citation of forms our practice has been to follow the transcription of the original data sources. As a result, in some cases the same sound has been transcribed differently for different languages. In particular, the glottal stop has been represented variously as *?,',* and *'*, while palatals such as $\check{c}, \check{s}, \check{z}$, etc. have in some cases been transcribed as the digraphs *ch, sh,* and *zh,* respectively. In the few cases where misunderstanding may result, the phonetic values have been indicated in a footnote. Following generative practice, the square brackets [ ] specifically refer to phonetic representations. Slanted brackets / / may refer to the underlying representation or intermediate stages in the derivation, as well as in certain cases to the phonetic representation of a morpheme, particularly when it is viewed in isolation.

Finally, we wish to acknowledge the generous support of the University of Illinois Research Board for part of the research reported in this book. We also wish to express our appreciation to Mohammad Imam Abasheikh, whose tireless work on his native language, Chi-Mwi:ni, has made possible the analyses of this fascinating language incorporated in this book.

Michael Kenstowicz
Charles Kisseberth

Topics in Phonological Theory

1

The Problem of the Abstractness of Underlying Representations

Assuming that phonological alternations are (in some cases, at least) appropriately characterized by postulating a single underlying representation (henceforth UR) from which each phonetic representation (henceforth PR) of that morpheme can be predicted by rule, the following fundamental question naturally arises: How direct is the relationship between an UR and a PR derived from it? In other words, to what extent may these two representations differ from one another?

It is widely accepted that URs utilize the same categorization of speech sounds as PRs: That is, morphemes are stored in the lexicon in terms of the same phonetic parameters (features) as appear in characterizations of their phonetic structure. This results in a fairly direct relationship between an underlying form and its surface form: in both cases the units making up the representations are viewed as a collection of specifications with respect to a certain set of phonetic features. Furthermore, generative phonologists generally assume that the UR of a morpheme is also the PR of that morpheme, if no rule applies to modify the UR. Theoretically, then, it is possible for a UR to be identical to a PR derived from it.

However, an examination of the work of generative phonologists reveals that in most, if not all, instances a UR and its PR are not identical. This lack of identity is the consequence of two essential factors. First, there is considerable redundancy in the sounds of a language; not all of the phonetic properties of

a PR are independently selected, and as a consequence those properties that
are not independently selected can be viewed as rule-governed and thus not to
be included in lexical representations (such representations being regarded as
the repository of what is idiosyncratic and unpredictable about the phonological
behavior of a morpheme). Second, sounds are very often affected by the contexts
in which they are placed; since morphemes can occur in different contexts,
they are often required to modify their basic shape.

Since a UR and a PR derived from it are generally not identical, we return
to the question: To what extent may they diverge? This question is basically
the same as that posed by Paul Kiparsky in his paper "How Abstract is
Phonology?" (1968). It is a fundamental question, and one that we cannot
answer as yet. Before examining the question in detail, however, some preliminary remarks about what counts as "evidence" for a given phonological
analysis are required.

Given a body of linguistic data, we wish to discover which analysis (or set
of analyses, should it happen that different speakers arrive at different analyses
of the same data) out of all the logically possible analyses best represents the
internalized knowledge of native speakers of the language. The most direct
means of establishing that a certain analysis is correct for a given speaker of the
language is to show that the behavior of this speaker cannot be accounted for
in a plausible fashion without assuming that his internalized grammar includes
the basic features of the analysis in question. For instance, to establish that a
particular pattern of morphophonemic alternation is the result of a rule rather
than simply a matter of memorization on the speaker's part, we would look
for evidence that the speaker goes beyond the data that he has actually encountered (and thus could have memorized) to apply the rule in situations that
the speaker has not previously encountered. We will refer to such behavioral
data as "external" evidence.

Various kinds of external evidence have been adduced in recent years to
support particular analyses of a speaker's knowledge of the pronunciation of
his language: (1) the combination of familiar elements in novel (not previously
encountered by the speaker) word-forms, where the pronunciation of the entire
combination cannot be explained simply in terms of the speaker's memorization
of the pronunciation of the elements themselves; (2) slips of the tongue, where
the resulting pronunciation cannot be explained simply as a rearrangement of
elements in the intended pronunciation; (3) the phenomenon of a "foreign
accent," where a speaker extends a rule of his own language to the pronunciation
of another language that he is attempting to speak; (4) language games (usually
involving the transposition of syllables, the insertion of sounds, the deletion
of sounds, etc.), where pronunciations in the "secret language" cannot always
be explained entirely in terms of a manipulation of the overt phonological
shape of words in the ordinary language; (5) language change—in particular,
cases where sense can be made out of a historical change of x to y only if one
assumes that speakers assigned a particular interpretation (analysis) to x and

to the system of which x was a part. (Some examples of the use of external evidence will be provided later in this chapter.)

Unfortunately, when we examine a particular phonological problem in a particular language, it is often the case that the external evidence available does not serve to establish the exact character of the analysis that speakers have internalized. For example, there may be external evidence that a certain alternation in the pronunciation of morphemes is rule-governed, but no external evidence that points to the exact form of the rule or the underlying representations on which the rule operates. Relevant external evidence is often difficult, if not impossible, to find. Under these circumstances it is natural that linguists would like to have recourse to other types of evidence to support their analyses of linguistic data. More specifically, they would like to be able to determine from the linguistic data itself the appropriate analysis. This is not an unreasonable goal. After all, language learners must arrive at an analysis based on an examination of a body of data alone. The language learner does not appeal to the kinds of external evidence cited earlier. He examines the data he is exposed to and uses certain principles (the nature of which we must discover) to arrive at an analysis. If we can learn what general principles the language learner utilizes in his grammar construction, then we can make use of these same principles in choosing an appropriate linguistic description. Let us refer to these principles as "internal" evidence.

In order to determine the principles speakers utilize in their grammar construction (what counts as internal evidence for speakers), obviously we must examine a certain number of examples of grammars that speakers have constructed and try to determine what considerations in the data led to the adoption of the grammars that were in fact selected. In order to know which grammars speakers have arrived at (and which ones they have rejected), we must have the relevant external evidence. There is no other evidence that we can use; we cannot use internal evidence, for our goal is to discover what in fact counts as internal evidence.

If we can amass sufficient external evidence to determine in a range of cases what sorts of analyses speakers have arrived at, then we can attempt to deduce from these examples what considerations about the data might be responsible for leading to the adoption of these grammars. The "relevant" considerations will constitute the internal evidence that speakers make use of in grammar construction. Once we have discovered the general principles that govern the choice of a grammar (and how speakers react to situations where these principles are in conflict), then we can make use of these principles (i.e., internal evidence) in deciding on an analysis in situations where external evidence is either unavailable or insufficient. If we can identify the relevant kinds of internal evidence, then we can conclude that an analysis (or set of analyses) that is supported by this evidence is correct, even in the absence of external evidence.

Although linguists have always made use of various kinds of internal evidence in justifying phonological descriptions, they have rarely attempted to justify the use of this internal evidence by demonstrating that external evidence leads the linguist to choose analyses that are in fact precisely those that the internal evidence supports. Thus the conclusions that linguists arrive at on the basis of this internal evidence are only as strong as the internal evidence itself. The various kinds of internal evidence that linguists appeal to cannot be fully accepted until they can actually be shown to play a role in the grammar-construction of speakers.

Various types of internal evidence have been invoked in the justification of phonological descriptions, most of which revolve around such notions as "generality," "economy," and "naturalness." In fact, many such examples can be found both in this chapter and in later chapters, for we shall continue to employ many of the traditional arguments to support proposed analyses. We do this recognizing that the analyses we propose are only as well-motivated as these arguments. We follow this course of action simply because we have little choice. While there is considerable external evidence that demonstrates that many aspects of the phonetic structure of languages are rule-governed, we have exceedingly little external evidence that goes beyond this to show the precise nature of the rules and the underlying representations that the rules presuppose. In the case of most of the examples discussed in this book, we simply lack adequate external evidence and are thus forced to appeal to internal evidence, despite the fact that this evidence itself needs justification.

It seems to us that it is possible to give at least some external evidence that tentatively establishes the relevance of the traditional kinds of internal evidence. But external evidence also exists that supports the relevance of certain other principles, not traditionally used in generative phonology at least (e.g., Vennemann, 1974, attempts to use evidence from linguistic change to support the principle that speakers identify the underlying form of a morpheme with the form of the morpheme that occurs in morphologically unmarked contexts). It may well be that all of these principles have some validity. The most critical problem is to determine the relative importance of these various considerations in situations where they conflict with one another. Until the relative importance of all the types of internal evidence can be established, we are obliged to take all of them into consideration.

Let us return at this point to the question of the abstractness of underlying representations: To what extent may the UR of a morpheme diverge from its associated PRs? An answer to this question would aid us in finding an answer to the question: What is an appropriate analysis of any given set of data? And an answer to the latter would essentially be a statement about the nature of language. Thus any restriction on the "distance" between a UR and its PRs would contribute substantially to the characterization of the nature of language.

Two types of restriction on the pairing of underlying and surface representations can be distinguished: absolute restrictions (which no language may violate) and relative restrictions (which may be violated, but only "under duress"). Clearly, absolute restrictions would be more powerful: They would simply eliminate from consideration many logically possible analyses of a set of data. Relative restrictions, on the other hand, could be violated—provided other considerations forced the violation. Relative restrictions would in a sense be just one among several kinds of relevant considerations employed by speakers in arriving at an analysis. Their relative strength (when in conflict with other kinds of evidence) would have to be determined.

In this chapter we will examine a number of possible restrictions that might be imposed on the grammars of individual languages and that would limit the extent to which the UR of a morpheme may depart from its associated PRs. In some cases these restrictions have been explicitly proposed by certain linguists; in other cases they have implicitly controlled actual linguistic analyses, without having been made explicit; in yet other cases the restrictions are simply logical possibilities that have not been explicitly stated nor implicitly accepted by anyone (to our knowledge). The degree to which the various restrictions discussed actually do limit the "distance" between a UR and its associated PRs varies greatly. From the more restrictive conditions it generally follows that for any given set of phonetic realizations of a morpheme there exists only a small class of possible underlying representations (in extreme cases, restrictive conditions reduce the class of possible underlying forms to one). The less restrictive conditions allow a larger set of possible URs.

As already noted, the most direct relationship between a UR and its PR is that of identity. The condition that would allow the least divergence between a UR and its PR would be one that says that URs and their associated PRs are in fact always identical. Let us call this the "identity condition" imposed on the relationship between underlying and surface forms. The identity condition denies the existence of the very distinction between underlying and surface representations. In so doing, it leaves unexplained the relationship between different phonetic realizations of the same morpheme. Furthermore, the identity condition claims that the lexical representation of a morpheme contains all of the phonetic detail of the surface form of the morpheme (even though these phonetic details may in fact be derivable by general rules), and thus in no way distinguishes between those phonetic details that are idiosyncratic (unpredictable, hence contrastive) and those that are not (predictable, hence noncontrastive).

Therefore, we must abandon the identity condition if we can demonstrate that: (1) differences in the phonetic realization of the same morpheme in different contexts are (in some cases) rule-governed, and that the most appropriate formulation of these rules requires deriving the various surface forms from a single phonological representation; and (2) certain aspects of the pronunciation of a morpheme must be assigned by rule, rather than simply memorized as part of the lexicon (even in cases where that morpheme has but one surface phonetic realization).

Evidence that certain phonetic phenomena are rule-governed is rather easily provided, and generally comes from the productive extension of the rule to "new" forms, forms not previously encountered by the speaker and thus not "memorized." Consider, for example, the following case from Chi-Mwi:ni, a Bantu language. Chi-Mwi:ni has both long and short vowels in its phonetic representations; furthermore, it is necessary to assume that both types of vowels occur as basic (underlying) elements in the language. Nevertheless, there are certain contexts where long vowels do not generally occur in phonetic representations. If one examines individual words in isolation, for instance, he does not find long vowels any further forward in the word than in the antepenultimate syllable. Examination of examples such as those in (1) suggests that there is a rule operative in the language that will shorten a vowel if it occurs in a preantepenultimate syllable in the word.

(1)   *x-so:m-a* 'to read'   *x-so:m-eł-a* 'to read to/for'
        x-som-eł-an-a 'to read to one another'

        ku-ba:ram-a 'to talk'   *ku-baram-ił-a* 'to talk for'

        ku-re:b-a 'to stop'   *ku-re:b-eł-a* 'to stop for'
        ku-reb-eł-an-a 'to stop for one another'

The roots /so:m/ 'read', /ba:ram/ 'talk', /re:b/ 'stop' all have long vowels that can not be predicted by rule. The long vowel of these roots is not maintained in all of their morphologically derived forms. In particular, the length of the root vowel is lost as soon as that vowel comes to be in preantepenultimate position as a consequence of the addition of suffixes. Given a root such as /so:m/, the length of the root vowel is maintained both in *x-so:m-a* and *x-so:m-eł-a*. In the first example, the root vowel is in the penultimate syllable of the word, and in the second example it is in the antepenultimate syllable. The length is lost, however, in *x-som-eł-an-a*, where the root vowel is in a preantepenultimate position. Given a root such as /ba:ram/, the long vowel is maintained only in *ku-ba:ram-a*, where it is in the antepenultimate syllable. The addition of another suffix induces vowel shortening, as in *ku-baram-ił-a*.

Not only does Chi-Mwi:ni appear to shorten vowels in preantepenultimate positions in the word, but the rule also seems to operate in certain kinds of phrases. Note the examples in (2):

(2)   *chibu:ku*   'book'   *chibuku ichi*   'this book'
      mu:nt^hu   'man'   *munt^hu iłó*   'the man who came'
      ku-vu:nḍ-a   'to break' *ku-vunḍ-a chiluti* 'to break a small stick'

The long vowel of the noun *chibu:ku* shortens when the demonstrative *ichi* follows, since the presence of the demonstrative puts the underlying long vowel in a preantepenultimate position. Similarly, the long vowel of the verb root /vu:nḍ/ 'break' shortens when *chiluti* follows; the addition of this object noun puts the root vowel in preantepenultimate position.

The fact that a speaker of Chi-Mwi:ni will shorten preantepenultimate long vowels even in phrases that he has never heard before provides evidence that the alternations cited in (2) are the consequence of a general rule, and not simply memorized. For example, even though a speaker has (presumably) never encountered the phrase meaning 'to read a small stick', he automatically assigns the phrase the pronunciation *xsoma chiluti*, with the vowel of the root /so:m/ shortened by virtue of its preantepenultimate position. This automatic extension of vowel shortening to novel forms like *xsoma chiluti* supports the argument that the occurrence of a short vowel in such cases is rule-governed.

Let us turn now to an example where the productive extension of a rule occurs in connection with a slip of the tongue. Various linguists (Sapir, 1925 represents one especially interesting example) have analyzed the velar nasal [ŋ] in English as arising from an underlying /n/ via a rule of nasal assimilation. Slips of the tongue as in the following examples (recorded in Fromkin, 1971) support the existence of such a rule: [wɪŋks ən . . .] instead of the intended *weeks and months*. In this example, the speaker has added a nasal consonant before the final consonant cluster of *weeks* in anticipation of the nasal consonant [n] in *months*, which occurs before a word-final consonant cluster. The inserted nasal, however, is pronounced [ŋ] rather than [n], showing apparently the effect of the proposed rule of nasal assimilation.

We find an additional example of the productive extension of a rule in Bakwiri (Hombert, 1973), a language of the Duala group of Bantu languages: Vowels are nasalized when they precede clusters of a nasal plus (voiced) stop, the only nasal clusters permitted in the language. This rule accounts for the vowel nasalization in examples like *kômbà* 'to take', *kôndì* 'rice', and *zâŋgō* 'father'. Young Bakwiri speakers play a language game that involves moving the last syllable of a word to a position before the initial syllable of the word. Thus *mɔ́zɔ́* 'viper' is pronounced *zɔ́mɔ́* in the game. This transposition of syllables, in some cases, creates a context for vowel nasalization. When the game is applied to *mbèzà* 'young man', for example, the result is [zã̀mbè]. The fact that the final vowel of *mbèzà* becomes nasalized when placed before the initial *mb* cluster supports the claim that Bakwiri has a RULE of vowel nasalization that applies to VNC clusters.

Although the productive extension of a rule provides the most common source of evidence that certain aspects of pronunciation are rule-governed, other types of BEHAVIORAL evidence can be given. Let us return to the analysis of [ŋ] in English. In a word such as *bank* [bæŋk], the surface [ŋ] never alternates: [ŋ] appears in every surface realization of the morpheme. What is the evidence, then, that *this* particular occurrence of [ŋ] should be derived from an underlying /n/? Why cannot underlying /ŋ/ be postulated here? (This does not, of course, preclude the possibility that *some* surface [ŋ] sounds derive from underlying /n/.) Once again, slips of the tongue can be used to support the claim that /n/ underlies the surface [ŋ] in [bæŋk]. The evidence this time is not a product of the extension of the rule of nasal assimilation to a sequence of sounds arising from the slip of the tongue (as in the case of [wɪŋks] discussed above), but rather of the occurrence of a slip of the tongue whose form can only be understood on the basis of accepting a particular underlying representation of a given word that differs from its surface form. As a case in point, consider the following slip of the tongue reported in Fromkin (1975): [bæn] *will* [peyk] instead of the intended *bank will pay*. The speaker in this example has taken the last consonant of *bank* and added it to *pay*. Note that the resulting form is [bǽn], with a final *n*, and not *[bǽŋ]. The appearance of *n* here can be accounted for if /n/ is, in fact, the source of [ŋ] in [bǽŋk]. For once the final consonant of *bank* is transferred to *pay*, the underlying /n/ is no longer in a context to undergo nasal assimilation.

Language games can, in some cases, provide similar evidence that a certain aspect of pronunciation should be derived by rule rather than be attributed to the underlying representation of a morpheme. For instance, Sherzer (1970) suggests that the word [bíriga] 'year' in Cuna, an Amerindian language, should be derived from underlying /birga/ via a vowel epenthesis rule. Part of the evidence for such an analysis comes from the observation that stress is generally predictable in the language, occurring on the penultimate syllable. [bíriga] appears to be an exception to this rule. But if the underlying representation /birga/ is accepted, then the stress can be accounted for neatly, provided that stress is assigned prior to the application of the vowel epenthesis rule. Sherzer provides behavioral evidence in support of this analysis. He notes that the Cuna Indians play a language game that involves moving the first syllable of a word to the end of the word. For example, the Cuna word [argan] 'hand' is pronounced [ganar] in the game. When Cuna speakers use [bíriga] in the game, they say [gabir] and not* [rigabi]. The form [gabir] is explicable if the underlying representation of 'year' is /birga/. We need only assume that it is at the underlying level, rather than at the surface, that Cuna speakers rearrange the syllables of a word when playing the game. If /biriga/ were the underlying representation of 'year', there would be no explanation of how moving the first syllable to the end could lead to [gabir].

In the preceding paragraphs we have briefly sketched several examples where various kinds of behavioral evidence (i.e., speech forms produced by speakers where the forms in question were not simply memorized, but rather involved some extension of the speaker's knowledge of his language) support the claim that some aspects of pronunciation are determined by rule, and that underlying representations distinct from surface forms need to be postulated. On the basis of such evidence, we reject the identity condition on the relationship between underlying and surface representations.

Let us consider now a somewhat weaker condition that may apply to underlying and surface representations.

(A)   *The UR of a morpheme consists of all and only the invariant phonetic properties of that morpheme's various PRs.*

While (A) is not fully precise as stated, it will be sufficient for our purposes. (A) claims that by comparing the various phonetic realizations of a morpheme, its UR can be determined by eliminating those phonetic properties that do not occur in all the phonetic forms. In particular, only those segments that occur in all the forms of a morpheme belong in the UR, and only those phonetic properties of a segment that are constant in all the phonetic realizations of that segment will be included in the UR. The UR is what is invariant in the various pronunciations of the morpheme. Notice that if this constraint on the shape of URs were valid, the UR of a morpheme would stand in a very direct relationship with its various phonetic shapes: the UR would be a subset of the phonetic properties of each of the associated PRs.

Principle (A) is an extremely restrictive constraint imposed on grammars. If one assumes that (A) can be stated more precisely, offering a unique answer to the question, "What are the invariant phonetic properties of any given set of phonetic realizations of a morpheme?", then the application of (A) automatically yields a single possible UR for any given set of PRs. A's restrictiveness lies in its requirement that the UR consist of *all* invariant properties (thus disallowing the omission of one or more invariant phonetic features) and *only* invariant properties (thus disallowing the assignment of some variant properties to the UR, as well as disallowing the assignment of properties that do not occur in any of the PRs to the UR).

An examination of the following data from the Yawelmani dialect of Yokuts, an Amerindian language spoken in California (Newman, 1944) presents an example of the application of (A).

(3)

ʔilk-al	'might sing'		ʔilik-hin	'sings'
logw-ol	'might pulverize'		logiw-hin	'pulverizes'
ʔugn-al	'might drink'		ʔugun-hun	'drinks'
pa ʔṭ-al	'might fight'		pa ʔiṭ-hin	'might fight'

The preceding data illustrate a very general pattern in Yawelmani, whereby verb roots that have the shape CVCC- before vowel-initial suffixes assume the shape CVCiC- before consonant-initial suffixes (the *i* vowel in the latter will be realized as *u* if the preceding vowel is a high back rounded vowel, by virtue of a very important rule of vowel harmony operative in the language). By assuming that the URs of 'sing', 'pulverize', 'drink', and 'fight' are /ʔilk/, /logw/, /ʔugn/, and /paʔṭ/, respectively, the disyllabic forms of these morphemes can be readily accounted for by postulating a phonological rule that inserts *i* in the environment C___CC. Such an analysis can be motivated on the grounds that (a) there are no cases of CCC clusters in the language, thus the proposed rule can be viewed as one that transforms underlying representations containing "unpronounceable" combinations of sounds into acceptable surface forms; and (b) there are no verb roots of the shape $CV_1CV_2(C)$-, where V_1 and V_2 are not identical; if the *i* in a form such as *pa ʔit-hin* were underlying, then we would have to allow underlying disyllabic verbs with nonidentical vowels—but then all such verbs would have *i* as their second vowel.

(A) would require that the second vowel of *ʔilik-*, *logiw-*, etc., be omitted from the URs of these morphemes, since this vowel is not invariant in all of the phonetic realizations of these morphemes (being absent in the alternants *ʔilk-*, *logw-*, etc). (A) thus requires these verbs to have the structure CVCC- in their underlying representations; the vowel that occurs in the CVCi/uC- alternant would have to be assigned by rule. Since this is just the sort of analysis that can be argued to be appropriate for the Yawelmani data, condition (A) in this case would require the URs of these morphemes to be just the ones that we have posited.

Although in certain cases (A) will predict the underlying form that appears to be correct on the basis of internal and/or external evidence, (A) has many weaknesses. Perhaps the most obvious one is that (A) requires all invariant properties to be assigned to the UR. There are, however, many instances where nonidiosyncratic (rule-governed) properties of the pronunciations of a single morpheme happen to be invariant as well. (A) would require these rule-governed features to be incorporated into underlying structure.

Recall, for example, vowel nasalization in Bakwiri. A vowel in this language is nasalized if it precedes a cluster of nasal plus (voiced) stop. In a morpheme such as *kõmbà* 'to take care', the first vowel of the root is nasalized in all of the pronunciations of the morpheme since it is always followed by an NC sequence. Condition (A) requires that this nasalization be included in the UR of *kõmbà*. But when the final syllable of the word moves to the beginning in the linguistic game, the pronunciation *mbákò* results. Note that the *o* is oral in this form. This can be explained if we assume that the UR of this morpheme is /kombà/ with an oral vowel and that the speech disguise rule applies to the UR before the nasalization is assigned. Such an analysis is prohibited by (A), however. Consequently, it appears that (A) is too strong.

Russian provides a second example demonstrating that (A) is too restrictive a condition. In Russian the two mid-vowels ε and *e* both appear in phonetic representations, but do not contrast. *e* occurs before palatalized consonants, while ε appears elsewhere (before nonpalatalized consonants and word finally). Furthermore, the language has a pervasive rule palatalizing consonants before front vowels, giving rise to alternations like the following.

(4)   *l'εs*   'forest'   *o-l'es'-ε*   'about the forest'
         m'εst-o   'place'   *o-m'es't'-ε*   'about the place'
         b'εl-yj   'white'   *b'el'-it'*   'to whiten'

The proper analysis of these data posits ε as underlying, since its associated rule is phonetically more plausible than the rule that would be required if *e* were underlying; in addition, underlying ε would parallel the open quality of *o* [ɔ], the other mid-vowel phoneme of Russian. The *e* variant is generated by a rule that raises ε before palatalized consonants, which are articulated by raising the body of the tongue to the hard palate.

(5)   ε ⟶ e/____C′

There are, however, many morphemes whose final consonant is always palatalized, showing that the opposition between C and C′ is contrastive in Russian. If a front mid-vowel precedes this consonant, then it is articulated as *e* in all occurrences of the morpheme. Some examples follow.

(6)   *t'ep'er'* 'now'   *z'd'es'*   'here'
          ol'en' 'deer'   *o-ol'en'-ε*   'about the deer'
          z'v'er' 'beast'   *o-z'v'er'-ε*   'about the beast'

Principle (A), if accepted as a condition on grammars, would require us to assign to these morphemes an underlying *e* root vowel, despite the fact that its occurrence is completely predictable in terms of the rule we have formulated as (5). Linguists who have analyzed Russian have considered the *e* in these words to be a phonetic variant of the underlying /ε/ phoneme and have consequently adopted an analysis that violates (A).

These counterexamples to (A) might be circumvented by modifying the principle as follows:

(A′)   *The UR of a morpheme consists of only (but not necessarily all) invariant phonetic properties of the phonetic realizations of the morpheme; invariant properties of morphemes that are predictable by rule may be omitted.*

(A′) has severe difficulties, however. Note the following data from Yawelmani.

(7)   *?aml-al* 'might help'   *?a:mil-hin*   'helps'
          moyn-ol 'might become tired'   *mo:yin-hin*   'becomes tired'
          ṣalk'-al 'might wake up'   *ṣa:lik'-hin*   'wakes up'

These examples appear to contain instances of the rule of vowel insertion (epenthesis) discussed earlier, whereby the vowel *i* is inserted in the environment C___CC. If this rule is to be invoked to account for the $\emptyset \sim i$ alternations in (7), then the verb roots meaning 'help', 'become tired', and 'wake up' must have the underlying shape CVCC-.

In addition to the $\emptyset \sim i$ alternation, a vowel-length alternation can also be observed in this data. The root vowel is short when followed by a consonant cluster, but long when the epenthetic *i* vowel separates the members of the consonant cluster. There is considerable evidence that Yawelmani contains a rule of vowel shortening that shortens long vowels that occur in the context

$$\underline{\quad} C \begin{Bmatrix} \# \\ C \end{Bmatrix}.$$

The data in (8) illustrate the application of this rule.

(8)   *ṣa:p-al* 'might burn'   *ṣap-hin*   'burns'
          do:s-ol 'might report'   *dos-hin*   'reports'
          me:k'-en 'will swallow'   *mek'-k'a*   'swallow!'
          c'o:m-ut 'was destroyed'   *c'om-k'a*   'destroy!'

If the verb root 'burn' is taken to be underlying /ṣa:p/, the proposed rule of vowel shortening will correctly predict that the root vowel will appear in a shortened form when a consonant-initial suffix is added. A rule that shortens vowels in the environment

$$\underline{\quad} C \left\{ \begin{matrix} \# \\ C \end{matrix} \right\}$$

is consistent with the observation that the sequences $V:C\#$ and $V:CC$ generally do not occur in Yawelmani surface forms. If, on the other hand, the underlying form of the verb root 'burn' is /ṣap/, then we have to postulate a rule that would lengthen the root vowel when a vowel-initial suffix is added. Numerous examples in the language contradict such a rule.

(9)   *xat-al*   'might eat'   *xat-xa*   'let's eat'
       xil-en   'will tangle'   *xil-hin*   'tangles'
       bok'-en   'will find'   *bok'-xo*   'let's find'
       hud-al   'might recognize'   *hud-mu*   'having recognized'

Accepting, then, that Yawelmani has a rule of vowel shortening, this rule would seem to be responsible for the vowel-length alternation observed in examples like *ʔaml-al/ ʔa:mil-hin*. In order to invoke the rule of vowel shortening to explain the data in (7), the roots must have the underlying shape CV:CC-. The derivation of *ʔaml-al* and *ʔa:mil-hin* would then be as follows:

(10)   /ʔa:ml-al/   /ʔa:ml-hin/
        inapplicable   *ʔa:mil-hin*   vowel insertion
        ʔaml-al   inapplicable   vowel shortening

Notice that vowel insertion is crucially ordered to apply before vowel shortening in this analysis. If vowel shortening were to apply first, /ʔa:ml-hin/ would be incorrectly changed to * *ʔaml-hin*; then vowel insertion would apply yielding * *ʔamil-hin*.

Therefore, the underlying form of the roots in (7) must be CV:CC- rather than CVCC- for two reasons. First, if CVCC- represented the basic form of these roots, then the long vowel in the CV:CiC- variant would have to be derived by a rule of vowel lengthening and could not be explained in terms of an independently motivated rule. As we have seen, an underlying CV:CC-structure accounts for the vowel length alternation between the variants CVCC- and CV:CiC- in terms of the rule of vowel shortening, which is needed in the grammar in any case. Secondly, if CVCC- were taken as the underlying structure, any rule that would be postulated to derive the long vowel in the CV:CiC- variant would be contradicted by data such as the following:

(11)   *ʔilk-al*   'might sing'   *ʔilik-hin*   'sings'
        pa'ṭ-al   'might fight'   *pa'iṭ-hin*   'fights'
        logw-ol   'might pulverize'   *logiw-hin*   'pulverizes'

If /moyn-hin/ results in *mo:yin-hin*, why doesn't /logw-hin/ result in * *lo:giw-hin*? There is no ready explanation. On the other hand, if the underlying form of 'become tired' is /mo:yn/ and that of 'pulverize' is /logw/, the difference between these two roots is easily explained by means of our vowel insertion and vowel shortening rules.

In summary, the available language-internal evidence points in the direction of postulating URs in the form of /ʔa:ml/, /mo:yn/, and /ṣa:lk'/ for the verbs in (7), which allow the alternations observed in the data to be subsumed under two independently motivated phonological rules. Any other analysis will require an additional rule or rules to account for these examples.

Now, consider what condition (A') says about the Yawelmani data. The initial vowel in such PRs as ʔaml- and ʔa:mil- is neither invariably short nor invariably long. Since (A') requires that only invariant phonetic properties be included in the UR of a morpheme, the UR of 'help' cannot be /ʔa:ml/—since vowel length is not present in all the surface forms of this root. Neither can the UR be /ʔaml/, where a stands for a *short* vowel—since the vowel of this root is not short in all its surface occurrences. The only representation permitted by (A') is /ʔAml/, where A stands for a vowel that is not specified as either long or short.

Given the UR /ʔAml/, a rule will be required that will render this vowel long in an example like ʔa:mil-hin. But the rule that would accomplish this would have to *fail* to lengthen the first vowel of pa'iṭ-hin. If this is to be done, the vowel-lengthening rule must somehow apply only to vowels that are unspecified in UR for length. In other words, the analysis required by (A') would involve a crucial contrast between an underlying short vowel (as in /pa't/) and a vowel unspecified for length (as in /ʔAml/). The required rule of vowel lengthening would apply to unspecified vowels, but not to short vowels.

The analysis required by (A') thus substitutes a contrast between unspecified and short vowels for the long/short contrast involved in the analysis that posits CV:CC- roots underlyingly in (7) and CVCC- roots underlyingly in (11). What is the basis for choosing between these two approaches?

The analysis required by (A') strikes us as objectionable. It claims, essentially, that phonological rules discriminate between segments that are 'unspecified' for some phonetic property and segments that are 'specified'. If this were in fact true, for any given phonetic property (vowel length, for instance), one would expect to find three distinct patterns of behavior: the pattern exhibited by those sounds that are positively specified for the relevant property in UR, the pattern exhibited by those sounds that are negatively specified, and finally the pattern exhibited by those sounds that are unspecified. This does not appear to be the case. In general, one finds only TWO patterns of behavior: in the present example, that of ʔa:mil-hin /ʔaml-al and that of pa'iṭ-hin/ pa'ṭ-al.

Postulating a contrast between A/a rather than between a:/a represents a case where a nonphonetic contrast (unspecified versus specified) is substituted for a phonetic contrast (long versus short), but without any justification from the phonetic reality per se.

The situation for (A′) becomes even more complex if we consider the following data from Pengo (Burrow 1970). (In the following transcriptions, *j* stands for a voiced palatal affricate.)

(12)

(2nd) singular imperative	(3rd) singular past	gerund	gloss
tu:b-a	*tu:p-t-an*	*tu:b-ji*	'blow'
tog-a	*tok-t-an*	*tog-ji*	'step on'
ṛa:k-a	*ṛa:k-t-an*	*ṛa:g-ji*	'offer worship'
hi:p-a	*hi:p-t-an*	*hi:b-ji*	'sweep'

The root 'blow' appears in two shapes, *tu:b-* and *tu:p-*. (A′) requires that the voicing of the final consonant not be indicated in the underlying form, since voicing is variable for this segment. The root 'sweep' also appears in two forms, *hi:p-* and *hi:b-*. Likewise, (A′) requires that the voicing of the final consonant of this root also be unspecified in the UR. Thus, we will have underlying representations for 'blow' and 'sweep' where both morphemes end in a labial stop unspecified for voicing. The proper value for voicing of these stops in preobstruent position will be given by a general rule of voicing assimilation. Observe, however, that a rule assigning voice to the final segment of 'blow' but voicelessness to the final segment of 'sweep' will be required when these morphemes appear in prevocalic position. But there is no way of predicting from the underlying form of these roots which one will end in a voiced consonant and which one in a voiceless one. If we maintain (A′), then we must claim that the differential behavior of 'blow' and 'sweep' with respect to the voicing or lack of voicing of the root-final consonant is not attributable to the phonetic makeup of these roots. Since it is likewise impossible to find a grammatical basis for this differential behavior, we must consider the difference to be a matter of an arbitrary, nonphonetic property. It would be necessary to divide the lexicon into two types of consonant-final roots: One type will be assigned the feature VOICE before a vowel-initial root suffix, the other will be assigned the feature VOICELESS.

A theory of phonology not adhering to (A′) would characterize the differential behavior of 'blow' and 'sweep' by claiming that the former is underlying /tu:b-/ and the latter /hi:p-/. The voicing-assimilation rule needed for any analysis of these examples requires both roots to end in a voiceless consonant when followed by -*t*- and a voiced consonant when followed by -*ji*. The fact that /tu:b-/ ends in [b] and /hi:p-/ ends in a [p] before a vowel would not derive from a rule, but from the underlying character of the root-final consonant.

(A′) thus requires an arbitrary, nonphonetic contrast to distinguish 'blow' and 'sweep', whereas the alternative view posits a contrast between underlying voiced and voiceless consonants. Notice that although one function of (A′) is to require a very direct relationship between a UR and its associated PRs, in this case it requires that the contrast *tu:b-a*/*hi:p-a* be accounted for by a totally arbitrary division of the lexicon, even though the surface phonetic contrast is in fact one of voicing. Principle (A′) requires that a surface phonetic contrast be replaced by a nonphonetic contrast with no independent justification, thus leading to considerable abstractness.

We can adduce some other considerations against the analysis resulting from (A′). Note the following data from Pengo.

(13) *pa:g-a*   'strike!'   *ba:g*   'luck'
      pez-a   'lift!'   *besa*   'instrument for leveling ground'
      ku:k-a   'call!'   *gu:h-a* 'swallow!'

While /pa:g-/ has an initial voiceless consonant in all of its manifestations, /ba:g-/ has an invariant voiced consonant in root-initial position. Such data could be handled within the framework of (A′) by assuming an underlying contrast between voiceless /p/ in *pa:g-a* and voiced /b/ in *ba:g*. But this would involve claiming that voicing is relevant in root-initial, but not in root-final position. However, we would have a rule that introduces a voicing contrast in root-final position, where the rule in question would be triggered by an arbitrary division of the lexicon into roots requiring voicing and roots requiring voicelessness. Clearly, such a rule is merely a roundabout way of introducing a voicing contrast in root-final position that is precisely parallel to the voicing contrast found in underlying root-initial position. In fact, if one were to adopt such an analysis, a logical extension of it would be to claim that both *pa:g-a* and *ba:g* begin with an underlying /P/, a labial stop unspecified for voicing. A rule is needed in any case to specify the /P/ of /tu:P-/ as voiced and the /P/ of /hi:P-/ as voiceless in prevocalic position. Why not let the same rules account for the difference in voicing in the initial consonants of *pa:g-a* and *ba:g*? All that would be required would be to divide the lexicon into two kinds of root-initial consonants, one type undergoing voicing prevocalically, and the other not.

In other words, if we were to follow the logic of (A′) all phonetic properties could be eliminated from the underlying form and we could depend solely upon a nonphonetic system of classifying the phonetic behavior of morphemes. Thus, the condition (A′), while superficially requiring a direct relationship between underlying and phonetic representations, would in fact permit totally abstract underlying forms (a network of nonphonetic subcategorizations) just in order to account for data like those from Pengo. Most phonologists have rejected such analyses for an obvious reason. Phonetic contrast is clearly a crucial aspect of language structure: It is the device that permits utterances to be distinguished and thus makes communication possible. But an approach that leads to reanalyzing phonetic contrasts (such as roots ending in voiced versus voiceless consonants) as nonphonetic contrasts (such as roots whose final consonants are subject to a rule assigning voice prevocalically versus roots whose final consonants are subject to a rule assigning voicelessness prevocalically) states that surface phonetic contrasts are derived from under-lying nonphonetic contrasts, with no evidence at all from the sound patterning of language to justify this position.

Principle (A′) encounters more severe difficulties in an example such as the following from Tonkawa, an Amerindian language formerly spoken in Texas (Hoijer, 1933). In this language verbal roots display extensive morphophonemic alternations. The following examples are entirely typical.

(14)

	A	B	C	D	gloss
	notx	*ntox*	*notxo*	*ntoxo*	'hoe'
	netl	*ntal*	*netle*	*ntale*	'lick'
	picn	*pcen*	*picna*	*pcena*	'cut'

Although these verb roots have a constant consonantal structure (*n-t-x-*, *n-t-l-*, *p-c-n-*), their vocalic structure is highly variable. It is possible, however, to reduce this variability to general rules. Notice, for example, that in the columns labeled A and B there is no vowel in root-final position, whereas in the columns labeled C and D there is a vowel in final position. The A and B forms occur when followed by a vowel-initial suffix, while the C and D forms occur when a consonant-initial suffix follows. It would therefore be possible to account for this particular alternation by stating that the final vowel in the C and D forms belongs to the underlying structure of the verb root, and that this final vowel is deleted when a vowel follows. Furthermore, note that a vowel occurs between the first and second consonant of the verb root in the A and C forms, but no vowel occurs between the second and third consonant. In contrast, the B and D forms reveal no vowel between the first and second consonants of the verb root, but have a vowel between the second and third consonant. The A and C forms occur when the root is word-initial or preceded by a consonant-final prefix. The B and D forms occur after prefixes ending in a vowel. In other words, the alternations follow a quite regular pattern. It is important to point out, however, that while it is possible to predict when a vowel will be pro-nounced and when it will not be, it is *not* possible to predict *which* vowel will occur. Taking 'cut' as an example, we have no way of determining whether the vowel *e* will occur between the first and second consonant, or whether *a* will occur between the second and third consonant, or whether *a* will follow the third consonant. The choice of vowel in each position is an idiosyncratic property of the verb root.

Given URs such as /notoxo/, /netale/, and /picena/, we can readily account for alternations found in (14). In case a vowel-initial suffix follows, the last vowel of these representations would be deleted. The second vowel would be lost in the case where the root is in the environment

$$\begin{Bmatrix} C \\ \# \end{Bmatrix} \underline{\qquad},$$

and the first vowel would be lost when the root is in the environment V____.

How would (A′) handle the Tonkawa data? According to (A′), no sound may appear in the UR of a morpheme unless it appears in all the phonetic realizations of that morpheme. Consequently (A′) would not allow any vowel to occur in the URs of 'hoe', 'lick', and 'cut', since none of the vowels that occur in the PRs of these morphemes occur in all of the PRs of the morpheme. The URs would thus have to be /ntx/ for 'hoe', /ntl/ for 'lick', and /pcn/ for 'cut'. But given such URs, there are no general phonological principles that could account for the surface phonetic patterning of these morphemes. It is idiosyncratic that /ntx/ 'hoe' has the vowel /o/ between /n/ and /t/ in *notx-*, whereas /ntl/ 'lick' has the vowel /e/ in this position. There are no phonological processes to which these facts can be attributed. If underlying representations are assumed to be the repository of those phonetic properties that cannot be attributed to the application of phonological rules, then the URs of 'hoe', 'lick', and 'cut' must contain not only an indication of the consonantal structure of these morphemes, but also a specification of the vowels that intervene between these consonants. The absence of some of these vowels in the various allomorphs is predictable by general rules. (A′) does not permit this, however; it requires that the vowels be inserted on the basis of nonphonetic information that would have to be associated with each morpheme. Instead of accounting for the contrast between *notx-* and *netl-* by including /o/ between /n/ and /t/ in the UR of 'hoe', but /e/ between /n/ and /t/ in the UR of 'lick', (A′) posits the URs /ntx/ and /ntl/. A rule is then needed that would insert a vowel between the first two consonants of an unprefixed root or after a consonant-final prefix (these are the contexts in which the CVCC(V)-alternant occurs); such a rule is possible because there are no roots with an initial consonant cluster in these contexts. But the quality of the vowel inserted by the rule would have to be an idiosyncratic property of each root. Nonphonetic information would thus have to be associated with each root morpheme in order to determine the quality of the inserted vowel. Thus, once again (A′) requires replacing a phonetic contrast (/notoxo/ versus /netale/) with a nonphonetic contrast (/ntx/ plus some nonphonetic information determining that /o/ will be inserted between the initial two consonants in the appropriate circumstances, as opposed to /ntl/ plus some nonphonetic information determining that /e/ will be inserted between the first two consonants, etc.). Again we find no reason for ignoring the surface phonetic contrast (/o/ versus /e/) in favor of the nonphonetic contrast.

One direction in which one might move in attempting to relax the constraints imposed by (A′), while at the same time severely restricting the possible URs for a morpheme, is to permit variant (alternating) features such as the voicing of Pengo obstruents to occur in the UR of a morpheme, but to establish at the same time criteria that will determine which value for the alternating feature is to be included in the UR and which value is to be assigned by rule. The criteria that we are about to discuss all assume that the UR of any morpheme is identical to one of the morpheme's PRs (excluding those features of the PR that are entirely predictable and thus do not have to be included in

URs at all—e.g., aspiration in English). These criteria differ with respect to WHICH PR is identified as the basis for establishing the UR.

Let us begin by considering the condition on grammars expressed as (B).

(B)   *The UR of a morpheme includes those variant (alternating) and invariant phonetic properties that are idiosyncratic (unpredictable). But it may include only those variant properties that occur in the PR that appears in isolation (or as close to isolation as the grammar of the language permits).*

A principle such as (B) seems to be implicitly assumed by many pedagogically based language descriptions, where one frequently finds the pronunciation of morphologically complex forms (the plural of a noun, for instance) described in terms of a change in the morphologically simpler form (the singular form of a noun, for instance). Two considerations seem to motivate (B). First, the UR of a morpheme is often obscured when that morpheme is conjoined to another, due to morphophonemic changes. If a morpheme can be examined in isolation, the obscuring effect can be eliminated and the underlying form revealed. Second, the unaffixed or minimally affixed form of a root often appears in a more basic semantic context (singular as opposed to plural, present tense as opposed to past, nominative as opposed to oblique cases, and so on), and there is a tendency to identify the UR of a morpheme with the alternant appearing in a more basic semantic context, perhaps on the grounds that this context is more frequent, especially during the initial stages of language learning.

(B) encounters substantial difficulties, however, because numerous phonological processes are induced by word-initial and word-final position. Consequently, an isolated form of a morpheme does not necessarily escape being affected by phonological rules and thus does not necessarily reveal the underlying form of a morpheme.

Consider the extremely well-motivated rule of word-final devoicing of obstruents in Russian. The noun roots in (15) below alternate, ending either in an unvoiced obstruent (in the nominative singular forms) or a voiced obstruent (in the dative singular and nominative plural forms).*

(15)

nominative singular	dative singular	nominative plural	gloss
xlep	xlebu	xleba	'bread'
sat	sadu	sady	'garden'
zakas	zakazu	zakazy	'order'
storoš	storožu	storoža	'guard'
rok	rogu	roga	'horn'

Given data of this type, one could either take the nom. sg. form as basic and

* These transcriptions ignore the effects of an automatic rule that changes unstressed *e* and *o* to *i* and *a*, respectively.

posit a rule that voices obstruents before vowel-initial suffixes, or take the dat. sg./nom. pl. form of the root as basic and posit a rule of final devoicing. The final devoicing approach is strongly supported by the fact that words do not end in voiced obstruents in Russian pronunciation. Furthermore, numerous examples like the following would falsify a rule that would voice obstruents before vowel-initial suffixes.

(16)

nominative singular	dative singular	nominative plural	gloss
čerep	čerepu	čerepa	'skull'
cvet	cvetu	cveta	'color'
les	lesu	lesa	'forest'
duš	dušu	dušy	'shower'
bok	boku	boka	'side'

The root-final obstruents in these examples all remain voiceless even when followed by a vowel-initial suffix. Under the final devoicing analysis, the final underlying voiceless obstruents of the roots in (16) would simply remain and not alternate. According to the analysis of Russian that posits a rule voicing obstruents before vowel-initial suffixes to account for the data in (15), all of the roots in (16) would have to be regarded as exceptions. The analysis of Russian that postulates a word-final devoicing rule clearly provides the most appropriate analysis of the data (and, of course, is the analysis that linguists have generally accepted).

Let us consider now how (B) requires us to analyze the Russian data. The noun roots in (15) have an alternating final consonant. The phonetic property involved (namely, voicing of obstruents) is not a predictable feature of Russian pronunciation (it is not possible to predict that the root final consonant of *sadu* is *d* while the root final consonant of *cvetu* is *t*). Consequently, the URs of the roots in (15) must be specified for voicing. (B) requires that the underlying value for an alternating feature must be that value that occurs in the isolated form of the morpheme. In the case of the roots in (15), that form is the nom. sg. (B) thus posits URs such as /xlep/, /sat/, /zakas/, and so on. But if these URs are accepted, the alternation in voicing observed in (15) would have to be accounted for by a rule that voices obstruents before vowel-initial suffixes. We have seen, however, that such an analysis is inconsistent with the large number of nouns like those in (16). In order to maintain (B), all such nouns would have to be marked as exceptions to the rule of voicing before vowel-initial suffixes. (B) requires replacing a perfectly straightforward phonetic contrast (roots ending in underlying voiced obstruents as opposed to roots ending in voiceless obstruents) with a nonphonetic contrast (roots that regularly undergo voicing as opposed to roots that exceptionally fail to undergo the rule).

Lardil, a language of Northern Australia provides a more extreme example of the sort of problem that (B) encounters. According to the analysis of Lardil proposed by Hale (1971), "The object of a nonimperative verb is inflected for accusative case and, simultaneously, for tense (in agreement with the tense of the verb). The subject of a sentence and the object of an imperative verb are uninflected (as in the citation form)." Thus, a noun appears inflected in an accusative nonfuture form or in an accusative future form.*

(17)

uninflected	accusative nonfuture	accusative future	gloss
mela	*mela-n*	*mela-ṛ*	'sea'
parna	*parna-n*	*parna-ṛ*	'stone'
wanka	*wanka-n*	*wanka-ṛ*	'arm'

The above examples suggest assigning to the acc. nonfut. suffix the shape -*n* and to the acc. fut. suffix the shape -*ṛ*. The noun roots would be identical to their uninflected form.

The examples cited in (18) below involve morphophonemic alternation.

(18)

ŋuka	*ŋuku-n*	*ŋuku-ṛ*	'water'
kaṭa	*kaṭu-n*	*kaṭu-ṛ*	'child'
muṇa	*muṇu-n*	*muṇu-ṛ*	'elbow'
kenṭe	*kenṭi-n*	*kenṭi-wuṛ*	'wife'
pape	*papi-n*	*papi-wuṛ*	'father's mother'
ŋiṇe	*ŋiṇi-n*	*ŋiṇi-wuṛ*	'skin'

Note that whereas *mela* 'sea' has the acc. nonfut. *mela-n*, *ŋuka* 'water' has the form *ŋuku-n*. If we were to analyze both of these roots as ending in /a/, there would be no general principles to predict that in the case of 'sea' this /a/ would remain constant, whereas in the case of the suffixed forms of 'water' it would change to /u/. If we adopt the inflected form of the root as the underlying structure, however, i.e., /mela/ versus /ŋuku/, then a rule that said that underlying /u/ is pronounced as /a/ in word-final position would predict that /ŋuku/, when uninflected, is pronounced as *ŋuka*. Such as analysis is supported on two grounds. First, there are no roots that end in /u/ both in the inflected and in the uninflected form: That is, there are no roots like *malu*, *malu-n*. The absence of such roots would be predicted by the rule changing /u/ to /a/ in final position. Second, if we analyse a root such as *pape*, *papi-n* as underlying /papi/, then its uninflected form could be accounted for by simply extending the rule that lowers /u/ to /a/, so that it also lowers /i/ to /e/.

(19)   Lowering   V $\longrightarrow$ [-high]/____ #

(We assume that subsidiary principles account for the fact that /u/ is lowered to an unrounded vowel.) (B) does not allow this analysis but instead requires that any variable phonetic property be represented in the UR as it appears in

---

* Lardil distinguishes four types of coronal consonants: laminal dental /th/, apico-alveolar /t/, laminal alveopalatal /tj/, and apical domal /ṭ/.

the unaffixed form of the morpheme. (B) thus chooses /ŋuka/ as the UR of 'water', merging it with /mela/. To account for the form *ŋuku-n* it would be necessary to posit a rule raising /a/ to /u/; nonphonetic information would be required in order to permit /ŋuka-n/ to undergo this raising, but not /mela-n/. Such an approach treats the absence of examples with invariant /u/, like the hypothetical *malu, malu-n*, as entirely fortuitous.

Consider next the following additional data.

(20)

thuŋal	*thuŋal-in*	*thuŋal-ur̯*	'tree'
kethar	*kethar-in*	*kethar-ur̯*	'river'
miyar̯	*miyar̯-in*	*miyar̯-ur̯*	'spear'
ṭupalan	*ṭupalan-in*	*ṭupalan-kur̯*	'road'
yaraman	*yaraman-in*	*yaraman-kur̯*	'horse'

A few comments on the shape of the suffixes are required. The acc. nonfut. has the shape -*n* in (17) and (18), while it has the shape -*in* in (20). This difference is apparently a consequence of the fact that the roots in (17) and (18) are vowel-final, while in (20) there is no evidence of a vowel-final stem. If the underlying form of the suffix is /-in/, a rule deleting the initial vowel after a vowel-final stem could be formulated. Now consider the acc. fut., which has the shape -*r̯* in (17) and in those words in (18) where the root ends in /u/. When the root ends in /i/, the acc. fut. is pronounced as -*wur̯*. In (20) this suffix is pronounced as -*ur̯*, except after nasal-final roots, where it is realized as -*kur̯*. If we take the UR of the suffix to be /-ur̯/, we can account for its allomorphy by inserting a *w* between root-final /i/ and this suffix, but dropping the suffix-initial /u/ after roots ending in other vowels: /papi-ur̯/⟶ *papi-wur̯*, but /mela-ur̯/⟶ *mela-r̯*. The examples in (20) require /k/ to be inserted between a nasal-final root and the suffix -*ur̯*. When the root ends in an oral consonant, the suffix reveals its underlying shape: /kethar-ur̯/⟶ *kethar-ur̯*.

The data in (21) present a new problem of analysis.

(21)

thur̯ara	*thur̯araŋ-in*	*thur̯araŋ-kur̯*	'shark'
per̯e	*per̯eŋ-in*	*per̯eŋ-kur̯*	'vagina'
ŋalu	*ŋaluk-in*	*ŋaluk-ur̯*	'story'
kur̯ka	*kur̯kaŋ-in*	*kur̯kaŋ-kur̯*	'pandja'

The suffixal shapes in (21) are just what we would expect after consonant-final roots; see (20). Indeed, the roots display a consonant in the inflected forms. But the consonant that appears in the inflected forms is absent in the uninflected form. If we were to assume that the consonant in question is part of the root, thus accounting for the shapes of the following suffixes, it would be necessary to postulate a rule that deletes certain consonants in word-final position. This rule would have to convert /thur̯araŋ/, /per̯eŋ/, /ŋaluk/, and /kur̯kaŋ/ to *thur̯ara, per̯e, ŋalu,* and *kur̯ka*. The rule could not be formulated so as to delete any word-final consonant, since /thuŋal/, /miyar̯/, and /yaramin/ in (20) do not lose their consonants. Consideration of additional data reveals that nonapical consonants delete finally, while apical consonants remain (for a systematic exception, see below). Thus, the data of (21) can be accounted for by a rule of the following form:

(22)   Nonapical Deletion   C ⟶ ∅/____ #
                                       [-apical]

While /ŋaluk-in/ will not be affected by any of the rules discussed, /ŋaluk/ will undergo nonapical deletion, yielding *ŋalu*. The fact that *ŋalu* ends in *u* confirms in part our analysis. Recall that there is motivation for a rule in Lardil that lowers /u/ to *a* in final position. If the root were in fact /ŋalu/, there would be no explanation for why lowering does not apply to this form. If /ŋaluk/ is the UR, however, the failure of lowering to apply can be attributed to the presence of the final /k/, which prevents lowering. That is, lowering is ordered to apply before nonapical deletion.

Our account of the data in (21) is based on positing the inflected form of the root as underlying. But if we were to accept (B), the uninflected form of the root would have to be selected as the underlying structure. This would require a rule to convert /ŋalu-in/ to *ŋaluk-in*, while converting /peṛe-in/ to *peṛeŋ-in* and at the same time permitting forms such as /mela-in/ to become *mela-n*. Nonphonetic information would thus be required to guarantee that /k/ is inserted in the case of /ŋalu-in/, but /ŋ/ in the case of /peṛe-in/. Nonphonetic information would also be needed to explain why /ŋalu/ and /peṛe/ undergo consonant insertion, while /mela/ does not.

(23) provides more relevant data.

(23)
yalul	yalulu-n	yalulu-ṛ	'flame'
karikar	karikari-n	karikari-wuṛ	'butterfish'
mayar	mayara-n	mayara-ṛ	'rainbow'
kaŋkaṛ	kaŋkari-n	kaŋkari-wuṛ	'father's father'
wiwal	wiwala-n	wiwala-ṛ	'bush mango'

The inflected forms of (23) have the shapes expected after vowel-final stems; see (17) and (18). A vowel precedes the suffix in each example: *yalulu-n*, *karikari-n*, and so on. But this vowel is not present in the uninflected form. If we consider this vowel to be part of the root, a rule is needed to convert /yalulu/, /karikari/ . . . to *yalul, karikar* . . . when these roots are uninflected. If we compare the examples where deletion of the vowel would occur—in (23)—with those where it would not—(17) and (18)—a crucial difference emerges: deletion occurs with roots that are trisyllabic or longer; it does not occur when the root is disyllabic. The following rule accounts for this difference.

(24)   Apocope   V ⟶ ∅/VC₁VC₁____ #

Note that *thuṛara* 'shark' in (21) does not become *thuṛar*. We have argued that this root is /thuṛaraŋ/, however; see *thuṛaraŋ-in*. The failure of apocope to apply to *thuṛara* can be accounted for by simply ordering apocope before nonapical deletion. Thus, the presence of final /ŋ/ in the UR of *thuṛara* is responsible for the retention of the final *a* in this word. One final point can be made in favor of our analysis of (23): The UR of *karikar* is /karikari/, clearly a reduplicated word. The fact that it is reduplicated is obscured in the uninflected form but transparent in inflected forms.

Principle (B) requires a radically different approach to the data in (23). The URs would have to be /yalul/, /karikar/, and so on. Nonphonetic information would be required in order to specify that these roots are separated by a vowel from the following suffix, while the roots of (20) are not. Additional nonphonetic information would be needed to specify which vowel appears in the inflected forms.

Consider now the following examples, which are interesting for several reasons.

(25)
ṭipiṭi	*ṭipiṭipi-n*	*ṭipiṭipi-wuṛ*	'rock-cod'
murkuni	*murkunima-n*	*murkunima-ṛ*	'nullah'
puṭu	*puṭuka-n*	*puṭuka-ṛ*	'short'
ŋawuŋa	*ŋawuŋawu-n*	*ŋawuŋawu-ṛ*	'termite'

In each of the examples the uninflected form is shorter by two segments than the corresponding inflected forms. The "added" syllables are *-pi, -ma, -ka, -wu* whose initial consonants are all nonapicals. This strongly suggests that the rule of nonapical deletion is operative here. Note furthermore that if the inflected form of the root is basic, the roots are all vowel-final and trisyllabic or longer. Thus, apocope could account for the absence of the vowel of the "added" syllables in question. All that would be required is that apocope be ordered to apply before nonapical deletion, an ordering that was suggested by *thuṛara*. The derivation of *murkuni* would be as follows.

(26)   /#murkunima#/
          ---------   lowering
          murkunim   apocope
          murkuni   nonapical deletion

Note that lowering must be applied before nonapical deletion, otherwise /i/ would be lowered to /e/; apocope must be applied before nonapical deletion so that /murkunima/ can become /murkunim/ by the former rule and thus subject to the latter rule. Observe that *murkuni* does not undergo apocope, showing that apocope cannot reapply. The analysis of this data permits us to recognize *ṭipiṭi* and *ŋawuŋa* as reduplicated forms as well.

Once again (B) precludes this analysis, since it posits the shorter form appearing in the uninflected column as basic. Rules would be necessary to affix /pi/ to /ṭipiṭi/, /ma/ to /murkuni/, and so on. On phonological grounds we could not predict which roots would take an additional syllable nor determine its vowel quality. Nonphonetic information would have to be specified in the UR to insure that the appropriate suffixes affix to the appropriate roots.

One additional rule of Lardil phonology needs to be mentioned. Examination of the language reveals no word-final consonant clusters.

(27)   *kantukan   kantukantu-n   kantukantu-ṛ*   'red'

When we take an example like (27) into consideration, we find that once again the uninflected form is shorter by two segments than the inflected form. In this case the missing syllable is /tu/. Here we cannot invoke our nonapical deletion rule to account for the missing consonant, since /t/ is an apical. We could, however, appeal to a rule of cluster simplification.

(28)   Cluster Simplification $C \longrightarrow \emptyset / C\_\_\_\#$

This rule must be assumed to apply after apocope:

(29)   /#kantukantu#/
            kantukant   apocope
            kantukan   cluster simplification

More complicated cases arise as well.

(30) *muŋkumu   muŋkumuŋku-n   muŋkumuŋku-ṛ*   'wooden ax'
      tjumputju   tjumputjumpu-n   tjumputjumpu-ṛ   'dragonfly'

In (30) the uninflected form is three segments shorter than the inflected form. The "added" structure in these examples is /ŋku/ in 'wooden ax' and /mpu/ in 'dragonfly'. In both cases the first consonant of the added structure is a nonapical consonant. The absence of this consonant can be attributed to nonapical deletion, whereas the absence of the second consonant could be traced to the operation of cluster simplification. The absence of the vowel would of course be due to apocope. The derivation of *muŋkumu* is as follows.

(31)   /#muŋkumuŋku#/
            muŋkumuŋk   apocope
            muŋkumuŋ   cluster simplification
            muŋkumu   nonapical deletion

Once again (B) would require that /muŋkumu/ and /tjumputju/ be taken as the underlying representations for 'wooden ax' and 'dragonfly', respectively. Rules would then be required to expand the former to /muŋkumuŋku/ and the latter to /tjumputjumpu/ when the inflected root shapes are formed. There are no general principles that would determine that these roots add two consonants and a vowel in the formation of the inflected root shapes, whereas other roots do not: /mela/ 'sea' adds nothing; /miyaṛ/ 'spear' adds nothing; /nalu/ 'story' adds just /k/; /yalul/ 'flame' adds just /u/; /murkuni/ 'nullah' adds /ma/ (one consonant and a vowel). No general rules can be given to determine how many consonants to add and whether or not to add a vowel. Furthermore, the nature of the consonant or the vowel cannot be predicted. Thus, positing the uninflected allomorph as the underlying representation, as required by (B), means relinquishing the phonetic basis for the alternation between the uninflected and the inflected root forms, even though obvious phonetic contrasts exist when the inflected root forms are examined.

The evidence from Lardil suggests that (B) is untenable as an absolute constraint on URs. Nevertheless, there are cases in which the UR of a morpheme is identified with the form in isolation, even at the expense of rather severe descriptive complexity. For example, Hale (1971) contrasts certain data from Maori with the Lardil data discussed above. Proto-Polynesian underwent a sound change whereby the final consonant of a word was deleted, giving rise to alternations in Maori such as the following.

(32)

active	passive	gloss
hopu	*hopukia*	'catch'
aru	*arumia*	'follow'
mau	*mauria*	'carry'
awhi	*awhitia*	'embrace'

Instead of positing the allomorph in the affixed form as the underlying structure (and utilizing a rule to delete word-final consonants), present-day speakers of Maori regard the unaffixed (active) forms of the roots as underlying, requiring the division of the lexicon into a number of arbitrary lexical classes ("conjugations"): *hopu* belongs to a class that takes the *-kia* form of the passive suffix, *aru* belongs to a class that takes the *-mia* form, and so on. More than a dozen such lexical classes are required.

The evidence that Maori speakers have reinterpreted the data in (32) and assigned the consonant that appears in the passive forms to the passive suffix rather than to the verb root derives from various observations that *-tia* is developing into the REGULAR passive suffix (all other forms, such as *-kia*, *-mia*, *-ria*, etc., are regarded as irregular). The following observations support the conclusion that *-tia* is the regular passive suffix: (a) If a speaker forgets the correct passive form of a verb, he may use a form where *-tia* is added to the active verb form—and he is understood when he does this; (b) if a noun is used as a verb in spontaneous speech, this denominal verb will form its passive by adding *-tia*; (3) loan words add *-tia* in forming a passive, even if these loan words end in a consonant. (Additional arguments provided by Hale lead to the same conclusion.)

Although historically a root such as that in *awhi/awhitia* ended in a consonant, the evidence cited above suggests that speakers reanalyzed forms such as this and associated the consonant with the suffix. The result was that the passive suffix had multiple allomorphs. For some reason (as yet undetermined), the

-*tia* allomorph has developed into the regular form of the suffix. This analysis has resulted in numerous exceptional forms, falling into a dozen or so "conjugations."

The reanalysis of the data in (32) that appears to have taken place in Maori suggests that although (B) may not be an absolute condition on grammars, it may play a significant role nevertheless in a speaker's grammar-construction. That is, (B) may be a relative condition placed on URs—a condition that may be violated, but only if the analysis of the data demands a violation. The difficult problem of course is to discover the factors which determine whether (B) will or will not be violated.

The most frequently used form of a morpheme is generally the minimally affixed form (since lack of affixation often coincides with a more basic semantic concept). Our discussion of (B) showed, however, that such forms cannot be regarded as reliable reflections of underlying structure. There is another way though, in which frequency might play a role in deciding what underlying value should be assigned to an alternating phonetic feature. Consider (B').

(B')   *The UR of a morpheme includes those variant and invariant phonetic properties that are idiosyncratic. But it may include only those variant properties that occur in the greatest number of "contexts".*

As formulated (B') is imprecise. What is meant, for example, by "contexts"? This question might be answered in different ways, but for our present purposes we will simply assume that the number of contexts in which a morpheme can occur is a function of the number of different affixes that can precede or follow it (within the "word"—assuming that we are dealing with rules whose domain of application is the word itself). Consider, for example, the Russian data discussed earlier. The final consonant of the root 'bread' appears voiced in *xlebu* (dat. sg.) and *xleba* (nom. pl.), but voiceless in *xlep* (nom. sg.). The voiceless consonant occurs in just one context (when no suffix follows the noun root); the voiced consonant occurs in two contexts (when followed by the dat. sg. -*u* and by the nom. pl. -*a*). Since these examples are representative of the general situation (i.e., the voiced form of the root occurs throughout the noun declension excepting the case where no suffix follows the root), (B') will correctly predict /xleb/ as the UR of 'bread'.

(B') likewise leads to the most comprehensive analysis of the Lardil data. Consider the noun meaning 'nullah'. It has the shape *murkuni* when there is no suffix, but takes the shape *murkunima*- before the acc. nonfut. and acc. fut. suffixes. Since the syllable /ma/ occurs in the greater number of contexts, (B') leads to the inclusion of these alternating sounds in the UR. This seems an accurate description of the Lardil data.

There are nevertheless many cases where the constraint on URs provided by (B') is too strong. For example, in Russian the vowels *o* and *a* contrast phonetically only when accented. When unaccented, *o* and *a* merge into *a*. There are many nouns belonging to the so-called oxytone accentual class, in which the stress falls on the first vowel of the suffix if there is one, but on the final vowel of the root when there is no suffix. For the entire masculine declension there are at most only two forms where the noun appears unaffixed and, hence, where a noun will be stressed on the root vowel. In all other forms the accent appears on the ending. In spite of this fact there are many examples in which the root vowel appearing under stress in the unaffixed form can be either *o* or *a*. For instance, the complete declension of *stol* 'table' and *vrak* 'enemy' is as follows.

(33)

	singular	plural	singular	plural
Nominative	stól	stal-ý	vrák	vrag'-í
Genitive	stal-á	stal-óf	vrag-á	vrag-óf
Dative	stal-ú	stal-ám	vrag-ú	vrag-ám
Accusative	stól	stal-ý	vrag-á	vrag-óf
Instrumental	stal-óm	stal-ám'i	vrag-óm	vrag-ám'i
Locative	stal'-é	stal-áx	vrag'-é	vrag-áx

Other examples include *vráč, vračá* 'physician'; *plášč, plaščá* 'cloak'; *etáš, etažá* 'story'; versus *kót, katá* 'tomcat'; *žívót, živatá* 'stomach'; *dvór, dvará* 'courtyard'. If (B′) were followed in the analysis of the data in (33), it would be necessary to posit an underlying /a/ for 'table' (since *a* occurs in more contexts than does *o*). We would also be obliged to posit underlying /a/ in 'enemy', since *a* appears in all contexts for this morpheme. Notice that once again we would be compelled to divide the lexicon into arbitrary classes in order to determine which underlying /a/'s appear as *o* when the stress falls on them, and which appear as *a*.

To cite one more example of this type, morphemes like /pek/ 'bake' and /žeg/ 'burn' in Serbo-Croatian exhibit the following patterns in the present tense.

(34)

	1st singular	peč-ē-m	žež-ē-m
	2nd	peč-ē-š	žež-ē-š
	3rd	peč-ē	žež-ē
	1st plural	peč-ē-mo	žež-ē-mo
	2nd	peč-ē-te	žež-ē-te
	3rd	pek-ū	žeg-ū

Here the *ē* is the thematic or stem vowel that is added to the root. It deletes by a general rule when the following person-number suffix begins with a vowel: *pek-ū* < /pek-ē-ū/, *žeg-ū* < /žeg-ē-ū/. (B′) requires us to set up the *peč-* and *žež-* alternants as underlying, since they occur most frequently. The associated rule in this analysis, however, which involves *č* and *ž* becoming *k* and *g* before *u*, is quite unnatural and furthermore would have to be limited to apply before just the /-u/ of the 3rd pl. morpheme, because *č* and *ž* freely occur before other *u* vowels in Serbo-Croatian. On the other hand, the analysis

setting up the velar stops k and g as basic involves a rule that is both phonetically natural and consistent with the general gap in Serbo-Croatian sound
structure that velars do not normally appear before front vowels except in
borrowed words. Finally, one needs a rule that changes velars to palatals
before front vowels for many other alternations in the language. For instance,
in the declension of certain nouns the vocative sg. ending is -*e*. Noun stems
ending in k and g change to *č* and *ž* in the vocative: *junak, junač-e* 'youth';
Bog, Bož-e 'God'. (B′) requires the alternants /junak/ and /bog/ be selected as
underlying forms, because they appear in the overwhelming majority of the
remaining forms in the paradigms of these nouns. Thus, if we apply (B′) consistently, we find that alternations occurring in exactly the same phonetic
context (palatals before *e*, velars elsewhere) must in some cases be analyzed
with underlying palatals and in others with underlying velars, without any
independent evidence for doing so.

It therefore appears that the surface alternant that best reveals the UR of
a morpheme need not be the alternant that occurs in isolation—see the earlier
discussion of (B)—nor the alternant that occurs in the most contexts—see the
discussion of (B′). The next hypothetical condition on URs that we shall
examine also belongs under the (B) heading in that it, too, tries to establish
general criteria for identifying the underlying value for an alternating phonetic
feature.

(B″)   *The UR of a morpheme may include both variant and invariant phonetic*
        properties. All of the variant properties selected to appear in the UR must
        occur in a single surface alternant of that morpheme, the basic alternant.
        The choice of the basic alternant is constrained by a principle of parallel-
        ism according to which the basic alternant for all morphemes of a given
        morphological class (noun, verb, particle, etc.) must occur in the same
        morphological context.

This parallelism condition is weaker than (B) and (B′) in that it does not fix
in advance the basic allomorph for all morphemes, but merely requires that if,
for example, the basic allomorph for a particular noun root is identified as
the nom. sg., then the allomorph appearing in the nom. sg. will be the basic
alternant for all other nouns.

(B″) is consistent with the Lardil data discussed above. We saw that the
morpheme /ŋuka/ ∼ /ŋuku/ 'water' has an /a/ ∼ /u/ alternation and that the
alternant /ŋuku/ appearing in the inflected form offers the best underlying
representation. (B″) requires that the allomorph appearing in the inflected
form be chosen as basic for all noun stems in Lardil. It correctly forces us to
set up the longer, nonreduced allomorph for a stem like 'nullah' /murkuni/ ∼
/murkunima/, since it is the latter allomorph that appears in the inflected form.

(B″) is consequently weaker than either (B) or (B′) in that it does not predict
in advance which morphological environment will yield the basic alternant of
a morpheme. Nevertheless, (B″) is still an extremely strong constraint placed

on URs because it claims that the basic alternants of a given morphological class will appear in the same context. There is, however, evidence that (B″) is too strong.

Consider the following data from Pengo, some of which we looked at earlier.

(35)

2nd singular imperative	3rd singular masculine past	gloss
cupa	cuptan	'spit'
tu:ba	tu:ptan	'blow'
eca	eccan	'shoot'
uja	uccan	'suck'
ho:ka	ho:ktan	'wash clothes'
maga	maktan	'sleep'

The 2nd sg. imperative is formed by suffixing -a to the verb root; the past tense is formed by suffixing -t- to the verb root ($t \longrightarrow c$ if preceded by c or j) and adding the subject marker (-an in the 3rd sg. masc.). The examples in (35) require positing the form of the verb root that appears in the imperative as basic; if the past-tense morpheme were basic instead, we could not account (phonologically) for the fact that /cup/ 'spit' retains a final /p/ in cupa, whereas /tu:p/ 'blow' converts final /p/ to /b/ in tu:ba (and so on for other examples). In other words, whereas obstruent-final roots may be either voiced or voiceless before the imperative suffix, they may only be voiceless before the past-tense marker -t-. It is possible to predict the past-tense form from the imperative form by means of a rule that devoices a voiced obstruent preceding a voiceless one, but not possible to predict the imperative form from the past by a phonologically conditioned rule. The imperative form thus represents the "position of maximal differentiation", while the past-tense represents a "neutralized position". The UR is the form that appears in the position of maximal differentiation, if there is to be a phonetic basis for a contrast such as cuP-a versus tu:B-a.

Having now constructed the argument where the imperative form of a verb root is posited as underlying, we now return to the parallelism constraint of (B″) that would require the imperative form to be basic for all verbs. With this in mind, let us examine the data in (36).

(36)

	2nd singular imperative	3rd singular masculine past	gloss
	aha	astan	'seize'
	gu:ha	gu:stan	'swallow'
	iha	istan	'strike'
cf.,	tuza	tustan	'wear'
	peza	pestan	'pick up'

There are no pairs such as *pesa/pestan* or *peha/pehtan*. In general [s] and [h] do not contrast in Pengo: [s] occurs word-finally and before voiceless consonants; [h] occurs prevocalically and before voiced consonants (though in some cases [h] will alternate optionally with [s] before voiced sonorant consonants). These examples indicate that not only are [s] and [h] in noncontrastive distribution, but that the same underlying sound unit may sometimes appear as [s] and at others as [h].

The parallelism requirement demands /ah/, /gu:h/, and /ih/ as the basic forms of 'seize', 'swallow', and 'strike'. Such URs would then require a rule like (37).

(37)   h ⟶ s/____ [−voice]

There are, however, considerations to suggest that /s/ rather than /h/ is the proper underlying representation, so that the URs for these morphemes would be /as/, /gu:s/, and /is/. In such an analysis the required rule would be as follows.

(38)   s ⟶ h/____ [+voiced]

Such URs would of course violate (B″), because the /s/ appears in the past-tense form and not in the imperative, whereas the URs of the roots in (35) appeared in the imperative and not the past-tense form.

A crucial argument for /s/ is provided by the following data.

(39)

Intransitive		Transitive		
2nd singular imperative	3rd singular masculine past	2nd singular imperative	3rd singular masculine past	gloss
laba	laptan	lapa	laptan	'fit into'
ruga	ruktan	ruka	ruktan	'hide'
maga	maktan	maka	maktan	'lie/lay down'
maza	mastan	maha	mastan	'turn'
vi:za	vi:stan	vi:ha	vi:stan	'finish'

In the first three of these forms the difference between the intransitive and transitive forms of the root is that the former ends in a voiced obstruent, the latter in the corresponding voiceless one. This pattern is extremely common in the language. At first glance 'turn' and 'finish' seem to violate this principle: We have *maza, maha* (not **masa*), and *vi:za, vi:ha* (not **vi:sa*). Instead of the expected /s/, we find /h/. To account for these forms it would seem that we need a second principle: Final /z/ in the intransitive form will be replaced by /h/ in the transitive form. But the additional statement is necessary only if /h/ is posited as basic from which the /s/ of *mastan*, for example, is derived. If /s/ is underlying and the imperative form of the root is derived from the past-tense form in these cases, the intransitive *maz-* and *vi:z-* will have the expected *mas-* and *vi:s-* as their transitive variants; /mas/ and /vi:s/ will then be converted to *mah-* and *vi:h-* before a voiced sound.

A second argument for underlying /s/ originates in another voicing alternation in Pengo. Vowel-final verb roots fall into two arbitrary classes: Class A devoices the initial underlying voiced obstruent of an immediately following suffix, while class B preserves the underlying voicing.

(40)

		I	II	III	IV	V	gloss
A		*ka:-*	*ka:-t-*	*ka:-pa-*	*ka:-ka-*	*ka:-hi-*	'watch'
		ḍo-	*ḍo-t-*	*ḍo-pa-*	*ḍo-ka-*	*ḍo-hi-*	'peck'
		ta-	*ta-t-*	*ta-pa-*	*ta-ka-*	*ta-hi-*	'bring'
B		*a:-*	*a:-d-*	*a:-ba-*	*a:-ga-*	*a:-zi-*	'be'
		ki-	*ki-d-*	*ki-ba-*	*ki-ga-*	*ki-zi-*	'do'
		va:-	*va:-d-*	*va:-ba-*	*va:-ga-*	*va:-zi-*	'come'

Column I gives the basic verb root; II, the verb stem used when the object, direct or indirect, is 1st or 2nd person; III, the intensive-frequentative verb stem; IV, the "motion" stem; V is a gerund. Note that in II we find *-t-* after the A roots but *-d-* after the B roots; in III, *-pa-* after A roots and *-ba-* after B roots; *-ka-* for A in IV but *-ga-* for B. In V, however, *-hi-* is the form that occurs following A roots, rather than the expected *-si-*, given that *-zi-* occurs after the B roots. This unexpected *-hi-* can be derived by the same principle that yields *-t-*, *-pa-*, and *-ka-*, *provided* we assume the *h* to be derived from underlying /s/. That is, /zi/ is converted to /si/ in roots of type A by the same principle that converts /ba/ to /pa/; /si/ is replaced by /hi/ via the general rule that changes /s/ to /h/ before a voiced sound. If the underlying form were /h/ and /s/ derived by rule from /h/, the appearance of *-hi-* in these examples would not follow from the general principles stated earlier.

If we are to account for the various voicing alternations and the $s \sim h$ alternation illustrated in (35), (36), (39), and (40) by general, motivated rules, then the UR of a verb root cannot be limited to a particular morphological category. The voicing alternations in (35) can be accounted for only if the imperative is posited as the UR of a given root, while the $s \sim h$ alternation is most appropriately described in terms of an underlying /s/, which appears in the past-tense form of the roots in (36).

The Russian data discussed earlier also provide a counterexample to (B″). Recall that the final-devoicing alternation (*trup*, *trup-u* versus *xlep*, *xleb-u*) requires that we take the allomorph appearing before various case suffixes as underlying, since the underlying voicing opposition is neutralized in word-final position. But nouns with oxytonic stress (*stól*, *stal-ú* versus *vráč*, *vrač-ú*) require that we posit as underlying the unaffixed nominative singular forms because only in this form of the paradigm does the stress fall on the root vowel, revealing the underlying /o/ versus /a/ contrast. In unstressed position underlying /o/ merges with underlying /a/ into phonetic *a*.

Thus, (B″) cannot be accepted as an adequate constraint on underlying representations because the phonologist must select the appropriate underlying form for each morpheme considered individually and not be tied to a particular context for all morphemes of a given class. This is true for a fairly obvious reason. The underlying representation of a morpheme will appear unaltered only in some environments. There is no reason to expect that there will be a single environment in which all morphemes of a given class will be unaffected by a given morphophonemic rule.

All of the principles under the heading (B) attempt to restrict the assignment of an underlying value for alternating phonetic features. They do this by claiming that certain surface alternants of a morpheme will be accurate indicators of what the UR of the morpheme is. A somewhat different approach to the problem of constraining URs is provided by the condition on grammars expressed as (C).

(C)   *The UR of a morpheme includes those variant and invariant phonetic properties that are idiosyncratic. But all of the variant properties assigned to the UR must occur together in at least one phonetic manifestation of the morpheme. This manifestation can be referred to as the **basic alternant**.*

(C) leaves us greater freedom to select the appropriate UR for any morpheme than the various conditions under (B) allowed. In deciding which value to assign to the underlying structure of an alternating phonetic feature, we are not limited to any particular form or forms of the morpheme nor does a decision about the UR of one morpheme commit us to a decision about any other morpheme.

Nevertheless, (C) is a strong restriction on URs and seems to have been followed by a number of linguists in the past (see McCawley, 1967). (C) claims that if there are two or more alternating phonetic features, the choice of an underlying value for one of these features will restrict the choice of an underlying value for all the other alternating features, since there must be at least one PR that directly manifests ALL the underlying values of these alternating features.

What remain as counterexamples to the (B) conditions can be accounted for by (C). For example, for the Pengo data (C) allows the form of the verb root that appears in the past tense as underlying in *gu:h-a, gu:s-t-an*, while the imperative may be selected as the basic alternant in the case of *tu:b-a, tu:p-t-an*. Similarly, the basic alternant for *xlep, xleb-u* in the Russian example may be the one appearing before a case suffix, while for *stól, stal-ú* (C) permits the unaffixed allomorph to be identified as the basic alternant.

There are, nevertheless, severe problems with (C). For instance, it accounts for the Russian data presented in the preceding pages of this chapter by positing as underlying the suffixed allomorph for noun roots manifesting the voicing alternation, while positing the unsuffixed alternant for end stressed nouns that exhibit the neutralization of the /o/ versus /a/ contrast. But there is no reason not to expect both of these alternations to occur in the same noun root. If they do, then (C) will not permit us to posit the *maximally general* UR—the UR that can be converted into the correct surface alternants by the rules of final devoicing and unstressed /o/ ⟶ *a*. Morphemes having these properties include *pirók, pirag-á* 'pie', and *sapók, sapag-á* 'boot'. In all forms of the paradigm except for the nom. and acc. sg., the accent is on the final syllable, inducing a change of the root vowel /o/ to *a*. But in the nom. and acc. sg., where the underlying /o/ shows up phonetically, the root is unsuffixed, so that the underlying /g/ is devoiced on the surface level. Thus, if we follow (C) in constructing the UR for 'boot', we must resort to arbitrary, nonphonetic information in order to describe its phonological behavior. On the other hand, if we do not require that all of the underlying values for alternating features appear in one basic alternant, we can assign this morpheme the UR /sapog/, and the correct phonetic alternants will be generated by the independently needed rules of final devoicing and unstressed /o/ neutralization.

Similarly, the Tonkawa data discussed earlier with respect to (A′) provide insuperable difficulties for (C) as well as for all of the (B) conditions. Recall that Tonkawa verb roots such as 'hoe', 'lick', and 'cut' were argued to have the URs /notoxo/, /netale/, and /picena/ respectively. Many similar verbs exist in the language. The vowels in these verbs all alternate with ∅. Furthermore, it is a fact that there are no surface realizations where ALL three vowels of one morpheme are pronounced. There is always at least one (and sometimes two) of the vowels subject to a deletion rule, regardless of the context. Consequently, to maintain that (C) is an appropriate condition on the grammar of Tonkawa would require URs to be set up for these verb roots where at least one of the vowels is omitted. But it will be totally arbitrary which vowel is omitted, and in any case nonphonetic information will be required in order to insert the omitted vowel in the PRs where it occurs.

Finally, Yawelmani verbal roots with the phonetic alternants CV:CiC- and CVCC- could not be assigned the underlying representation CV:CC-, since distinctive length only appears when *i*, which we argued to be inserted and not part of the UR, is present. Condition (C) would require setting up one of the surface alternants as the UR, with the accompanying complications discussed earlier.

The preceding examples show that (C) is too restrictive a condition, since it bars a number of (internally) motivated analyses. How might (C) be modified so as to accommodate these examples, but at the same time impose significant restrictions on URs? (D) provides a possible approach to the problem.

(D)   *The UR of a morpheme includes all those variant and invariant phonetic properties that are idiosyncratic. Given a morpheme with the underlying shape* /P/$_i$, /P/$_j$, . . . /P/$_n$, *there must be a* [P]$_j$ *(where* [P]$_j$ *is one of the phonetic realizations of* /P/$_j$) *such that* [P]$_j$ *contains all of the feature specifications of* /P/$_j$.

(D) requires that all of the underlying specifications of variant features as well as of idiosyncratic invariant features for any segment must occur together in a single phonetic realization of that segment. This condition resembles (C) except that it is narrowed in scope, applying just to the relationship between underlying segments and their phonetic reflexes, as opposed to the relationship between the entire UR of a morpheme and its associated PRs. Hence, (D) is less restrictive than (C) in that it permits one segment in the UR to be revealed in one PR and another segment in some other PR. At the same time it imposes a relatively strong limitation on URs by requiring that each segment in an UR be more or less directly manifested on the surface.

Condition (D) permits the appropriate UR for 'boot' in Russian—namely, /sapog/. The segment /o/ appears in the phonetic form *sapók*, while the /g/ appears in the phonetic form *sapag-á*. Since (D) requires only that each underlying element surface directly in one phonetic alternant and not that all of the segments be manifested in the SAME phonetic alternant, /sapog/ is an acceptable UR as far as (D) is concerned. Similarly, (D) allows the UR /picena/ for 'cut' in Tonkawa, since each of the sounds in this UR appears in at least one of the surface forms of the morpheme (though there is no surface alternant where all the sounds are pronounced).

Although (D) permits appropriate descriptions of all the language data so far discussed in this chapter, it still seems too restrictive. If (D) were accepted as an absolute condition on grammars, what appear to be well-motivated analyses would be disallowed. One such example is developed in considerable detail below.

In Yawelmani, only three long vowels occur (in general) in surface structure, whereas five short vowels occur.

(41)	Yawelmani long vowels		e:	a:	o:	
	Yawelmani short vowels	i	e	a	o	u

Of the five short vowels, only four are clearly underlying sounds; the vowel *e* is a surface variant of the long vowel *e:*, arising from the rule of vowel shortening discussed earlier—see. *me:k'-al* 'might swallow', but *mek'-hin*, 'swallows'. (See the following discussion for additional information regarding the vowel /e/.)

In many languages, long and short vowels occur 'paired'; that is, for any given short vowel there is a corresponding long vowel structurally parallel to it (though not necessarily of precisely the same quality). At first glance, Yawelmani appears to have an asymmetric vowel system, since the three surface long vowels *e:*, *a:*, and *o:* do not pair neatly with the four underlying short vowels. What we propose to do here is to present a substantial amount of evidence supporting the claim that the underlying long vowel system in Yawelmani is *i:*, *a:*, *o:*, and *u:*. We will argue that surface *e:* derives from underlying *i:*, while surface *o:* has its source in two different underlying segments, *o:* and *u:*. Postulating underlying *i:* and *u:* will be shown to violate (D), since most morphemes containing an underlying i: or u: do not have surface realizations where these segments appear in an unaltered form. An underlying i: may appear on the surface as e:, e, i, o:, or o (as the consequence of various phonological and morphological rules of the language), but generally not as i:. An underlying u: may appear on the surface as o:, o, or u, but generally not as u:. Those morphemes where underlying i: and u: never appear as such violate (D).

Let us refer to the proposed analysis of Yawelmani that postulates underlying high long vowels as the "abstract" analysis. The first set of data supporting the abstract analysis involves the phenomenon of vowel harmony, which occurs extensively in Yawelmani. Examination of verb roots and suffixes containing underlying short vowels provides considerable evidence for a rule of vowel harmony of the following form.

(42)
$$\text{vowel harmony} \quad \begin{bmatrix} V \\ \alpha\text{high} \end{bmatrix} \longrightarrow \begin{bmatrix} +\text{round} \\ +\text{back} \end{bmatrix} \Big/ \begin{bmatrix} V \\ +\text{round} \\ \alpha\text{high} \end{bmatrix} C_0 \underline{\quad\quad}$$

Verbally stated, this rule claims that a vowel will become rounded and back if it is preceded by a rounded vowel of the same height within the word.

Alternations such as those listed below support this rule.

(43)

nonfuture	nonfuture passive	precative	dubitative	gloss
xat-hin	xat-it	xat-xa	xat-al	'eat'
xil-hin	xil-it	xil-xa	xil-al	'tangle'
bok'-hin	bok'-it	bok'-xo	bok'-ol	'find'
dub-hun	dub-ut	dub-xa	dub-al	'lead by hand'
max-hin	max-it	max-xa	max-al	'procure'
giy'-hin	giy'-it	giy'-xa	giy'-al	'touch'
k'o?-hin	k'o?-it	k'o?-xo	k'o?-ol	'throw'
hud-hun	hud-ut	hud-xa	hud-al	'recognize'

With one exception, there are no nonalternating suffixes in Yawelmani. Suffixes containing a high vowel, like -hin/-hun, have the unrounded variant following the vowels i, a, or o, whereas the rounded variant appears after u. Suffixes containing a nonhigh vowel, like -xa/-xo, exhibit the unrounded variant after i, a, or u, whereas the rounded variant appears after o. These facts can be accounted for nicely if we assume that the high vowel suffixes have an underlying i and the low vowel suffixes have a underlying a, and the rule of vowel harmony rounds a vowel that is preceded by a rounded vowel of the same height. Thus i will harmonize with a preceding u while a will harmonize with a preceding o. (It should be pointed out that $e(:)$ and $o(:)$ in Yawelmani are phonetically [$\varepsilon(:)$] and [$\mathrm{o}(:)$].)

Let us consider now verb roots containing long vowels in the underlying structures. These long vowels may, of course, appear shortened on the surface as a result of vowel shortening as discussed earlier.

(44)

nonfuture	nonfuture passive	precative	dubitative	gloss
ṣap-hin	ṣa:p-it	ṣap-xa	ṣa:p-al	'burn'
mek'-hin	me:k'-it	mek'-xa	me:k'-al	'swallow'
dos-hin	do:s-it	dos-xo	do:s-ol	'report'
c'om-hun	c'o:m-ut	c'om-xa	c'o:m-al	'destroy'

These examples obviously present obstacles to our rule of vowel harmony, as formulated earlier. In particular, the root *c'o:m-* 'destroy' reveals a discrepancy when it is compared with *do:s-* 'report'. Both of these roots contain the vowel *o:* on the surface level (which is shortened to *o* when a consonant cluster follows). Vowel harmony predicts that a suffix containing the vowel *i* will not change to *u* after a nonhigh rounded vowel, while a suffix containing *a* will change to *o*. Examination of the data reveals that *do:s-* behaves as expected: We find *do:s-it* and *do:s-ol*. *c'o:m-* poses a problem. Surprisingly, an *i* vowel after this root is changed to *u*, while an *a* vowel remains unaffected: *c'o:m-ut*, but *c'o:m-al*. *do:s-* and *c'o:m-* are not isolated examples.

(45)
wo:n-ol	'might hide'	won-hin	'hides'
sonl-ol	'might pack on back'	so:nil-hin	'packs on back'
hotn-ol	'might take the scent'	ho:tin-hin	'takes the scent'

versus

ṣo:g-al	'might pull out a cork'	ṣog-hun	'pulls out a cork'
wo:ʔy-al	'might fall asleep'	wo:ʔuy-hun	'falls asleep'
doll-al	'might climb'	do:lul-hun	'climbs'

(A number of these roots have the underlying structure CV:CC- and are subject to the rule of vowel epenthesis when followed by a consonant-initial suffix. The epenthetic *i* vowel undergoes vowel harmony, supporting the hypothesis that epenthesis must precede harmony.)

It is very simple to characterize the behavior of a root like *c'o:m-*; it behaves as though it contains a *high* rounded vowel and not a non-high rounded vowel. *do:s-*, on the other hand, behaves like a root containing a nonhigh rounded vowel. This difference in behavior can be readily accounted for if surface *o:* is derived from two different underlying vowels, *u:* and *o:*. For then one would posit the UR /c'u:m/ 'destroy' but /do:s/ 'report'. Given a UR like /c'u:m/, it would be necessary to include in the grammar a rule of vowel lowering that would have the effect of lowering *u:* to *o:*. Since *u:* does not generally occur in the language, the rule of vowel lowering would not have to be restricted contextually at all. All *u:* vowels would be lowered. (Actually, we will generalize vowel lowering so that it lowers *i:* to *e:* as well as *u:* to *o:*.)

The derivation of *c'om-hun* versus *c'om-xa* is given in (46).

(46)   /c'u:m-hin/   /c'u:m-xa/
           c'u:m-hun   inapplicable   vowel harmony
           c'o:m-hun   *c'o:m-xa*   vowel lowering
           c'om-hun   *c'om-xa*   vowel shortening

It is crucial that vowel harmony precede vowel lowering; if lowering were to apply first, incorrect derivations would result.

(47)   /c'u:m-hin/   /c'u:m-xa/
           c'o:m-hin   *c'o:m-xa*   vowel lowering
           inapplicable   *c'o:m-xo*   vowel harmony
           *c'om-hin   **c'om-xo*   vowel shortening

It is also crucial that vowel lowering precede vowel shortening; otherwise the following incorrect derivations would result.

(48)   /c'u:m-hin/   /c'u:m-xa/
           c'u:m-hun   inapplicable   vowel harmony
           *c'um-hun   **c'um-xa*   vowel shortening
           inapplicable   inapplicable   vowel lowering

Vowel lowering would not apply to an intermediate representation like /c'um-hun/ or /c'um-xa/ since only long high vowels lower, not short high vowels (cf., *hud-hun* 'recognizes', not **hod-hon*).

Vowel harmony, then, furnishes a certain amount of evidence for deriving some surface *o:* vowels from underlying *u:*. Other surface *o:* vowels are derived from underlying *o:*. Vowel harmony also provides evidence for deriving surface *e:* and its variant *e* from underlying *i:*. Consider, for instance, the behavior of the future suffix in the data below.

(49)   *?ayy-en*   'will pole a boat'   *c'o:m-on*   'will devour'
       ?edl-en   'will get hungry'   *t'uyt'uy-on* 'will shoot repeatedly'
       bok'-en   'will find'   *wo?y-on*   'will fall asleep'

Notice that the future suffix, which always appears in word-final position, has two surface alternants: *-en* and *-on*. This variation would certainly appear to be the consequence of the vowel harmony rule. But given that *e* is a nonhigh vowel, one would expect it to appear rounded after nonhigh rounded vowels and remain unrounded after high rounded vowels. This is not what happens, however. *bok'-en* shows that the vowel of the future suffix fails to round after a nonhigh rounded vowel. *t'uyt'uy-on* indicates that this suffix does harmonize with a high rounded vowel. The *-on* variant also occurs in examples like *c'o:m-on* and *wo?y-on*; we have already seen that these roots have an underlying *u:* (/c'u:m/ and /wu:?y/).

While the future suffix appears to exhibit a strange pattern of behavior, a simple explanation is still possible—if we admit *i:* as an underlying vowel in Yawelmani. Recall that *e* is clearly derived from the vowel *e:* in most instances via the rule of vowel shortening (which operates in the context

$$\underline{\quad} C \left\{ \begin{matrix} \# \\ C \end{matrix} \right\}).$$

If *e:* is derived from underlying *i:*, then the underlying representation of the future suffix will be /i:n/. Given this underlying form, the surface realizations of this morpheme will follow automatically from the rules already discussed.

(50)

/bok'-i:n/	/c'u:m-i:n/	
inapplicable	c'u:m-u:n	vowel harmony
bok'-e:n	c'o:m-o:n	vowel lowering
bok'-en	c'o:m-on	vowel shortening

The morphophonemic behavior of the future suffix can be accounted for by independently motivated rules only if *i:* is admitted as an underlying vowel in Yawelmani.

There are a few other morphemes whose vowel harmony pattern suggests that *e:* should be derived from an underlying high vowel. Compare *moyo'n-e:-* 'make tired' (cf., /mo:yn/ 'be tired') with *hubu?s-o:-* 'make choose' (cf., /hubs/ 'choose'). Causative verbs can be constructed in Yawelmani (in some, but not all, cases) by suffixing the vowel *-e:-* to the verb root. The root itself is modified in the process, but this modification is not relevant here. The crucial point is that the causative suffix *-e:-* is subject to vowel harmony. It does not, however, harmonize after a nonhigh rounded vowel (cf., *moyo'n-e:-*), rather it harmonizes after a high rounded vowel (cf., *hubu?s-o:-*). This behavior can be readily accounted for if the causative suffix has an underlying *i:* vowel, but not otherwise.

We have shown so far that the rule of vowel harmony can account for all the alternations between unrounded and rounded vowels, but only if surface *e:* (~*e*) is derived from *i:* and some surface *o:* (~*o*) vowels derive from *u:*. Let us turn now to additional data, unrelated to vowel harmony, that support our "abstract" analysis.

The structure of verb roots in Yawelmani is highly restricted. There are two basic types: monosyllabic and disyllabic roots. Monosyllabic roots have the structure CV(:)C(C). That is, they all begin with one and only one consonant, which is followed by a vowel that may be long or short, which in turn is followed by at least one and possibly two consonants. The disyllabic roots require closer scrutiny. Examples are given in (51).

(51)

dubitative	nonfuture	gloss
p'axa:t'-al	p'axat'-hin	'mourn'
hiwe:t-al	hiwet-hin	'walk'
?opo:t-ol	?opot-hin	'arise from bed'
ṣudo:k'-al	ṣudok'-hun	'remove'
pana-l	pana:-hin	'arrive'
?ile-l	?ile:-hin	'fan'
hoyo-l	hoyo:-hin	'name'
c'uyo-l	c'uyo:-hun	'urinate'

All of the above roots can be analyzed as having the basic structure CVCV:(C)-. The long vowel in these roots is shortened in the context

$$\_\_\_C \left\{ \begin{matrix} \# \\ C \end{matrix} \right\}$$

by vowel shortening. In the case of a root like /ʔopo:t/, this shortening occurs when a consonant-initial suffix is added. In the case of a root like /hoyo:/ this shortening occurs as a consequence of another rule that elides the initial vowel of the dubitative suffix -al when preceded by a vowel. When the suffixal vowel is deleted in /hoyo:-al/, the final vowel of the root precedes a word-final consonant and thus shortens.

An examination of all disyllabic verb roots demonstrates that only FOUR combinations of vowels occur in such roots: (a) $CaCa:$(C)-, (b) $CiCe:$(C)-, (c) $CoCo:$(C)-, and (d) $CuCo:$(C)-. Note that the (a) and (c) patterns can be characterized very simply: The first and the second vowels have the same quality, but the first is short while the second is long. The (b) and (d) patterns do not fit this description on the surface level, but if we adopt the abstract analysis then they too can be explained by the same generalization. If $e:$ derives from underlying $i:$, then the (b) pattern is really $CiCi:$(C)- at the underlying level. The two vowels do have the same quality underlyingly. Similarly, if surface $o:$ comes from either basic $o:$ or basic $u:$, then the (d) pattern can be set up as $CuCu:$(C)- in its underlying structure. All disyllabic roots now have the structure $CV_1CV_1:$(C)- at the underlying level.

This analysis of disyllabic roots is supported by the observation that roots of type (c) and (d) exhibit quite different behavior with respect to vowel harmony. The final $o:$ of $CoCo:$(C)- type roots behaves like nonhigh vowels, yielding forms such as $ʔopo:t$-ol and $ʔopot$-hin, whereas the final $o:$ of $CuCo:$(C)- type roots behaves like a high vowel, yielding forms such as $ṣudo:k'$-al and $ṣudok'$-hun. If $CoCo:$(C)- type roots have this same shape in their underlying structure, it follows that they will induce following nonhigh vowels only to harmonize but not affect high vowels. On the other hand, if $CuCo:$(C)- type roots are derived from underlying representations of the form $CuCu:$(C)-, it follows that they will induce following high vowels to harmonize but not affect nonhigh vowels.

The evidence provided by disyllabic roots for the "abstract" analysis is actually more persuasive than one might think. We have indicated so far that there are just four types of disyllabic verb roots in the language, and that these four types can be subsumed under one generalization if the "abstract" analysis is accepted. Furthermore, the way in which the vowel of the suffix harmonizes with the vowel of the root supports the underlying structure proposed. We can reinforce these arguments further, however, because of the intricate nature of Yawelmani morphology. Although verb roots may either be of the shape CV(:)C(C)- or $CV_1CV_1:$(C)- in their underlying structure, there are a variety of suffixes in the language which require a preceding root to assume a particular shape. In particular, there are some suffixes that require that all verb roots become disyllabic. The following chart illustrates the manner in which various verb roots are altered to a disyllabic pattern.

(52)

verb root	disyllabic stem shape	gloss
giy'-	*giy'e:-*	'touch'
hud-	*hudo:-*	'recognize'
bok'-	*bok'o:-*	'find'
xat-	*xata:-*	'eat'
ṭo:k'-	*ṭok'o:-*	'strike'
c'o:m-	*c'umo:-*	'destroy'
me:k'-	*mik'e:-*	'swallow'
ʔilk-	*ʔile:k-*	'sing'
luk'l-	*luk'o:l-*	'bury'
lown-	*lowo:n-*	'attend a feast'
do:ll-	*dulo:l-*	'climb'
mo:yn-	*moyo:n-*	'get tired'

For instance, the noun-forming suffix *-iwse:l-* requires that a preceding verb root be transformed into a disyllabic stem shape. The verb *luk'l-* 'bury' thus appears in the shape *luk'o:l-* in the noun stem *luk'o:l-uwso:l-* 'cemetery (literally, place for burying one another)'. The verb root *lown-* 'attend a feast' appears in the shape *lowo:n-* in the noun stem *lowo:n-iwse:l-* 'place where they attend one another's feast'. The noun-forming suffix *-hne:l-* also requires that a preceding verb root be transformed into a disyllabic stem shape. The verb root *c'o:m-* 'destroy' (which has already been shown to behave as though it contains a high rounded vowel) assumes the disyllabic stem shape *c'umo:-* in the noun stem *c'umo-hno:l-* 'place of x's being destroyed'. The verb root *ṭo:k'-* 'strike' (which triggers the kind of harmony that one would expect from a nonhigh rounded vowel) assumes the disyllabic stem shape *ṭok'o:-* in the noun stem *ṭok'o-hne:l-* 'place that was struck'. Note that in the preceding two examples, the initial consonant cluster of *-hne:l-* induces the shortening of the final vowel of the disyllabic stem.

Let us consider now the significance of the data just introduced. First of all, it can be readily observed that the disyllabic stems in (52) once again fall into the four patterns observed earlier. Secondly, there is a systematic correlation between the vowel of the underlying verb root and the disyllabic shape that this verb root assumes. For example, all verbs that have a short *i* vowel in their underlying representation (e.g., *giy'-* 'touch' and *ʔilk-* 'sing') assume the disyllabic pattern C*i*C*e*:(C)-. Similarly, all verbs that have a short *u* vowel in their underlying representation (e.g., *hud-* 'recognize' and *luk'l-* 'bury') assume the disyllabic pattern C*u*C*o*:(C)-. Furthermore, all verb roots that have a long *o:* vowel that behaves like a high vowel with respect to vowel harmony (e.g., *c'o:m-* 'destroy' and *do:ll-* 'climb') assume the disyllabic pattern C*u*C*o*:(C)- as well. In contrast, roots that have a short *o* vowel (e.g., *bok'-* 'find' and *lown-* 'attend a feast') or a long *o:* that behaves like a nonhigh vowel with respect to vowel harmony (e.g., *ṭo:k'-* 'strike' and *mo:yn-* 'get tired') assume the disyllabic stem pattern CoCo:(C)-.

Given the "abstract" analysis of Yawelmani proposed here the formation of the disyllabic stem in (52) from the underlying verb root is entirely straightforward. One simply takes the underlying vowel of the root and uses it in both vowel slots in the disyllabic formula $CV_1CV_1:(C)$, maintaining at the same time the original consonantal structure. For example, the root *giy-* will become *giy'i:-*, the root *hud-* will become *hudu:-*, and so on. The rule of vowel lowering will derive the correct surface form *diy'e:-* and *hudo:-*. Similarly, *luk'l-* will be altered to *luk'u:l-* whereas *lown-* will be altered to *lowo:n-*; vowel lowering will lower the *u:* of *luk'u:l-*, but only after vowel harmony operates. The derivation of *luk'o:l-uwso:l-* will thus be as follows.

(53) luk'l-iwsi:l-/

luk'u:l-iwsi:l-	morphological rule that produces the disyllabic stem
luk'u:l-uwsu:l-	vowel harmony
luk'o:l-uwso:l-	vowel lowering

It should be pointed out here that the fact that a root like *c'o:m-* 'destroy' adopts the disyllabic shape *c'umo:-* strongly confirms the proposal that this root has the UR /c'u:m/. For we now have two totally independent reasons for assuming this underlying representation: (1) the kind of vowel harmony that *c'o:m-* induces and (2) the disyllabic stem shape that it assumes.

The existence of suffixes that require that a preceding verb root adopt the pattern CVC(C)- provides yet more evidence for the "abstract" analysis of Yawelmani vowels. The following chart illustrates how various underlying verb roots are transformed so as to fit into the required stem shape.

(54)

verb root	CV̆C(C)- stem shape	gloss
me:k'-	*mik'*	'swallow'
do:s-	*dos-*	'report'
c'o:m-	*c'um-*	'destroy'
wa:xl-	*waxl-*	'weep'
şe:nṭ'-	*şinṭ'-*	'smell'
wo ʔy-	*wu ʔy-*	'fall asleep'
c'uyo:-	*c'uy-*	'urinate'
hoyo:-	*hoy-*	'name'
ʔile:-	*ʔil-*	'fan'

For example, the causative suffix *-a:la:-* requires that a preceding verb root adopt the CV̆C(C)- stem pattern. The root *me:k'-* 'swallow' assumes the shape *mik'-* in *mik'-a:la:-* 'make swallow'. The root *c'o:m-* 'destroy' (which would have an underlying *u:*, given the "abstract" analysis) assumes the shape *c'um-* in *c'um-a:la:-* 'make destroy', while the root *do:s-* 'report' (which would have an underlying *o:*) has the shape *dos-* in *dos-a:la:-* 'make report'. These examples illustrate very clearly that when an underlying long vowel is shortened so as to conform to the CV̆C(C)- stem pattern, surface *e:* is shortened to *i* and surface *o:* is shortened to either *u* or *o*. There is, however, a definite pattern to the shortening of *o:*. Those surface *o:* vowels that act like high vowels with respect to vowel harmony shorten to *u*, while those surface *o:* vowels that behave like nonhigh vowels with respect to vowel harmony shorten to *o*. This pattern follows automatically from the "abstract" analysis, if it is the underlying (and not the surface) vowel that is shortened to form the CV̆C(C)- stem. Given URs like /mi:k'/, /c'u:m/, and /do:s/, the correct CV̆(C)- stems will result if we simply shorten the underlying long vowel of these roots.

If the "abstract" analysis of Yawelmani is accepted, the stem shapes that are required by various suffixes in the language can all be seen to involve a crucial shortening or lengthening of the underlying root vowel. (In some instances other changes are involved as well—vowel replacements, consonantal increments, etc.) Limitations of space require that we forego further illustration of this general point. It should be noted, however, that all of the stem forms not discussed here agree perfectly with the "abstract" analysis.

We mentioned earlier than the long vowels *i:* and *u:* do not generally occur in Yawelmani phonetic representations. One exception to this statement results from a contraction of *iw* to *i:* and of *uw* to *u:* in certain instances of these sequences (but not all). These surface *i:* and *u:* vowels are not subject to the proposed rule of vowel lowering. We could account for this fact by ordering vowel lowering *before* the contraction rule that produces *i:* from *iw* and *u:* from *uw*. There is, however, a second exception to the statement that *i:* and *u:* do not occur phonetically. Consider the following data.

(55)

verb root	causative stem	gloss
di ʔṣ-	*di ʔi: s-e:-*	'make, repair'
ʔugn-	*ʔugu: n-o:-*	'drink'
be: wn-	*biwi: n-e:-*	'sew'
mo: yn-	*moyo: n-e:-*	'get tired'
p'axa: t'-	*p'axa: t'-e:-*	'mourn'

The causative stem illustrated in (55) occurs only with verb roots that possess three consonants in their underlying representation. In these cases, a short vowel appears between the first two consonants and a long vowel of the same quality appears between the second and third. The long *i:* in a form like *di ʔi: s-e:-* and the long *u:* in a form like *ʔugu: n-o:-* do not undergo vowel lowering. Whereas long high vowels in other stem formations are subject to vowel lowering, the causative stem as exemplified must somehow avoid this rule.

Because of the existence of causative stems like *di ʔi: s-e:-* and *ʔugu: n-o:-*, it cannot be said that the "abstract" analysis of Yawelmani involves postulating vowels that never occur in the language. Long, high vowels do occur. Nevertheless, the "abstract" analysis violates (D). An underlying form such as /c'u:m/ has various surface realizations: *c'o:m-*, *c'om-*, *c'um-*, *c'umo:-*, etc. All of the phonetic features of the underlying *u:* (namely, [+syll, +high, +long, +round]) are manifested in the various surface forms of this morpheme. But it is not the case that all of the features of *u:* are found together in a single surface reflex of this underlying segment. *u:* never occurs as a surface realization of the underlying *u:*.

Consequently, if the "abstract" analysis of Yawelmani is an appropriate one (and on the basis of internal evidence it seems to be), then (D) must be rejected, since it would disallow this analysis of Yawelmani vowels. Yawelmani is somewhat unique in terms of the AMOUNT of evidence that can be marshalled in favor of an abstract analysis that violates (D). There are, however, other cases where there is a certain amount of evidence in favor of analyses that violate this condition.

In the main dialect of Pengo examined in Burrow (1970) all obstruents occur in voiced/voiceless pairs: *b*/*p*, *d*/*t*, *z*/*s*, *ḍ*/*ṭ*, *j*/*c*, *g*/*k*. We will refer to this as dialect A. There are certain other dialects of Pengo that substitute *j* for the *z* of dialect A. Thus these dialects (call them the B dialects) lack a voiced *z* phonetically, although they retain the voiceless *s*. As will be seen below, there is evidence that B dialects have undergone a sound change whereby *z* has been replaced by *j*. The principal phonological consequence of the *z* > *j* change on the internal structure of the B dialects is that there are two morphophonemically distinct surface *j* sounds.

The discussion of Pengo earlier in this chapter noted that the language contains a rule of voicing assimilation. For example, the root *uj-*, 'suck', has the past tense stem *uc-c-* in both the A and B dialects as a consequence of this voicing assimilation process. In dialect A there is another root *noz-*, 'wash', which has the past stem *nos-t-*; in dialect B this root is *noj-*, but it also has the past stem *nos-t-*. Thus, some roots in dialect B ending in *j* devoice to *c* while others devoice to *s*. The roots that devoice to *s* are precisely the ones that are pronounced as *z* in dialect A.

Given the distinct morphophonemic behavior of the *j* of *uj-* and that of *noj-* in B dialects, we must incorporate sufficient apparatus to account for the difference between *uc-c* (clearly from *uj-t-*) and *nos-t* (from ?) into the grammar of Pengo. We might of course mark *noj-* as distinct in that it undergoes a special *c* ⟶ *s* rule: thus, *noj-t-* would first become *noc-t-* by voice assimilation, then *nos-t-* by the special rule. Alternatively, specially marked *j*'s could be shifted to *s* directly before voiceless consonants. But in either analysis this additional rule would be limited to specially marked forms, since the *j* of *uj-* must not become *s* in the past stem.

There is an obvious alternative solution to the problem of the morphophonemic behavior of *noj-*: One could assign to it, and other roots like it, the underlying structure /noz/. All that would then be required is to posit a rule

$z \longrightarrow j$, applied after voice assimilation. We would then obtain derivations like the following.

(56) /noz-a/   /uj-a/   /noz-t-/   /uj-t-/

		nos-t-	uc-t-	voice assimilation
	noj-a			$z \longrightarrow j$
			uc-c-	other

This analysis posits an underlying element /z/ that does not actually appear phonetically as z: its underlying voicing is apparent in the *noj-* alternant, its underlying continuant character in the alternant *nos-*. But there is no alternant in the B dialects where it appears phonetically both voiced and a continuant. Notice that this analysis also provides the B dialects with a symmetrical underlying system where each obstruent appears both voiced and voiceless. The imbalance in the system—the lack of a z phonetically—is treated simply as a phonetic gap not a phonological one.

Additional morphophonemic evidence in favor of the proposed analysis is that Pengo verb roots fall into two classes, A and B. A verbs induce a devoicing of an immediately following voiced consonant, while B verbs do not. Vowel-final roots may belong to either type. In A dialects, the gerund suffix is *-zi* for B verbs, but *-hi < -si* (as above) for A verbs, yielding, *a:zi* (root *a:-* 'be'), *o:-zi* (root *o:-* 'take away'), *va:-zi* (root *va:-* 'come'), but *ka:-hi* (root *ka:-* 'watch'), *do-hi* (root *do-* 'pick'), *ro-hi* (root *ro-* 'jump'). In B dialects, however, *-zi* has been replaced by *-ji*. If *-ji* were the underlying gerund suffix in these dialects, it would have to be converted to *-si* ($> -hi$); our independently motivated rule however, simply devoices a voiced obstruent after a type A verb. Thus, *-ci would be the expected form of the gerund suffix after A verbs. If we posit *-zi* as the underlying form—in B as well as in A dialects—then the general devoicing of consonants after A roots will yield the correct *-si* (ultimately *-hi*). The rule $z \longrightarrow j$ will apply after this devoicing rule. The required derivations are as follows.

(57)   /a:-zi/(B root)   /ka:-zi/(A root)

	/a:-zi/(B root)	/ka:-zi/(A root)	
		ka:-si	devoicing
	a:-ji		$z \longrightarrow j$
		ka:-hi	$s \longrightarrow h$

Another case where an analysis that violates (D) appears to be internally motivated is provided by Huamelultec Chontal, a Hokan language (Waterhouse, 1949). In this language 3rd sg. verbal forms have no overt affix marking person and number. However, stems that ordinarily begin with an alveolar consonant assume a special shape in the 3rd sg. form that begins with the corresponding alveopalatal consonant. Stems that do not have an initial alveolar have the same form in the 3rd sg. as in other verbal forms. Some examples of the alternation are as follows.

(58)

ceepa ya?	'I went'	*čeepa*	'he went'
simpa ya?	'I saw'	*šimpa*	'he saw'
ɬo?pa ya?	'I moved it'	*ƚʸo?pa*	'he moved it'
tepa ya?	'I bit it'	*tʸepa*	'he bit it'
n'apa ya?	'I bought it'	*ñ'apa*	'he bought it'
napa ya?	'I hit'	*ñapa*	'he hit'
loopa ya?	'I played'	*lʸoopa*	'he played'

These alternations can be readily accounted for by a rule that converts a stem-initial alveolar to the corresponding alveopalatal when the verb is in the 3rd sing. It is of some interest that there is a rule in Huamelultec Chontal that effects a parallel change of alveolars to alveopalatals after a high vowel or *y*. However, to our knowledge there is no independent evidence in this dialect that would warrant positing a 3rd sg. prefix containing a high vowel or *y*, which could serve to condition the observed changes. Consequently, we will assume that a morphologically conditioned rule is adequate to account for the appearance of the alveopalatal consonant in 3rd sg. forms.

Waterhouse (1949) notes an additional complication with respect to 3rd sg. verbal forms that has direct relevance to (D). Although the affricate *c* and the continuant *s* are contrastive in the speech of older speakers of the language (cf., *acala?* 'egg white' and *asalá?* 'wings'), younger speakers are gradually losing this contrast, replacing *c* by *s*. The degree to which *c* had merged with *s* at the time of Waterhouse's description varied from speaker to speaker. For some the merger was complete—*s* always occurred instead of the *c* of the older speakers. For others the merger was partial, but with *s* most likely to replace *c* in frequently used words. Despite this variation speakers consistently employed *č* in the 3rd sg. forms of verbs with initial *c* (in the speech of older people) and *š* in the 3rd sg. forms of verbs with initial *s* (in the speech of both older and younger speakers. Morphophonemically, then, the *s* of younger speakers, derived from an earlier form *c*, behaves differently from the *s* that derives from an earlier *s*. For younger speakers who have completely replaced *c* by *s* we find the following pattern of alternation of stem-initial alveolars.

(59)

other persons	3rd singular
t	tʸ
n	ñ
l	lʸ
ɬ	lʸ
s	č
s	š

One explanation would assume that even younger speakers who never pronounce *c* (always merging it with *s*) nevertheless maintain a *c/s* contrast in underlying representations; the rule that palatalizes stem-initial alveolars in 3rd sg. forms operates in terms of this underlying contrast, not in terms of surface pronunciation. This underlying *c* would palatalize as *č*, whereas underlying *s* would palatalize as *š*. A rule would then be required that shifts *c* to *s* unconditionally (but in dialects where the merger is not complete, this rule would perhaps have to be viewed as lexically determined—only certain words would undergo it).

While this analysis is not, to our knowledge, motivated by any facts of the language other than those observed above, it does not appear unreasonable, given that speakers who merge *c* and *s* are exposed to speakers who maintain the contrast. As long as there are speakers who preserve this postulated underlying contrast as a phonetic contrast, the analysis does not seem particularly abstract. It does, however, violate (D), since underlying /c/ is (in at least some cases) realized as /s/ or as /č/, but never as /c/. The underlying features of /c/—an alveolar affricate—never occur together: The alveolar place of articulation is realized in the *s* phonetic variant, the affricate manner of articulation in the *č* phonetic variant.

This particular example of a possible counterexample to (D) is probably more typical than, say, the Yawelmani example. The evidence in favor of the postulation of /c/ in those dialects where *c* does not occur phonetically is provided essentially by a single phenomenon—the fact that some surface *s* sounds palatalize as *č* rather than *š*. This evidence seems sufficient, given that there are speakers who do pronounce *c*'s in the relevant forms. But it would seem that eventually there could be a situation where all speakers merge *c* with *s*, while preserving a contrast between *č* and *š* in the 3rd sg. forms. In this situation the evidence for the abstract *c/s* contrast would be limited to just one phenomenon. Is that a sufficient basis for positing an underlying contrast? This is, of course, the crucial problem that arises if it is accepted that the extent to which underlying forms may depart from surface forms is not regulated by a restriction like (D). How much evidence is necessary to warrant a representation that deviates significantly from surface forms? In supporting abstract representations we have discussed examples where the internal evidence was fairly extensive; the Huamelultec Chontal example, however, is more typical.

If we abandon (D) as unduly restrictive, in its precluding internally well-motivated analyses, we might attempt to restrict URs by another constraint.

(E)   *The UR of a morpheme includes all those variant and invariant phonetic properties that are idiosyncratic. Furthermore, given a morpheme with the UR* /P/$_i$, /P/$_j$, ... /P/$_n$, *for all* /P/$_j$, *it must be the case that each feature value of* /P/$_j$ *occurs in a* [P]$_j$ *(though not all of the feature values are required to occur together in the same* [P]$_j$*).*

(E) simply requires that each underlying feature specification of a segment occur in at least one of the corresponding phonetic reflexes of that segment.

(E) is a sufficiently weak condition on underlying representations to permit internally well-motivated descriptions of a number of counterexamples to (D).

For example, a Yawelmani UR /c'u:m/ with the surface allomorphs c'o:m- and c'um- (among others) would be permitted, since the underlying sound /u:/—a long high rounded vowel—manifests all of its underlying feature values on the surface. The values [+long, +round, +syllabic] are all manifested in the c'o:m- alternant, while the [+high] value is realized in the c'um- alternant.

(E) would also permit the analysis of Pengo that posits /noz/, with surface variants noj- and nos-. The underlying /z/ is a voiced continuant; the underlying voicing is manifested in the noj- alternant, the underlying continuancy is manifested in the nos- alternant. Similarly, (E) would allow a Huamelultec Chontal UR like /ceepa/, with surface allomorphs seepa and čeepa. A voiceless alveolar affricate, /c/ manifests its alveolar place of articulation in the seepa alternant and its affricate character in the čeepa alternant.

Nevertheless, (E) is still not weak enough to account for all the analyses that can be strongly motivated on internal grounds. It was noted above that (E) permits UR like /c'u:m/ for the surface forms c'umo:- and c'um- in Yawelmani. But (E) does not allow every aspect of the abstract analysis of Yawelmani sketched in this chapter. Recall that it was suggested that the future morpheme, which has the PRs -en and -on, should be represented as /-i:n/. Such a representation would violate (E), however, since the underlying long high vowel would never be realized phonetically as either high or as long. This suffix is always a terminal suffix. Thus, if it has the underlying shape /i:n/, it will always be subject to the rule that shortens a long vowel before a consonant at the end of a word. The vowel of this suffix is never realized as high in any surface alternant, since there are no morphological processes that would affect it in such a way as to permit the underlying height of the vowel to be manifested.

Perhaps it will be useful here to review the internal evidence that supports a representation such as /i:n/. First of all, the vowel e is generally unambiguously derived from a long vowel in Yawelmani by means of the general vowel-shortening process; in most cases a surface e alternates with a surface e:. Consequently, e is not an underlying sound in the Yawelmani system, but rather a variant of /e:/, which itself is derived from /i:/ according to our interpretation presented earlier. Thus, if the vowel of -en/-on is NOT represented as an underlying long vowel, then a phonemic e will have to be postulated for this one morpheme, which would always occur in the environment ____C#, one of the contexts in which a vowel is shortened.

Another argument is that the suffix -en does not behave as though it possesses a nonhigh vowel. Its behavior is systematically different from a suffix like -al. Whereas -al rounds to -ol after a rounded nonhigh vowel, -en remains unchanged in that environment. Furthermore, whereas -al does not change after a high rounded vowel, -en changes to -on in that environment. These facts will follow automatically if -en derives from /-i:n/. The latter UR has a high vowel, which will predictably round after a high rounded vowel, but not after a nonhigh rounded vowel. Thus, if the behavior of the future suffix is to be accounted for by independently motivated rules of the grammar, it is necessary to assume an UR /-i:n/, in direct violation of (E).

Another particularly convincing example violating (E) is provided by Efik (Welmers, 1968 and Cook, 1969). Consider the following forms.

(60)   *sió*   'take out'   *dùòp*   'ten'
         tiɛ̌   'sit'   *kìèt*   'one'
         bìà   'yam'   *níɔ́ŋ*   'become tall'
         kùì   'shut out, screen'

The problem that concerns us here is the analysis of the [i] and [u] vowels that occur prevocalically in the above examples. These vowels are very similar to the [i] and [u] vowels cited below, though somewhat shorter.

(61)   *díp*   'hide (trans.)'   *dúk*   'enter, use (vehicle)'
         bìt   'be damp'   *búp*   'ask'
         étigi   'okra'   *ótu*   'group'
         dù   'be (location)'

Prevocalic [i] and [u] cited in (60) are distinctly vocalic in nature, in contrast to the following prevocalic [y] and [w] consonants.

(62)   *yàk*   'let, permit'   *wàgá*   'get torn'
         yìp   'steal'   *wèt*   'mark, write'
         yóm   'look for, want'   *wùt*   'show'

The question that arises is whether prevocalic [i] and [u] are to be treated as vowels in their underlying representation, or are they better treated as the corresponding consonants /y/ and /w/. Depending upon how this question is answered, the examples in (60) will have the syllable structure

$$C \begin{Bmatrix} y \\ w \end{Bmatrix} V(C)$$

or

$$C \begin{Bmatrix} i \\ u \end{Bmatrix} V(C).$$

In either case a unique syllable structure results, since otherwise there are neither syllable-initial consonant clusters nor vowel sequences. Thus, either analysis of prevocalic [i] and [u] necessitates positing a unique underlying syllable structure, so the proper analysis of these elements cannot be decided on the basis of general considerations of permissible syllable structures. We must bring other considerations to bear on the matter.

Tonal phenomena provide some evidence suggesting that prevocalic [i] and [u] should be treated as underlying consonants. In Efik syllables that unambiguously contain a single vowel show the following tonal shapes: V́, V̀, V, V̂, V̌—high tone, low tone, mid tone, falling tone, or rising tone.

(63) high: *fĭk*   'press down',   *dé*   'sleep'
      low: *kèm*   'be equal to', *kɔ̀ŋ*   'become high'
      mid: *káma*   'hold',   *éto*   'tree, wood'
      falling: *à-ŋâ*   'cat',   *i-kɔ̂* 'language, word'
      rising: *bĕ*   'go past',   *kă*   'go'

If prevocalic [i] and [u] were underlying vowels, one might expect to find the resulting two-vowel sequence to contain any sequence of the tones mentioned above. That is, one might expect [i] and [u] to have one of the five tonal shapes cited above and the following vowel to have another. But in fact the surface vowel sequences *i*V and *u*V reveal precisely the same tonal shapes that are permitted on a syllable containing a single vowel. Thus, we find only *i*V́ (equivalent to V́), *i*V̀ (equivalent to V̀), *i*V (equivalent to V), *i*V̂ (equivalent to V̂), and *i*V̌ (equivalent to V̌). Examples of all types are cited in (60).

The vowel sequences *i*V and *u*V thus have the same tonal possiblities as single vowels but these do not correspond to the range of possibilities exhibited by sequences where two vowels are involved, as in (64).

(64)   *à-ŋâ*   'cat'   (there is no corresponding *i*V̂)
        éto   'tree, wood'   (there is no corresponding *i*V)
        èka   'mother'   (there is no corresponding *i*V)

Thus, there is evidence that as far as their tonal properties are concerned, *i*V and *u*V are analogous to *V* rather than to *V . . . V*.

Negative verb forms provide more evidence that prevocalic [i] and [u] should be treated as underlying /y/ and /w/. Note the following examples, where the *ŋ-* is the 1st sg. subject pronoun prefix, -*k*V- is a past tense marker, and -*g*V is the negative morpheme.

(65)   *ŋ́-ke-di-ge mí*   'I didn't come here'
        ŋ́-ka-ă-ga dó   'I didn't go there'
        ŋ́-ke-sé-ge fî   'I didn't look at you'
        ŋ́-ko-dù-go dó   'I wasn't there'
        ŋ́-kɔ-bɔ̀-gɔ́ òkúk 'I didn't receive money'
        ŋ́-ka-tá-ga unàm   'I didn't eat meat'
        ŋ́-ka-diá-ga ùdiá 'I didn't eat (food)'

The past-tense marker shows the following regular alternation and consequently supports analyzing prevocalic [i] and [u] as underlying consonants rather than vowels.

(66)   *-ke-*   if following vowel is *i* or *e*
        -ko-   if following vowel is *u*
        -kɔ-   if following vowel is *ɔ*
        -ka-   if following vowel is *a*

But notice that a root like *-diá-* takes the *-ka-* form of the past, which indicates that phonetic [i] does not behave as a vowel with respect to this rule. But if we posit /dyá/ in the underlying structure, the principles in (66) will correctly predict the -ka- form of the past-tense marker.

A comparison of the data in (65) with that in (67) provides another argument.

(67) ń-ke-ȳéne-ke òkúk   'I didn't have any money'
      ń-ke-kèmé-ke ńdinam útom ɛ̀mì   'I wasn't able to do this work'
      ɛ̀ȳé í-kpɔ̀ri-ké ísɔ̀ŋ káŋa   'he hasn't swept the floor yet'

In (67) there are bisyllabic stems (-ȳéne, -kèmé, -kpɔ̀ri). The negative marker has the shape -kV (the quality of the vowel being determined by the same principle as that in the past tense morpheme) in these forms, whereas after monosyllabic stems, as in (65), it has the shape -gV. The root -díá in (65) behaves like a monosyllabic stem rather than like a bisyllabic stem.

Thus, there are at least three different aspects of Efik phonological structure that independently support the position that prevocalic [i] and [u] arise from underlying /y/ and /w/. Such an analysis implies the UR /dyá/ for the morpheme 'eat', where the second segment is specified [-vocalic]. However, this /y/ is always realized phonetically as [+vocalic], in direct violation of condition (E).

Another counterexample to (E) is found in Turkish (Lees, 1961). Turkish has an underlying voicing opposition for stops:

(68)   /p/ para   'money'   /b/ boru   'pipe'
       /t/ tat   'taste'   /d/ dip   'bottom'
       /č/ čilek 'strawberry' /ǰ/ ǰezir 'root'
       /k/ kuš   'bird'   /g/ göz   'eye'

As the following examples show, this opposition is neutralized in preconsonantal and final positions.

(69)

absolute	plural	objective	gloss
ip	ip-ler	ip-i	'rope'
dip	dip-ler	dib-i	'bottom'
at	at-lar	at-ı	'horse'
at	at-lar	ad-ı	'name'
sač	sač-lar	sač-ı	'hair'
ač	ač-lar	aj-ı	'tree'
kök	kök-ler	kök-ü	'root'
ek	ek-ler	ek-i	'joint'
gök	gök-ler	gö-ü	'heaven'
čilek	čilek-ler	čile-i	'strawberry'

The last four items are the ones of interest to us here. The roots for 'root' and 'joint' are clearly /kök/ and /ek/. But for 'heaven' and 'strawberry' we need to posit a root-final consonant that will appear phonetically as [k] in preconsonantal and final positions, but as ϕ before a vowel-initial suffix. This consonant cannot be /k/, if we are to distinguish the morphophonemic behavior of 'heaven' and 'strawberry' from that of 'root' and 'joint'. Examination of Turkish phonetics reveals that *g* does not occur intervocalically, despite the fact that in initial position it freely contrasts with /k/, as we have seen. This clearly suggests that we posit /g/ as the final consonant in 'heaven' and 'strawberry'; in this manner not only may these words be distinguished from 'root' and 'joint', but the absence of *g* intervocalically represents an imbalance on the phonetic level rather than one on the underlying level. That is, in UR /g/ has the same distribution as each of the other stops.

Thus, the internal evidence from Turkish suggests that the URs for 'heaven' and 'strawberry' are /gög/ and /čileg/ and that there is a rule deleting *g* in intervocalic position. However, this analysis violates (E) because the underlying [+voice] feature characterizing the final segments of /gög/ and /čileg/, and thereby distinguishing them from /kök/ and /ek/, never appears in any phonetic realization of the /g/. This segment appears as [k], and hence [-voice], before a consonant and in final position, and as ϕ before a vowel.*

In order to weaken (E) to the point where analyses such as those sketched above are permitted, it is necessary to move in the direction of only requiring that some of the underlying features of any given segment be manifested phonetically. In the Turkish URs /gög/ and /čileg/ all of the features of the final segments are realized phonetically except for that of [+voice]. Similarly, in the Efik example all of the features of the underlying /y/ in /dyá/ are realized phonetically except for that of [-vocalic]. In the case of the UR /-i:n/ in Yawelmani, however, the distinctive features for /i:/ are [+high, -round, +long], and of these, only the [-round] specification is realized phonetically. Of course, certain nondistinctive properties of /i:/, such as [-back], are also realized phonetically. But the point is that in this case not even a majority of the distinctive features of the underlying segment are directly attested in phonetic representations. It would seem, then, that there is no basis for determining how many of the underlying features of a segment must be directly attested in phonetic representation. Let us therefore propose (F) as a condition imposed on the relationship between an underlying structure and its phonetic manifestations.

(F)   *Given a morpheme with the UR* /P/ᵢ /P/ⱼ · · · /P/ₙ, *for all* /P/ⱼ, *at least one of the features of* /P/ⱼ *must appear in a corresponding* [P]ⱼ *of at least one PR of that morpheme.*

---

* It turns out that this example from Turkish is not nearly as convincing as our discussion in the text indicates, since the overwhelming majority of velar stops that delete occur in polysyllabic roots, while the majority of nondeleting ones occur in monosyllabic roots. It is thus possible to posit an underlying /k/ for both types of root and formulate a rule deleting intervocalic /k/ when it is the final sound of a polysyllabic root. Zimmer (1975) mentions some external evidence from experiments with nonsense words that supports the contention that the k/∅ alternation is determined by the number of syllables in a root instead of the hypothetical contrast between /k/ and /g/.

This condition permits any underlying element provided at least one of the distinctive features of that element is present in a surface form of the morpheme. It is an exceedingly weak constraint, violated only when the phonetic representation of a segment shares no features with its underlying representation. This might occur in two ways: Either all of the underlying feature values of a segment would have to change their values (an unlikely situation), or the underlying segment would have to never appear in phonetic representations at all. This latter situation—which represents an obviously extreme form of abstractness—is the one we shall focus on, since analyses hypothesizing such a state of affairs have in fact been presented for a variety of languages, both from generative and nongenerative points of view. We must restrict ourselves to a selected number of cases where evidence in favor of analyses violating (F) can be adduced.

One analysis that violates (F) is the analysis of English that derives all occurrences of phonetic [ŋ] from underlying /ng/ sequences. This account of the velar nasal is motivated by the following considerations. For one thing, [ŋ] has a more restricted distribution than *m* or *n*, since it nevers occurs word-initially (*map*, *nap*, but not **ŋap*) nor internal to a morpheme before a vowel (*smear*, *sneer*, but not **sŋeer*). A restricted distribution often indicates that a sound is derived rather than underlying (since the restricted distribution would follow automatically from the fact that the rule in question operates only in certain contexts). Second, the sequences [nk] and [ng] do not occur in English phonetic structure. On the other hand, [ŋk] and [ŋg] do occur (*link*, *plank*, *finger*, *anger*). These data can be accounted for by postulating a rule that /n/ assimilates to the point of articulation of a following velar. Such a rule could, of course, be regarded as just one aspect of a more general nasal assimilation process. Third, although [ŋ] occurs in final position, **[ŋg]* does not (we have *sing* [sĩŋ], but not **[sĩŋg]*). This distributional fact enables us to derive [ŋ] by a rule that deletes *g* in the environment ŋ____#. This rule must be applied after the nasal assimilation rule that converts /n/ to [ŋ] when a velar follows. *g* deletes not just in absolute word-final position, but also before certain suffixes as well—e.g., the *-er* agentive suffix (*singer*), the verbal suffixes *-ing* (*singing*) and *-ed* (*hanged*). Finally, we observe that there are some examples of alternation that support a rule deleting *g* word-finally after [ŋ]. For instance, *long* ends in a velar nasal, but in *longer*, the comparative form of the adjective, a *g* is pronounced after the velar nasal. This alternation requires a rule of *g* deletion, since there would be no way to insert the *g* by a general rule (for example, *thin* does not acquire a *g* in *thinner*).

Deriving the [ŋ] of *long* from an underlying /ng/ sequence does not violate condition (F) since the underlying /g/ is actually pronounced in one of the surface alternants of this morpheme. But deriving the [ŋ] of *sing* from /ng/ does violate (F), since the underlying /g/ is never pronounced in any form of the morpheme—it is always realized as ∅, although it does effect the change of a preceding underlying /n/ to [ŋ].

In addition to the internal evidence found in English, which supports deriving [ŋ] from underlying /ng/, there is some external evidence cited in Fromkin (1975). She notes the occurrence of slips of the tongue of the following sort: [swĩn] *and* [sweyg] for the intended *swing and sway* (phonetically, [swĩŋ] and [swey]). This slip of the tongue provides evidence for an underlying /g/ in *swing*, even though the /g/ is not pronounced. This underlying /g/ in *swing* seems to have been transposed to the end of the following word, *sway*, preventing the assimilation of the underlying nasal. The result is that the underlying /n/ shows up phonetically. Another slip of the tongue supporting an underlying /g/ is [sprɪg] *time for* [hĩntlər] instead of the intended *Springtime for Hitler*. This example seems to involve the transfer of the underlying /n/ of *Springtime* to *Hitler*. In transferring the /n/ to the later word, the underlying /g/ is left behind, resulting in [sprɪg].

Marshallese provides another example that violates condition F (Bender 1968, 1969, 1970). According to Bender's analysis this language has a linear vowel system composed of the following four phonemic members: *i, &, e,* and *a*. Each of these vowels is subject to rounding, fronting, and backing, depending upon the consonants adjacent to it, so that in reality the phonetic inventory of vowels in Marshallese is much larger than the phonemic inventory (see Bender, 1968, for details). In what follows we will ignore phonetic adjustments of the vowels and retain the phonemic representation.

Bender argues that the higher mid-vowel *&* is not contrastive in Marshallese, but instead is a predictable variant of either *i* or *e*. Before exploring the details, we must discuss a pervasive rule of Marshallese phonology—apocope. Examination of the following data reveals a rule deleting the final vowel of a word.

(70)

Noun	his Noun	my Noun	gloss
naj	*naji-n*	*naji-h*	'child'
giy	*giyi-n*	*giyi-h*	'tooth'
qen	*qena-n*	*qena-h*	'catch'
jem	*jema-n*	*jema-h*	'father'
kilep	*kilepá-n*	*kilepa-h*	'bigness'
jeneq	*jeneqa-n*	*jeneqa-h*	'footprint'

We may now turn to the data of interest here, the limited distribution of the vowel *&*. This vowel is essentially limited in occurrence to the following types of roots.

(71)

Noun	his Noun	my Noun	gloss
w&b	*wibe-n*	*wib&-h*	'chest'
p&t	*pite-n*	*pit&-h*	'pillow'
k&l	*kile-n*	*kil&-h*	'technique'
w&n	*weni-n*	*weni-h*	'turtle'
b&g	*begi-n*	*begi-h*	'night'

For the moment let us ignore the third column. As far as the first two columns are concerned, these alternations may be accounted for in one of two ways. First, *i* will change to *æ* when it is followed by an *e* that will eventually delete, and *e* will change to *æ* when it is followed by an *i* that will delete. Another possible treatment is to metathesize the word-final vowel into the preceding syllable instead of simply deleting it. The resultant *ie* and *ei* sequences may then be converted into *æ* directly. Fortunately, for our purposes it does not matter which of these two treatments is adopted. In either case underlying / # wibe # / and / # weni # / will be converted into phonetic *wæb* and *wæn*. The important point is that the vowel *æ* is derivable in all cases from a combination of *i* and *e*.

In the third column stems such as *weni-* 'turtle' and *begi-* 'night' exhibit an unmodified stem-final vowel before the 1st-person possessive morpheme: *weni-h, begi-h*. On the other hand, stems such as *wibe-* 'chest' and *pite-* 'pillow' deflect their final vowel to *æ* in the 1st person possessive: *wibæ-h, pitæ-h*. If we are to give a maximally general account of the distribution of the *æ* vowel (to account for it with the rules already at our disposal), we must assign the underlying representation /-hi/ to the 1st person singular possessive morpheme. The /i/ is of course needed to deflect the preceding /e/ to *æ*. It has no effect on any other preceding vowel and is deleted by the general rule of apocope.

In the data at our disposal the 1st person possessive morpheme always appears at the end of a word. As such, its vowel never shows up phonetically. However, because of the particular nature of the vowel alternations in the language, we are able to see its effects quite clearly. The proposed analysis of Marshallese violates (F), since it postulates an underlying sound for the 1st person possessive morpheme that is never pronounced in any of the morpheme's overt forms. The available internal evidence, however, supports that analysis.

Lithuanian (Kenstowicz, 1972a) provides another example along the same lines. Before discussing the relevant points, however, we must dispense with several preliminaries. To begin with, the language has the following phonetic vowel inventory.

(72)

	long		short	
	i:	u:	i	u
	e:	o:		
	ε:	a:	ε	a

The long open vowels *ε*: and *a*: are predictable variants of the corresponding short vowels, appearing in accented nonfinal syllables. Alternations like the following demonstrate this point. (In the following citations the acute accent marks the accented syllable; the tone of the syllable is not indicated, as this is not relevant to our discussion.)

(73)

nominative singular	instrumental singular	locative singular	gloss
kɛ́:las	kɛlú	kɛlɛ́	'road'
mɛ́:tas	mɛtú	mɛtɛ́	'time'
lá:pas	lapú	lapɛ́	'leaf'
rá:tas	ratú	ratɛ́	'wheel'

We account for these alternations by the following rule of secondary lengthening.

(74)
$$\overset{\acute{}}{V} \longrightarrow [+\text{long}]/\underline{\quad}C_0V$$
$$[+\text{low}]$$

Removing ɛ: and a: from the underlying vowel system leaves a rather asymmetrical vowel inventory: each of the two high vowels occurs in a long-short contrast, but for the nonhigh vowels, e: is paired with ɛ and o: is paired with a. Given the tendency for balanced underlying vowel systems, we might expect there to be internal evidence in Lithuanian that would reduce these two pairs to a simple long-short opposition, the differences in vowel quality being predictable by rule. The following data are suggestive.

(75)

present		past					
1st singular	3rd singular	1st singular	3rd singular	gloss			
minú	mína	mi:naú	mí:ne:	'trample'	cf., miná	'mob'	
girú	gíra	gi:raú	gí:re:	'praise'			
tupú	túpa	tu:paú	tú:pe:	'perch'	tupiklá	'perch'	
dumú	dúma	du:maú	dú:me:	'blow'	dúmple:s	'bellows'	
drɛbú	drɛ́:ba	dre:baú	dré:be:	'splash'			
gɛrú	gɛ́:ra	ge:raú	gé:re:	'drink'			
lɛmú	lɛ́:ma	le:maú	lé:me:	'doom'	lɛ́:manas	'critical'	
vagú	vá:ga	vo:gaú	vó:ge:	'steal'	vagís	'thief'	
karú	ká:ra	ko:raú	kó:re:	'hang'	karó:lai	'necklace'	

The derived nominals suggest that the underlying root vocalism is exhibited in the present tense and that the past-tense vocalism is derived. Comparing the present and past-tense roots, it will be observed that not only is the vowel of the latter a lengthened variant of the former, but when the underlying root vowel is open ɛ or a, the derived long vowel of the past appears as e: and o:, respectively. This is actually a general trait of Lithuanian. There are several other morphological rules that lengthen vowels. Wherever they apply to ɛ and a, the mid-vowels e: and o: result. This suggests that we abstract the raising of open long vowels from each of these rules and formulate it as a separate process. The rule of raising states this in approximate terms.

(76)   raising   [ɛ:, a:] → [e:, o:]

This rule permits us to derive all occurrences of *e:* and *o:*, which in turn permits us to postulate a completely symmetrical underlying vowel system for the language.

(77)

	short		long	
	i	*u*	*i:*	*u:*
	ɛ	*a*	*ɛ:*	*a:*

Phonetic *e:*'s and *o:*'s arise from long open *ɛ:* and *a:* by vowel raising, while phonetic *ɛ:* and *a:* arise from *ɛ* and *a* by secondary lengthening, which is ordered after raising.

The secondary-lengthening rule is not the only source of long open vowels in Lithuanian. There is another rule that deletes a dental nasal before a continuant consonant, compensatorily lengthening the preceding vowel. This rule must be ordered after raising because lengthened open vowels resulting from the loss of a nasal do not become mid-vowels. We may illustrate the operation of this rule by showing the range of allomorphs for the prefix *san-*.

(78)   *sámbu:ris*   'assembly'   *bú:ris*   'crowd'
         sándo:ra   'covenant'   *dó:ra*   'virtue'
         sántaka   'confluence'   *tɛké:ti*   'to flow'
         sáŋkaba   'coupling'   *ká:be:*   'hook'
         sá:vo:ka   'idea'   *vó:kti*   'to understand'
         sá:skambis   'harmony'   *skambé:ti*   'to ring (bell)'
         sá:šlavo:s   'sweepings'   *šlá:ve:*   'he swept'
         sá:žine: 'conscience'   *žinó:ti*   'to know'

We may express the nasal-loss rule informally as follows:

(79)   V*n* continuant ⟶ V: continuant

Turning to the relevance of these data to the validity of condition (F), note that a crucial feature of the analysis we have presented is that all occurrences of long open vowels in phonetic representation are the result of either nasal loss or secondary lengthening. An underlying long open vowel will never be realized on the surface level because raising will convert it to a mid-vowel. As such, our analysis seems to run into difficulties when confronted with forms like the following:

(80)

nominative singular	genitive plural	gloss
á:žualas	*a:žualú:*	'oak'
kɛ́:sas	*kɛ:sú:*	'moss-grown hillock'
žá:šis	*ža:šú:*	'goose'

If these roots are assigned URs with short open vowels, we can account for the long root vowels in the nom. sg. forms by secondary lengthening. But this account fails to explain why the root vowels are long in the gen. pl., where the accent is not on the root. On the other hand, if the roots are assigned underlying long open vowels, raising will convert them into phonetic mid-vowels. There is, however, another source for long open vowels—nasal loss. If these roots are assigned the URs /anžual-/, /kɛns-/, and /žanš-/, their superficially anomalous behavior can be explained. This analysis is supported by the existence of two additional "gaps": first, there are no *n* plus *continuant* clusters within a morpheme in phonetic representations; second, all unaccented *a:* and *ɛ:* vowels are followed by a continuant. These gaps are natural consequences of the analysis just proposed. Note, however, that a UR like /žanš/ violates (F). The *n* never appears phonetically in any allomorph; it is always deleted because of the following *š*.

So far, in the examples of "ghost" segments from English, Marshallese, and Lithuanian it has been possible to pinpoint the exact phonetic nature of the abstract segment. There are, however, cases where this appears impossible. A particularily clear example is provided by "*h* aspiré" words in French (Schane, 1972). Final consonants in French are deleted in phrase-final position as well as word-internally in preconsonantal position. If the following word begins with a vowel, the final consonant of the preceding word is normally pronounced, a process called *liaison* in traditional terminology. Thus, we have *les garçons* [legarsõ], but *les amis* [lezami]. There is however a group of words that induces the deletion of a preceding consonant despite the fact that they always begin with a vowel phonetically.

(81)　　　　　*les héros*　　[leero]　　'hero'
　　　　　　　les haches　　[leaš]　　'ax'
　　　　　　　les haricots　[leariko]　'bean'
　　　　　　　les hibous　　[leibu]　　'owl'

Although one might simply mark these morphemes in the lexicon as conditioning consonant truncation exceptionally, other relevant facts cast some doubt upon the validity of such an approach. For instance, words beginning with a vowel normally induce the deletion of the final vowel of a preceding word: *le garçon*, but *l'ami*, where the /ə/ of the article has been deleted. Morphemes that exceptionally induce the truncation of a preceding consonant (the *h* aspiré words) consistently fail to trigger the deletion of a preceding vowel despite the fact that they always begin with a vowel.

(82)　　　　　*le héros*　[ləero]　　*le haricot*　[ləariko]
　　　　　　　la hache　[laaš]　　*le hibou*　　[ləibu]

Merely marking these morphemes as triggering consonant truncation exceptionally fails to explain why they also automatically fail to induce vowel deletion. On the other hand, if we say that these morphemes begin with an underlying consonant, and if this consonant is deleted after all relevant rules have applied, then both exceptional properties of these morphemes can be linked with one another. In fact all phonological rules of French that are sensitive to vowel- versus consonant-initial words consistently treat the *h* aspiré words as if they began with a consonant. To cite just one more example, prenominal adjectives ending in a nasal consonant normally delete the nasal if the following word begins with a consonant, but retain the nasal if the following word is vowel-initial (with no nasalization of the preceding vowel; see Dell, 1973): *bon vélo* [bõvelo] 'good bicycle' versus *bon ami* [bɔnami] 'good friend'. The *h* aspiré words behave like consonant initial words: *bon heros* [bõero].

In order to account for the consistent behavior of the *h* aspiré words, it would appear that they must be entered into the lexicon with an initial consonant that is deleted after all relevant rules have applied. The problem is, which consonant? Historically, these words derive by and large from Germanic borrowings with an initial *h*. However, except for a few eastern dialects and stage pronunciations, *h* has been deleted everywhere in French. Although one could identify the ghost segment as /h/, it appears that there is no real motivation for doing so. A glottal stop, which also does not occur in French, would suffice. In fact any otherwise nonoccurring consonant could be selected. In view of these facts Schane (1972) has suggested that the underlying consonant merely be represented as [+consonantal] without any further specification, a kind of *archisegment*.

Selkirk and Vergnaud (1973) have called attention to some additional facts that call the whole question of the abstract consonant into question. Specifically, they point out that most morphological derivatives of *h* aspiré words behave as if they began with a vowel. Thus, while we have *les héros* [leero], we also have *l'héroïne*, not **la héroïne*. A phonological analysis would require a very peculiar rule deleting the abstract consonant when a derivational suffix is added. On the other hand, if the *h* aspiré words are treated as being exceptional in some way, their behavior in derivative formations can be seen as a manifestation of the tendency to regularize morphologically derived forms. (For example, *sit* in English has the marked past-tense from *sat*, while the past tense of *babysit* can be heard as either *babysat* or *babysitted*, the latter form exhibiting the regular past-tense suffix). This would appear to argue for treating the *h* aspiré words like *héros* as exceptional in some way. But even if we mark such forms as exceptions (via some lexical marking system), this still fails to explain the systematicity of their behavior.

The *h* aspiré words in French thus represent what is perhaps a more typical case of a possible violation of (F) than do our earlier examples. First of all, the evidence does not lead to any NECESSARY "ghost" segment. That is, there exists more than one hypothetical underlying sound that could produce the correct surface results, and there exists no evidence warranting the choice of one over the others. Second, not all of the implications of the ghost segment are borne out. Consequently, postulating a consonant at the beginning of *héros* implies that this consonant will also appear in forms derived via suffixation from *héros*. But since this implication does not hold in French, there is some doubt cast on the proposed ghost segment.

In this chapter we have examined a series of possible conditions imposed on the abstractness of underlying representations—that is, on the extent to which the UR of a morpheme may differ from its associated set of phonetic realizations. We have seen that the weakest possible condition—namely, (F)—cannot be maintained if certain internally supported analyses are to be accepted. The failure to find any absolute condition determining the relationship between an UR and its PRs leaves open the possibility of describing any case of contrasting patterns of morphophonemic behavior in terms of an underlying phonological contrast. Perhaps it will be useful to consider in detail one example where postulating an underlying phonological contrast does not appear to us to provide the best description of the observed contrasts in morphophonemic behavior. (See Chapter Two for many other examples.)

Menomini, an Algonquian language, provides some interesting material in this respect. The sound *n* in Menomini displays two different patterns of behavior. One *n* alternates with *s* before nonlow front vowels and *y*, while the other *n* does not. (It should be noted here that *t* is converted to *č* in this same environment in Menomini.)

(83) *en-ōhnɛ-t*   'if he walks hither'   *es-yā-t*   'if he goes hither'
      w-ēn-owawan 'their hands'   *w-ēs* < /w-en-e/   'his head'
      ōn-an   'canoes'   *ōs* < /on-e/   'canoe'

(84) *o-tān-an*   'his daughter'   *o-tān-ew*   'he has a daughter'
      a ʔsɛnyāk   'stones'   *kōn-ēwew*   'it is snowing'
      kōn   'snow'   *kūnyak*   'lumps of snow'

Thus, in the phonological description of Menomini there must be some difference in the URs of the morphemes in (83) and (84) in order to be consistent with the fact that the *n*'s in the former set palatalize to *s* while those of the latter do not. In Bloomfield (1939) these morphemes are differentiated by representing the *n*'s of (83) as /n/ in their underlying structure, and those of (84) with the capital letter morphophoneme /N/. The palatalization rule is then defined to operate on /n/ and ordered after it is a rule that converts the nonpalatalizing /N/s to *n*.

Unlike Bloomfield and many structuralists, generative phonologists have assumed that segments in the UR are to be represented in the same fashion as in the PR: that is, as matrixes of distinctive features that indicate whether or not a given segment possesses a particular phonetic property. Consequently, generative phonologists can differentiate the two different *n*'s in Menomini in only two ways: They may be assigned different underlying feature matrixes (distinguished by an underlying phonetic contrast that is later neutralized in all positions), or the morphemes of the language can be subcategorized by an arbitrary nonphonetic lexical classification on the basis of whether or not they undergo the palatalization rule. (In effect, the latter option involves marking in the lexicon all the morphemes containing /N/s in Bloomfield's analysis as exceptions to the palatalization rule.)

Now unlike our earlier discussion of counterexamples to (A)–(F), the first option is not nearly as attractive for these Menomini examples, because an underlying phonetic contrast cannot be substantiated. The only difference between the two n's is that some undergo the rule of palatalization while others do not. In all other respects the two n's behave exactly the same. Thus, if we were to try to differentiate them in terms of an underlying phonetic contrast, the choice of which phonetic differentiation to make would be totally arbitrary. This situation can be profitably compared with the one in Yawelmani, where surface $o:$ shows two different patterns of behavior. One behaves like a low vowel with respect to vowel harmony and the other like a high vowel. We suggested that the proper way to differentiate the phonological behavior of the two different kinds of $o:$'s was in terms of an underlying contrast that never appeared directly on the phonetic surface: The first type was posited as /o:/, the second as /u:/. This underlying contrast was supported by several other criteria besides vowel harmony, all of which allowed us to pinpoint exactly in phonetic terms the underlying difference between the two kinds of $o:$'s. In the Menomini case, however, there are no synchronic facts that permit such a phonetic differentiation of the two kinds of n's. The only relevant synchronic facts are that some n's palatalize to s and some do not.

In spite of the difficulty in positing an underlying phonetic differentiation in cases like this, early generative phonology was so biased in favor of proposing phonological explanations for contrasting morphophonemic behaviors (rather than treating them as the result of nonphonetic factors, such as grammatical conditioning or lexical subclassification) that we find such analyses proposed even in the most implausible circumstances. This was especially true when the historical antecedents of the language were known. Thus, in his doctoral dissertation on Menomini, Bever (1967) differentiated the two n's by deriving the palatalizing one from /θ/ and the nonpalatalizing one from /n/. In Bever's analysis the palatalization rule is defined as transforming /t/ and /θ/ to č and s, respectively, before /y/, /i/, and /e/. Subsequently, another rule changes all remaining /θ/s to n. To some extent this analysis recapitulates the historical development, since many of the palatalizing /n/s come from Proto-Algonquian *θ, while the nonpalatalizing /n/s come from *n. Aside from this fact, which is irrelevant in a synchronic description, Bever tries to motivate the selection of /θ/ on grounds of simplicity. To differentiate the two /n/s one needs to set up a consonant that otherwise does not occur in Menomini. This consonant must appear as s in the palatalizing environments and as n elsewhere. The choice of the underlying segment can be restricted to some extent by attempting to formulate rules that will effect these changes to n and s as simply as possible.

θ differs from s just by the feature of stridency (and the rule of palatalization renders a consonant [+strident]; see the change of t to $\check{c}$). θ differs from n by the feature of nasality. If /θ/ is selected as the underlying segment, the rules required in the analysis will be rather simple, involving minimal feature changes.

The latter argument is extremely weak because it is based on an inadequate conception of the role of simplicity in phonology. In addition, it fails to eliminate one of the two liquids, which do not occur in Menomini either, as candidates for the UR of the palatalizing n's. There are, besides, other pertinent facts that render this analysis not only implausible but actually incorrect. They have to do with the fact that the merger of PA *θ to n was not direct, but went through an intermediate stage of *l. In an important study Piggott (1971) has shown that in PA *t alternated with $\check{c}$ and *θ with s before front nonlow vowels and glides. In most of the Algonquian languages *θ became l, merging with PA *l. At this stage there were some l's (derived from *θ) that alternated with s; other l's (derived from *l) did not. Now, if we were to follow the logic of Bever's analysis for this stage of the language, the alternating l's would be derived from /θ/ and the nonalternating ones from /l/, with a subsequent rule changing all /θ/s that did not palatalize to l. But this kind of analysis would be inconsistent with the fact that in all of the Central Algonquian languages the $l \sim s$ alternation was generalized to the l's that derive from PA *l. This is a totally unexpected change as far as a phonological analysis is concerned, but finds a ready interpretation according to a lexical analysis that differentiates the two kinds of l's by means of an arbitrary lexical classification: the tendency for arbitrary nonphonetic properties to be lost in linguistic change. (Cf., the fact that many of the nouns and verbs that formed their plurals or past tense by umlaut or ablaut in earlier stages of English now take the regular -(e)s plural and weak past -(e)d endings.) At some time after the merger of *θ with *l, *l merged with *n to yield the present-day Menomini situation. We thus might expect in the future development of Menomini that either the $n \sim s$ alternation will be generalized to the n's that derive from *n or perhaps the alternation will be lost entirely from the language. In either case both of these changes would be comprehensible according to a lexical analysis of the $n \sim s$ alternation, but not according to a phonological one.

It is clear that phonological theory must impose some constraints on underlying representations so that unmotivated analyses like the one for Menomini can be excluded. The problem of abstractness thus remains one of the most important issues facing contemporary generative phonology.

In this chapter we have discussed a large number of possible conditions imposed on underlying representations and have presented (internally) well-motivated counterexamples to each one; as a result we must exclude the possibility of accepting any of these constraints as absolute conditions on underlying structures. However, the number of cases in which evidence is available to support an abstract phonological solution is small when compared to the number of cases in which such evidence is unavailable. In most cases our only recourse will be to lexical analyses. This means that the weaker conditions we have discussed—especially (D), (E), and (F)—function as rules of thumb setting upper limits on the amount of abstractness in URs that most phonologists implicitly follow. These conditions are violated only infrequently, and then only when a fair amount of evidence is available to motivate a more abstract analysis. Furthermore, even when internal evidence is available, this still leaves unanswered the fundamental question of whether or not the native speaker actually constructs his internalized grammar along such abstract lines. At present there is little evidence one way or the other on this issue as well as on most other issues facing contemporary phonological theory. But this only reflects the speculative nature of the still-developing discipline of linguistics.

2

The Nonphonetic
Basis of Phonology

1.0 THE SUBVERSION OF THE PHONETIC BASIS
OF PHONOLOGICAL ALTERNATIONS

Phonological alternations generally have their ultimate source (historically speaking) in sounds being affected by the phonological context in which they occur. In other words, synchronic phonological alternations are largely the consequence of sound changes that have occurred in the history of the language, and these sound changes are generally phonologically conditioned, altering a given sound only in a specific environment. Furthermore, the sound changes in question are generally phonetically motivated; that is, not only does the change take place in a specific phonological context, but there is also a phonetic explanation for why the change in question occurs in the context that it does.

The sound changes that occurred historically, and the conditions under which they occurred, often become obscured through subsequent historical evolution. The phonetic basis of the original change may thus be lost, resulting in an alternation that from a synchronic point of view must be accounted for by a rule that lacks phonetic motivation. In some cases the alternation may continue to be conditioned by phonological factors alone (though not the same phonological factors as originally induced the alternation), while in other cases (partial) nonphonetic conditioning may arise. In this chapter we consider several different ways in which the original basis of an alternation may become altered in the course of language change.

1.1 TELESCOPING

It often happens that the intermediate steps in a series of historical changes are lost (i.e., cannot be motivated) in a synchronic grammar of the resulting language. If a language changes As to Bs in the environment X at a certain point in history, and then later changes Bs to Cs, the result may be that some As will alternate with Cs synchronically. If the intermediate stage of B cannot be motivated in a synchronic description, there will have to be a rule taking As directly to Cs. Such a rule can be said to have "telescoped" (Wang, 1968) the two historical changes, A > B and B > C. Although each of the historical steps may be phonetically motivated, the telescoped rule will not necessarily be. A couple of examples will illustrate this point.

Some of the Slavic languages provide an illustration of telescoping on the basis of the "fall of the yers" and its interaction with vowel length. In Proto-Slavic there was a contrast between long and short vowels. During the time when Proto-Slavic was subdividing into the individual Slavic languages, it underwent a sound change whereby the short (lax) high vowels *ĭ* and *ŭ*, the so-called "yers", deleted in certain positions and merged with other (usually mid) vowels in other positions. (This will be discussed in more detail later in this chapter.) Final position was one of the places where the yers fell. Associated with the fall of the yers was a compensatory lengthening of the preceding syllable. In some of the Slavic languages a Proto-Slavic long vowel as well as a compensatorily lengthened vowel underwent certain changes while the corresponding short vowel remained unchanged. In general these changes involved raising or diphthongization, the most common fate of long vowels. For example, in Ukrainian long *e:* was raised to *i:*. But in Ukrainian the contrast between long and short vowels was subsequently lost. The interaction of these various changes is illustrated in the historical developments of the words *sviča* 'candle' and *mid, med-u* (gen. sg.) 'honey'.

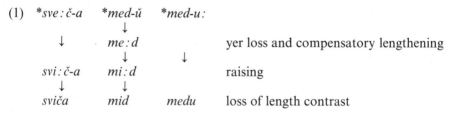

(1) **sve:č-a   *med-ŭ   *med-u:*

↓ . me:d yer loss and compensatory lengthening

svi:č-a mi:d raising

sviča mid medu loss of length contrast

Because the contrast in vowel length has been lost, we are now left with an *e ~ i* alternation in place of the historical series *e > e: > i*. And since there is no evidence either for positing an abstract length contrast in present-day Ukrainian or for positing the suffix *ŭ* in *med-ŭ*, we are left with the following telescoped rule raising *e* to *i* before one or more word-final consonants.*

---

* This environment is identical to the environments in which there was a word-final yer in Proto-Slavic, since in Proto-Slavic all words ended in a vowel, and the only vowels that have been lost word-finally are the yers.

(2) $\qquad$ e $\longrightarrow$ i/___C$_1$ #

This rule has very little of the phonetic motivation that is associated with the historical development of the $e \sim i$ alternation.

This distortion of the historical basis for the alternation is even more dramatically illustrated by consideration of the historical development whose present-day reflex is the $o \sim i$ alternation, found in such forms as *mist*, *most-u* 'bridge'. Long $o:$ was raised to long $u:$, which later diphthongized to *uo* in some dialects and shifted to $\ddot{u}:$ in others. In the latter case it lost its length and, in most dialects, its roundness as well yielding i (Pan'kevich, 1938). Thus in Standard Ukrainian we find o alternating with i, an alternation that represents the terminal points of the diachronic chain $o > o: > u: > \ddot{u}: > i$. Again each step is phonetically plausible in itself: raising of long vowels, fronting of $u:$ (cf., French, Swedish), unrounding of $\ddot{u}$ (cf., Greek). But the final product—the telescoped rule [e, o] $\longrightarrow$ i/___C$_1$ #—is not. Since there is no evidence for the intermediate stages synchronically, the speakers of the language have no reason to construct a grammar encompassing these intermediate stages; rather, there is every reason to shift the mid-vowels directly to i, even though the result is a phonetically unexpected change of o to i in a phonetically unexpected environment (___C$_1$ #).

1.2 INVERSION

The phonetic basis of an alternation may also be obscured if language learners invert the direction of the change. That is, suppose that a language changes As to Bs in the environment X. If subsequent speakers (for whatever reason) happen to interpret the Bs as underlying forms, they will be forced to postulate a rule that converts Bs to As in environments other than X. (We are assuming, of course, that the original sound change has resulted in synchronic alternations between As and Bs.) The resulting rule will not necessarily have the same phonetic motivation as the original change. The development sketched above has been termed "rule inversion" (Vennemann, 1972a).

Schuh (1972) discusses an example of rule inversion in Hausa. Hausa underwent a sound change traditionally known as Klingenheben's law, whereby certain consonants weakened to sonorants in syllable-final position. Consider the following data.

(3) $\quad$ *K $\longrightarrow$ w $\qquad\qquad$ (*K = k, g, $\hat{k}$)

talawcii	'poverty'	*talaka*	'poor person'
batawyee	'a twin'	*tagwaaye*	'pair of twins'
hawree	'tusk'	*haƙoorii*	'tooth'

*T $\longrightarrow$ $\tilde{r}$ ($\tilde{r}$ = trilled r) $\qquad$ (*T = alveolar obstruent)

kirga < *kiřga*	'to count'	*kididdiga*	'to reckon'
biyař	'five'	*baadu*	'five' dialectal
ařnee	'pagan'	*asnee*	'pagan' dialectal

$$*P \longrightarrow w \qquad\qquad (*P = p, b, \hat{b}, m)$$

hawsii	'barking of dog'	*hapsii*	dialectal
alluwraa	'needle'	*'al'ibra*	Arabic
zawna	'to sit'	*zama*	'remain'

This sound change has produced morphophonemic alternations in cases where various morphological rules insert a vowel between two consonants. If the first consonant in a cluster was weakened (historically) as a result of Klingenheben's law, the original form of the consonant will often appear in morphologically related items where a vowel occurs between the two consonants (by virtue of a morphological rule). For instance, a process of vowel insertion is involved in plural formation: *aa* is inserted between medially abutting consonants, and the final vowel shifts to long *ee*. Some examples: *askaa* 'razor', *asaakee* (pl.); *bawnaa* 'buffalo', *bakaanee* (pl.). Schuh claims that in the synchronic grammar of Hausa, nouns such as 'buffalo' are analyzed with the weakened consonant (resulting from Klingenheben's law) as underlying. Underlying forms such as /bawn/ require a lexically conditioned rule that shifts underlying *w* to the appropriate velar or labial in the plural. It is obviously an inversion of the original sound change, one that presupposes a lexical analysis instead of a purely phonological one. It is therefore of some interest to see what evidence supports this analysis.

Schuh points out first that the change of syllable-final *k* to *w* is no longer productive in Hausa. Instead, Hausa now assimilates a velar completely to the following consonant. This is illustrated in borrowings (*lacca*, from English 'lecture') and by productive reduplications like *daddaka* 'to pound well' < *dak-daka* < *daka* 'to pound'; *bubbuga* 'to beat well' < *bug-buga* < *buga* 'to beat'. By itself this evidence is far from compelling. One could claim that there is a rule in Hausa changing labials and velars to *w*, but that the rule is restricted to certain morphological contexts (contexts that would not include reduplicated verbs).

Second, he cites a form *gwawroo* 'bachelor', whose plural is *gwagwaaree*. He sees the UR as /gwawr-/ as opposed to /gwagwr-/, since etymologically the *w* derives from a labial and not a velar (cf., dialectal *gwabroo*). By itself this example does not constitute very strong support in favor of underlying *w* either. The language learner could easily formulate the rule that labial/velar $\longrightarrow$ *w* before another consonant on the basis of singular-plural pairs like 'buffalo'. When he encounters a form like the singular of 'bachelor' and perceives a *w* preceding the consonant, he knows that the *w* is the surface reflex of either a velar or labial, but he does not know which one. It is not surprising that he would make a few false guesses.

In order for the rule inversion analysis to be compelling one needs to cite some fact that corresponds to our assumption about rule inversion, but that is difficult to explain with a noninverted description. The third piece of evidence Schuh cites appears to be of this nature. There is a new, innovating pattern of plural formation in Hausa where instead of saying *bakaanee* as the plural of *bawnaa*, 'buffalo', the alternative *bawnaayee* is now possible. "In this type of plural, if the first syllable has a long vowel nucleus, *-aa-* is found after the medial consonant and a suffix *-yee* is added" [p. 393]. Other examples include the following:

(4)

singular	plural	alternative plural	gloss
buuzuu	*bugaajee*	*buuzaayee*	'Tuareg'
juujii	*jibaajee*	*juujaayee*	'rubbish heap'
sawrii	*samaarii*	*sawrayii*	'young man'

The historically underlying roots are /bugz/, /jibj/, and /samr/. The *z* palatalizes to *j* before a front vowel, and the weakened *w* velarizes a preceding *i* to *u* (/jiwb/ ⟶ /juwb/), and then vocalizes to *u* (/buwz/ ⟶ /buuz/).

Evidently, the type of plural formation found in (4) occurs only with roots containing long vowel nuclei. The fact that forms with *w* from a labial or velar via Klingenheben's law fit this pattern indicates that these forms have been analyzed as having long vowel nuclei. This treatment could be explained if these roots were formed with underlying /w/, since preconsonantal *w* would naturally combine with a preceding vowel to form a long vocalic nucleus. On the other hand, if we claimed the roots in (4) were /bugz/, /jibj/, and /samr/, there would be little reason to expect them to behave like roots with a long vocalic nucleus. Consequently, these alternate plural forms lend some support to the inversion analysis.

Obstruent weakening resulting from Klingenheben's law took place in many other positions besides that of the second radical consonant in nouns (note the forms cited above). Naturally, the question arises as to whether the alternation was also reanalyzed with an underlying sonorant in these positions. Schuh cites no evidence that they were. Assuming that no such evidence exists, we are left with a situation in which the same alternation $x \sim y$ is possibly analyzed in one category with x as underlying and in others with y. From a traditional generative point of view this kind of situation would be considered quite complex and bizarre. Nevertheless, it may not be as unusual as it seems on first impression, since Vennemann (1972a) has claimed that rule inversion will most often occur when the allomorph indicative of the historically original representation appears in a morphological category that is *marked* or more complex, while the historically derived allomorph appears in a morphologically more basic category. Thus in Hausa the historically derived allomorph appears in the singular and the allomorph reflecting the historically earlier pronunciation appears in the plural. According to Vennemann, rule inversion will most often occur in such situations, and it will never happen that rule inversion will make a historically derived allomorph appearing in a morphologically more complex category the underlying representation. Assuming for the moment that this asymmetry is in fact true, it is quite possible for there to be cases in which an alternation is analyzed with different underlying forms in different paradigms.

For example, in Polish there was a sound change whereby Proto-Slavic *e
and *ē were backed to o and a, respectively, before nonpalatalized dentals.
Subsequently, remaining *ē's were merged with e by a general loss of vowel
length. As a result of these changes there arose declensions of nouns whose
etymological structure consisted of an *e or *ē followed by a nonpalatalized
dental consonant, in which a back vowel o or a appeared in the overwhelming
majority of cases in the declension, including the nom. sg. This is a result of
the fact that most of the case endings began with back vowels that caused no
palatalization of the preceding root-final consonant, thus permitting the
backing rule to apply. For example, the noun gwiazd-a 'nail' from *gw'ēzd-
shows the historically derived allomorph with a in all cases of the paradigm
except for the dative/locative sg. gwiezd-ie, where the -e ending has palatalized
the root-final consonants, inhibiting the backing of the root vowel. Similarly,
zioł-o 'herb' from *z'el- has the back vowel in all its allomorphs but the loc. sg.
ziel-ie, where the etymological stem vowel appears.

The following facts might be used to argue that the historically derived back
vowel allomorphs have been reanalyzed as underlying forms (Becker, 1974).
First, this allomorph appears in the overwhelming majority of the forms in
the declension. Second, with the loss of the length contrast between *e and *ē,
there would be no way to predict synchronically when an e will show up as an
a or an o in the back vowel allomorphs, if e is posited as underlying. Finally,
the back vowel allomorphs have been extended throughout the paradigm for
the vast majority of nouns. Thus, a form like ściana 'wall' < *st'ēn- has the
dat./loc. ścian-ie instead of the expected ścien-ie; likewise, cios 'blow' from *t'es
has the loc. form cios-ie and not cies-ie. Only about twenty nouns exhibit the
alternation in present-day Standard Polish, while well over a hundred show
analogical extension of the back vowel allomorph. For the few forms retaining
the alternation we might then postulate a minor rule (see below for a discussion
of minor rules).

(5)   a, o ⟶ e/C'___palatalized dental

When we turn to verbs, we find a different situation. All of the verbs that
show an alternation between e and a back vowel in inflection belong to the
class of consonant-stem verbs, which have no conjugation marker and to which
the inflectional ending is added to the root directly. Here one can argue that
the etymological front vowel allomorphs have been retained as the underlying
forms. First, the majority of inflectional endings contained front vowels that
caused a palatalization of the root-final consonant, permitting the front vowel
alternant to surface phonetically. This can be seen by examination of the
following paradigm for the verb *n'es- 'carry'.

(6)   infinitive   nieś-ć
           1st singular   nios-ę   1st plural   nies-iemy
           2nd   nies-iesz   2nd   nies-iecie
           3rd   nies-ie   3rd   nios-ą

In addition to the front vowel allomorph being more frequent, it also occurs in the 3rd sg., which is generally regarded as the most "basic" form in the verb paradigm. It should also be noted that the vast majority of verbs in this class have the root structure C*eC-; there are only a very few with C*ēC-, which have *a* instead of *o* in the back vowel allomorph. Thus, with an underlying front vowel allomorph, one could still account for the vast number of front-back alternations, unlike the nouns. Finally, there has been no analogical extension of the back vowel allomorphs of verbs, contrary to what we observed with the nouns. These facts suggest an analysis of the *e*~*o* alternation for the verbs that can be handled by the following rule.

(7)   e ⟶ o/___ nonpalatalized dental

In general, as we have seen, it is difficult to prove that rule inversion has actually occurred. Therefore we are not actually proposing that *e* is the underlying vowel in Polish verbs, while *o* and *a* are the underlying vowels in the nouns. However, we see no reason for believing that such diverging reanalysis of a once historically unitary alternation could not (naturally) occur. Obviously the matter deserves further investigation.

We should perhaps point out that we discussed an example in Chapter 1 that might be regarded as a kind of rule inversion—namely, the treatment of the relationship between active and passive verb forms in Maori. Recall that historically word-final consonants delete; thus root-final consonants deleted when no suffix followed the root, but were retained when a suffix followed. Active verbs have no suffix added to the root, whereas passive verbs do. Thus the consonant that historically occurred at the end of a verb root appears only before the passive suffix. There is considerable evidence, however, that speakers have reinterpreted this consonant as part of the passive suffix. Instead of an underlying root consonant and a rule of word-final consonant deletion, speakers now posit no underlying consonant at the end of the root but instead restructure the passive suffix with an unetymological initial consonant.

1.3 PARADIGM REGULARIZATION

A third way in which an alternation that was originally phonetically justified may be lost is through analogical extensions of the alternation. Many of these analogical extensions appear to be motivated by a tendency to "regularize" paradigms (i.e., eliminate allomorphy so that a given morpheme will retain a constant phonological shape throughout the paradigm). Although this idea goes back to traditional historical linguistics, the systematic study of the phenomenon within the context of synchronic phonological descriptions is still in a rudimentary stage; the term "paradigm" remains a largely pretheoretical concept. Consequently, we make no attempt to define the notion here, relying on the reader's intuitive understanding of the concept.

A regular paradigm can be achieved by a variety of means. These include, first, complete loss of a rule or curtailment of the scope of a rule's application; second, generalization of a rule beyond the bounds of its original context; third, change of the environment of a rule to correspond to the paradigm itself; fourth, change in the order of application of separate rules; fifth, change in the pattern of interaction of different applications of the same rule.

Some of the analogical developments resulting from the fall of the yers in the Slavic languages can be viewed as directed toward the achievement of more regular paradigms. As mentioned earlier, the yers were lax high vowels ĭ and ŭ which merged with mid-vowels when the following syllable contained a yer and dropped out word-finally or when the following syllable contained a vowel that was not a yer. In East Slavic (Russian and Ukrainian) ŭ, when vocalized, became o, while ĭ became e before palatalized ("soft") consonants and o elsewhere (Isačenko, 1970).

Within noun paradigms this development gave rise to some rather radical allomorphy. For instance, in Modern Russian there are about a dozen monosyllabic roots that, from a synchronic point of view, contain a "fleeting" vowel. For example, the word meaning 'forehead' shows the shape /lob/ in the nom. and acc. sg., where no case ending follows, but the shape /lb/ before all the remaining case endings (such as *lb-y* nom. pl.). Historically, the morpheme was /lŭb/, while the nom. and acc. sg. case endings were ŭ. By regular development the root yer of /lŭb-ŭ/ was vocalized to o, while the ending was deleted. In the remaining forms of the paradigm, such as the nom. pl. /lŭb-y/, the endings began with non-yer vowels; as a result, the yer of the root was deleted.

In Old Russian there were many more monosyllabic roots that contained etymological yers and that showed the fleeting-vowel alternation. But in the historical development of Russian most of these have generalized the vocalized allomorph throughout the paradigm. For instance, Isačenko (1970) cites the following examples (cognates from some of the West Slavic languages are also shown, where many more forms have retained the original historical development of retention and loss of the fleeting vowels).

(8)

	Common Slavic	Russian	West Slavic		gloss
	čĭst-ĭ/čĭst-i	čest'/čest-i	Czech	čest/ct-i	'honor'
	mĭst-ĭ/mĭst-i	mest'/mest-i	Czech	mst-a	'vengeance'
	tŭšč-ĭ/tŭšč-a	tošč'/tošč-a	Polish	tszcz-y	'meagre'

This, then, is an example where the curtailment of a rule leads to a more regular paradigm. Of course, once the vocalized alternant was regularized throughout the paradigm, the UR of these morphemes was presumably reanalyzed to contain nonalternating mid-vowels. It is important to note, however, that many of the forms that have generalized the vocalized allomorph in the inflectional paradigm still retain vestiges of the zero allomorph in derived forms: *mest'*, *mest-i* 'vengeance' and *mstitel'* 'avenger'. Thus, the extension of the vocalized allomorph does not necessarily extend beyond the inflectional paradigm.

Paradigm regularization is connected with the analogical development of the fleeting-vowel alternation in yet another way. Kiparsky (1963) has pointed out that in a series of consecutive yers the original pattern of vocalization and deletion in Russian was that even-numbered yers were vocalized and odd-numbered ones dropped, counting from the end of the word. This is illustrated by forms like the following.

(9)   *lĭstĭcĭ   ⟶   l's'tec   'flatterer'
        *rŭpŭtŭ   ⟶   rpot   'grumble' (Old Russian)
        *sŭnĭmŭ   ⟶   snem   'meeting, gathering'

The Modern Russian fleeting-vowel alternation retains the original alternating pattern of vocalization and deletion only in restricted circumstances. Essentially, it is to be found only when the adjacent fleeting vowels are separated by a stem boundary. For example, the fleeting vowel of a prefix will be vocalized if the initial syllable of the following stem contains a fleeting vowel that has been deleted. Thus, the prefixes so-, oto-, and razo-, from *sŭ, *otŭ, and *razŭ contain fleeting vowels that we shall distinguish from nonfleeting e and o by the slash mark. Before roots that contain no fleeting vowels the prefixes always show the allomorphs s-, ot- and raz-.

(10)   s-pisat'   'list, register'   cf.,   pisat'   'write'
        ot-padat'   'fall off'   padat'   'fall'
        raz-nosit'   'peddle, hawk'   nosit'   'carry'

But preceding roots such as čęt- (<*čĭt-) 'read', žęg- (<*žĭg-) 'burn', bęj- (<*bĭj-) 'beat', and bęr- (<*bĭr-) 'take'—which contain fleeting vowels—the presence or absence of the prefix vowel depends upon the fate of the fleeting root vowel: If the root vowel is vocalized, the prefix vowel is lost; if the root vowel is deleted, the prefix vowel is vocalized. Within the simple verb paradigm the fleeting vowels are vocalized in the root in various forms of the paradigm, depending upon the phonological and, in some cases, arbitrary lexical properties of the root, as well as the nature of the inflectional ending. Forms such as čęt- and žęg- vocalize the root vowel in the infinitive and the masculine past: both of these endings (-t' < *tĭ and -l < *-lŭ) originally contained yers, evoking the vocalization of the preceding root vowel, which in turn prevents the vocalization of the fleeting vowel in the prefix. For comparison, we cite the 1st sg. present and fem. past forms, whose endings contained full vowels, evoking a deletion of the root yers, which allows the fleeting vowels of the prefixes to surface.

(11)   'count'   'kindle'
        infinitive   s-čes-t'   /sϕ-čęt-t*ĭ/   raz-žeč   /razϕ-žęg-t*ĭ/
        masculine past s-čo-l   /sϕ-čęt-l*ŭ/   raz-žog   /razϕ-žęg-l*ŭ/
        1st singular   so-čt-u   /sϕ-čęt-u/   razo-žg-u /razϕ-žęg-u/
        feminine past   so-č-la   /sϕ-čęt-la/   razo-žg-la /razϕ-žęg-la/

The phonology of these rather complex forms involves rules deleting various consonants as well as a rule that shifts the vocalized fleeting vowel *e* to *o* before a nonpalatalized consonant. But the effects of these other rules should not obscure the important point that vocalization of the fleeting vowel of the prefix depends upon the fate of the fleeting vowel in the root. (See Lightner, 1974, for a discussion of some descriptive problems connected with the precise formulation of this rule.)

The dependence of prefix vowels on the root vowel is further supported by verbs like *bę́j-* (<*bĭj-) 'beat' and *bę́r-* (<*bĭr-) 'take'. Here the vocalization of the root vowels is not completely determined by the (etymological) character of the endings (whether or not they contained a yer), as was the case with *čę́t-* and *žę́g-*. *bę́j-* is subject to a rule which contracts *ej* to *i* in preconsonantal position. This rule is ordered before the rule vocalizing the fleeting vowels, and since the contracted *i* behaves like a full vowel, the result is deletion of the prefix vowel. The forms *ot-bit'* 'repel' and *raz-bit'* 'smash' illustrate this point.

(12) | infinitive | *ot-bi-t'* | /otφ-bę́j-t*ĭ/ | *raz-bi-t'* | /razφ-bę́j-t*ĭ/ |
|---|---|---|---|---|
| masculine past | *ot-bi-l* | /otφ-bę́j-l*ŭ/ | *raz-bi-l* | /razφ-bę́j-l*ŭ/ |
| 1st singular | *oto-b'j-u* | /otφ-bę́j-u/ | *razo-b'j-u* | /razφ-bę́j-u/ |
| feminine past | *ot-bi-la* | /otφ-bę́j-la/ | *raz-bi-la* | /razφ-bę́j-la/ |

On the other hand, *bę́r-* has a special inflection. First, in the nonpresent it has a verb suffix /-a/ occurring between the root and the inflectional ending. Being a full vowel, /-a/ causes deletion of the root vowel. As expected, this permits the fleeting vowel of the prefix to surface. Second, it is subject to a special minor rule (historically related to Indo-European ablaut) that vocalizes the root vowel in the present tense, even though in this context fleeting vowels normally delete, because the endings of the present tense contain full, nonfleeting vowels. Here, too, the fleeting vowel of the prefixes is deleted, in accordance with the generalization that the fate of prefix vowels depends upon the fate of the root vowels. The verbs *otobrat'* 'take away' and *razobrat'* 'analyze, take apart' serve as examples.

(13)

infinitive	*oto-br-a-t'*	/otφ-bę́r-a-t*ĭ/	*razo-br-a-t'*	/razφ-bę́r-a-t*ĭ/
masculine past	*oto-br-a-l*	/otφ-bę́r-a-l*ŭ/	*razo-br-a-l*	/razφ-bę́r-a-l*ŭ/
1st singular	*ot-ber-u*	/otφ-bę́r-u/	*raz-ber-u*	/razφ-bę́r-u/
feminine past	*oto-br-a-la*	/otφ-bę́r-a-la/	*razo-br-a-la*	/razφ-bę́r-a-la/

These forms rule out the possibility of trying to condition the allomorphy of the prefixes on the basis of the particular morphological category of the verb and show that the shape of the prefix depends upon the fate of the root vowels.

When we turn to consecutive fleeting vowels within a stem, the pattern of retention and loss is different. If a fleeting vowel in a stem is followed by another fleeting vowel also in the stem, the first will always vocalize, regardless of the

fate of the second. This is shown most clearly by diminutive formations such
as the following. The root *den'* meaning 'day' contains a fleeting vowel and
hence is inflected like *lob*, discussed earlier: *den', dn'-a* (< *dĭn'-ĭ*). A diminutive
form of this morpheme can be constructed by appending the diminutive suffix
-ok (< *ŭk*), which also contains a fleeting vowel. Since fleeting vowels are
vocalized before zero endings like the nom. sg., we would expect formations
like *dn'-ok, den'-k-a* if the alternating pattern were in effect. Instead, we find
den'-ok, den'-k-a with retention of the fleeting vowel of the root in both forms.
The same nonalternating pattern occurs when the diminutive suffix is reduplicated: *den'-oč-ok, den'-oč-k-a* (where the voiceless velar stop of the diminutive
palatalizes before the diminutive suffix). Reflection upon many similar cases
reveals a clear generalization: Within a stem a fleeting vowel will always
vocalize before another fleeting vowel of the stem; only a stem-final fleeting
vowel will delete, depending on the character of the inflectional suffix. When
we ponder the reason for this nonalternating pattern here, as opposed to the
alternating pattern across the stem boundary, a clear generalization emerges.
The nonalternating pattern within the stem provides the stem with a more
constant shape within the inflectional paradigm, as illustrated in the following
table.

(14)

	nonalternating	alternating
	den'ok	*dn'ok*
	den'k-a	*den'k-a*
	den'očok	*den'čok*
	den'očk-a	*dn'očk-a*

One might speculate that the alternating pattern is more difficult psychologically
in that the fate of the first vowel in a form like /dén'-φk-φk/ would depend
upon the fate of the final fleeting vowel, which in turn depends upon the nature
of the inflectional ending. In other words the number of "computations"
involved in determining the pronunciation of a fleeting vowel would increase
with the distance between the first and last members in a string of fleeting
vowels in the alternating pattern. But retention of the alternating pattern for
just the FINAL vowel of the stem involves only one "computation"—one looks
at the following ending.

Thus far we have seen examples in which regular paradigms have been
achieved by curtailment or loss of a rule and by a change in the pattern of
multiple application of a rule. In Chapter 4 we will discuss an example in which
a regular paradigm is obtained by switching the order of application of two
rules. We close this section with an example where paradigm regularity has
been achieved by the extension of a rule beyond the phonetic limits that
originally defined it.

In the history of Russian a rule was added that backed the vowel *e* to *o*
when followed by a nonpalatalized consonant. It is commonly believed that

this was a rule of assimilation since nonpalatalized consonants in Russian are actually velarized. This rule leaves many traces in the structure of present-day Russian (Lightner, 1969). There are many roots with an underlying /e/ that surfaces phonetically when the root-final consonant is followed by a suffix that induces palatalization (historically, all these suffixes began with front vowels). When no such suffix follows, *e* appears as *o*.

(15)   /gr'ez/   *gr'oz-a*   'dream'   *gr'ez'-it'*   'to dream'
        /kol'es/   *kol'os-a* 'wheels'   *kol'es'-n'ik*   'wheelwright'
        /v'ed/   *v'o-l*   'he lead'   *v'ed'-en'ije*   'leading'
        /dal'ek/   *dal'ok*   'distant'   *dal'eč'-e*   'distantly'

However, within a paradigm of a regular noun such as the masculine /m'ed/ 'honey' or the feminine /gr'ez-a/ 'dream' there is only one inflectional suffix that begins with a front vowel, which palatalizes the root-final consonant. This is the locative singular ending /-e/ (this ending also functions as the dative singular ending for feminine nouns). Here we might expect the shift of *e* to *o* to be inhibited by the palatalized consonant, but it is not. Thus, the correct forms are *m'od'-e* and *gr'oz'-e*, not *m'ed'-e* and *gr'ez'-e*. Evidently, then, the rule shifting *e* to *o* has been extended beyond its natural phonetic context—before nonpalatalized consonants—to apply before palatalized consonants within the inflectional paradigm, which yields a more constant shape of the root throughout the paradigm. In this regard it is interesting to note that a few nouns have irregular plural forms resulting from the intercalation of a suffix of the historical shape /-ĭj/, which causes a palatalization of the preceding consonant. This suffix inhibits the shift of *e* to *o*: /p'er/, 'feather', which appears as *p'er'-ja* in the nom. pl., can be compared with a regular form like /s'el/, 'village', which becomes *s'ol-a* in the plural. Perhaps the reason the /-ĭj/ suffix inhibits the shift of *e* to *o*, while the /-e/ does not, is that the former appears in all the plural forms—and hence half of the inflectional paradigm—while /-e/ appears in only one, marginal, case form. In any case this example shows that the notion "paradigm" will have to be much more rigorously defined in order for the appeal to paradigm regularity to have much explanatory force.

1.4 GRAMMATICALIZATION

A fourth way in which the phonetic basis of an alternation can be lost happens when the original conditioning factors are obscured through subsequent historical developments and the change becomes associated with a particular grammatical category or categories. We can refer to this as the grammaticalization of a rule.

The Slavic languages provide a wealth of examples in which once purely phonological rules have become grammaticalized. In Slovak, for example, there is a rule that lengthens a vowel before one or more word-final consonants.

(16) $V \longrightarrow [+\text{long}]/\underline{}C_1 \#$

(16) accounts for such alternations as *lip-a* 'linden tree', *li:p* gen. pl., and *kopyt-o* 'hoof', *kopy:t* gen. pl. It is a completely productive rule, as evidenced by borrowings like *pižam-a, piža:m* 'pajama', and *embarg-o, emba:rg* 'embargo'. Historically, the rule results from the compensatory lengthening effect of the fall of a yer in the following syllable. In Proto-Slavic all words ended in vowels, many of which were yers. All final yers dropped, causing a lengthening of the preceding syllable. Since no other word-final vowels but yers were deleted, words that now end in consonants in Slovak (and Slavic generally) originally ended in a yer. If the lengthening had remained purely phonological, we would expect all these words to terminate in long syllables. This is not the case; rather, vowel lengthening is restricted to certain morphological categories. Limiting the discussion to nouns, we find the following restrictions: for feminine nouns three of the seven cases ended in yers in the plural: the genitive, dative, and locative. Each of these categories has retained lengthening. In the singular no words ended in yers, so there is no lengthening. For neuter nouns the same three cases in the plural (the genitive, dative, and locative) evidence lengthening, while the instrumental singular ending *-om* that originally ended in a yer (*-*omĭ*) now shows no lengthening: *kopyt-o, kopyt-om*, but not *kopyt-o:m*. For masculine nouns, the genitive, dative, and locative plural, as well as the instrumental and nominative singular all terminated in yers, and hence could be expected to exhibit lengthening. In the present-day language length has been lost in all these cases, except for a handful of masculine nouns that retain lengthening in the nominative singular: *mra:z, mraz-u* 'frost'; *nuož* (< **no:ž*), *nož-a* 'knife'. Thus, this lengthening has become limited to plural nouns in the feminine and neuter inflectional categories. Perhaps the grammaticalization of this process was to be expected, since the phonetic basis for the rule was lost; once the yers fell from final position, they never appeared again. Hence, the phonetically motivated compensatory lengthening had to be replaced by a lengthening rule whose context was the rather arbitrary $\underline{}C_1 \#$.

Another example of the grammaticalization of a once phonetic rule has been discussed by Hooper (1974). In Spanish all vowels are said to have two phonetic variants: a tense, or close, allophone appearing in open syllables, and a lax, or open, variant appearing in closed syllables, which is indicated by capital letters in the following discussion. This rule interacts in a potentially critical fashion with another rule that is present in many of the Spanish dialects. This second rule weakens syllable-final *s* to *h* or *∅*. The question is, What is the value—tense or lax—of vowels appearing in syllables that were once closed by the *s*, which has since been lost? Etymologically, of course, they were lax, since the *s* closed the syllable. The question becomes more interesting by virtue of the fact that *s* is the plural marker for nouns. Hooper discusses three dialects that illustrate different responses to this labile interaction of the two rules.

In Uruguayan Spanish we find the two rules applying in their historical order with no evident restructuring.

(17)

orthography	standard Spanish	dialectal	gloss
clase	[klase]	[klase]	'class, sg.'
clases	[klasɛs]	[klasɛ]	'class, pl.'
pan	[pan]	[pan]	'bread, sg.'
panes	[panɛs]	[panɛ]	'bread, pl.'

There are two possible analyses for these data. One, proposed by Saporta (1965), essentially recapitulates the historical development. The plural marker is /-s/ (-es after consonant stems). The tense-lax rule applies first, yielding the lax vowel [ɛ] in the plural; subsequently, the s of the plural is deleted because it closes the syllable. The preceding is a fairly abstract analysis, however. Another possible analysis states that the plural morpheme has been restructured as underlying /-ɛ/, or possibly as /-e/ with a special rule that laxes the plural ending. The limited data available for this dialect do not permit one to decide, however, which analysis is more appropriate.

On the other hand, the second dialect discussed by Hooper—Western Andalusian—applies the tense-lax rule in accordance with surface phonetic structure. That is, a vowel that appears in a syllable originally closed by s, where the s has been lost, is now pronounced as tense. Consequently, in this dialect the singular and plural of nouns like 'class' are identical. This dialect could be described in two ways. One analysis would claim that this dialect has ordered the s-loss rule before the tense-lax rule. The s of the plural ending will not, therefore, induce laxing, since it will be deleted prior to the application of the tense-lax rule. An analysis of this type makes sense only if some evidence can be brought to bear showing that speakers still posit an s in the underlying structure of the plural morpheme. The second analysis of the Western Andalusian data would be that there is no underlying s in the plural (for speakers of this dialect), and therefore it is entirely to be expected that the final vowel of the plural of 'class' will not be pronounced as lax.

In a third dialect, Eastern Andalusian, Hooper shows that the tense-lax rule has become grammaticalized into a kind of harmony rule that renders all the vowels of a word lax in the plural (as well as other morphological categories that once were marked by an s, such as the 2nd sg. of the verb).

(18)

orthography	singular	plural	gloss
pedazo	pedaθo	pɛdʌθo	'piece'
alto	alto	ʌltoʰ	'tall'
cabeza	kabeθa	kʌbɛθʌ	'head'
selva	selva	sɛlvʌ	'forest'
tonto	tonto	tontoʰ	'stupid'
piso	piso	pɪsoʰ	'floor'
fin	fin	finɛʰ	'end'
grupo	grupo	grʊpoʰ	'group'

Note that in this dialect the tense-lax difference in vowels is no longer dependent upon syllable structure: see *pedaθo, selva,* and their plurals. Although one might still attempt to predict the final vowel of the plural by means of the tense-lax rule, positing an underlying /-s/, and then following this with another rule that causes all vowels to harmonize with the final one, forms like *rafaɛl* 'Rafael', and *tomʌh* 'Thomas', show that vowel harmony is not a general process. Apparently, vowel harmony is found only in words where the etymological *s* marked a morphological category such as the plural of nouns or the second person of verbs. Thus, in this dialect the tense-lax rule has been grammaticalized in a rather dramatic fashion.

2.0 GRAMMATICAL INFORMATION IN PHONOLOGICAL RULES

It has been one of the hallmarks of generative phonology that phonological rules are permitted to have access to grammatical information (though the usual assumption has been that it is only surface syntactic structure that is relevant to the application of phonological rules, rather than deep syntactic structure and/or semantic structure). Thus even though generative phonologists have, until quite recently at least, generally preferred giving purely phonological, abstract solutions (such as those discussed in Chapter 1) over solutions incorporating grammatical conditioning, they have nevertheless accepted the proposition that grammatical factors do play a role in phonology. In this section we wish to illustrate some of the major kinds of grammatical information that influence the application of phonological rules.

2.1 GRAMMATICAL CATEGORIES

Perhaps the simplest sort of grammatical consideration of relevance in determining phonetic form is the syntactic category to which a lexical item belongs. The application of many phonological rules is often restricted to a particular syntactic category. For example, in English (Chomsky and Halle, 1968) stress assignment rules are sensitive to the contrast between nouns versus verbs and adjectives. A relevant sample of the stress patterns to be found in simple nouns appears in (19).

(19)	(i)	(ii)	(iii)	(iv)
	América	*aróma*	*agénda*	*capríce*
	metrópolis	*balaláika*	*synópsis*	*paróle*
	ásterisk	*angína*	*asbéstos*	*regíme*
	lábyrinth	*muséum*	*uténsil*	*cocáine*

If the final syllable of a noun contains a tense vowel, it will take the stress (iv).

If the final syllable contains a lax vowel, then stress will fall on the penultimate syllable if that syllable contains a tense vowel (ii) or a lax vowel followed by two or more consonants (iii). If the final vowel is lax and the penultimate syllable consists of a lax vowel followed by at most one consonant, then stress may appear on the antepenult (i). In verbs and adjectives, on the other hand, the principles of stress assignment are different, as inspection of (20) reveals.

(20)

	(i)	(ii)	(iii)
	astónish	caréen	eléct
	elícit	devóte	lamént
	detérmine	surmíse	usúrp
	sólid	supréme	diréct
	vúlgar	remóte	imménse
	frántic	ináne	absúrd

In these categories stress appears on the final syllable if it contains a tense vowel (ii) or ends in more than one consonant (iii). This differs from nouns where the number of consonants in the final syllable plays no determining role in the placement of stress (cf., ásterisk versus eléct). Also, if the final syllable of a verb or adjective contains a lax vowel followed by at most one consonant, the stress will fall on the penult but no further to the left, while in nouns it falls on the antepenult (cf., astónish versus análysis).

The category "noun" plays a critical role in a phonological alternation involving tone in Igbo (cf., Welmers and Welmers, 1969, and Welmers, 1973, for discussion). In the following data, $\acute{V}$ indicates a high-tone vowel, $\grave{V}$ indicates a low-tone vowel, and '(C)$\acute{V}$ indicates a "down-stepped" high tone—i.e., a vowel whose high tone is lowered relative to a preceding high tone. (A high tone is automatically lowered after a low tone, but this automatic down-stepping is not indicated. The ' preceding a high tone thus indicates a lowering of a high tone not induced by a phonetic low tone.)

Nouns of the shape $\acute{V}C\acute{V}$ are converted to $\acute{V}'C\acute{V}$ after a preceding high tone in two syntactic contexts. The first context occurs when the noun is immediately preceded by a verb, the second context when the noun is preceded by another noun that it modifies. (We have simplified somewhat the statement of conditions under which the rule applies, but in ways that are irrelevant to the present discussion.) The following examples will illustrate the application of this tonological alternation.

(21)   isolation form of noun

ánụ	'meat'	wètá á'nụ	'bring meat'
écí	'tomorrow'	gàá é'cí	'go tomorrow'
éwú	'goat'	ánụ é'wú	'goat meat'
ńrí	'food'	égó ń'rí	'money for food'

Only nouns of the shape $\acute{V}C\acute{V}$ mutate to $\acute{V}'C\acute{V}$ after a high tone; adjectives do not change after a noun ending in a high tone: *ákwúkwǫ́ ǫmá* 'a good book', *ùwé ǫ́cá* 'a white garment', *éféré úkwá* 'a large plate'.

The syntactic categories "noun" (as opposed to "pronoun") and "direct object" (as opposed, for example, to "indirect object") play an important role in Hausa phonology. For example, certain types of verbs in Hausa show an alternation between a final long and a final short vowel. The short vowel variant appears when the verb is followed immediately by a noun functioning as its direct object. Some examples follow.

(22)

	nā kāmà̄	'I caught'
	nā kāmà̄ shi	'I caught it'
	nā kāmà kɪfī	'I caught a fish'
	nā kāmà̄ wà Mūsā kīfī	'I caught Musa a fish'
	nā karàntā	'I read'
	nā karàntā shi	'I read it'
	nā karàntà littāfī	'I read the book'
	sun karàntā manà shī	'they read it to us'

(In the Hausa data, V̄ indicates a long vowel, V̀ indicates a low tone, and the absence of a tone mark indicates high tone. Indirect object nouns are preceded by *wà* while indirect object pronouns are preceded by *ma*. Direct objects are not marked.)

The traditional analysis of the vowel length alternations cited in (22) is to posit the isolation form of the verb as underlying (*kāmà̄*, *karàntā*) and posit a rule that shortens the final long vowel when it is followed by a direct object noun (like *kɪfī*, *littāfī*, in the examples above), but not when a direct object pronoun (like *shi*) or an indirect object phrase (like *wà Mūsā* and *manà*) follows. This traditional analysis has been criticized in Newman (1973), where the short vowel variant of the verb is posited as underlying instead and rules formulated that lengthen the final vowel in various contexts (one of which is before a direct object pronoun). Leben and Bagari (1975) have attempted to support the traditional analysis. But in any case direct object nouns behave differently from direct object pronouns and indirect object phrases.

In Dakota verb roots fall into two syntactic types, neutral and active; this classification determines (in part) the shape of pronominal elements prefixed to the root. Dakota places considerable emphasis on the stative aspect of any action; for example, the root 'to scrape' belongs to the neutral rather than the active type, and thus means 'to be in a scraped condition'. As a consequence of this tendency to emphasize the stative aspect of an action, the active verb roots in the language are limited almost entirely to actions having animate subjects or objects. (For discussion see Boas, 1939, pp. 1, 23). The neutral/active classification in Dakota plays a significant role in delimiting the application of a phonetic process whereby *k*-sounds are replaced by a corresponding *č* (transcribed by the symbol *c* in the orthography employed below) when a front vowel precedes. Active verb roots beginning with *k* palatalize when a prefix ending in a front vowel precedes, but neutral verb roots resist this change, even if they are transitivized by an instrumental prefix.

(23)   Active verb roots

k'á	'to mean'	*ni-c'á*	'he means thee'
k'ú	'to give'	*ni-c'ú*	'he gives it to thee'
k'į	'to carry on the back'	*ní-c'į*	'he carries thee on his back'
kilówą	'he sings to another'	*ni-cílową*	'he sings to thee'

Neutral verb roots

k'áta	'he is warm'	*ni-k'áta*	'you are warm'
		na-íc'i-k'ata	'he makes himself warm by walking'
kįza	'he squeaks'	*ni-kįza*	'you squeak'
		na-ní-kįza	'he makes you squeak by kicking you'
k'įta	'to be scraped off'	*na-ní-k'įta*	'he scrapes (mud) off you with the foot'

Syntactic and morphological features such as singular-plural, present-past tense, or particular inflectional classes often act as conditioning factors in the application of phonological rules. For example, there is a class of "oxytone" or finally accented nouns in Russian in which the accent is on the first syllable of the case ending, if there is one, and otherwise on the final syllable of the stem. In the masculine inflectional class the accent remains on the ending in both the singular and plural, while in the feminine and neuter plural the accent is regularly retracted one syllable from the ending to the final vowel of the stem. The operation of this retraction rule is evident in the following paradigms.

(24)

		masculine	feminine	neuter
Singular	Nominative	*sapóg*	*kolbas-á*	*dolot-ó*
	Genitive	*sapog-á*	*kolbas-ý*	*dolot-á*
	Dative	*sapog-ú*	*kolbas-é*	*dolot-ú*
	Accusative	*sapóg*	*kolbas-ú*	*dolot-ó*
	Instrumental	*sapog-óm*	*kolbas-ój*	*dolot-óm*
	Locative	*sapog-é*	*kolbas-é*	*dolot-é*
Plural	Nominative	*sapog-í*	*kolbás-y*	*dolót-a*
	Genitive	*sapóg*	*kolbás*	*dolót*
	Dative	*sapog-ám*	*kolbás-am*	*dolót-am*
	Accusative	*sapog-í*	*kolbás-y*	*dolót-a*
	Instrumental	*sapog-ámi*	*kolbás-ami*	*dolót-ami*
	Locative	*sapog-áx*	*kolbás-ax*	*dolót-ax*
		'boot'	'sausage'	'chisel'

The stress-retraction rule must clearly be able to distinguish inflectional classes in order to correctly retract the stress in *kolbasá* and *dolotó* but not in *sapóg*. In addition, it must be able to distinguish singular from plural so that it retracts the stress only in the plural of the first two words.

In a significant number of cases phonological processes appear to depend upon a distinction between root and affixal morpheme. A phenomenon known as Dahl's law, operative in the Bantu language Rundi, will serve as an illustration. (The Rundi data are taken from Rodegem, 1970; Meeusen, 1959, provides a description of Rundi morphophonemics.) A number of morphemes in Rundi containing the voiceless stops *t* and *k* have alternant pronunciations with the voiced stops *d* and *g*. Some examples follow:

(25) Infinitive prefix *ku-/gu-*:

ku-bárir-a	'to tell'	*gu-cúr-a*	'to forge'
ku-duug-a	'to climb'	*gu-fásh-a*	'to help'
ku-gab-a	'to administer'	*gu-kéek-a*	'to suspect'
ku-rim-a	'to cultivate'	*gu-piim-a*	'to measure'
ku-zím-ir-a	'to lose one's way'	*gu-s-a*	'to resemble'

(26) Noun prefix *iki-/igi-*:

iki-bira	'forest'	*igi-teésha*	'obstacle'
iki-daági	'the German language'	*igi-cu*	'cloud'
iki-gúzi	'price'	*igi-faáru*	'rhinoceros'
iki-maányu	'piece'	*igi-húgu*	'country'

(27) 1st plural subject/object marker *tu-/du-*:

tu-baaz-a	'we work wood'	*du-teek-a*	'we cook'
tu-mesuur-a	'we launder'	*du-cur-a*	'we forge'
ku-tu-bárir-a	'to tell us'	*ku-du-fásh-a*	'to help us'
ku-tu-raab-a	'to examine us'	*ku-du-kúund-a*	'to like us'

The morphemes illustrated above can be shown to possess underlying voiceless stops, since there exist other morphemes that possess invariably voiced stops, whereas there are no grammatically parallel morphemes that have an invariably voiceless stop.

(28)   3rd plural subject marker *ba-*:

ba-gur-a	'they buy'	*ba-som-a*	'they read'
ba-bon-a	'they see'	*ba-kor-a*	'they do'
ba-rim-a	'they cultivate'	*ba-taang-ur-a*	'they begin'

(29)   Noun prefix *ibi-*:

ibi-bira	'forests'	*ibi-cu*	'clouds'
ibi-gúzi	'prices'	*ibi-húgu*	'countries'
ibi-maányu	'pieces'	*ibi-kóokó*	'wild animals'

Granting that the underlying representations of the morphemes in (25)–(27) are /ku-/, /iki-/, and /tu-/, we appear to require the following rule, since the voiced alternant of these morphemes appears when the following consonant (stop or continuant) is voiceless.

(30)   Dahl's law [-voiced] ⟶ [+voiced]/____V [-voice]

But (DL) is clearly too strong in that it predicts the voicing of consonants in contexts where it does not occur. In particular, recall the examples *ku-tu-bárir-a* and *ku-tu-raab-a*, where the infinitive prefix *ku-* remains voiceless even though the following consonant is also voiceless. A number of other examples of this sort can be given.

(31)   *ku-tá-baríir-a*   'to not saw' (*-ta-*, negative morpheme)
        tu-tá-gum-á   'unless we stay'
        tú-ta-a-kubuur-a   'unless we sweep (today)'
        tú-ta-á-kubuur-a   'unless we swept (yesterday)'

From these examples we see that a voiceless consonant in a prefix is not voiced when the voiceless consonant that follows is also in a prefix. Thus, the infinitive prefix /ku-/ is unchanged in *ku-tá-baríir-a*; the 1st pl. subject marker /tu-/ is unchanged in *tu-tá-gum-á*. Indeed, the only examples of Dahl's law (with one restricted class of exceptions not dealt with here) involve a prefix followed by a voiceless consonant in the root morpheme.

Examples such as *tŭ-ta-a-kubuur-a* and *tŭ-ta-á-kubuur-a* provide an additional complication. Notice that the negative prefix /ta-/ remains unaffected by Dahl's law. The reason appears to be that this prefix is separated, in forms such as these, from the root by another morpheme consisting of a single vowel; the preceding examples involve *-a-*, which marks action within the present day, and *-á-*, which marks action that occurred on the preceding day. It might be possible to make use of the fact that in all examples where a voiceless consonant in a prefix is followed by a voiceless consonant in a root, but remains unaltered, there is an intervening *long* vowel. This long vowel always derives, however, from the presence of a morpheme consisting of a single vowel. All the prefixes in Rundi have underlying short vowels, and as a consequence, when Dahl's law applies, it happens always to be across short vowels. Even though reference to the length of the intervening vowel is a possible consideration, it seems to us that the important point is that Dahl's law operates only on a prefix containing a voiceless consonant that immediately precedes a root with an initial voiceless consonant. (DL)′ states this principle.

(32)   (DL)′ [-voiced] ⟶ [+voiced]/____X $\begin{bmatrix} \text{[-voiced]} \end{bmatrix}$
                                                      Root

        condition: X does not contain a morpheme boundary

In this section we have presented a sampling of the types of categorical information that appear to determine the application of phonological rules. We have not attempted to be exhaustive; given that phonological rules seem to be very easily grammaticalized, it is likely that most, if not all, (surface?) grammatical contrasts could, under the appropriate circumstances, become relevant to the operation of a phonological rule.

2.2 BOUNDARIES

Perhaps the most common situation in which grammatical structure determines whether or not a phonological rule of the form A $\longrightarrow$ B/C____D will apply to the sound sequence C'A'D' has to do with the location of C', A', and D' relative to the beginning and/or end of a grammatical unit (such as morpheme, word, or phrase). Let us refer to the beginning and end of grammatical units as the boundaries of such units. Thus we can speak of morpheme boundaries, word boundaries, phrase boundaries, and so on.

Boundaries appear to exhibit two essential functions with respect to the application of phonological rules: an inhibiting function and a conditioning function. A boundary can be said to inhibit the application of a rule of the form A $\longrightarrow$ B/C____D to the sound sequence C'A'D' if the occurrence of the boundary in question between C' and A' or between A' and D' prevents the rule's application. A boundary can be said to condition the application of a rule if the rule is restricted so as to apply only when C', A', or D' is located at a particular kind of boundary.

The word boundary is perhaps the grammatical boundary that most frequently affects the application of phonological rules. Consider, first of all, the inhibiting function of a word boundary. Many (perhaps most) phonological processes affecting a sound sequence C'A'D' will apply only if this sequence is within the same word. That is, phonological rules tend not to apply "across" words, only within words. Phonological rules have the word as their (most usual) DOMAIN. A few examples will suffice to illustrate this point.

Vowel harmony, for instance, is often a word-level phenomenon, operating within words but not between words. Recall that in Yawelmani a vowel is rounded when preceded by a rounded vowel of the same height. This rule operates only within words. Thus in a sentence like *wonxo na*ʔ 'let me hide (it)', the nonhigh vowel in the 1st sg. subject pronoun *na*ʔ remains unrounded even though the preceding word ends in a rounded nonhigh vowel.

Palatalization is also often a word-level phenomenon. For example, in Chimalapa Zoque (Knudson, 1975) the consonants /c/ and /s/ palatalize to /č/ and /š/ in the environment ____(C)*i*. (/č/ and /š/ apparently do not occur in native words except by virtue of the process of palatalization.) Examples involving alternation include: *tic-pa* but *tič-i* 'dry'; *ʔ-iy is-pa* 'he sees it' but *ha ʔy iš-i* 'he does not see it'. Examples not involving alternation include: *ʔušpi* 'alligator', *čiŋ-pa* 'is bathing'. The palatalization rule does not apply across word boundaries. Thus we find examples such as *capac kini* 'red nose', *capac i ʔni* 'red cloud', *te šis pic yik* 'the meat is very black' where /c/ and /s/ are followed by a word beginning (C)*i* . . . , but they remain unaltered.

We will cite here two other processes in Chimalapa Zoque that are restricted to the domain of the word. These processes are especially interesting in that although they do not apply across word boundaries in careful speech, they do so in casual speech. This illustrates the not uncommon situation where the domain of a rule is extended from the word to the phrase in casual speech.

Suffixes in Chimalapa Zoque beginning with a glottal stop are subject to certain morphophonemic rules. The /ʔ/ of such suffixes will metathesize with a preceding stem-final sonorant. This process is exemplified in (33).

(33)

	noun		noun + possessive *ʔiy*
	kom	'post'	*ko ʔm-iy*
	pin	'person'	*pi ʔn-iy*
	nopal	'cactus'	*nopa ʔl-iy*
cf.	*ciku*	'badger'	*ciku- ʔy*
	verb		verb + intransitivizer *ʔoy*
yem-pa	'is fanning (fire)'		*ye ʔm-oy-pa*
won-pa	'is stripping (bark)'		*wo ʔn-oy-pa*
may-pa	'is counting'		*ma ʔy-oy-pa*

If a voiceless obstruent occurs in final position in the preceding stem, the /ʔ/ of the suffix will combine with the obstruent to produce a voiced obstruent (plus a "half-lengthening" of the preceding vowel).

(34)

	verb		verb + *ʔoy*
pup-pa	'is sowing'		*pu·b-oy-pa*
kit-pa	'is bending (corn)'		*ki·d-oy-pa*
ʔuk-pa	'is drinking'		*ʔu·g-oy-pa*

A glottal stop in word-initial position does not, however, metathesize with a preceding word-final sonorant in careful speech. Instead, the glottal stop simply deletes. Thus *ʔaŋmayyi* 'he studied' deletes its initial *ʔ* in a careful pronunciation of *ka pin aŋmayyi* 'the man studied'. In casual speech, however, one finds *ka pi ʔn aŋmayyi*, where the initial *ʔ* of the verb has metathesized yielding the noun form *pi ʔn*. Similarly, in careful speech, a *ʔ* at the beginning of a word does not combine with a voiceless stop at the end of a preceding word to yield a voiced obstruent. The glottal stop is simply deleted in this environment. Thus we find *pa ʔak anasa* 'sweet orange' in careful speech (with deletion of the glottal stop in *ʔanasa*), but *pa ʔa·g anasa* in casual speech.

In addition to constituting the domain in which phonological rules operate, word boundaries also condition the application of phonological rules in many languages. A great variety of phonological rules are typically formulated by referring to the beginning or end of a word; for example, word-final devoicing of obstruents (as in Russian); simplification of initial or final consonant clusters, either by means of an epenthetic vowel or the deletion of one of the consonants (cf., the discussion of Yawelmani and Lardil in Chapter 1); stress rules that assign stress to a particular vowel in the word, counting either from the beginning or the end (e.g., the second vowel from the end of the word is regularly stressed in Yawelmani); and so on.

It may be that not all these examples constitute real cases where a word boundary is truly conditioning a rule's application. For instance, stress assignment rules are really not "triggered" by the presence of a word boundary; rather, in some intuitive sense, the boundary serves as a reference point. One might well claim that the word boundary simply defines the domain of the stress rule and that the rule stresses a particular syllable counting from the beginning or the end of the rule's domain.

In many cases word boundaries may coincide with syllable boundaries, a fact that might allow (in some cases) the substitution of a syllable boundary for a word boundary in the formulation of rules. (The notion "syllable" in this context would have to be an abstract one rather than phonetic, since the rules in question would be applying to underlying or intermediate representations and not phonetic representations.) Yawelmani provides a good example illustrating this point. In Yawelmani a vowel is shortened when followed by two consonants or by one consonant at the end of a word. The phonetic syllable structure of Yawelmani is very simple: a syllable exhibits the canonical shapes CV or CVC. Consequently, the vowel shortening process can be stated as follows: a long vowel shortens before a syllable-final consonant. This rule will shorten the long vowel in a structure like . . V:CC. . . (since the C immediately following the long vowel is in syllable-final position) as well as a . . .V:C# structure (since word-final consonants always belong to the preceding syllable in Yawelmani).

Even though in some cases, word boundaries might be dispensed with in favor of syllable boundaries, it does not appear to be the case that this can always be done. Sounds located near or at the beginnings or ends of words undergo rules that other sounds do not. We cite a few cases below.

Recall that in Lardil a word-final vowel is deleted if it appears in a trisyllabic or longer word. This rule could not be reformulated to claim that a syllable-final vowel deletes if preceded by at least two vowels in the word; such a reformulation would incorrectly predict that the vowels in the third syllable of the following words would delete (assuming that a VCV sequence in Lardil syllabifies as V.CV): *yaraman-in* 'horse (acc.)', *murkunima-n* 'nullah (acc.)', *ŋawuŋawu-n* 'termite (acc.)'. This example is typical of many other rules deleting word-final, but not syllable-final, vowels. The rule that lowers word-final /i/ and /u/ to /e/ and /a/ respectively in Lardil can also be shown to be restricted to word-final, and not syllable-final, vowels. If this rule were reformulated to affect a syllable-final high vowel, the italicized vowels in the following examples would incorrectly be lowered: *pulumunitami-n* 'young female dugong (acc.)', *ṭipiṭipi-n* 'Rock-cod sp.', *ŋawuŋawu-n* 'termite (acc.).

One additional example illustrating the necessity for recognizing word boundaries as possible conditioning factors in phonological rules is provided by Chi-Mwi:ni, a Bantu language closely related to Swahili. This language exhibits considerable evidence for postulating a rule whereby a vowel at the end of a word is lengthened. Although there are rules of vowel shortening in Chi-Mwi:ni (discussed later in this chapter) that counteract the effects of this word-final vowel-lengthening rule, the existence of this rule is supported by the fact that any word in the language will reveal a final lengthened vowel when appearing in an environment other than those that induce vowel shortening.

Word-final vowel-lengthening can be observed in the following phrases where a verb is followed by a noun. (It should be noted here that in phrase-final position, all vowels are short in Chi-Mwi:ni; thus all words pronounced in isolation will end in a final short vowel. Consequently, the effects of word-final vowel lengthening are observable only in phrase-medial position.)

(35)   *xpała*   'to scale'   *xpała: nsi*   'to scale fish'
       kuja   'to eat'   *kuja: ṇama*   'to eat meat'
       nava:łe 'that he dress'   *navałe: ŋguwo* 'that he put on clothes'
       hujó   'one who eats'   *hujo: zijó*   'one who eats *zijo*'
       huso:mó 'one who reads' *husomo: chuwó* 'one who reads a book'

In each example, the verb form in isolation terminates in a short vowel, but this final vowel is lengthened when a noun follows the verb.

Noun plus adjective combinations also reveal the application of the word-final vowel-lengthening process.

(36)   *ŋguwo*   'clothes'   *ŋguwo:mpʰiya* 'new clothes'
          chisu   'knife'   *chisu: chiłe*   'long knife'
          mashu:ŋgi 'hair'   *mashuŋgi: małe* 'long hair'

Similarly, various "connectors", i.e., conjunctions, prepositions, particles, undergo lengthening when followed by a noun or verb.

(37)   *kama* 'if'   *kama:we*   'if you'
          na   'by'   *na: muke* 'by the woman'
          ka   'with'   *ka: chisu* 'with a knife'
          kolko 'than'   *kolko: ye*   'than him'

Although word-final vowels are lengthened in Chi-Mwi:ni, syllable-final vowels are not; thus if one attempted to substitute syllable boundary for word boundary in the formulation of the vowel lengthening rule, one would incorrectly predict that the italicized vowels in the following examples would be lengthened: *xałamu* 'pen', *ku-big-a* 'to hit', *mi-ti* 'trees'.

Although the boundaries between words generally have been accepted as serving both as the domain in which rules are allowed to operate and also as a conditioning factor serving to trigger a rule's application, Chomsky and Halle (1968; henceforth, *SPE*) assume boundaries between morphemes exhibit a conditioning function only. They propose that the morpheme never constitutes the domain for a phonological process (as opposed to morpheme structure conditions, which do retain the morpheme as their domain). *SPE* claims that given a rule of the form $A \longrightarrow B/C\underline{\quad}D$, where C and D refer to segments and not boundaries, this rule will apply to a structure $C'A'D'$ regardless of whether a morpheme boundary appears between C' and A' or between A' and D'. In other words, the presence of a morpheme boundary can never inhibit the application of a phonological rule. Of course, the absence of a morpheme boundary can prevent a structure from meeting the structural description of a rule, if that structural description requires the presence of a morpheme boundary at a particular point.

It certainly seems to be true that phonological rules are not ordinarily inhibited from applying by virtue of the presence of a simple morpheme boundary. But we are not convinced that the morpheme never serves as the domain for phonological rules. Possible counterexamples follow.

Langdon (1975) cites an example from Yuma, an Amerindian language, where a rule of vowel raising appears to be restricted just to morpheme-internal (actually, root-internal) contexts. Before we enumerate examples supporting the rule of vowel raising, it is necessary to observe that in Yuma there is a pattern of vocalic ablaut whereby a nonplural verb stem is converted into a plural stem. The ablaut is basically a reversal of the length of the vowel of the verb root: Thus CVC roots occur as CV:C in the plural, and CV:C roots as CVC. The plural stem may be marked by affixation in addition to the vowel length reversal.

The vowel-raising rule that concerns us raises a short /a/ vowel to /e/ if a labialized consonant (including *w*, but excluding the labials *p*, *v*, *m*) or a palatalized consonant precedes. If short /a/ is located between two palatalized consonants, it is raised to /i/. Consider the following examples.

(38)

singular stem	plural stem	gloss
ačéw	*u:čá:wv*	'create' (root /čáw/)
awá:	*awéč*	'go' (root /wá:/)
a:vkʸéw	*a:čvu:kʸá:w*	'carry a long object' (root /kʸáw/)
xačinʸ	*xačá:nʸ*	'be a young female' (root /čánʸ/)

The /a/ of the root /čáw/ undergoes raising in the nonplural stem since it is preceded by a palatalized consonant. In the plural stem, the root vowel is lengthened to /a:/ and thus escapes raising (which is a process limited to short /a/). The root vowel in /čánʸ/ is raised to /i/ in the nonplural since palatalized consonants appear on either side; again, the plural stem escapes raising due to the vowel lengthening. The root /wá:/ has an underlying long vowel, and thus escapes raising in the nonplural stem; but since the plural stem requires reversal of the underlying length, the derived short /a/ is subject to raising because of the preceding labilized consonant.

Langdon cites the following data as evidence that vowel raising applies only to an /a/ preceded by a labialized or palatalized consonant within the same morpheme.

(39)

nonplural stem	plural stem	gloss
ká:m	kačám	'conquer' (root /ám/)
á:r	natu:wárv	'want' (root /á:r/)

These two examples involve vowel-initial roots that exhibit short /a/ in the plural stem, but in which short /a/ is not raised despite the preceding palatalized consonant in the case of 'conquer' and the preceding labialized consonant in the case of 'want'. The consonants in both instances do not belong to the root. It is also the case that /a/ is not raised to /i/ between palatalized consonants unless both consonants belong to the same morpheme as /a/. Compare the nonplural stem kayá: 'sharpen an edge' with the plural stem kaču:yéču. The root is /yá:/, and when the long /a:/ is shortened in the plural stem it is raised to /e/ because of preceding /y/. Note that raising to /i/ does not take place, even though a palatalized consonant /č/ follows. This /č/ is not part of the root, indicating that raising /a/ to /i/ occurs only between two palatalized consonants that both belong to the same morpheme as /a/. Vowel raising in Yuma thus appears to be a morpheme-internal process; in fact, it apparently occurs only in roots.

Another possible case where a phonological rule does not apply across a morpheme boundary is discussed in Beach (1938). In Hottentot, the phoneme /p/ is pronounced as a weakly aspirated, voiceless stop in initial position: [pʰ]i 'him', [pʰ]eru 'wonder'. In final position /p/ is usually unreleased: sao[p⌐] 'your father', ne[p⌐] 'this'. Intervocalically the situation is slightly more complex. In morphemes of the shape /(C)VpV/, speakers sometimes slightly voice /p/; in the Korana dialect /p/ is not only voiced in this environment but also weakened to a bilabial fricative: tsa[ß]a 'thin', kxo[ß]a 'cease', o[ß]a 'have chapped hands'. The weakening of intervocalic /p/ is restricted, however, to cases where the sequence . . .VpV. . . occurs within the same morpheme. The initial /p/ of a suffix is pronounced as a voiceless stop: xo-[p]a 'cheek (masc. acc. sg.)', o-[p]a 'and him', kxo-[p]a 'hide' (see Beach, 1938, pp. 292–294, for discussion of these examples).

Whereas morphemes do not very commonly constitute the domain of a phonological rule, they frequently condition the application of phonological rules. Rules may, for instance, be restricted to apply only to morpheme-initial segments and not to phonetically identical segments that appear morpheme-internally. The Quichua dialect of Puyo Pongo in Eastern Ecuador provides an example of such a rule (Orr, 1962). In this language voiced and voiceless stops contrast after nasals when the nasal and the stop belong to the same morpheme.

(40)　　*šiŋki*　　　'soot'　　*čuntina*　'to stir the fire'
　　　　čuŋga　　　'ten'　　*indi*　　'sun'
　　　　pampalʸ ina 'skirt'　　*ñukanči* 'we'
　　　　hambi　　'poison'　　*punja*　　'day'

However, when a suffix ending in an underlying voiceless occlusive is added to a morpheme ending in a nasal, the suffix-initial occlusive is voiced. (Also, basic /n/ assimilates to /m/ before a bilabial.) The genitive suffix /-pa/ appears in this shape in *sinik-pa* 'porcupines', and *čilis-pa* 'streamless region's', but has the allomorph /-ba/ in *kam-ba* 'yours' (cf., *kan* 'you'), and *hatum-ba* 'the big one's' (cf., *hatun* 'big'). The locative affix /-pi/ shares the same behavior: *sača-pi* 'in the jungle', and *punja-pi* 'in the daytime', but *hatum-bi* 'in big one's', and *atam-bi* 'on the frog' (cf., *atan* 'frog'). The objective suffix /-ta/ and the interrogative suffix /-ču/ have a similar distribution

(41)　　*wasi-ta*　'house'　　cf.　*kan-da*　'you'
　　　　ayča-ta　'meat'　　　　*atan-da*　'the frog'
　　　　puru-ta　'gourd'　　　　*wakin-da* 'others'

　　　　ali-ču　'is it good?'　　*kan-ju*　'you?'
　　　　lumu-ču　'manioc?'　　　*tiyan-ju* 'is there?'
　　　　mana-ču　'isn't it?'　　　*čarin-ju* 'does he have?'

These data reveal that a voiceless occlusive will voice after a nasal whenever the nasal and the occlusive belong to different morphemes. If they belong to the same morpheme, no assimilation takes place.

　　The preceding example illustrates a process that affected morpheme-initial segments only; Eastern Pomo (McLendon, 1975), an Amerindian language of California, has a rule that applies only to segments in morpheme-final position. This language possesses both aspirated and unaspirated voiceless stops; for example, *pʰa:lá* 'the one who goes last', but *pá:laʔ* 'shovel'; *xóbi:tʰà:* 'gunpowder', but *pʰa:táy* 'no good, inadequate'; *cʰé:c* 'mother's brother', but *cá:r* 's.t. clean'; *čʰé:* 'where', but *mi:čé* 'pounding basket'; *kʰól* 'worm', but *kóy* 'sore'. These examples show that both aspirated and unaspirated stops may occur in prevocalic position. There is a rule in Eastern Pomo, however, that deaspirates a voiceless stop when it occurs in morpheme-final position and is followed by a vowel-initial suffix. The application of this rule can be observed in (42).

(42)　*xápʰa:tipʰ*　'driftwood'　　　*xápʰa:tip-ay*　'with driftwood'
　　　c'ótʰ　　'tule bog'　　　　*c'ót-ay*　　'with a tule bog'
　　　čʰicʰ　　'root'　　　　　　*čʰic-ay*　　'with a root'
　　　xóčʰ　　'two'　　　　　　*xóč-a*　　'two (things)'
　　　ba:tʰinkʰ　'get big'　　　　*ba:tʰink-a*　's.o. got big'
　　　bé:kʰ　　'they'　　　　　　*bé:k-i-bàyle* 'their husband'
　　　ká:wkʰ　'person(s)/people'　*ká:wk-i-Yà*　'human bones'

Aspirated voiceless stops occur morpheme-initially before a vowel (cf., $p^{h}a$:$lá$) and morpheme-internally before a vowel (cf., k'i:$c^{h}áy$ 'waist'), but not morpheme-finally before a vowel. Deaspiration occurs only before vowel-initial suffixes, not consonant-initial ones; for example, $bé$:k^{h} 'they' is unaffected in $bé$:k^{h}-qay 'they, too'.

Phrase boundaries also play a critical role in phonology, both in terms of constituting the domain in which some phonological rules apply and also in terms of conditioning the application of certain rules. The extent of the "phrases" involved may vary (sentences, particular syntactic constructions, and so on), and it is conceivable that in a given language distinctions might have to be made between different types of phrases. We will not, however, deal with this issue here.

Perhaps the most typical kinds of rules that require syntactic phrases as their domain are those that assign or modify accentual features such as tone and stress. A good example of an accentual rule operating within phrases is provided by Zarma, a language spoken in Niger, where the tonal sequence ´`` is modified to ´´`, ´ indicating high tone and ` indicating low tone (Tersis, 1972). Several examples of the application of this rule in various phrases follow.

(43)

gá:sú	'calabash'	bè:rì	'large'	gá:sú bé:rì	'a large calabash'
hánsì	'dog'	kòmsó	'skinny'	hánsíkòmsó	'a skinny dog'
ńgà	'his'	cè	'foot'	bõ̀	'on'
ńgá cè bõ̀	'on his foot'				
írì	'we'	kà	'come',	írí kà	'we are coming'
Sùú:rù	(proper name)	gòó	'exist'	Sùú:rú gòó	'Suru exists'

It can be readily observed that the sequence ´`` is modified to ´´` regardless of the location of word boundaries. In the case of the phrase 'a large calabash', the ´ occurs on the last vowel of 'calabash' and the `` sequence occurs on the adjective 'large'; in the phrase 'a skinny dog', the ´` sequence occurs in 'dog' and the second ` occurs on the first vowel of 'skinny'.

Accentual rules are not the only ones that may have the phrase as their domain. For instance, in Chi-Mwi:ni various rules that shorten vowels can be shown to operate not just within words but also within syntactic phrases. Vowel length is phonemic in Chi-Mwi:ni—i.e., underlying representations must contain information as to whether a given vowel is basically long or short. Consider the near minimal pairs in (44).

(44)

ku-ba:ram-a	'to talk'	ku-balam-a	'to promise'
x-pe:ɫ-ek-a	'to be able to be swept'	ku-peɫek-a	'to send'
m-ko:ko	'mangrove'	m-kono	'hand/arm'
ŋ-gi:sha	'anchor'	ŋ-gisi	'squid'

In addition to underlying long vowels there are also long vowels that arise by rule. The rule of word-final lengthening discussed above constitutes one example.

Since the long vowels derived by rule behave identically to underlying long vowels with respect to these examples, we will not always distinguish between these two sources of long vowels in subsequent discussions.

If Chi-Mwi:ni words are studied in isolation, it is readily observable that long vowels do not occur in any position except in the penultimate or the antepenultimate syllable. The absence of long vowels in preantepenultimate syllables must be attributed to the application of a phonological rule that shortens vowels in syllables preceding the antepenultimate. The existence of this rule is rather easy to demonstrate. Consider, for instance, the verb root /so:m/ 'read' in the following examples: *x-so:m-a* 'to read', *x-so:m-esh-a* 'to teach', *x-som-esh-añ-a* 'to teach one another'. In *x-so:m-a* the long vowel of the root is in the penultimate syllable and retains its length; in *x-so:m-esh-a* the root vowel is in antepenultimate position and also retains its length; but in *x-som-esh-añ-a* the root vowel is in a preantepenultimate syllable and loses its length. Additional examples illustrating this same loss of length due to the addition of suffixes are given below.

(45) *ku-re:b-a* 'to stop'   *ku-re:b-eł-a* 'to stop for'
      ku-reb-eł-an-a 'to stop for one another'

x-sa:meh-a	'to forgive'	*x-sameh-an-a*	'to forgive one another'
x-fa:ñ-a	'to do'	*x-fañ-ił iz-a*	'to do for, with'
bo:z-eł-e	'he stole'	*boz-eł-e-ni*	'what did he steal?'
jo:hari	'jewel'	*johari-y-e*	'her jewel'

The shortening of vowels prior to the antepenultimate syllable can be explained by the following rule.

(46) preantepenultimate shortening (PAS)
$$V \longrightarrow [\text{-long}]/\underline{\hspace{1em}}C_0VC_0VC_0V$$

PAS will shorten any vowel that is followed by AT LEAST three vowels in the word. Thus given a representation such as /x-so:m-esh-añ-a/, PAS will shorten the vowel of the root since it is followed by three vowels.

PAS is not limited to words, however. If one studies various kinds of syntactic phrases in Chi-Mwi:ni, one finds that long vowels do not occur in syllables preceding the antepenultimate syllable WITHIN THE PHRASE. Consider the following phrases consisting of nouns plus modifiers.

(47) | | | | |
|---|---|---|---|
| *nu:mba* | 'house' | *numba: ŋk^{h}ułu* | 'large house' |
| *miṭu:ŋgi* | 'clay water jars' | *miṭuŋgi mikułu* | 'large clay water jars' |
| *mp^{h}u:nda* | 'donkey(s)' | *mp^{h}unda: mbiłi* | 'two donkeys' |
| *miṭa:na* | 'rooms' | *miṭana miwiłi* | 'two rooms' |
| *sanḍu:xu* | 'box' | *sanḍuxu: nzito* | 'heavy box' |
| *ziła:tu* | 'shoes' | *ziłatu zizito* | 'heavy shoes' |

Recall that in Chi-Mwi:ni a word-final vowel is lengthened when that vowel is not at the end of a phrase. This rule is responsible for the long vowels in *numba: ŋkʰuɫu, mpʰunda: mbiɫi,* and *sanḍuxu: nzito*. Notice, however, that in the phrases *miṭungi mikuɫu, miṭana miwiɫi,* and *ziɫatu zizito* the last vowel of the noun is not lengthened. This lack of length can be attributed to the application of PAS, since in each case the last vowel of the noun is in preantepenultimate position in the phrase. The final vowel of the noun in an example like *mpʰunda: mbiɫi* is in the antepenultimate position (which allows retention of vowel length).

The observant reader will also have noticed that although these nouns in isolation contain long vowels, these same long vowels are shortened in the noun plus modifier phrases. This shortening can be attributed (unambiguously) to PAS in examples like *miṭuŋgi mikuɫu* (from /miṭu:ŋgi mikuɫu/). In the case of examples like *numba: ŋkʰuɫu* (from /nu:mba ŋkʰuɫu/) the situation is not quite so clear, since there is another rule (which we will discuss below) that can account for the shortening of the long vowel in *nu:mba*.

Verbs followed by noun phrases also provide evidence that PAS operates at the level of the phrase rather than simply at that of the word. In isolation the verb *bo:zeɫe* 'he stole' exhibits a long vowel, but vowel length disappears in a phrase such as *bozeɫe xaɫamu* 'he stole a pen'. The long /o:/ of the verb shortens because it occurs further forward in the phrase than antepenultimate position. Notice also that the last vowel of the verb is not lengthened in *bozeɫe xaɫamu* even though word-final vowels are assigned length in phrase-medial position (cf., *bozeɫe: chisu* 'he stole a knife'). This fact can also be explained by invoking PAS, since in *bozeɫe xaɫamu* the final vowel of the verb is in a pre-antepenultimate syllable in the phrase.

Although long vowels can occur either in penultimate or antepenultimate position within a phrase, long vowels can never appear in both positions at the same time. It is rather a simple matter to motivate a rule in Chi-Mwi:ni that shortens a long vowel when followed by another long vowel. We refer to this rule as pre-length shortening (PLS). This rule operates within words. For example, a long vowel in a verb root is shortened when the passive suffix /o:w/ is added.

(48)   *ku-bo:ɫ-a*   'to steal'   *ku-bol-o:w-a*   'to be stolen'
        ku-ɫe:t-a   'to bring'   *ku-ɫet-o:w-a*   'to be brought'
        k-i:mb-a   'to sing'   *k-imb-o:w-a*   'to be sung'
        ku-vu:nḍ-a   'to break'   *ku-vunḍ-o:w-a*   'to be broken'

Note that the shortening of the vowel of the verb root in these passives cannot be attributed to PAS since the root vowel is in antepenultimate position, a position that does not require shortening.

When a locative suffix *-ni* is added to a noun stem, the final vowel of the noun is regularly lengthened. If the preceding vowel is long, it is shortened—a shortening that can be attributed to PLS.

(49)   *nu:mba*   'house'   *numba:ni*   'in the house'
         shko:mbe   'cup'   *shkombe:ni*   'in the cup'
         mi:ko   'kitchen'   *miko:ni*   'in the kitchen'
         me:za   'table'   *meza:ni*   'on the table'

PLS is not restricted to the word, but rather applies within a phrase. Notice, for example, that the final vowel of the verb in *uziłe nu:mba* 'he bought a house' is short, despite the fact that word-final vowels are lengthened in phrase-medial position (cf., *uziłe: nsi* 'he bought fish', *uziłe: chisu* 'he bought a knife'). The absence of length on the final vowel of the verb in *uziłe nu:mba* can be attributed to the application of PLS. Similarly, the absence of length on the final vowel of the noun in *numba ke:nda* 'nine houses' (cf., *numba: mbiłi* 'two houses') can be accounted for by PLS.

Chimalapa Zoque (Knudson, 1975) provides another example of a phonological rule that operates across word boundaries. The consonants /c/ and /s/ are palatalized to /č/ and /š/ if a /y/ precedes. The /y/ does not necessarily have to belong to the same word.

(50)   *cecpa*   'is carving'   *kuy čecepa*   'is carving wood'
         sawa   'wind'   *waya?y šawa*   'cold wind'
         cɨkpa   'is making'   *?ɨy čɨkpa*   'is making it'
         se?tpa   'is frying'   *?ɨy še?tpa*   'is frying it'

In addition to functioning as the domain in which a rule operates, phrase boundaries may also condition the application of phonological rules. Typically what we discover is that a certain phonological process will affect word-initial or word-final segments whenever the word is in phrase-initial or phrase final position. A few instances follow.

In Sierra Popoluca (Foster and Foster, 1947) there is a rule that inserts ?, the glottal stop, following a phrase-final short vowel. This inorganic ? disappears (is not inserted) when the word-final short vowel is in phrase-medial position; it thus contrasts with an underlying ?, which remains in both phrase-final and phrase-medial positions. Compare (51) and (52).

(51) /?á:či/ ⟶ [?á:či?] 'uncle'   ?a?ná:či putpa? 'my uncle goes out'

(52) /či?/ ⟶ [či?] 'give'   ?ančí?pe?m 'I give it to that one'

The morpheme meaning 'uncle' ends in a vowel underlyingly, but acquires a glottal stop when it appears phrase-finally; no glottal stop is inserted phrase-medially, however, as can be seen from *?a?ná:či putpa?*. The morpheme meaning 'give' ends in a glottal stop underlyingly, consequently this glottal stop appears in both phrase-medial and phrase-final position. The insertion of glottal stops in Sierra Popoluca can be handled by the following rule, where $ indicates a phrase boundary.

(53) $\emptyset \longrightarrow ?/\check{V}\_\_\_\$$

A rather common phenomenon associated with phrase-final position is devoicing of obstruents and/or sonorants. For instance, in Chimalapa Zoque (Knudson, 1975) sonorant consonants are devoiced prepausally if they are preceded by a glottal stop. Consider these examples (a capital letter indicates voicelessness of sonorants). *kama ʔM* 'hard' (cf., *kama ʔm te kuy* 'the tree is hard', where the word-final *m* is syllabic and not devoiced); *pono ʔN* 'weak' (cf., *te pono ʔn pɨn* 'the weak man', where word-final *n* is syllabic and not devoiced).

Up until now we have restricted our discussion of boundaries to those that are relatively straightforward in the sense that they have an obvious motivation on a higher morphological/syntactic level (notions such as morpheme, or formative, word, and phrase are fundamental units of linguistic analysis that can be justified without appeal to the manner in which they affect phonological rules). The use of boundaries in phonology has not, however, been restricted to these simple cases. Other types of boundaries have been utilized in phonological description, and some discussion of the use of such boundaries is required.

There are many examples in which a phonological rule that is normally triggered or blocked by a word boundary is also triggered or blocked within a string of sounds that would normally be considered a word (either from a phonetic point of view, in the sense that it cannot be interrupted by a pause, or from a syntactic/morphological point of view). For example, in Russian there is a rule that deletes the glides *j* and *w** in preconsonantal position.

(54)				
	znaj-u	'I know'	*živ-u*	'I live'
	znaj-e-te	'you (pl.) know'	*živ-e-te*	'you (pl.) live'
	znaj	'know!' (imp. sg.)	*živ-i*	'live!' (imp. sg.)
	zna-t'	'to know'	*ži-t'*	'to live'
	zna-l	'he knew'	*ži-l*	'he lived'
	zna-xarka	'sorceress'	*ži-tel'*	'resident'

However, when we turn to the 2nd pl. imperatives, we find that the rule does not operate. The plural imperative of 'know' is *znaj-te*, not *zna-te*. A verb stem ending in an underlying *w*, like *slav-* 'praise' (cf., *slav-i-t'* 'to praise'), has a plural imperative form *slaf'-te*, and the corresponding singular imperative form is *slaf'*. The voiceless *f'* in the latter two forms can be derived quite straightforwardly from *v* (< /w/) by independently necessary rules of voicing assimilation and final devoicing. The difficulty with the imperative plural forms lies in explaining why the underlying glides *j* and *w* do not delete, even though they stand before a consonant.

In his famous description "Russian Conjugation" (1948) Roman Jakobson explained the lack of deletion in these forms by positing that between the per-

---

* Historically, and in many synchronic analyses of Russian, the surface obstruent *v* derives from an underlying /w/. For discussion see Lightner, 1972.

sonal endings and the imperative stem there is, in effect, an internal word boundary. This would impart the following structure to *znaj-te* and *slaf'-te*: /#znaj#te#/ and /#slaw#te#/. Given this structure, the glide-deletion rule would be blocked, for as formulated, it will not apply across a word boundary. Forms like the infinitive and past tense would not have an internal word boundary: /#znaj-t'#/, /#znaj-l#/.

At first blush the positing of an internal word boundary may seem ad hoc. But Jakobson provides additional evidence for this step. One such piece of evidence concerns another rule of Russian that depalatalizes a consonant before a following nonpalatalized, or "hard", consonant: cf., *otmet'i-t'* 'to mark'; *otmet'i-t-sa* 'to mark (reflexive)', where the addition of the reflexive marker *-sa* causes depalatalization of the underlying *-t'* of the infinitive suffix. In the imperative singular the nonreflexive and reflexive forms of this verb are *otmet'* and *otmet'-sa*, respectively. Note that in the latter the final *t'* of the stem is palatalized, even though it is followed by the reflexive marker *-sa*. Once again, if we assume that imperative verb forms in Russian have a special syntactic structure such that there exists an internal boundary between the stem and the personal endings, the blocking of the depalatalization rule can be explained: /#otmet'#sa#/.

So far we have shown the internal word boundary to have only a delimiting function—it blocks the application of a rule that would otherwise apply if the boundary were not present. But we know that there is a rule in Russian that is triggered by a word boundary—the final devoicing rule. If the imperative is truly of the structure /stem#personal ending/, then we might legitimately expect the internal # to trigger the devoicing of a stem-final voiced obstruent in the imperative. Forms such as *slaf'* and *slaf'te* (stem *slav'-*, cf., *slav'-i-t'* 'praise') unfortunately do not testify to this. The devoicing of the underlying *v* in the former could be triggered by the "normal" rather than the internal #. And the devoicing of the latter could be derived from /#slav'-te#/ by the regular voicing-assimilation rules that assimilate one obstruent to a following one. What is needed is an imperative form in which the first sound of the personal ending normally permits a voicing contrast before it, e.g. a sonorant consonant. Unfortunately, in Russian, *-te* is the only personal ending that can be added to the imperative stem.

But in other Slavic languages such a situation happily does arise. Czech is such a language (Jakobson, 1949). Like Russian, Czech has a rule of final devoicing. But unlike Russian, it is possible to add the 1st pl. ending *-me* to the verb stem in the imperative. This suffix begins with a nasal, a sound in Czech that normally permits a voicing contrast in a preceding consonant: *lid-mi* 'people, instr. pl.', *písmo* 'letter'.

When we turn to the 1st pl. imperatives in Czech, we do indeed find that the stem-final obstruents devoice, just as in final position: *hod-it* 'to go', *hot'-me* 'let's go'; *lež-et* 'to lie down', *leš-me* 'let's lie down'. These forms can be explained if we assume that, just as in Russian, there is an internal word boundary located between the imperative stem and the personal ending. According to this analysis / # hod' # me # / will be converted to / # hot' # me # / by a rule of final devoicing. It should be noted that similar to Russian, Czech exhibits the glide deletion rule that independently substantiates the existence of this internal word boundary in the imperative: cf., *dělaj-i* 'they do', *děla-t* 'to do', *děla-l*, 'did', *dělej* 'do!, sg.', *dělej-me* 'let's do', *dělej-te* 'do! (pl.)'. When we consider other Slavic languages, there are further phenomena which support the notion of internal word boundaries for the imperative (see Jakobson, 1965; Halle, 1973, pp. 329–330).

The data from Russian and Czech suggest first that the person-number endings are joined to the preceding stem in the Slavic imperative in a rather different fashion from the way such endings are appended in other forms of the verb, and second, that this difference can in part be identified with an internal word boundary, which has various phonological effects.

To cite another example let us consider the following data from Polish (Schenker, 1966). In Polish stress is regularly placed on the penultimate vowel of the word. For instance, the root for 'hippopotamus' appears unsuffixed in the nom. sg. and hence has prefinal stress: *hipopótam*. When the gen. sg. suffix *-a* is added, the stress appears on the final vowel of the root: *hipopotám-a*. When the disyllabic instrumental pl. suffix is added, the stress does not appear on the root at all: *hipopotam-ámi*. Finally, the addition of the trisyllabic gen. sg. nonfeminine suffix yields the stress pattern *hipopotam-owégo*.

This penultimate stress rule has some interesting "exceptions" in the past tense of verbs. In Polish, the past tense of a verb is formed by the addition of the past-tense suffix *-l* plus a gender-number suffix.

	singular	plural
masculine	$-\phi$	$-i$
feminine	$-a$	$\{-y\}$ [ɨ]
neuter	$-o$	

The stem *pisa-* 'write' exhibits the following paradigm in the past.

(55)   *pisał*   'he wrote'
       pisáła   'she wrote'
       pisáło   'it wrote'
       pisáli   'they (masc.) wrote'
       pisáły   'they (fem./neut.) wrote'

The lateral *l* is palatalized in Polish when it appears before front vowels and glides. Nonpalatalized *l* is realized as [w] as a result of a later rule and is indicated by the barred *ł*.

Polish indicates 1st and 2nd person in the past tense by adding to the past stem elements that, at least historically, are remnants of the verb 'to be',

(56)

		singular		plural	
		masculine	feminine	masculine	feminine
	1st	pisá-ł-e-m	pisá-ł-a-m	pisá-l-i-śmy	pisá-ł-y-śmy
	2nd	pisá-ł-e-ś	pisá-ł-a-ś	pisá-l-i-ście	pisá-ł-y-ście
	3rd	písa-ł	pisá-ł-a	pisá-l-i	pisá-ł-y

Note that in the 1st and 2nd pl. forms stress is placed on the antepenultimate vowel of the verb, instead of the normal penultimate position. This aberrant stress placement can be explained by postulating an internal word boundary between the verb stem and the elements -*śmy* and -*ście*: /# #pisa-l-i#smy# #/ and /# #pisa-l-i#scie# #/. The regular penultimate stress rule will now correctly accent these forms.

The fact that the elements -*śmy* and -*ście* are synchronically clitics in Polish provides independent evidence for this internal word boundary. As such, they are attached to the first major constituent of a clause. For instance, there is an adverb *trochę* 'awhile'; the sentence 'they wrote for awhile' is rendered *tróchę pisáli*. But 'we wrote for awhile' is expressed as *tróchęśmy pisáli*, where the 1st pl. marker has been appended to the adverb, since it occupies phrase-initial position. Note that in *tróchęśmy* we have antepenultimate stress, just as in *pisáliśmy*. It is clear that these elements -*śmy* and -*ście* do not affect the positioning of the stress, acting as if they were not part of the word for purposes of the stress-placement rule, even though they are always pronounced as part of the word to which they are attached with no intervening pause.

Some further support for this treatment derives from the following considerations. Certain speakers of Polish (especially of the younger generation) fail to apply the rule that places the clitic on the clause-initial constituent; instead, they attach it to the verb. There is a growing tendency among these speakers to place stress on the penultimate vowel, so that we find them saying *pisaliśmy* and *pisaliście*. This might be explained by claiming that since the person markers are no longer treated as having a variable syntactic position by these speakers, but are always affixed to the verb form, they are reinterpreted as suffixed to the verb in the same way as the past-tense suffix and the gender markers: That is, they are joined to the word only by a morpheme boundary, /# #pisa+1+i+śmy# #/ and /# #pisa+1+i+ście# #/, and thus are assigned regular penultimate stress.

In addition to cliticization, reduplication processes often are associated with internal word boundaries. The Venezuelan language Warao (Osborn, 1966) provides a good illustration of this point but before showing it, we must dispense with a few preliminaries. First, Warao has a basic phoneme /r/, an apical flap, which is realized as [d] in word-initial position. Second, /w/ appears unaltered in initial position, but has a bilabial fricative allophone [β] medially (since there are no consonant clusters in Warao, and since all words end in vowels, medial position is always intervocalic). Finally, the stress system of Warao is such that a heavy stress regularly falls on the penultimate syllable; a weaker, secondary stress is placed on every other syllable counting forward from the heavily stressed one: *nàhoròahàkutái* 'the one who ate'; *yàpurùkitàneháse* 'verily to climb'; *enàhoròahàkutái* 'the one who caused him to eat'; *yiwàranáe* 'he finished it' (where the acute and grave accents represent heavy and weak stress, respectively). These stress patterns are implemented by the following two ordered rules.

(57)   penultimate stress: V ⟶ V́/___(C)V #

(58)   secondary stress: V ⟶ V̀/___(C)V (right to left iterative)
$$[\text{-str.}]$$

We can now proceed to the data of interest. These are reduplicated forms, which in Warao are especially frequent in nouns referring to animals. For instance, the word for 'lemur' is *koráikorái*. This form is superficially anomalous, since the regular stress rules predict the accentual pattern **kòraìkorái*. Note, however, that this word is exceptional in a peculiar way: not only does it not have the expected stress pattern, it also contains two primary stresses. Thus, with respect to the stress rules, this form behaves as if it is composed of two words rather than one, despite the fact that phonetically it is pronounced as a single word with no internal pause. This suggests that we assign such reduplicated items a constituent structure in which we establish an internal word boundary between the two elements of the reduplicated item. If primary stress assignment operates only within words (and not across word boundaries), stress will be correctly assigned to *koráikorái*: The two instances of *a* both occur here in the environment specified in (57).

Notice that we are in a position to test the validity of this analysis of the stress patterns for reduplicated nouns because other rules of Warao are sensitive to the presence of a # boundary—namely, rules generating allophones of /r/ and /w/. All other things equal, our analysis predicts that reduplicated nouns with morpheme initial /r/ and /w/ will exhibit the word-initial allophones [d] and [w] in what is phonetically a medial position. The forms for 'alligator' and 'fish' show this to be correct. The underlying form of the former is /ruru/, and that of the latter /wara/. They are phonetically realized as [dúrudúru] and [wárawára], respectively. If these words were analyzed as possessing no internal word boundary, not only would they have an exceptional stress pattern, but in addition the occurrence of medial [d] and [w] would be inexplicable, since these allophones are regularly limited to word-initial position. But in the analysis that assigns reduplicated forms an internal word boundary, they are completely regular in all respects.

The preceding examples show that in many languages certain morphemes or morpheme classes appear to be more loosely attached to the word than others, and the recognition of internal word boundaries appears to be justified. Notice that these boundaries exhibit the same dual function as word boundaries: They prevent the application of rules in some cases while they trigger the application of rules in others. Furthermore, they very often correlate with independently motivated grammatical distinctions.

Yet another kind of boundary, internal to words, has been rather commonly postulated—namely, a "prefix" boundary at the juncture of a prefix and a following root. For example, Chomsky and Halle in *SPE* utilize such a boundary to explain the stress behavior of prefixes such as *trans-*, *per-*, and *con-*. The following rule is postulated in *SPE* to account for the stress pattern of such verbs as *fúrnish*, *wórship*, and *cóvet*.

(59) $$V \longrightarrow \acute{V}/\underline{\hspace{1cm}}C_0 \, (\check{V}C_0^1)]$$

This rule abbreviates the following two rules:

(60) a. $V \longrightarrow \acute{V}/\underline{\hspace{1cm}}C_0\check{V}C_0^1]$

   b. $V \longrightarrow \acute{V}/\underline{\hspace{1cm}}C_0]$

(60a) stresses the penult if the ultima ends in a lax vowel plus at most one consonant. Any word that fails to undergo (60a) is then subject to (60b), which stresses the last vowel of a word.

Notice that words such as *permít*, *transfér*, *confér*, *transmít*, and *compél* show final stress even though their ultima ends in $\check{V}C$. These words appear to be exceptions to (60a). Chomsky and Halle attribute this exceptional accentual behavior to the morphological structure and posit a special boundary, symbolized as $=$, between the prefix and the root. Furthermore, *SPE* suggests that a phonological rule will not normally apply across any boundary other than the morpheme boundary unless some special provision is made (e.g., mentioning the possible presence of the boundary in the structural description of the rule). Consequently, the stress rule (60a) will not apply to a form such as $/\#\mathrm{con}=\mathrm{fer}\#/$ since the sequence $VC_0\check{V}C_0^1]$ does not occur. (60b) will, however, be able to apply to $/\#\mathrm{con}=\mathrm{fer}\#/$ since the sequence $\check{V}C]$ is present.

These verb-forming prefixes exhibit another phonological peculiarity that justifies isolating them in a separate class, which is marked by a prefix boundary: Underlying /s/ voices intervocalically when the preceding vowel belongs to a member of this class of prefixes. Compare the voicing of /s/ in *resist*, *resemble*, *resolve*, *design*, and *presume* with the cognate *consist*, *semblance*, *solve*, *consign*, and *consume*. The voicing of the /s/ is limited to the prefixal context, as is shown by three facts: First, intervocalic /s/ within morphemes does not voice (*asylum*, *misogynist*, *parasol*); second, intervocalic *s* fails to voice when there is a boundary present, and the word is not a complex verb (*para+site*, *philo+sophical*, *meta+soma*); third, intervocalic *s* also does not voice when the *s* and the preceding vowel are separated by an internal word boundary (*photo#synthesis*, *proto* # *Siouan*, *re* # *settle*). Thus, intervocalic *s* seems to voice only when it is preceded by the prefix boundary.

To illustrate one more example, according to Lightner (1972) a prefix boundary is needed in the description of Russian in order to account for the following facts. First, the final vowel of a prefix does not delete before a vowel-initial root, despite the fact that there is a general vowel-truncation rule in Russian V $\longrightarrow$ $\emptyset$/____V—cf., *na*=*učit'* 'teach' (cf., *učit'* 'learn'); *pere*=*odevat-sa* 'to change one's clothes' (cf., *odevat-sa* 'get dressed'); *pere*=*ubeždat'* 'make someone change his mind' (cf., *ubeždat'* 'persuade'). If these forms are provided with a prefix boundary as shown, then the vowel truncation rule will be correctly blocked. In addition, there is another general rule in Russian that inserts a prothetic *j* before a word-initial *e*. This rule also applies when a root-initial *e* is preceded by a prefix: cf., /exat'/ $\longrightarrow$ [jexat'] 'to go'; *pri*=*jexat'* 'arrive'; *pod*=*jexat'* 'approach'. To handle data such as the preceding the prothetic *j* rule must be formulated as follows

(61) $$\emptyset \longrightarrow j / \begin{Bmatrix} \# \\ = \end{Bmatrix} \text{____} e$$

The reader may wonder why, instead of setting up a special prefix boundary =, we do not simply posit an internal word boundary. The answer is that for a number of rules the boundary between the prefix and the root does not behave like a word boundary. For example, a prefix-final voiced obstruent does not devoice in this position: *pod*=*igrat'* 'to play' does not become *potigrat'*.

Note that the above rule is formulated to insert the *j* after, instead of before, the prefix boundary. There is some question as to whether this is correct, for we have no convincing evidence that the position of an inserted segment relative to a boundary ever matters for the application of some subsequent rule. If it is generally the case that the position of the inserted segment relative to the boundary makes no difference, this in turn suggests that there is something inappropriate about viewing boundary symbols as actually present in the string of segments. For some discussion of this and related matters see Pyle 1972.

The boundaries we have discussed so far appear in many languages. Morpheme, word, and phrase boundaries seem to be universal. Many languages seem to have internal word boundaries. The prefix boundary is rather problematical, since in most languages phonological rules regularly apply across the boundary between a prefix and root. In these languages, then, there is no evidence for a boundary of the strength of = (which, recall, inhibits a rule from applying unless special provisions are made) at the boundary of a prefix and a root. Thus if we posit a = boundary in some cases, we must do it on a language specific basis.

There are other instances where one might postulate a boundary of a language-particular sort. In Chi-Mwi:ni one could argue for a special boundary that would precede object prefixes. (Object prefixes are not an obligatory feature of the Chi-Mwi:ni verb, thus not all verbal forms will contain such a prefix.) In the following discussion, we will demonstrate that three phonological rules in Chi-Mwi:ni fail to apply across the boundary before an object prefix.

Prefixes of the shape C*i*/*u*-, where C is an obstruent, delete their vowel if a voiceless obstruent follows. The consonant of the prefix then becomes a continuant (if it was originally a stop) and becomes voiceless (if it was originally voiced). This rule, which we will refer to as vowel drop, operates when the prefix precedes a root beginning with a voiceless obstruent. For example, the infinitive prefix /ku/ is converted to /x/ in examples such as *x-pik-a* 'to cook', *x-fuɬ-a* 'to wash', and *x-kos-a* 'to make a mistake', but not in *ku-bo:l-a* 'to steal', *ku-viv-a* 'to be ripe', and *ku-gaf-a* 'to make a mistake'. Similarly, the 1st pl. subject prefix /chi/ is converted to /sh/ (=[š]) in examples such as *sh-pe:z-eɬ-é* 'we swept', *sh-tokos-e:z-é* 'we boiled', but not in *chi-mo:z-eɬ-é* 'we shaved' or *chi-nu:nsh-iɬ-é* 'we smelled something'. The subject prefix /zi/ (which is used when the subject is a plural noun belonging to certain "noun classes") changes to /s/ in *s-fof-e:ʈ-e* 'they went to graze', *s-pish-il-a* 'they were cooked', but not in *zi-vu:nz-il-a* 'they were broken (by someone)' or *zi-bo:z-el-a* 'they were stolen'.

The preceding examples illustrating vowel drop show the rule applying before roots that begin with a voiceless obstruent. The rule also applies before prefixes that begin with a voiceless obstruent. For instance, the 1st pl. subject prefix is converted to /sh/ preceding the future prefix /ʈa/ but not before the present tense prefix /na/: *sh-ʈa-x-pik-a* 'we will cook', but *chi-na-x-pik-á* 'we are cooking'. The past continuative prefix /chi/ both undergoes vowel drop (as in *wa-sh-pik-a* 'they used to cook') and also triggers it (as in *sh-chi-bo:ɬ-a* 'we used to steal').

Vowel drop fails to apply, however, when a prefix of the relevant type precedes an object prefix that begins with a voiceless obstruent. For example, the 1st pl. subject prefix remains unchanged before the 2nd sg. object prefix /xu/: *chi-xu-mer-e:l-é* 'we looked for you'. Similarly, the subject prefix /zi/ is unchanged before the 1st pl. object prefix /chi/ in *zi-chi-be:ɬ-e* 'lit., they were lost to us—i.e., we lost them'. (The reader will have noted that subject and object prefixes may, in some cases, be identical in phonological shape; thus /chi/ is both the 1st pl. subject and the 1st pl. object prefix.) The past continuative prefix /chi/ also remains unchanged preceding an object prefix that has an initial voiceless obstruent: *chi-xu-big-a* 'he used to hit you', *chi-chi-won-a* 'he used to see us'.

The question that arises is whether or not object prefixes will themselves undergo vowel drop when followed by a voiceless obstruent. The 2nd sg. object prefix /xu/ is immune to the rule of vowel drop: *wa-ʈa-xu-pik-iɬ-a* 'they will cook for you', *wa-xu-som-esh-e:z-e* 'they taught you'. But /xu/ is apparently simply an exception, since other object prefixes undergo vowel drop. For instance, /chi/ is both the 1st pl. object prefix and also an object prefix agreeing with singular nouns of a certain noun class; in both cases it is converted to /sh/ before roots that have an initial voiceless obstruent—cf., *wa-sh-pik-il-i:l-e* 'they cooked for us', *wa-sh-kaɬa:nz-iɬ-e* 'they fried it'. /zi/ is an object prefix agreeing with various plural nouns, and it is converted to /s/ in examples such as *wa-s-pasi:ɬ-e* 'they skinned them' and *wa-s-ṭi:nz-iɬ-e* 'they cut them'.

The juncture occurring between a prefix and an object prefix is, then, one that inhibits the application of the rule of vowel drop, whereas the juncture between an object prefix and the root does not inhibit the rule's application. There is another rule in Chi-Mwi:ni that is closely related to vowel drop that is also blocked at the juncture before an object prefix. This rule affects prefixes of the shape Ci/u-, where C is a sonorant. The vowel of such prefixes is deleted, regardless of the nature of the following consonant. For instance, the 3rd sg. object prefix referring to humans is /mu/ in its underlying shape, but surfaces as /m/ in examples like *wa-m-bo:z-eɬ-e* 'they stole from him', *wa-m-som-esh-e:z-e* 'they taught him', and *wa-m-gi:s-iɬ-e* 'they pulled him'. Similarly, the 1st sg. subject and object prefix /ni/ surfaces as /n/ (or a morphophonemic variant resulting from nasal assimilation) in *n-vu:nz-iɬ-é* 'I broke something', *n-som-e:ɬ-é* 'I read', *m-pʰish-iɬ-é* 'I cooked', *ŋ-gi:s-iɬ-é* 'I pulled', *wa-m-pʰik-il-i:l-e* 'they cooked for me', and *wa-ŋ-gi:s-iɬ-e* 'they pulled me'.

The vowel of prefixes like /mu/ and /ni/ is deleted both before voiceless and voiced consonants, thus differing from the rule of vowel drop that applies to prefixes with an obstruent consonant, like /chi/ and /ku/. We will refer to the rule that omits the vowel from "sonorant" prefixes like /mu/ and /ni/ as vowel deletion. Vowel deletion is restricted so as to not apply in the context ___CV#—cf., *ku-ni-j-a* 'to eat me', *ku-mu-j-a* 'to eat us', *ni-f-e* 'that I die', *ni-n-e* 'that I drink'. (It is interesting that vowel drop is also blocked from applying in this same context—cf., *ku-f-a* 'to die', *ku-t-a* 'to crush soaked grain'. Vowel drop and vowel deletion are very closely related rules, despite the fact that they differ in terms of whether they are sensitive to the nature of the consonant following the Ci/u- prefix.) Besides being inhibited in the environment ___CV#, vowel deletion is also inhibited before an object prefix. Thus we find *ni-m-som-el-e:l-é* 'I read to him' (where /ni/ fails to undergo vowel deletion while /mu/—the object prefix—undergoes the rule) and *ni-xu-pik-il-i:l-é* 'I cooked for you' (where again /ni/ does not undergo vowel deletion before an object prefix).

There is another rule, in addition to the processes of vowel drop/vowel deletion, that is blocked at junctures preceding object prefixes. We will refer to this rule as vowel coalescence. When certain prefixes of the shape Ci/u- precede a vowel, the vowel of the prefix coalesces with the following vowel to yield a long vowel having the vowel quality of the second vowel in the sequence. For example, the infinitive prefix /ku/ undergoes vowel coalescence in examples such as *k-a:sh-a* 'to light' (cf., *ash-á* 'light (it)!'), *k-o:ɬok-a* 'to go' (cf., *oɬok-a* 'go!'), *k-i:z-a* 'to refuse' (cf., *iz-á* 'refuse!'). /ku/ undergoes vowel coalescence regardless of the quality of the vowel that follows. Vowel coalescence fails to apply, however, when /ku/ is followed by an object prefix beginning with a vowel (there are two such prefixes in Chi-Mwi:ni, /i/ and /u/). Thus we find *ki-'i-ṭi:nḍ-a* 'to cut it' and *ku-'u-fu:ŋg-a* 'to close it'. A glottal stop separating the vowel of the infinitive prefix and the vowel of the object prefix is inserted in these examples; no coalescence occurs. (Note that /ku/ changes to /ki/ before /i/; although this vowel assimilation occurs before several object prefixes, it occurs nowhere else.) The glottal stop in the preceding examples is clearly inserted; it is absent, for example, when /i/ and /u/ object prefixes precede vowel-initial roots, since in this context /i/ and /u/ prefixes undergo glide formation accompanied by compensatory lengthening of the following vowel: *ki-y-u:ł-a* 'to buy it', *ku-w-a:sh-a* 'to light it'.

The rule of glide formation mentioned above also affects the /i/ and /u/ prefixes when they function as subject prefixes: *i-som-e:l-a* 'it was read', but *y-anḍish-il-a* 'it was written'; *u-vu:nz-il-a* 'it was broken', but *w-ash-i:z-a* 'it was lit'. This process does not obtain at a juncture preceding an object prefix. In other words, if the subject prefixes /i/ or /u/ precede the object prefixes /i/ or /u/, glide formation does not occur. Note the following examples.

(62)   *ijiwe i-'u-poṭel-el-e: muti*   'the stone fell on the log'
        muti u-'i-burbuk-il-il-e nu:mba   'the tree fell on the house'
        ijiwe i-'i-poṭel-el-e me:za   'the stone fell on the table'
        uŋga u-'u-ṭawañik-il-il-e mkate   'the flour spilled on the cake'

We have demonstrated that a number of phonological rules in Chi-Mwi:ni fail to apply across the juncture separating a prefix from a following object prefix; the same rules apply, however, between the juncture of object prefixes and the following root, as well as between all prefixes and a following element other than an object prefix. These facts could be accounted for by claiming that there is a boundary &, stronger than the simple morpheme boundary, separating the object prefix from everything else preceding it in the word. The rules that we have discussed would then have to be designated as rules that operate only across boundaries weaker than the & boundary. The recognition of a special boundary at the juncture before the object prefix does not, however, appear to be one that has any universal application. If it does not, and if the preceding data are properly described in terms of a boundary located before the object prefix, then the determination of boundaries would have to be regarded as a language-specific task.

The reader may well have noted that the examples presented concerning boundaries intermediate between the morpheme and the word boundary raise certain fundamental questions: (1) Does the mere fact that a given rule fails to apply across the boundary between two particular morphemes or morpheme classes constitute evidence that a boundary "stronger" than the simple morpheme boundary occurs at this juncture? (2) Does the fact that a given rule applies only to structures containing a particular morpheme or morpheme class constitute evidence that a boundary different from the morpheme boundary is present? In other words, are ALL instances where the grammatical (particularly, morphological) identity of an element is relevant to a rule's application to be analyzed in terms of boundaries, or is there a distinction between phenomena properly described by making reference to boundaries and phenomena properly described by means of direct reference to morphological identity? And if there is a distinction, how do we know when we are dealing with boundaries and when we are not?

In our opinion, the failure of a morpheme to undergo a rule whose structural description it apparently meets is not necessarily a matter of the cohesion of this morpheme to its neighbors; nor does the fact that a certain morpheme (class) uniquely triggers a phonological rule imply that there is something special about how it relates to its neighboring morphemes. In many cases we know how the grammaticalization of a rule developed historically, but there is little evidence that this process of grammaticalization is INVARIABLY associated with changes in the internal cohesion of elements in the word or phrase. (This is not to deny that in some cases such changes in cohesion may be involved.) If it is true that both grammatical identity and grammatical cohesion can affect a rule's application, then we are left with the difficult problem of attempting to determine when phonological phenomena should be analyzed in terms of postulating a special boundary and when appeal to grammatical identity alone should be made.

It seems to us that the basic concept underlying the notion of boundaries is the degree of *cohesion* (morphologically and/or syntactically defined) that linguistic forms exhibit. The morpheme is regarded as the minimal grammatical element; its component parts cannot be separated into smaller units and thus are fused together in the closest fashion possible. Morphemes cohere to form larger units—words, but in some cases it is possible to distinguish different degrees of cohesion within the word. For example, derivational affixes often cohere more tightly with the root than inflectional affixes. And often there will be various enclitic morphemes that are attached more loosely to the word than the inflectional morphemes. The degree of cohesion of elements within a word is often reflected in linear structure: Elements closer to the root in a linear sense tend to cohere more closely to the root than elements farther away.

Boundaries can thus be viewed as devices for indicating the degree of cohesion of elements: If no boundary except the morpheme boundary separates two elements, we are dealing with especially close-knit morphemes; if word, but not phrase, boundaries separate morphemes, then these morphemes belong to different words that are part of the same phrase; a phrase boundary separates words that belong to different phrases. Insofar as the existence of boundaries intermediate between the morpheme and the word can be demonstrated, they separate morphemes that belong to the same word but are not as closely knit as those separated only by the morpheme boundary.

According to this view, boundaries are concerned with the degree of cohesion between elements. The grammatical IDENTITY of an element is something quite different. Clearly, if one could freely posit boundaries and freely utilize them in rules, the distinction between boundaries and grammatical identity would vanish: A special boundary could be associated with each (nonlexical) morpheme in the language. The concept of boundary is thus rather vacuous unless some restrictions on positing boundaries in a string of morphemes and on referring to boundaries in phonological rules can be established.

One very reasonable constraint on the general use of boundaries which will inhibit the application of phonological rules can be expressed as follows: Boundaries must be hierarchical in structure, ordered from "weakest" (i.e., expressing the closest bond between morphemes and thus having the least inhibiting effect on phonological rules) to "strongest" (i.e., expressing the weakest bond between morphemes and thus having the greatest inhibiting effect on phonological rules). Furthermore, if a phonological rule is inhibited by a boundary of a certain strength, all boundaries of greater strength will inhibit the rule from applying as well.

A quite reasonable constraint on the positing of special boundaries would be that they must be grammatically motivated and grammatically consistent. There are various aspects of the condition that boundaries be grammatically motivated. The basic requirement is that the boundary must occur at the juncture between morphemes. Placing a boundary within a morpheme is obviously a violation of the requirement that the boundary be grammatically motivated. But there are other facets to the problem. It is generally agreed that derivational affixes are grammatically more closely bound to a root than inflectional affixes (this is reflected in the course of language change whereby derivational affixes very frequently coalesce with a root to form unanalyzable elements, whereas the reanalysis of component parts rarely occurs in the case of inflectional affixes). Consequently, if one requires that boundaries must be grammatically motivated, one would presumably be prevented from establishing a stronger boundary between a derivational affix and a root than between an inflectional affix and a root. In other words, the relative strength of boundaries must conform to grammatical facts.

An interesting question arises in connection with the constraint that boundaries must be grammatically motivated. The most problematical area with respect to the postulation of boundaries has to do with boundaries intermediate between the morpheme and the word. What kinds of cohesion occur within the word? First of all, there are differences in the extent to which an element is *part* of the word. The establishing of internal word boundaries attempts to explain this phenomenon. Secondly, there are differences in the extent to which morphemes are linked to the root. Thus roots plus (lexical) derivational affixes often form a stem to which inflectional endings are added. The derivational affixes are more closely bound to the root than they are to the adjacent inflectional affixes. And the inflectional affixes are not bound directly either to the root or to the derivational affixes, but rather to the whole stem. A stem boundary might be posited between the stem and the inflectional affixes, yielding a stronger break at this juncture than occurs between the root and the derivational affixes. The question that arises is whether there are other kinds of cohesion in addition to cohesion to the word and cohesion to the root.

Recall the example from Chi-Mwi:ni involving object prefixes, where we saw that certain rules of Chi-Mwi:ni phonology fail to apply across the juncture between a prefix and a following object prefix. One could claim that these rules must (in some way) make reference to the category "object prefix", or one could posit a special boundary at this juncture. It does not seem to be correct to say that morphemes to the left of the object prefixes are less a part of the word than the object prefix. In an example such as *wa-na-xu-big-a* 'they are beating you (sg.)', the subject prefix *wa-* and the tense prefix *-na-* are obligatory elements that cannot be omitted. Furthermore, subject prefixes and tense prefixes undergo the same rules as object prefixes; they all behave then like prefixes.

Can one claim that the object prefixes are more closely linked to the verb root than the subject prefixes and the tense prefixes? Grammatically it is difficult to see any justification for such a claim. But in any case, one generates inappropriate forms if one claims that there is a stronger boundary between subject or tense prefixes and the root than there is between the object prefixes and the root. For the various phonological rules that fail to affect a prefix that precedes the object prefix do affect the same prefixes when they precede the root. For instance, /ni/ 1st sg. reduces to /n/ in *n-chʰor-e:l-é* 'I engraved' where it precedes a /ch/ at the beginning of a root, although /ni/ does not reduce in *ni-chi-j-i:l-é* 'I ate it' where it precedes the object prefix /chi/. Consequently, the boundary between a subject or tense prefix and the root does not inhibit the application of the rules in question.

If there are only two kinds of cohesion (to the word and to the root) at the word level, then the Chi-Mwi:ni data would appear not to be properly treated by making reference to boundaries. If other kinds of cohesion are to be allowed, what are they?

Let us turn now to the constraint that boundaries must be grammatically consistent. This constraint might be expressed as follows: All elements of the same grammatical function are separated from adjoining elements by the same boundary. Given a requirement of this sort, differential behavior among members of the same class of grammatical elements could not be attributed to a difference in boundary strength. The reason behind this sort of a condition is simple: If one is free to associate different boundaries with morphemes of the same grammatical group, then the grammatical basis of the boundary is destroyed.

It might be useful to discuss a specific example at this point to illustrate the issue. In Chi-Mwi:ni, we have seen that the 1st sg. subject prefix has the phonological shape /ni/—cf., *ni-xu-pik-il-i:l-é* 'I cooked (it) for you'. The 2nd pl. subject prefix also has the phonological shape /ni/—cf., *ni-sh-pik-il-i:l-é* 'you (pl.) cooked (it) for us'. Despite the underlying phonological identity, the 1st sg. and the 2nd pl. subject prefixes (and object prefixes as well) exhibit quite distinct morphophonemic behavior. Although both prefixes undergo vowel deletion (see preceding example), the resulting sequences of nasal plus consonant exhibit different behaviors. For instance, the nasal of the 1st sg. prefix assimilates to a following stop, while the nasal of the 2nd pl. prefix does not: *m-bo:z-eł-é* 'I stole' versus *n-bo:z-eł-é* 'you (pl.) stole'; *ŋ-gur-i:l-é* 'I moved' versus *n-gur-i:l-é* 'you (pl.) moved'.

Furthermore, a voiceless stop is aspirated following nasal of the 1st sg. prefix, but not after the nasal of the 2nd pl. prefix: *m-pʰish-ił-é* 'I cooked' versus *n-pish-ił-é* 'you (p.) cooked', *n-tʰesh-eł-é* 'I laughed' versus *n-tesh-eł-é* 'you (pl.) laughed', *ŋ-kʰos-e:z-é* 'I made a mistake' versus *n-kos-e:z-é* 'you (pl.) made a mistake'.

Root-initial liquids shift to /d/ following the nasal of the 1st sg. prefix, but not after the nasal of the 2nd pl. prefix: *n-do:s-eł-é* 'I dreamed' versus *n-ło:s-eł-é* 'you (pl.) dreamed'; *n-deb-e:ł-é* 'I stopped', versus *n-reb-e:ł-é* 'you (pl.) stopped'; *n-das-ił-é* 'I left off' versus *n-las-ił-é* 'you (pl.) left off'.

There are additional differences, but the preceding examples suffice to establish the point that the 1st sg. and the 2nd pl. prefixes must be distinguished in terms of their morphophonemic behavior. Since both prefixes appear to be /ni/ in their underlying representations, a phonological distinction is not present. Consequently, some appeal to the morphological identity of the morphemes or to boundaries is called for. But if one claims that a difference in boundaries exists between the 1st sg. subject prefix and the 2nd pl. subject prefix, he is grammatically inconsistent in his placement of boundaries.

One can imagine situations where an argument could be given that such a violation of grammatical consistency is necessary. For instance, if certain phenomena were associated unambiguously with the presence of a particular (grammatically motivated) boundary, then another morpheme exhibiting exactly the same phenomena might be claimed to have the same boundary associated with it (even though other morphemes of the same type do not). The identification of this boundary would not be made on the basis of grammar but rather on the basis of analogous phonological behavior. Whether or not such a placement of a boundary on the basis of analogous phonological behavior (and thereby violating grammatical consistency) is valid, the general condition of grammatical consistency seems a reasonable one.

A strong set of constraints imposed on the positing of special boundaries would prevent the arbitrary use of boundaries to describe phonological alternations (or the lack thereof). But serious problems remain. For example, suppose that one is able to establish on grammatical grounds that a certain set of morphemes cohere less strongly to a given word than other morphemes. Now suppose that we associate a special boundary & with these morphemes. If these morphemes should happen to undergo a phonological process to which no other morphemes are subject, one could formulate the rule so that it is triggered by the boundary &. But it is not obvious that this boundary is really the important factor, as opposed to the morphological identity of the morphemes involved. That is, what is the evidence that the degree of cohesion is central to triggering the rule's application in such a case? Why not just consider the rule to be triggered by the grammatical category to which these morphemes belong? In those cases where grammatically different sets of morphemes undergo a given rule and they all have a certain boundary associated with them, formulating the rule in terms of the boundary is justified, since it permits expression of a generalization. In such a situation, all that the various sets of morphemes have in common is the degree to which they cohere to neighboring morphemes. Thus degree of cohesion must be the relevant factor. But when a grammatically unified set of morphemes is the only one having a particular boundary associated with it, then reference to that boundary makes no new generalization that cannot be made simply by referring to the grammatical identity of the set of morphemes in question.

The preceding remarks leave us with one final question: In cases where phonological phenomena could be ascribed either to boundaries or to grammatical identity, is there a basis for choosing one solution over the other? Under what conditions do speakers tend to associate the blocking or triggering of a phonological rule with the cohesiveness of elements as opposed to the grammatical categories to which the elements belong?

2.3   REMOTE SYNTACTIC INFORMATION IN PHONOLOGY

Most generative phonological descriptions assume that phonological rules apply to surface structures (possibly modified by so-called "readjustment rules" as proposed in *SPE*); that is, the rules are assumed to operate on structures that exist after all syntactic processes have been applied, having access only to information about syntactic structure that is actually present in surface structure. It is difficult to test the validity of these assumptions fully without a much better understanding of the notion "surface structure" and of the interrelationship between syntax and morphology than is presently available. Nevertheless, it is possible to cite a certain amount of evidence that suggests that phonological rules do apply "in terms of" syntactic configurations that exist prior to the application of certain syntactic rules.

Pashto, one of the national languages of Afghanistan, provides an interesting example where a phonological rule apparently must be applied prior to the application of syntactic rules. In Pashto, the formatives /wə́/, perfective marker, and /nə́/, negative marker, are stress-bearing elements that combine in a closely knit group with a following verb (the verb itself is unstressed in this context). Some examples follow.

(63)   sāt-ə́m   'I am keeping'   škaw-úm   'I am cutting'
        wə́-sāt-əm   wə́-škaw-um
        nə́-sāt-əm   nə́-škaw-um

        kar-ə́m   'I am growing s.t.'
        wə́-kar-əm
        nə́-kar-əm

[Note: -əm indicates a 1st sg. subject; -um is a phonological variant
of -əm that occurs after a labial consonant.]

The preceding examples all involve consonant-initial verb stems. In the
Pashto dialect we have studied, the majority of verbs fall into this category.
Verb stems that originally began with nonlow vowels have acquired a y or w
on-glide. There are, however, some two dozen or so verb stems that begin with
a low vowel (historically, this vowel may have been a prefix, but its prefix status
cannot be demonstrated synchronically). This low vowel is generally /a/, though
some verbs show fluctuation between /a/ and /ā/ (=[ɔ]). When /ə́/ of the perfective and negative markers precedes such verb stems, a vowel coalescence
occurs; /ə́/ plus /a/ or /ā/ yields /ā́/.

(64)   áxl-əm   'I am buying'   áley-əm   'I am singeing
                                                          the feathers/hair off'
        wā́-xl-əm   wā́-ley-əm
        nā́-xl-əm   nā́-ley-əm

        ā́čaw-um   (or áčaw-um) 'I am throwing something.'
        wā́-čaw-um
        nā́-čaw-um

The perfective and negative markers are not always adjacent to the verb stem
in surface structure. The pronominal clitic ye, for example, may intervene.
Notice the following examples where ye follows the negative marker and
precedes the verb stem.

(65)   nə́ ye sāt-əm   'I am not keeping it'
                nə́ ye škaw-um   'I am not cutting it'
                nə́ ye kar-əm   'I am not growing it'
                nā́ ye xl-əm   'I am not buying it'
                nā́ ye ley-əm   'I am not singeing it'
                nā́ ye čaw-um   'I am not throwing it'

These examples reveal that the coalescence of the /ə́/ of the negative marker
with the stem-initial /a/ or /ā/ takes place, even though the clitic ye intervenes
between the negative marker and the verb stem.

Clitics in Pashto, including ye, are placed after the first stressed constituent
in a clause. The stressed perfective and negative markers count as the first
constituent if they occur clause-initially, as in the examples above. We can

easily explain an example like *na ye xləm* if we assume that the coalescence of the /ɔ/ of the negative marker with the initial /a/ of the verb stem applies prior to the insertion of the clitic *ye*.

Furthermore more than one clitic may intervene between the perfective or the negative marker and a following verb stem. The future marker *ba* functions as a clitic in Pashto. When *ba* and *ye* both occur in a single clause, they both follow the first stressed constituent, *ba* preceding *ye*.

(66) *wú ba ye sā̄t-əm*   'I will keep it'   *wā́ ba ye xl-əm*   'I will buy it'
      wú ba ye škaw-um   'I will cut it'   *wā́ ba ye ley-əm*   'I will singe it'
      wú ba ye kar-əm   'I will grow it'   *wā́ ba ye čaw-um*   'I will throw it'

The /ɔ/ of the perfective marker assimilates to /u/ when a labial consonant follows; this assimilation occurs not only when the perfective marker precedes /ba/, but also when it precedes a labial-initial verb stem: *wú bered-ə* 'he got scared'.

Let us now consider examples like *wā́ ba ye xləm*. In this case the /ɔ/ of the perfective morpheme has coalesced with the initial /a/ of the verb stem, even though the perfective morpheme is separated from the verb stem (on the surface) by two clitics. Furthermore, note that the /ɔ/ of the perfective morpheme has not assimilated to /u/, even though a labial consonant follows. We can again explain such data, if we permit vowel coalescence to precede the insertion of the clitics *ba* and *ye* between the perfective morpheme and the verb stem. The labialization of /ɔ/, on the other hand, must follow the placement of clitics, for its appearance in the shape *ú* is dependent upon the nature of the consonant that immediately follows in surface structure. It is rounded before the clitic *ba* in *wú ba ye sātəm* and unrounded in cases where a clitic not beginning with a labial appears between it and a labial-initial verb stem: *wɔ́ de berāw-ə*, 'you scared him', where the ergative clitic for second person *de* occurs between the perfective morpheme and the verb stem.

Even more involved cases may arise. Consider, for example, what happens when both the perfective and the negative markers occur together.

(67)   *wɔ́ nə sā̄t-əm*   'I did not keep it'
              wɔ́ nə škaw-um   'I did not cut it'
              wɔ́ nə kar-əm   'I did not grow it'
              wā́ nə xl-əm   'I did not buy it'
              wā́ nə ley-əm   'I did not singe it'
              wā́ nə čaw-um   'I did not throw it'

Notice that the negative marker must follow the perfective marker. Nevertheless, the /ɔ/ of the perfective coalesces with the initial /a/ or /ā/ of the verb stem while the /ɔ/ of the negative marker is unaffected. We can demonstrate that the negative marker is more loosely bound syntactically to the verb than the perfective marker—for example the negative marker can be postposed after the verb, but the perfective marker cannot. Thus one could plausibly argue that the negative moves into the position it occupies in the preceding examples. If this analysis is appropriate, then examples like *wá̃ nə xləm* can be explained by ordering the vowel coalescence rule before the insertion of the negative marker following the perfective marker.

Consider now the data in (68).

(68)		
	wú ba ye nə sāt-əm	'I will not keep it'
	wú ba ye nə škaw-um	'I will not cut it'
	wú ba ye nə kar-əm	'I will not grow it'
	wá̃ ba ye nə xl-əm	'I will not buy it'
	wá̃ ba ye nə ley-əm	'I will not singe it'
	wá̃ ba ye nə čaw-um	'I will not throw it'

In these examples three formatives intervene between the verb root and the perfective marker—the modal clitic /ba/, the pronominal clitic /ye/, and the negative marker /nə/. Nevertheless, the /ə̃/ of the perfective coalesces with the initial /a/ of verb roots such as /axl/: *wá̃ ba ye nə xləm*. Vowel coalescence appears to apply before the movement of the negative into position before the verb root and before the placement of the clitics in their position following the first stressed element in the clause.

Another example of this sort is to be found in Abaza, a Caucasian language (cf., Allen, 1956). There is a rule in this language that voices a fricative when it terminates the pronominal complex and the following root begins with a voiced obstruent. Thus, the pronouns meaning 'I', 'you', and 'we' are /s/, /šʷ/, and /ḥ/ (a pharyngeal spirant), respectively. They appear unchanged, in their underlying shape, before roots beginning with a sonorant (cf., *ds-nqʼʷaqʷ-d* 'he challenged me'), but preceding voiceless, obstruent-initial roots they are voiceless (*pšə-, xə-*) and voiced before voiced, obstruent-initial roots: (*ba-*).

(69)			
	s-pšə-d	*šʷ-pšə-d*	*ḥ-pšə-d*
	y-s-xəd	*y-šʷ-xə-d*	*y-ḥ-xə-d*
	y-z-ba-d	*y-žʷ-ba-d*	*y-ʕ-ba-d*

We appear to require a rule of roughly the following form

$$(70) \qquad \begin{bmatrix} +\text{cont} \\ -\text{son} \end{bmatrix} \longrightarrow [+\text{voice}]/ \underline{\qquad} \begin{bmatrix} \begin{bmatrix} -\text{son} \\ +\text{voice} \end{bmatrix} \end{bmatrix}$$
root

According to Allen (1956, p. 147):

> The voicing process is applicable to a pronominal complex even in the negative form, where one of the exponents of negation (indicated by *m*) intervenes between the pronominal and radical exponents.

We, therefore, find voicing of a pronominal spirant when the root begins with a voiced obstruent (despite the intervening *m*, a sonorant that normally permits the underlying voice feature to surface) in forms like the following.

(71)   *dg^y-z-m-ba-d*   'I did not see him'
        dg^y-ž^w-m-ba-d   'you did not see him'
        dg^y-ʕ-m-ba-d   'we did not see him'

Allen points out that the voicing process is blocked if any other morpheme intervenes between the pronominal prefix and the root, like the potential morpheme /zə-/ or the causative /r-/. *d-s-zə-ba-d* 'I could not see him', *y-l-ḥ-r-ba-d* 'we showed it to her'. All of these facts can be explained if we assume that the voicing assimilation rule applies as stated above, but that it is also able to make reference to a more remote syntactic structure which exists before the point at which the negative morpheme is inserted between the pronominal complex and the root. The validity of this analysis depends of course upon the assumption that the remote syntactic structure required for the most general operation of the voicing assimilation rule can be motivated on independent syntactic grounds. We have not had the opportunity to investigate the matter, but it is a fact that for many languages (such as English) the negative morpheme is best analyzed syntactically as originating at the beginning or end of the clause and then inserted within it by transformation. This is quite suggestive since it is the negative element in Abaza that is transparent to voicing assimilation.

Morin (1970) discusses a number of examples of this type as well. One of them involves mutation in Breton. In this language the possessives *ma* 'my', *he* 'her', and *o* 'their' induce a spirantization of an initial *p*, *t*, and *k* to *f*, *z*, and *x* in a following noun: *ar penn* 'the head' versus *ma fenn* 'my head'; *an ti* 'the house' versus *he zi* 'her house'; *ar karantez* 'the love' versus *o c'harantez* 'their love'. After the quantifier *oll* 'all, whole', voiceless stops do not ordinarily mutate except when *oll* is preceded by *ma*, *he*, or *o*; then the initial consonant of a following noun does suffer mutation: *an oll plijadur* 'all the pleasure', *ma oll flijadur* 'all my pleasure'; *an oll karantez* 'all the love', *he oll c'harantez* 'all her love'. On the other hand, mutation does not occur if any other word appears between *ma*, *he*, or *o*, and the following noun: *eur mell ti* 'a big house' versus *he mell ti* 'her big house'. In order to explain why *oll* permits mutation to apply through it, as it were, Morin hypothesizes that *ma oll flijadur* comes from an underlying structure *oll [ma plijadur]*. Mutation will apply to such a remote representation weakening *p* to *f*. Subsequently, *oll* is inserted between *ma* and *flijadur*.

Another example of a similar nature that Morin discusses concerns mutation in Irish. After the preposition *gan* 'without', the initial consonant of a following noun mutates optionally: *maher* 'mother', *gan vaher/gan maher* 'without mother'. But when two or more nouns are conjoined in a series and preceded by *gan*, all of them may mutate: *gan briste, pien agus maher* 'without trousers, pen nor mother' or *gan vriste, fien agus vaher*, with the same meaning. Mutation cannot take place when the nouns are simply conjoined and not preceded by a preposition. Since such phrases presumably derive from a more remote syntactic structure in which each noun is preceded by the preposition (*gan briste, gan pien, agus gan maher*), the proper pattern of spirantization can be obtained if the mutation rule is applied before the rule of conjunction reduction.

It is perhaps worth noting that in all of the preceding cases it is not necessary to assume that the phonological rule in question is actually APPLIED prior to the syntactic rule(s). Rather, we have shown that the CONDITIONS that determine whether or not a given phonological rule applies are conditions that exist prior to certain syntactic operations. Thus if phonological rules were permitted to operate *on* surface structures only when the surface structure involved had a particular shape at a deeper level, then these examples could be accounted for without actually ordering phonological rules before syntactic rules. (For a detailed discussion of related matters, see Chapter 6.)

Most of the examples discussed in this section have involved phonological rules that have applied because two formatives were contiguous at some point prior to surface structure. Certain syntactic rules causing elements to move (negative morphemes, clitics, etc.) obscure contiguity. These examples suggest, then, that phonological rules must be allowed to operate in terms of structures that exist prior to syntactic movement rules.

There are, obviously, other kinds of syntactic rules that could interact with phonological rules in a similar fashion. Syntactic deletion rules could, for example, destroy the context which invokes the application of a phonological rule. If the phonological rule does apply, then we could say that it is applied in terms of the syntactic structure prior to deletion. The example from Irish involving the interplay of conjunction reduction and spirantization offers one relevant example.

3.0 LEXICAL INFORMATION IN PHONOLOGY

Whether or not a given phonological rule *n* will apply to a particular phonological structure can be shown to be determined by a variety of factors. The most characteristic of these factors is the phonetic nature of the structure itself. A rule will apply to a given structure only if that structure contains a sound appearing in the environment required by the structural description of the rule. A second factor that may limit the applicability of a rule to a given structure is the syntactic/semantic makeup of that structure. Numerous examples illustrating this point were discussed in the preceding section. Another factor (discussed at length in Chapter 6) is the derivational source of the structure. For instance, in Lardil (see Chapter 1) only underlying word-final high vowels are subject to lowering. High vowels that come to stand in word-final position as the result of the deletion of a consonant do not undergo the lowering rule. This difference in the derivational source of a high vowel (underlying versus derived) can be expressed in the form of rule ordering.

Each of the factors discussed above that restrict the application of a given phonological rule is independently motivated, in the sense that each represents information necessary to the grammar, independently of the formulation of rule n. Phonetic information is needed in order to characterize the pronunciation of the structure involved. Syntactic/semantic information is independently required in order to describe the grammatical behavior of the structure. Also, the contrast between whether a segment is basic or derived by a particular rule x is information that is independent of whether or not some other rule n applies.

However, it is often the case that the phonological behavior of a morpheme cannot be determined solely on the basis of such independently necessary information. In such circumstances it is necessary to provide additional, unpredictable information ad hoc in order to characterize fully the phonological structure of the morpheme. Generative phonologists have taken the position that this information is to be included in the lexicon, whose role is that of the repository of all of the unpredictable, idiosyncratic features determining the phonological (as well as syntactic and semantic) behavior of a morpheme. Despite a fair amount of study of the nature of this unpredictable information, a great many questions remain unanswered. In the remainder of this section we will briefly survey the major types of lexical information that appear to be necessary to phonological theory.

3.1   LEXICAL EXCEPTIONS

Perhaps the simplest kind of situation in which an ad hoc lexical specification is mandatory in order to determine properly the application of a phonological rule involves lexical exceptions. Here we have in mind the situation in which most lexical items that satisfy the phonetic and grammatical requirements of a rule do in fact undergo the rule, although a small number unpredictably do not. Consequently, in order to assign the correct phonetic representation to the morphemes they must be blocked from undergoing the rule. This seems to be most properly handled by including in the lexical representation of these morphemes the ad hoc information that they are exceptions to the rule.

We will begin a brief discussion of how this is to be accomplished by examining what seems to us the strongest possible position that can be taken on the treatment of exceptions (short of denying that there are exceptions!). This is the position proposed in *SPE* where each morpheme in the lexicon is to be assigned a feature [α rule n], where α is a variable ranging over the values $+$ and $-$, for each of the phonological rules in the language. In the unmarked, regular case each lexical item is specified the value $\alpha = +$; in the irregular case of exceptions, $\alpha = -$. Then, by general convention, the specification α is assigned to each segment in the morpheme. *SPE* then proposes that given any phonological rule of the form *n*:

(72)   (n) A $\longrightarrow$ B/X____Y

this rule will apply to a string X′A′Y′ (where X′A′Y′ are not distinct from X, A, and Y, respectively), only when A′ contains the specification [+rule n]. If a segment has been assigned the specification [−rule n], by virtue of appearing in a morpheme that has been marked in the lexicon as an exception to rule *n*, *n* will not apply to that segment.

For example, in Ukrainian there is a rule that deletes the dental stops *t* and *d* before the past tense suffix *-l*. This accounts for the varying shapes of the morpheme /krad-/ 'steal' in *krad-u* 'I steal' and *kra-l-a* 'she stole'. The morpheme /zblid-/ 'turn pale' is an exception to this rule: *zblid-l-a* 'she turned pale'. Given the system developed above, the morpheme /krad-/ would be assigned the feature [+dental stop deletion], while /zblid-/ would be marked [−dental stop deletion] in the lexicon of Ukrainian. By general convention the specifications of + and − would be assigned to each segment of the morpheme. Dental stop deletion would not then apply to the *d* of /#zblid-l-a#/, since it is marked as [−DSD]. But the rule would apply to the *d* of /#krad-l-a#/ since it is specified [+DSD].

The position we have just outlined makes a very strong claim, in the sense that it is very restrictive: it claims that only a certain limited class of exceptions may occur. This is entirely fitting, since, as with so many other aspects of theoretical phonology, *SPE* was the first serious attempt to develop a theory of exceptions. And with first attempts, the best policy is to make the strongest, most restrictive claim consistent with the data available. For it throws into relief the kinds of data that could serve as possible counterexamples, and thereby provides a clear guide to future research.

Since the publication of *SPE* further work in the area of exceptions has revealed that the *SPE* position is too strong. In what follows we shall give a brief survey of the kinds of exceptions that have been clearly established, discussing what mechanisms seem to be required in order to deal with them.

The *SPE* position admits just one basic kind of exceptional behavior—this can be referred to as "negative input exceptions"; that is, a segment (actually, the morpheme containing the segment, according to the *SPE* analysis) is specified negatively as failing to undergo a specific phonological rule. There are, of course, other logically possible types of exceptional behavior. For example, a morpheme may fail to CONDITION the application of a phonological rule, even though the morpheme contains the sort of segmental structure that ordinarily requires the rule to apply. Exceptions of this type are in fact rather common.

Chi-Mwi:ni provides a quite straightforward example. There is a morphophonemic rule in Chi-Mwi:ni which affects just the perfective suffix *-i(:)ɫ-*; the *ɫ* of this suffix (*ɫ* is a liquid that contrasts with both *l* and *r*; in articulating *ɫ*, the tip of the tongue strikes lightly a small area to the front of the alveolar ridge, without lateral contact) is converted to *z* if the preceding verb stem ends in *s*, *sh* (=[š]) *z*, or *ñ*.

(73)　　*x-fiłis-a*　　'to go bankrupt'　　*fiłis-i:z-e*　　'he went bankrupt'
　　　　x-kos-a　　'to make a mistake'　　*kos-e:z-e*　　'he made a mistake'
　　　　k-a:nz-a　　'to begin'　　*anz-i:z-e*　　'he began'
　　　　x-ṭez-a　　'to play'　　*ṭez-e:z-e*　　'he played'
　　　　ku-ra:sh-a　'to follow'　　*rash-i:z-e*　　'he followed'
　　　　x-ṭosh-a　　'to think'　　*ṭosh-e:z-e*　　'he thought'
　　　　x-fa:ñ-a　　'to do'　　*fañ-i:z-e*　　'he did'
　　　　x-kakañ-a　'to change'　　*kakañ-i:z-e*　'he changed'

But:　*ku-ji:b-a*　　'to answer'　　*jib-i:ł-e*　　'he answered'
　　　　x-so:m-a　　'to read'　　*som-e:ł-e*　　'he read'
　　　　ku-haḍ-a　　'to say'　　*haḍ-i:ł-e*　　'he said'
　　　　x-ṭaraj-a　　'to hope'　　*ṭaraj-i:ł-e*　　'he hoped'

Although the change of the perfective *ł* to *z* is restricted to one morpheme, the rule appears to be productive; it does apply even in cases where the verb root has been borrowed from Arabic or Somali (the two languages that have affected Chi-Mwi:ni vocabulary most extensively). The root /fiłis/ in *fiłis-i:z-e* is an Arabic loan and /ra:sh/ in *rash-i:z-e* is a Somali loan.

There are, however, a handful of exceptional forms.

(74)　　*ku-bariz-a*　　'to appear'　　*bariz-i:ł-e*　'he appeared'
　　　　ku-ja:su:s-a　'to spy'　　*jasus-i:ł-e*　'he spied'
　　　　ku-'a:sis-a　'to found s.t.'　　*asis-i:ł-e*　'he founded (it)'

Even though the *ł* in *bariz-i:ł-e* does not undergo the expected change to *z*, it is clearly not the perfective suffix itself that is an exception; rather the root /bariz/ is exceptional in that its final *z* does not trigger the change of the perfective *ł* to *z*.

In the *SPE* system, the failure of the *ł* in *bariz-i:ł-e* to shift to *z* must be accounted for by specifying somehow the *ł* as [-rule *ł*-to-*z*]. The prefective suffix cannot be assigned this property in the lexicon, otherwise we could not account for why the rule applies in (regular) examples like *fiłis-i:z-e*, *kos-e:z-e*, *anz-i:z-e*, etc. In the *SPE* analysis it would be necessary to assign to the perfective suffix the property [-rule *ł*-to-*z*] when preceded by the morphemes /bariz/, /ja:su:s/, /'a:sis/, etc. Although this would be technically possible, it does seem to miss the point, since in this analysis the morphemes /bariz/, /ja:su:s/, /'a:sis/ are not marked in the lexicon as exceptional in any way. But they are clearly exceptional in that they fail to condition application of the *ł*-to-*z* rule. Let us refer to a morpheme like /bariz/ as a "negative environment exception."

If we accept that a morpheme may be exceptional either because it fails to undergo a rule, even though in the appropriate environment, or because it

fails to condition a rule, even though containing the relevant segmental structure, the following question arises: Does a morpheme that exceptionally fails
to undergo a rule also necessarily fail to condition that same rule (assuming
that the structure of the morpheme is such that it can both undergo the rule
and also condition it)? and vice versa? We can depict this range of questions
in the following table.

(75)

	undergoes rule n	conditions rule n
(i)	+	+
(ii)	+	−
(iii)	−	+
(iv)	−	−

The evidence seems to be that all four cases are possible. In the following
paragraphs we briefly discuss examples of each of the four types.

The following data from Piro, an Arawakan language of Peru (Matteson,
1965) are especially interesting in this regard. This language has a rule of vowel
drop of roughly the following form.

(76) $$V \longrightarrow \emptyset / VC\underline{\qquad} + CV$$

That is, a morpheme-final vowel deletes in a two-sided open syllable. To illustrate, the nominalizing suffix -*lu* causes the deletion of the final vowel of a
preceding verb stem.

(77) *yimaka* 'teach'   *yimak-lu*   'teaching'
      kakona 'to build a shelter for a *kakon-ru** 'a shelter in which a
                hideout in hunting'   hunter hides'
      kama   'to make'   *kam-lu*   'handicraft'

The addition of the possessive suffix -*ne*, which is used in combination with a
pronominal prefix, may also elicit an application of vowel drop to a preceding
stem.

(78) *xipalu* 'sweet potato'   *n-xipal-ne* 'my sweet potato'
      čalu   'fish net'   *n-čal-ne*   'my fish net'
      kahli   'clay'   *n-kahli-ne* 'my clay'
      xinri   'palm species'   *n-xinri-ne* 'my palm species'

In the last two examples the stem-final vowel does not delete because it is preceded by two consonants, instead of VC. Similarly, all morphemes that begin
with a consonant cluster inhibit the deletion of a preceding vowel. The "gener-
alizer" suffix -*kta* illustrates this constraint on the vowel deletion rule: *hiyaho*
'so, then', *hiyah-ni* 'therefore', but *hiyaho-kta-la* 'correctly'. Compare also
hima 'it is said', *hiya:himni* 'therefore it is said' (from *hiyaho-hima-ni* with

---

* Upon deletion of the vowel, the *l* shifts to *r* by a general rule that need not concern us.

degemination of the *h-h* cluster resulting from vowel deletion and the compensatory lengthening of the preceding vowel), but *mak-hima-kta* 'but in general it is said'.

Having established VC___ + CV as the context for vowel drop, we now proceed to the matter of interest. The causative suffix *kaka-* is perfectly regular with respect to the rule. It provides the context for the deletion of a preceding vowel (*čokoruha* 'to harpoon', *čokoruh-kaka* 'to cause to harpoon') and will itself lose its final vowel when followed by a CV morpheme: *salwa-kak-lu* 'cause him to visit'. *kaka* is thus a morpheme belonging to case (i) of the table in (75).

Piro also has several suffixes that fail to condition the deletion of a preceding vowel, but that nevertheless delete their vowel when a suffix follows. One such suffix is *-ta*, a verbal theme formative. This suffix occurs in the word *hata-ta* 'to illuminate', which is composed of the root *hata* plus the thematic *-ta*. Note that the final vowel of the root appears in a two-sided open syllable but fails to delete. The failure of the vowel to delete cannot be accounted for by simply marking the root *hata* as an exception to vowel drop, for it deletes its vowel when followed by other suffixes: *hat-nu* 'light, shining' from /hata-nu/, a suffix used to form abstract nouns. The suffix *-ta* is thus exceptional in failing to condition the deletion of a preceding vowel. However, the vowel of *-ta* itself may delete by vowel drop: *yono-t-na-wa* 'to paint oneself', is composed of a root *yono* 'to paint', followed by *-ta*, followed in turn by the reflexive elements *na-wa*. Another suffix having the same properties as *-ta* is the anticipatory suffix *-nu*. It fails to cause deletion of a preceding vowel as shown in words like *heta-nu* 'going to see' from *heta* 'to see' (cf., *het-lu* 'to see it'). But *-nu* loses its vowel before a suffix like *-lu: heta-n-ru* 'going to see him', from /heta-nu-lu/. The suffixes *-ta* and *-nu* belong to the second category of (75). They regularly undergo the rule of vowel drop, but exceptionally fail to condition the rule.

Piro also has a suffix that belongs to the fourth category, *-wa* meaning 'yet, still'. This suffix is doubly exceptional in both failing to undergo and failing to condition the very same rule. Forms like *heta-wa* 'still see' show that this suffix fails to condition vowel drop (cf., *het-lu* 'see it' and *het-ya* 'see there' illustrating that *heta* cannot be simply marked as an exception to vowel drop). Words like *heta-wa-lu* 'to see him yet' and *hišinka-wa-lu* 'to be still thinking about it' indicate that *wa* also fails to undergo vowel drop, since the 3rd person pronominal suffix *-lu* normally conditions the deletion of a preceding vowel, as we have seen from forms like *het-lu* 'see it'.

Slovak provides an example of the third type of exception—a morpheme conditioning a rule but exceptionally failing to undergo. Slovak contains a rule called the rhythmic law (RL), which shortens a vowel after a syllable containing a long vowel. This rule is followed by diphthongization that converts underlying [é, ǎ, ó] to [ie, ia, uo]. (A long vowel in Slovak is marked by an acute accent.) The 3rd pl. ending of the second conjugation, which is an underlying /-ǎ/, is an exception to RL. It is always realized as the diphthong /-ia/, regardless of whether the preceding stem ends in a long or short vowel.

(79)

	3rd person singular	3rd person plural	gloss
	rob-i	rob-ia	'work'
	vid-i	vid-ia	'see'
	kúp-i	kúp-ia	'buy'
	hlás-i	hlás-ia	'announce'

Consequently, the 3rd pl. morpheme must be marked as an exception to RL. It fails to undergo the rule. But when an underlying long vowel follows the 3rd pl. morpheme, it is regularly shortened. This can be shown by present active participles, which are formed by the addition of the suffix -c to the 3rd pl. form of the verb plus the "soft stem" gender endings, which are underlying /-i/, /-á/, and /-é/, for masculine, feminine, and neuter, respectively. The underlying length of these gender endings is revealed in adjectives like cudz-i 'foreign'. But when added to the participle stem, they regularly are realized as short.

(80)

	masculine	feminine	neuter	gloss
	cudz-i	cudz-ia	cudz-ie	'foreign'
	robiac-i	robiac-a	robiac-e	'working'
	vidiac-i	vidiac-a	vidiac-e	'seeing'
	kúpiac-i	kúpiac-a	kúpiac-e	'buying'
	hlásiac-i	hlásiac-a	hlásiac-e	'announcing'

To account for the shortening of the masc. ending in a form like robiac-i from /rob-ắ-c-í/, it seems that we must assume that the 3rd pl. morpheme /-ắ/ triggers an application of RL.

To be consistent with the preceding data we must provide for at least two types of exception features. Any morpheme will be assigned a value of + or − for the feature F_c, denoting whether or not it conditions a rule. Any morpheme will be assigned a value + or − for another feature F_u specifying whether or not it undergoes a rule. This procedure will then be carried out for each rule of the grammar. A question that arises in this connection is: Given a rule A $\longrightarrow$ B/X___Y, if a morpheme must be marked as exceptional for one side of the environment, will it also necessarily be an exception to the other side? The examples from Piro discussed earlier are relevant here. The only morphemes that are environmental exceptions to the rule dropping a morpheme-final vowel in the context VC___CV are those which prevent the deletion of a preceding vowel. To our knowledge, there are no morphemes that block the deletion of a following morpheme-final vowel. In other words, the CV portion of the rule has exceptions but the VC portion does not. Consider the problem of characterizing the behavior of a morpheme such as the anticipatory suffix -nu, which prevents the deletion of a preceding vowel (heta-nu) but itself undergoes the rule (heta-n-ru). If -nu is marked [-F_c] application of the rule will CORRECTLY be blocked in heta-nu. But the rule will INCORRECTLY be prevented from applying to /heta-nu-lu/ to yield heta-n-ru, the reason being that the consonant of *-nu* must be permitted to substitute for the consonant in the lefthand environment VC of the rule. But if it is specified [-F$_c$] it cannot. It therefore appears that we must expand our exception feature apparatus further to permit exceptions to different portions of the structural description of a rule. We will forgo doing this here until additional appropriate data can be assembled.

Negative input exceptions and negative environment exceptions represent the two most common types of exceptions. There is a small amount of evidence supporting the claim that two additional types must be recognized: "positive input exceptions" and "positive environment exceptions." The former involves cases where a segment UNDERGOES a rule even though it is not the appropriate segment-type; the latter involves cases where a morpheme CONDITIONS a rule's application even though the morpheme is not of the segmental structure appropriate for conditioning the rule. In other words, both types involve a "mistaken" application of a rule—the rule applies when it ought not to (rather than failing to apply when it should, as in the case of negative exceptions).

Chi-Mwi:ni provides examples that might be considered positive input exceptions. There is a morphophonemic rule in Chi-Mwi:ni that converts stem-final voiceless stops to *s* or *sh* before the perfective suffix *-i(:)ł-*.

(81) | | | |
|---|---|---|
| *ku-łap-a* | 'to swear an oath' | *las-ił-e* |
| *ku-gi:ṭ-a* | 'to pull' | *gi:s-ił-e* |
| *ku-ło:t-a* | 'to dream' | *ło:s-eł-e* |
| *x-pik-a* | 'to cook' | *pish-ił-e* |

Stem-final voiced stops are also converted to *z* before the perfective suffix, provided the voiced stop is preceded by a nasal. Otherwise, the voiced stop remains unaffected.

(82) | | | |
|---|---|---|
| *ku-ło:mb-a* | 'to beg' | *ło:nz-eł-e* |
| *x-ṭi:nd-a* | 'to cut' | *ṭi:nz-ił-e* |
| *x-shi:nd-a* | 'to win' | *shi:nz-ił-e* |
| *x-fu:ŋg-a* | 'to close' | *fu:nz-ił-e* |

But | | | |
|---|---|---|
| *ku-ja:rib-a* | 'to try' | *jarib-i:ł-e* |
| *ku-re:b-a* | 'to stop' | *reb-e:ł-e* |
| *ku-ru:ḍ-a* | 'to return' | *ruḍ-i:ł-e* |
| *ku-ḍo:ḍ-a* | 'to complain' | *ḍoḍ-e:ł-e* |
| *x-taraj-a* | 'to hope' | *taraj-i:ł-e* |
| *ku-ja:j-a* | 'to itch' | *i-jaj-i:ł-e* |
| *x-ṭig-a* | 'to castrate' | *ṭig-i:ł-e* |
| *ku-ra:g-a* | 'to be late' | *rag-i:ł-e* |

(It is perhaps worth pointing out that stems ending in a post-vocalic voiced stop are usually originally of non-Bantu origin, although now thoroughly integrated into the Chi-Mwi:ni phonological and morphological systems.) There is, however, one root in the language that ends in a post-vocalic voiced stop that does change before the perfective suffix: /big/ 'hit' has the perfective form *bish-iɬ-e* 'he hit'. The final /g/ of this root changes to /sh/, just as final /k/ of /pik/ does in *pish-iɬ-e*. One might therefore claim that /big/ is a positive input exception in that it undergoes the change to /sh/ even though it does not end in /k/ (which is the only consonant that regularly changes to /sh/ before the perfective suffix). Instead of recognizing /big/ as a positive input exception, one could simply treat the alternation between /big/ and /bish/ as suppletion. But to do so denies the connection between the occurrence of the /bish/ allomorph preceding the perfective suffix and the existence of a rule that regularly produces /sh/ exactly in this environment.

We have noted that voiced stops, if preceded by a nasal, mutate to *z* before the perfective suffix. The consonant *ɬ* also shifts to *z*.

(83)   ku-mo:ɬ-a   'to shave'   mo:z-eɬ-e
                    x-paɬ-a   'to scrape'   paz-iɬ-e
                    x-pe:ɬ-a   'to sweep'   pe:z-eɬ-e
                    x-kuɬ-a   'to grow'   kuz-iɬ-e

No other voiced sounds change (regularly) in the environment of the perfective suffix. The root /law/ 'go out' is, however, exceptional in that its final /w/ mutates to /z/ before the perfective: *laz-iɬ-e*. Stem-final /w/s ordinarily are unaffected—cf., *duguw-i:ɬ-e* 'he limped', *oɬow-e:ɬ-e* 'he got wet', *ow-e:ɬ-e* 'he bathed'. Thus the root /law/ could be considered a positive input exception in that its final /w/ undergoes the change to /z/ that is ordinarily restricted just to final /ɬ/ or voiced stops preceded by a nasal. Again, one could claim that the alternation between /law/ and /laz/ is a case of suppletion, but this ignores the fact that the /laz/ alternant is just the kind of shape that is regularly produced before the perfective suffix.

Let us turn now to some possible examples of positive environment exceptions. Once again, Chi-Mwi:ni provides relevant data. The various examples of perfective verbal forms cited earlier illustrate the operation of a rule of vowel harmony. Various suffixes in Chi-Mwi:ni of the form -*i*/*u*C- display a pattern of vowel harmony whereby a high vowel appears when the final vowel of the preceding stem is *i*(:), *u*(:), or *a*(:), whereas a mid-vowel appears if the preceding vowel is *e*(:) or *o*(:).

(84)   Perfective suffix -i(:)ɬ-:

        ɬim-i:ɬ-e   'he cultivated'   tetem-e:ɬ-e   'he shivered'
        kun-i:ɬ-e   'he scratched'   som-e:ɬ-e   'he read'
        gaf-i:ɬ-e   'he made a mistake'

        "Applied" ("prepositional") suffix:

        x-ʈi:nd-iɬ-a   'to cut for/with'   ku-pe:l-el-a   'to sweep for/with'
        x-ful-il-a   'to wash for/with'   x-so:m-eɬ-a   'to read for/with/to'
        x-pak-iɬ-a   'to rub for/with'

Causative suffix:

ku-miz-ish-a	'to make swallow'	*x-ṭek-esh-a*	'to make laugh'
x-ṭuf-ish-a	'to make spit'	*x-koɬoɬ-esh-a*	'to make cough'
ku-ra:g-ish-a	'to delay someone'		

The alternations illustrated above can most readily be accounted for if we assume that the high vowel variants occur in the underlying representation, and that a rule of vowel harmony operates on these suffixes to lower the basic high vowel to a mid-vowel when a mid-vowel precedes.

The verb /ubl/ 'kill' contains a high vowel and thus would not be expected to trigger vowel harmony, since only mid-vowels cause a following high vowel (in an -*i/u*C- suffix) to lower to mid. Nevertheless, /ubl/ does condition the application of vowel harmony: *ubl-e:l-e* 'he killed', *k-ubl-el-a* 'to kill with' (rather than the expected **ubl-i:l-e* and **k-ubl-il-a*). Thus /ubl/ conditions the application of vowel harmony to a suffix, even though /ubl/ does not contain a mid-vowel and thus should not condition the rule's application. We can consider, then, /ubl/ to be a positive environment exception.

Another possible case of a positive environment exception occurs in Chi-Mwi:ni. Recall the rules of vowel drop and vowel deletion. The former deletes the high vowel of a CV- prefix where C is an obstruent, before a voiceless obstruent: *ku-big-a* 'to hit', *x-pik-a* 'to cook'. The latter deletes the high vowel of a CV- prefix, where C is a sonorant, regardless of the nature of the following consonant: *m-so:m-a* 'one who reads' from /mu-so:m-a/, *m-ṭek-a* 'one who laughs' from /mu-ṭek-a/. Both rules are constrained so as not to delete the prefix vowel when it occurs in the context ____CV# : *ku-f-a* 'to die', *mu-f-a* 'one who dies'; *ku-t-a* 'to grind', *mu-t-a* 'one who grinds'.

There is one morpheme that behaves rather exceptionally with respect to both of these rules. The root /p/ 'give' induces the deletion of a preceding prefix vowel: *x-p-a* 'to give', *m-p-a* 'one who gives'. Since vowel drop and vowel deletion do not ordinarily apply in the environment ____CV#, /p/ is exceptional in triggering the application of these rules. We might therefore consider marking this morpheme as a positive environment exception in the lexicon.

3.2   MAJOR VERSUS MINOR RULES

So far we have dealt with exceptions in which the number of morphemes that fail to undergo a rule is relatively small compared to the number that do undergo the rule. We have proposed to handle these exceptions by including an ad hoc piece of information in their lexical entry, which must be memorized when learning the phonological structure of these morphemes. This proposal is supported by the behavior of language learners, who often extend the rule to exceptional items: For instance, the forms *fishes, sheeps, mans* are found in child language. In such situations the language learner has failed to learn (or at least remember) that these morphemes do not undergo regular rules of plural formation. Thus most of the nouns that formed their plurals by umlaut in Old English have joined the regular class of -*s* plurals. Under the treatment we have proposed, this regularization can be interpreted as the loss of an ad hoc piece of information, which is in accordance with the general tendency of linguistic structures to simplify.

However, there are examples in which a phonological rule applies only to a relatively small number of lexical items. The vast majority of morphemes fail to undergo the rule. Lightner (1968) discusses a number of examples like this from Russian. One of them involves a rule of deverbal nominalization that changes the root vowel to *o* in some roots, but not in others.

(85)

	root vowel changes		root vowel remains	
vy-bor	'choice', cf. *vy-br-at'* (1st sg. *vy-ber-u*) 'to choose'	*pod-kup*	'bribery', cf. *pod-kup-at'* 'to bribe'	
u-boj	'slaughter', cf. *u-bi-t'* 'to kill'	*ob-ed*	'dinner', cf. *ob-ed-at'* 'to dine'	
za-por	'lock', cf. *za-per-et'* 'to lock'	*beg*	'running', cf. *beg-at'* 'to run'	
pri-tok	'flow, influx', cf. *pri-teč* (1st sg. *pri-tek-u*) 'to flow'	*na-mek*	'hint', cf. *na-mekat* 'to hint at'	

In order to handle the forms in the first column we require a rule of roughly the following form: $V \longrightarrow o$ in derived nominals. However, it would be incorrect to mark the roots of the second column as exceptions to the rule, for the overwhelming majority of verbal roots in Russian suffer no such vowel change in the derived nominals. The language learner must memorize the few morphemes that do undergo the vowel change. Hence, it is the forms in the first column that must be treated as exceptional and specified with an extra ad hoc piece of information.

In order to achieve a state of affairs in which the relatively few forms undergoing the rule are treated as exceptional and require an extra piece of nonphonetic information in the lexicon to trigger their exceptional behavior, Lightner proposes following Lakoff's (1965) treatment of analogous phenomena in syntax by making a distinction between *major rules* and *minor rules*. Major rules apply to the overwhelming majority of morphemes that meet a given structural description. Idiosyncratic exceptions to major rules are handled by adding ad hoc information to their lexical entries: [−rule *n*]. Most of the rules discussed so far are major rules. Minor rules apply to only a small subset of the total number of forms that match a given structural description. The vast majority of morphemes do not undergo minor rules. By general convention all morphemes are assumed to be exceptions to a minor rule. Hence, in order for a minor rule to apply, the morpheme in question must be specified as [+rule *n*] in the lexicon.

To be more precise, we will assume that for each minor rule *n* in the grammar, there is a corresponding lexical redundancy rule of the form: [u rule *n*] ⟶ [−rule *n*], where *u* means "unmarked for rule *n*." Therefore, all regular morphemes (morphemes that, in the case of a minor rule, do not undergo the rule) will be specified by general convention as exceptions to the rule. Those few morphemes that undergo the rule will have to be marked as [+rule *n*], either by an ad hoc listing in the lexicon or perhaps by another redundancy rule.

Applying this treatment to the Russian data discussed earlier, the *V*∼*o* rule will be a minor one. A regular morpheme from the second column such as *kup-* (cf., *pod-kup*) will be [u V∼o] in the lexicon. It will be exempt from the *V*∼*o* rule by virtue of the following redundancy rule: [u V∼o] ⟶ [−V∼o]. On the other hand, an irregular morpheme such as *tek-* 'flow' (cf., *pri-tok*) will be marked as [+V∼o] in its lexical entry. It will not undergo the above redundancy rule and hence *will* undergo *V*∼*o*. Finally, as Lightner observes, for roots that contain a "fleeting" vowel followed by a sonorant such as *ber-* (cf., *vy-br-at'*, *vy-bor*), there is a generalization that can be extracted: Such roots always exhibit an *o*-nominal form. Consequently, roots of this shape may also be [u V ∼ o] in the lexicon. Their [+V ∼ o] specification may be supplied by another redundancy rule.

In the preceding example morphemes had to be specified in the lexicon as (idiosyncratically) undergoing a minor rule. There is evidence that morphemes must also be specified as (idiosyncratically) conditioning a rule. For example, in Polish the velars [k, g, x] shift to the palatals [č, ž, š] preceding the overwhelming majority of derivational suffixes that begin with front vowels.

(86) | | | | |
|---|---|---|---|
| *miȩk* | 'soft' | *miȩ*[č-ić] | 'to soften' |
| *sług* | 'servant' | *słu*[ž-ić] | 'to serve' |
| *śmie*[x] | 'laughter' | *śmie*[š-ić] | 'to make laugh' |
| *rȩk-a* | 'hand' | *rą*[č-ina] | 'little hand' |
| *strug* | 'plane' | *stru*[ž-iny] | 'shavings' |
| *ci*[x] | 'silent' | *ci*[š-ina] | 'silence' |
| *pisk* | 'squeak' | *pisz*[č-eć] | 'to squeak' |
| *drog* | 'expensive' | *dro*[ž-eć] | 'to become expensive' |
| *dy*[x-ać] | 'to pant' | *dy*[š-eć] | 'to pant, puff' |

For inflected forms, front-vowel suffixes fall into four types according to their effect on preceding velars. First, there are suffixes such as those in (86); second, there are suffixes that induce the shift of [k, g, x] to [c, dz, š/ś]; third, some suffixes front the velars *k* and *g* (but not *x*) to *k'* and *g'*. Finally, there are front-vowel suffixes which leave a preceding velar unchanged. For instance, in the declension of *a*-stem nouns, the second type of palatalization occurs before the dative and locative singular suffixes -*e*, while the accusative singular -*e* causes no change.

(87)

	nominative singular	dative/locative singular	accusative singular	gloss
	ręk-a	rę[c-e]	rę[k-e]	'hand'
	nog-a	no[dz-e]	no[g-e]	'leg'
	mu[x-a]	mu[š-e]	mu[x-e]	'flea'

Suffixes of the second and third type occur in the declension of "virile" nouns (masculine nouns referring to persons).

(88)

	nominative singular	instrumental singular	nominative plural	gloss
	urędnik	urędni[k'-em]	urędni[c-i]	'official'
	bóg	bo[g'-em]	bo[dz-i]	'God'
	mni[x]	mni[x-em]	mni[š-i]	'monk'

A few of these nouns take the vocative suffix -e, in which case the first kind of palatalization occurs (e.g., bo[ž-e] 'God!'). Finally, in the inflection of verbs we find front-vowel suffixes of the first and fourth types: mo[g-e] 'I can', mo[ž-e] 'he can'; pie[k-e] 'I bake', pie[č-e] 'he bakes'.

As might be expected, there is a historical explanation for the different effects these front-vowel suffixes have. The first type derive from Proto-Slavic front-vowel suffixes, while the others derive from historical back vowels which fronted at different stages in the development of the language. There is, however, little if any evidence that these morphophonemically different but phonetically identical vowels are anything but front vowels in underlying representation and that the differences are not to be handled by lexical markings. Since most front-vowel suffixes cause the first type of palatalization, this would be a major rule. The second and third types of palatalization are elicited by only a handful of suffixes, and hence could be handled by a minor rule. The fourth type, which causes no change, is simply a negative environment exception.

The above data from Polish illustrate the insufficiency of the analysis of minor rules given above earlier. Any noun or verb root ending in a velar will undergo the minor palatalization rules. Thus it would be incorrect to say that these rules are "minor" with respect to the particular morphemes that undergo them. Rather, they are "minor" with respect to the particular morphemes that *condition* their application. It seems, then, necessary to recognize two classes of minor rules: minor input rules and minor environment rules. A minor input rule applies only to morphemes specifically marked as undergoing the rule (all morphemes that are unmarked are predictably specified as failing to undergo the rule). All morphemes will (normally) undergo a minor environment rule, but only if the segments in the environment are specifically marked as conditioning the rule's application; morphemes that are not marked as conditioning the rule will be predictably specified as not conditioning the rule's application.

So far we have examined situations in which the morphemes requiring special lexical markings with respect to a particular phonological rule have been relatively small in number compared to the morphemes requiring no special marking. There are, however, many cases requiring ad hoc lexical categorization in which the number of morphemes failing to undergo the rule is approximately equivalent to the number that do undergo the rule. In these situations it makes no real sense to speak of one class as being "regular" and the other "exceptional". Such situations can be accounted for in essentially the same fashion as before—by ad hoc lexical categorization. The only difference is that we cannot identify one class as being unmarked or regular.

A relatively simple example can be found in Halle's study of Russian accent (1973): There is a general rule that places stress on the inflectional ending of a word whose stem is unaccented. Subsequent to this there is another rule, which Halle calls METATONY, which retracts the stress one syllable from the ending to the stem. In the present tense of verbs this rule operates in all persons but the 1st sg. However, whether or not any given verb undergoes the rule is to a large extent unpredictable. Compare the paradigms of the following verbs.

(89)

		toropít' 'to hurry'	govorít' 'to speak'
singular			
	1	toroplj-ú	govor'-ú
	2	toróp-iš	govor-íš
	3	toróp-it	govor-ít
plural			
	1	toróp-im	govor-ím
	2	toróp-ite	govor-íte
	3	toróp'-at	govor'-át

Verbs like *toropít'* that undergo the retraction rule include *kupít'* 'to buy', *xodít'* 'to go', *kormít'* 'to feed', *varít'* 'to cook'. Verbs with the stress pattern of *govorít'* include *rešít'* 'to decide', *tvorít'* 'to create', *mutít'* 'to muddle', *žurít'* 'to scold'. Further investigation of these verbs reveals that there is no independent property that makes it possible to predict whether or not they undergo retraction.

In a situation such as the preceding the plus and minus specifications for the metatony rule must be specified ad hoc in the lexicon for the members of both classes of stems, since neither /torop, + metatony/ nor /govor, − metatony/ can be identified as the regular case. In this example, the +/− metatony specifications would have to be considered environmental features, since the metatony rule takes the form of deleting the accent from a suffix, according to Halle's analysis. He assumes that prior to the metatony rule another rule has redundantly specified all syllables preceding the rightmost accented syllable as being redundantly accented. *toróp-iš* thus derives from

/tóróp-iš/. Metatony yields /tóróp-iš/, and a later rule deletes all but the right-most accent in a word to yield *toróp-iš*.

As in the previous examples of major and minor rules, the $+/-$ specification for a rule like metatony is sometimes predictable for a given class of morphemes. In the present case there are about sixty Russian verb stems ending in *a* which are unaccented, i.e., which are accented on the inflectional ending in the present tense. All such unaccented verb stems terminating in the vowel *a* undergo the metatony rule. Thus, *pisá-t'* 'to write', *piš-ú*, but *piš-eš* (from /piš-éš/), *piš-et* (from /piš-ét/), and so on. The [+ metatony] specification for these morphemes can be predicted by a redundancy rule.

Rules that have approximately as many exceptions as items that undergo the rule frequently arise as the result of the historical merger of two sounds or sound classes. For example, in Modern Hebrew there is a rather complex morphophonemic rule that spirantizes *p*, *b*, and *k* to *f*, *v*, and *x*, in postvocalic position, although the rule also operates in a number of other (grammatically determined) environments. However, only about half of the *k*'s in Hebrew obey this rule. The roughly 50 percent that do not alternate derive historically from the uvular stop *q*. In the standard Ashkenazi (European) dialect, historical *q* has everywhere merged with *k*. Examples of this process follow.

(90)

	past	present	future	infinitive	gloss
	patar	*poter*	*ji-ftor*	*li-ftor*	'solve'
	bagad	*boged*	*ji-vgod*	*li-vgod*	'betray'
	karat	*koret*	*ji-xrot*	*li-xrot*	'make a covenant'
	palaš	*poleš*	*ji-floš*	*li-floš*	'infiltrate'
	baxan	*boxen*	*ji-vxon*	*li-vxon*	'examine'
	karax	*korex*	*ji-xrox*	*li-xrox*	'bind (a book)'
	paraš	*poreš*	*ji-froš*	*li-froš*	'resign'
	balaš	*boleš*	*ji-vloš*	*li-vloš*	'inspect'
	kavaš	*koveš*	*ji-xboš*	*li-xboš*	'conquer'
but	*kašar*	*košer*	*ji-kšor*	*li-kšor*	'tie'
	kara	*kore*	*ji-kra*	*li-kro*	'read'
	kana	*kone*	*ji-kne*	*li-knot*	'buy'

A number of generative analyses of Hebrew have posited these nonalternating *k*'s as /q/, positing a rule merging /q/ to *k* after the spirantization rule has applied. Barkai (1972) has shown that these analyses cannot be maintained, for there is no evidence in the present day standard dialect that the nonalter-nating *k*'s should be set up as /q/ rather than any other nonoccurring sound in the inventory of the language, say /č/. In other words, the choice of /q/ is completely arbitrary. It thus differs from the kinds of examples discussed in Chapter 1, where the phonetic makeup of the abstract segment could be pinpointed from other aspects of phonological behavior. As far as the speaker of Modern Standard Hebrew is concerned, *k*'s arbitrarily fall into two classes—those that alternate with *x* and those that do not. This situation is accurately reflected in a linguistic description which distinguishes the two types of *k*'s by ad hoc lexical markings.

So far in this section we have examined situations in which the arbitrary lexical categorization of morphemes has been relevant to only a single rule. In these cases there is no correlation between a morpheme's plus or minus specification for one rule and its behavior with respect to another rule. There are, however, situations in which the arbitrary $+/-$ specification is relevant for more than a single rule and consequently forms some sort of system. In such circumstances it has been customary in generative phonology to subclassify the relevant morphemes in terms of an arbitrary diacritic feature to which the various rules dependent upon the classification may refer. An interesting example in which this kind of treatment is called for is to be found in Pike's (1948) analysis of Mixteco, a language of Mexico. Mixteco morphemes are in general disyllabic. Eight accentual patterns occur in the language (acute and grave accents represent high and low pitch, respectively, while the macron indicates mid pitch).

(91)   1. *sáná*   'turkey'
        2. *ñíʔī*   'steam bath'
        3. *báʔù*   'coyote'
        4. *kūčí*   'pig'
        5. *bēʔē*   'house'   perturbed to   *béʔē*   (i.e., pattern 2)
        6. *kūtù*   'nose'   perturbed to   *kūtú*   (i.e., pattern 4)
        7. *sùčí*   'child'   perturbed to   *súčí*   (i.e., pattern 1)
        8. *mìnī*   'puddle'   perturbed to   *mínī*   (i.e., pattern 2)

Morphemes with the tone patterns 5 through 8 take on the alternate tone patterns indicated above when preceded by certain morphemes. Pike calls this process "tone perturbation." However, which morpheme *causes* perturbation is not in general predictable. For example, the noun *ʔīsò* 'rabbit' exhibits pattern 6 when pronounced in isolation. Its shape is altered to ¯´ when preceded by the verb *kēē* meaning 'to eat': *kēē ʔīsó* 'the rabbit will eat'. However, there is a homophonous verb *kēē* meaning 'go away'. When it precedes *ʔīsò*, the noun is not perturbed; it retains its basic shape: *kēē ʔīsò* 'the rabbit will go away'. According to Pike the fact that *kēē* 'eat' perturbs the tonal shape of *ʔisò*, but *kēē* 'go away' does not, cannot be attributed to any phonological or grammatical difference between the verbs in question. This contrast between "perturbing" and "nonperturbing" morphemes is not restricted to isolated examples; it pervades the entire system. Another example: *sùčí* 'child' has underlyingly a low-toned first vowel and a high-toned second vowel; in *tàká sùčí* 'all the children' it retains this basic shape, but in *máá súčí* 'that child' its initial vowel shifts to high tone—cf., *kēē sùčí* 'the child will go away' but *kēē súčí* 'the child will eat'. Examples such as this show that a perturbing morpheme's influence is not restricted to a particular tonal shape in the second morpheme. A morpheme like *kēē* 'eat' will alter each one of the basic patterns 5 through 8 in the manner indicated in the table.

Pike does not present enough data for us to formulate precisely the tone sandhi rules. However, from his discussion it is clear that whether or not a morpheme causes perturbation is to a fair extent unpredictable. This requires us to postulate a diacritic feature, say [±P]. The tonal alternations will then be triggered by a preceding morpheme, specified [+P]. For many morphemes the specification for the feature [P] will simply have to be listed in the lexicon. Undoubtedly the contrast between *kēē* 'eat', a perturbing morpheme, and *kēē* 'go away', a nonperturbing morpheme, will have to be handled in this manner. However, as Pike observes, the assignment of [±P] is not totally unpredictable. Morphemes with the tone patterns high-low (type 3), mid-high (type 4), and low-mid (type 8) never cause perturbation. They are thus [−P]. This value can be predicted by a lexical redundancy rule. Except for possibly one other basic tonal shape, morphemes exhibiting all other basic shapes will have to be marked idiosyncratically as either [+P] or [−P] in the lexicon. The one exception seems to be pattern 1, namely high-high. Except for certain pronouns, morphemes with a high-high underlying shape consistently cause perturbation. It might be possible, then, to treat high-high morphemes as predictably [+P], with the few pronouns in question exceptionally marked [−P] in the lexicon.

With regard to the latter point it is interesting to note that a [−P] morpheme that assumes a high-high pattern as a result of perturbation fails to cause the perturbation of a following morpheme, as illustrated in a phrase such as *tàká sùčí* 'all the children', where *tàká* is [−P]. (If it were [+P] instead, we would expect *sùčí* to be perturbed to *súčí*.) Now consider the phrase *híín táká sùčí* 'with all the children'. Here *híín* has perturbed the following *tàká*, to *táká*, a general property of morphemes whose underlying shape is high-high. But note that [*táká*], also of the pattern high-high, fails to perturb the following *sùčí*. Thus, the redundancy that high-high morphemes are marked [+P] applies only to the basic tone pattern of a morpheme, not to the pattern that results from the perturbation rule.

The Mixteco example thus differs from the Russian and Hebrew ones discussed earlier in that the [+/−P] specification of a morpheme is relevant for four separate tone rules. The use of the diacritic feature [P] represents an attempt to distinguish this kind of systematicity from the earlier examples where the +/− specification described the behavior of a morpheme with respect to just a single rule. The use of diacritic features is perhaps more common for representing the distinct behavior of native versus borrowed lexical items, but many accentual phenomena seem to require such a device as well.

This concludes our survey of the role of grammar and the lexicon in determining phonological structure. The investigation of this topic, at least within generative phonology, is a relatively recent phenomenon, conditioned in large part by the increasing concern for the problems of abstractness discussed in Chapter 1. Hence, a great deal of study remains before we shall be able to assert with any confidence just what syntactic and lexical properties do and do not play a role in determining phonological structure. Also we have not dealt at all with the important but largely overlooked question of the influence of phonological structure on syntax and morphology. In the coming years consideration of this question along with continuation of the kinds of studies reported in this chapter will constitute one of the most important lines of linguistic research and will strengthen the growing conviction that semantics, syntax, phonology, and the lexicon are much more intimately connected and interdependent than was previously believed.

3

Constraints on
Phonological Representations

In generative studies phonological rules have characteristically been motivated by alternations. Nevertheless, in all languages there are numerous aspects
of phonological structure that are not (directly) involved in alternations. For
example, in English the feature specifications [+round] and [−round] co-occur
with [+back] and [−back], respectively, for the vowels *u* and *i*. While the
opposite combinations [+round, −back] and [−round, +back] are impossible
in English, they do occur in many other languages (e.g., Turkish). Although
this is unrelated to any alternations in English, it must nevertheless be expressed
in any adequate grammar. Similarly, it is a significant observation about the
sound pattern of English that no word begins with two successive stops. Once
again, this fact is unrelated to any alternations.

In this chapter we take up the difficult question of how to account for such
constraints on possible feature combinations within a segment and on possible
sequences of segments that are not directly involved in alternations. Our
discussion will focus on four central issues: (1) the relation of these constraints
to rules expressing alternations; (2) the domain for which these constraints
hold (is it the syllable, the morpheme, the word?); (3) the level at with these
constraints are to be stated (is it the UR, the PR, or some intermediate stage?);
(4) the form in which these constraints are to be stated.

In any given language only certain features of pronunciation are distinctive—
that is, unpredictable and thus capable of distinguishing between lexical items

131

in underlying representations. The remaining features are nondistinctive—that is, predictable and thus incapable of distinguishing one underlying form from another. Of course, such nondistinctive features may in some instances function to distinguish words in pronunciation even though never doing so in the lexicon itself. For example, aspiration of voiceless stops in Chi-Mwi:ni is a nondistinctive feature—all instances of aspiration in phonetic representations can be assigned by rule. In particular, voiceless stops are aspirated in the following environments: (1) after a homorganic nasal in the same morpheme; (2) after the (homorganic) nasal of the 1st sg. subject and object prefix; and (3) after the (homorganic) nasal of the noun class prefix of nouns such as *m-pʰaka* 'cat(s)', *n-tʰeṭe* 'spark(s)', *ŋ-kʰuku* 'chicken(s)'. Nevertheless, aspiration may in some cases be an essential phonetic device for distinguishing (phonetically) between different lexical items. Thus, underlying /n-paka/ 'cat(s)' and /mu-paka/ 'boundary' are pronounced *mpʰaka* and *mpaka*, respectively. In their underlying representations these two items have identical roots (/paka/), but differ in their prefixes (/n/ versus /mu/). Phonetically these items are distinguished by virtue of the fact that the root-initial voiceless stop is aspirated in the case of 'cat', but unaspirated in the case of 'boundary'. The prefixes are both pronounced as *m* because the /n/ prefix of 'cat' assimilates to the point of articulation of a following stop and the /mu/ prefix of 'boundary' undergoes the vowel deletion rule discussed in Chapter 2. A root-initial /p/ will aspirate following the /n/ noun class prefix, but not following the /mu/ noun class prefix. 'cat' is thus distinguished from 'boundary' by virtue of the aspirated stop at the beginning of the root rather than by virtue of the shape of the prefix. Because of examples of this sort we must distinguish between features of pronunciation that are distinctive in underlying structure and those that are distinctive *only* in surface structure. The present discussion is concerned with features that are nondistinctive in the underlying structure; it is irrelevant whether these features sometimes assume a distinctive function phonetically.

Given that nondistinctive features are predictable, and in many cases demonstrably rule-governed (in that external evidence as well as internal justification can be brought to bear to show that the observed regularity is not accidental, but rather one that follows from a principle actually governing the speech of speakers of the language), it has generally been assumed that a grammar will in fact omit any specification of such features in underlying structure. Rules will be formulated instead to assign these nondistinctive features their correct phonetic values. The assumption that nondistinctive features are not specified in underlying structure means that a given feature may have one of three values in the lexicon: +, −, or 0, where '0' means 'unspecified'. (We are assuming here that all features are binary rather than scalar in underlying structure, but this assumption is not crucial to the points that we wish to make.) Given that a feature has the value 0 in the lexicon, this 0 specification must ultimately be mapped onto a + or − value (or perhaps an even more detailed specification along some scale). The present chapter is devoted to a consideration of a variety of problems that arise in connection with providing such a mapping.

Let us begin by considering a typical example of a nondistinctive feature. In the Chawchila dialect of Yokuts (Newman, 1944) vowels are generally voiced; but in word-final position a vowel *may* appear devoiced phonetically (this occurs most frequently in fast speech and when the word-final vowel is followed by pause). Voicing is thus a nondistinctive feature for vowels in Chawchila; consequently all vowels will be represented as [0 voice] in the lexicon. Now we may ask how vowels in phonetic representations are assigned their value for the feature voice. Note that the vast majority of vowels will have to be assigned the value [+voice]; only word-final vowels can be assigned the value [−voice], and this assignment is optional. In such situations it has generally been assumed that [+voice] should be regarded as the basic value for vowels and [−voice] the value that is derived by virtue of a rule applying in a specific context. This approach assumes that the underlying value of a nondistinctive feature is assigned by a rule that applies independently of the context in which a given segment appears. For example, Chawchila would have rules such as (1) and (2).

(1) $[+\text{syll}] \longrightarrow [+\text{voice}]$ (2) $[+\text{syll}] \longrightarrow [-\text{voice}]/\underline{\hphantom{xx}}\#$ (optional)

Rule (1) applies to all vowels in the lexicon, changing their [0 voice] specification to [+voice]. If rule (2) is applied, it will replace a [+voice] specification (assigned by rule (1)) with a [−voice] specification. Rule (2) applies only in a particular context, unlike (1), which applies independently of context. It is thus parallel to morphophonemic rules that alter distinctive feature values, since morphophonemic rules also tend to be context-sensitive. Like ordinary morphophonemic rules, (2) may be regarded as a rule stating how a sound's pronunciation is affected by the context in which it occurs. Rule (1), on the other hand, is basically a rule stating what sounds may occur in the lexical representations of morphemes. In other words (1) can be viewed as expressing a constraint on the possible sounds occurring in underlying structure. It states that an underlying vowel in Chawchila must be voiced. Given this approach then, (1) is a rule concerning the lexicon, and can thus be viewed as a rule that applies to the lexicon, converting a [0 voice] specification to [+voice] prior to the insertion of morphemes into syntactic representations.

Let us refer to rules like (1) as "segment-structure rules". Such rules predict nondistinctive feature values, but in so doing they also express limitations on what sounds occur in the underlying structure of a given language. Given that such rules apply to the lexical representations of morphemes, we can also refer to rules like (1) as "morpheme-structure rules" (MSRs) in that they define the sounds available for the lexical representation of morphemes. We shall see below that segment-structure rules constitute just one type of morpheme-structure rule.

In summary then, one (quite plausible) approach to the assignment of nondistinctive features assumes that each nondistinctive feature has a normal value. This normal value is assigned by a set of morpheme structure rules (specifically, segment-structure rules) that apply directly to the lexical representation of a morpheme prior to the insertion of that representation into syntactic structures. These MSRs simply replace 0 specifications by either + or −. After the MSRs have been applied, each segment of the morpheme is specified for all the relevant phonetic features. The function of the phonological rules proper is to adjust the pronunciation of each segment as required by the context in which that segment appears in an utterance.

Where necessary, we will refer to the phonological representation that occurs in the lexicon (prior to the application of the morpheme structure rules) as the *lexical representation* of a morpheme, and the representation that results from applying the MSRs as the *underlying representation*. In most contexts, however, we will use these terms interchangeably.

The contrast between distinctive and nondistinctive features is rather more complex than indicated so far. There are in particular many features that are distinctive (for a given sound type) in some contexts, but not in others. For example, in Ki-Rundi vowel length is distinctive; one cannot in general predict whether a vowel will be long or short. Minimal pairs such as *gu-sib-a* 'to neglect' versus *gu-siib-a* 'to abstain' and *ku-gum-a* 'to be solid, firm' versus *ku-guum-a* 'to be impulsive', illustrate the distinctiveness of vowel length. However, the vowel in a morpheme-internal VNC sequence (where N stands for a nasal consonant) is invariably long phonetically, ignoring word-initial position where vowels are regularly shortened. Furthermore, it is (to our knowledge) not necessary to set up an underlying contrast of VNC versus VVNC (where VV represents a long vowel). Therefore, while vowel length is generally distinctive in Ki-Rundi, this contrast is *neutralized* in the context ____NC. We are not dealing here with a simple case where an underlying contrast is neutralized phonetically, but rather with a case where an underlying contrast that occurs in one context is neutralized in another context. In order to clarify this distinction consider again the situation in Yawelmani (see Chapter 1). Vowel length is distinctive in the underlying representation of Yawelmani, but the contrast is neutralized phonetically in the context ____CC, where vowels are regularly shortened: Underlying /go:b/ 'take in' contrasts with underlying /gop/ 'take care of an infant' in that the former root exhibits a long vowel when a vowel-initial suffix follows, while the latter root has a short vowel. Both roots, however, exhibit short vowels when a consonant-initial suffix follows. Although vowel-length contrasts are neutralized phonetically in the environment ____CC, it is not the case that *no underlying* contrast between V:CC and VCC exists morpheme-internally. Recall that in order to account for the root alternation in an example like *ʔa:mil-hin* 'helps' versus *ʔaml-al* 'might help', it is necessary to posit an underlying root /ʔa:ml/. In this representation a long vowel occurs before a consonant cluster. This representation contrasts with one like /pa't/ 'fight', where the vowel is short (thus, *pa'iṭ-hin* 'fights' and *pa'ṭ-al* 'might fight', with the root vowel short in both forms). Consequently, the underlying vowel length is contrastive in the context ____CC, but not phonetically. The situation in Ki-Rundi is different, for not only is the vowel-length contrast neutralized phonetically before an NC cluster, but no contrast exists on an underlying level either.

In Ki-Rundi an underlying contrast (long versus short) is neutralized in a particular phonological environment (before an NC cluster). In many cases the neutralizing context may be (in part or wholly) grammatical rather than phonological in nature. For instance, in Lɔmɔ́ngɔ (Hulstaert, 1957) seven vowels occur in root morphemes: *i, e, ɛ, a, ɔ, o,* and *u*. But in affixes, *ɛ* and *ɔ* do not occur except as phonetic variants of *e* and *o* under the influence of a vowel-harmony rule. Assuming that the mid-vowel contrast is one of tenseness, we can say that while this contrast is distinctive in roots, it is neutralized in affixes. Only the tense mid-vowels are permitted in the underlying representations of affixes.

Given that a vowel in a morpheme-internal VNC sequence will invariably be long in Ki-Rundi and that a mid vowel in Lɔmɔ́ngɔ will invariably be tense (in underlying structure) if it is in an affix, it is natural to attempt to express these regularities in the form of a rule. The Ki-Rundi rule can be formulated as in (3).

(3) $[+\text{syll}] \longrightarrow [+\text{long}]/\_\_\_[+\text{nasal}]\,[-\text{syll}]$

A rule such as (3) can be regarded as a statement about the possible underlying sounds occurring in particular contexts within a morpheme. Rule (3) says that only long and not short vowels occur in the context ____NC. It seems appropriate to treat (3) as simply another type of morpheme-structure rule—one that requires a segment to exhibit a particular property by virtue of the position of the segment within a morpheme, or the type of morpheme in which the segment is located. For convenience we will refer to such morpheme-structure rules as *sequential-structure* rules, as opposed to the segment structure rules such as (1). This label, although commonly used, is not wholly appropriate—there is no "sequence" involved in the Lɔmɔ́ngɔ case cited earlier, for instance. Perhaps "context-sensitive" versus "context-free" would be more precise than "sequential structure" and "segment structure," but we shall continue to use the more widely accepted terminology.

Like the segment-structure rules, the sequential-structure rules can be viewed as applying directly to the lexical representations of morphemes, replacing a 0 specification with either a plus or minus specification. Their role in the grammar then would be to convert (in conjunction with the segment-structure rules) minimally specified lexical representations into fully specified underlying representations. By "minimally specified" we mean that the lexical representations will contain only those feature values that are unpredictable. All predictable information will be omitted. The MSRs (both sequential and segment-structure rules) will provide all of the omitted values. The result of applying the MSRs will thus be morphemes fully specified for all relevant phonetic features.

We now turn to a number of problems that arise in connection with the analysis of morpheme-structure rules sketched above.

1   THE DUPLICATION PROBLEM

The hypothesis that morpheme-structure rules apply, in a block, directly to the lexicon makes MSRs totally distinct from the phonological rules proper They are distinct for three reasons: First, MSRs have a morpheme in isolation as their domain, whereas a phonological rule applies to a morpheme as it is situated in a particular string of words and morphemes; second, MSRs simply supply predictable feature values that have been omitted from lexical representations, while phonological rules alter feature values; third, all MSRs apply prior to the application of any regular phonological rule. One consequence of maintaining this distinction is that "generalizations" are necessarily left unexpressed: What appears to be a single phenomenon in some sense must be treated as two unrelated phenomena. This is what we call the DUPLICATION PROBLEM.

Consider segment-structure rules first. Recall that in Yawelmani the following vowels occur in underlying structure: *i, i:, u, u:, a, a:, o, o:*. The vowels *i*(:) and *u*(:) are [+high] whereas *a*(:) and *o*(:) are [−high]; *u*(:) and *o*(:) are [+round] whereas *i*(:) and *a*(:) are [−round]. Notice that in this vowel system the feature [back] is predictable. The following segment-structure rules will correctly specify the feature [back] for Yawelmani vowels.

(4) $\begin{bmatrix} +\text{syll} \\ +\text{round} \end{bmatrix} \longrightarrow [+\text{back}]$ (5) $\begin{bmatrix} +\text{syll} \\ -\text{high} \end{bmatrix} \longrightarrow [+\text{back}]$

(6) $\begin{bmatrix} +\text{syll} \\ -\text{round} \\ +\text{high} \end{bmatrix} \longrightarrow [-\text{back}]$

If MSRs apply directly to the lexicon, they all will have applied before the application of any phonological rule. This means that no MSR can participate in assigning to the UR of an utterance its correct PR. Once MSRs have converted the lexical representation of a morpheme to its underlying representation, they have fulfilled their function in the grammar.

But now consider the rule of vowel harmony in Yawelmani. As a consequence of this rule, an underlying *i*(:) shifts to *u*(:), and an underlying *a*(:) shifts to *o*(:). These changes occur when the vowel in question is preceded by a rounded vowel of the same height. Clearly, an assignment of the feature [round] is involved, suggesting the following formulation.

(7)
$$\begin{bmatrix} +\text{syll} \\ \alpha\text{high} \end{bmatrix} \longrightarrow [+\text{round}] / \begin{bmatrix} +\text{syll} \\ \alpha\text{high} \\ +\text{round} \end{bmatrix} C_0 \underline{\quad\quad}$$

As formulated above, the rule does not in fact yield the correct phonetic shapes. The vowel *i* is a high front vowel; when it is assigned the feature [+round] by (7), it will become a high front rounded vowel [ü]. The actual pronunciation is, however, that of a high back rounded vowel, [u].

We could revise the rule so that it specifies a vowel as both rounded and also back when preceded by a rounded vowel of the same height. One might legitimately ask, however, whether such a revision does not overlook the fact that in Yawelmani all rounded vowels are back, not just the rounded vowels that arise from the process of harmony. It is of course just this fact that the MSR in (4) expresses. Thus, if (4) is in fact a rule of Yawelmani, should it not be allowed to predict that when the vowel *i* is rounded by harmony, the resulting rounded vowel is pronounced as a back vowel? If (4) is not permitted to assign the feature [+back] to the harmonized vowel, it will be necessary to include in the harmony rule itself the information that a rounded vowel is pronounced as a back vowel. It is this repetition of information that constitutes what we are labeling the duplication problem.

Chamorro (Topping, 1968) provides another example of the duplication problem that also involves a connection between backness and rounding in vowels. The language has an underlying six-vowel system: *i, u, e, o, ä, a.* (In unstressed syllables *i* and *e* reduce to ɪ, *u* and *o* to ʊ, and *ä* and *a* to ə.) In this system *i* and *u* are [+high], the other vowels are [−high]; *ä* and *a* are [+low,], the other vowels are [−low]; *i, e,* and *ä* are [−back], the other vowels are [+back]. The feature [round] in this system is nondistinctive and can be assigned by the following MSRs.

(8)
$$\begin{bmatrix} +\text{syll} \\ +\text{low} \end{bmatrix} \longrightarrow [-\text{round}]$$

(9)
$$\begin{bmatrix} +\text{syll} \\ -\text{low} \\ \alpha\text{back} \end{bmatrix} \longrightarrow [\alpha\text{round}]$$

In other words, low vowels are also unrounded, but nonlow vowels have the same value for rounding as they have for backness. Note that in the Chamorro system rounding is assigned on the basis of backness, while in Yawelmani backness is assigned (in part) on the basis of whether a vowel is rounded or not. Chamorro represents perhaps the more common situation. In Chamorro [back] must be taken as the underlying feature, since it is the feature that distinguishes between *ä* and *a*, whereas in Yawelmani it is the feature [round] that must be taken as underlying, since it is this feature that distinguishes between *a* and *o* (recall that *o* in the Yawelmani data stands for a low back rounded vowel).

With this much background we can now turn to the rule of vowel fronting in Chamorro, which effects the shifting of an *u, o,* or *a* in the first syllable of a root to *i*, *e*, and *ä*, respectively, if that root is preceded by a front vowel. We have, for example, *gumə* 'house', but *i gimə* 'the house'; *tomʊ* 'knee', but *i temʊ* 'the knee'; *lahɪ* 'male', but *i lähɪ* 'the male'.

Clearly, the vowel changes involved in these examples represent a case of back vowels fronting under the influence of a preceding front vowel. We are dealing here with an instance of assimilation. It would appear to be appropriate, therefore, to formulate vowel fronting in Chamorro roughly as follows (ignoring the limitation on the rule to position in the first root syllable)

(10)
$$[+\text{syll}] \longrightarrow [-\text{back}]/ \begin{bmatrix} +\text{syll} \\ -\text{back} \end{bmatrix} C_0 \underline{\quad\quad}$$

The above formulation does not, however, yield the correct phonetic results. It simply fronts the vowel; it does not account for the fact that when *u* and *o* are fronted, they become *i* and *e*, not *ü* and *ö*. We can achieve the correct phonetic shapes by modifying (10) to say that the fronted vowel is also assigned the feature specification [−round]. But once again it can legitimately be asked whether the inclusion of this information into the vowel fronting rule does not ignore the fact that in Chamorro all front vowels are unrounded as a consequence of the MSRs (8) and (9). If there are rules in the language that require front vowels to be unrounded, ought those rules not be capable of accounting for the fact that when a rounded vowel is fronted, it becomes unrounded?

Given the existence of numerous examples parallel to those discussed above, some method of dealing with the problem of duplication must be found. Within the framework of generative phonology the first solution proposed was to allow the MSRs to be ordered *after* particular morphophonemic rules. In other words it was not required that the MSRs apply in a block to the lexicon. A given MSR could be ordered to apply after one or more morphophonemic rules. Clearly, if a MSR is applied after some of the regular phonological rules the language, then it is not applying to the lexicon, but rather to a morpheme that is part of a word or phrase that has already been altered in shape as a consequence of the operation of phonological rules that applied earlier in the derivation. Given this approach, MSRs are not in fact rules *about* the lexicon exclusively; rather, they are rules that may be true about any stage in the derivation between the lexical representation and the phonetic representation.

Let us refer to the solution to the duplication problem now under discussion as the *ordering solution*. Given the Yawelmani facts sketched earlier, the ordering solution would avoid duplication by simply stating that rule (4) is ordered after the rule of vowel harmony. Thus, vowel harmony will round the vowel *i* following a rounded high vowel, and then rule (4) will apply, specifying the resulting rounded vowel as also a back vowel. Similarly, in Chamorro rule (9) will be ordered after vowel fronting. The latter rule will convert *u* to a front vowel if a front vowel precedes, and then (9) will specify the resulting front vowel as being unrounded.

Given that some MSRs would have to be ordered after some of the morphophonemic rules of a language, one might propose that the MSRs do apply in a block, but only after all of the morphophonemic rules have been applied. Such a position cannot, however, be maintained. Consider, for example, rule (5), which says that all nonhigh vowels in Yawelmani are [+back]. This rule is valid for underlying representations and will apply correctly if it applies to the lexicon. But if (5) were to be applied after all the morphophonemic rules of Yawelmani, it would not produce the correct results. In particular, the rule of vowel lowering specifies high long vowels as being nonhigh. An underlying *i:* is converted by this rule to *e:*. If (5) were applied after vowel lowering, *e:* would incorrectly change to a back vowel; (5) must not be permitted to apply to the nonhigh vowels that result from vowel lowering. Therefore, to achieve the correct results (5) must be ordered before vowel lowering.

The reason that the MSRs cannot be ordered after all the morphophonemic rules of a language is very clear: Morphophonemic rules will often create sounds that are not permitted to occur in the underlying structure. Such sounds will be in violation of a MSR. The MSR that is violated must be prevented from affecting these sounds.

Sequence-structure rules also lead to the duplication problem. Recall the Ki-Rundi MSR in (3) above: it requires that a vowel preceding an NC cluster be marked [+long]. There must be a morphophonemic rule in Ki-Rundi that lengthens a vowel that is located before an NC cluster. The data in (11) illustrate the application of this rule.

(11) *ku-ror-a*   'to look at'   *kuu-n-dor-a*   'to look at me'
      ba-tabáare   'that they help'   *baa-n-tabáare*   'that they help me'
      umu-gabo   '(married) man'   *umuu-ntu*   'person'

The prefixes /ku/, /ba/, and /umu/ all end in a short vowel in the UR; but if they appear before an NC cluster, their final vowel is lengthened. The rule that accounts for this lengthening must obviously apply not to the lexicon, but rather to the words and phrases that result from insertion of lexical items into syntactic structures. It would seem, then, that the MSR (3) exactly duplicates the morphophonemic rule that lengthens vowels in the environment ____NC. But if (3) must be applied to the lexicon while the morphophonemic rule applies to syntactic structures where morphemes have been conjoined to form words and phrases, this duplication cannot be avoided.

Once again an ordering solution is possible that would avoid this duplication. Suppose that (3) were not applied directly to the lexicon, but rather at some point among the set of morphophonemic rules. If this were allowed, there would be no need to invoke a second rule to account for the morphophonemic variation in (13). Rule (3) would be sufficient, since it specifies a vowel as [+long] if it is in the context ____NC. It would thus be able to affect a vowel specified as [0 long] and also a vowel specified as [−long], making both [+long] in position before an NC cluster. Given this approach, a single rule will both assign nondistinctive features to lexical representations and also alter distinctive features by virtue of the context in which they appear. One consequence of this approach, however, is that sequential-structure rules must be permitted to apply among the set of morphophonemic rules.

The Ki-Rundi example is by no means an isolated case. It is common to discover that a constraint that determines the pronunciation of one sound in conjunction with others in adjoining morphemes will also constrain the kinds of sequences of sounds that occur in the URs of single morphemes. For example, in a language that requires an obstruent at the end of one morpheme to assimilate the voicing of an obstruent at the beginning of the next morpheme, it is often true that all obstruent clusters in the URs of morphemes agree in voicing. Similarly, in a language that requires that a nasal in morpheme-final position assimilate the point of articulation of an obstruent at the beginning of the next morpheme, it is often the case that in the URs of morphemes a nasal is always homorganic to a following obstruent.

Given the ordering solution, therefore, a sequential-structure rule will not apply in many cases to the lexicon, but rather will be ordered among the morphophonemic rules. In this situation, however, the sequential-structure rule is indistinguishable from an ordinary morphophonemic rule. It differs only in that it has a double function: besides altering a plus or minus specification for a particular feature (the function of an ordinary morphophonemic rule), it will also convert a 0 specification to a plus or minus value (the function of an ordinary MSR).

What we have seen so far is that the ordering solution requires both segment-structure and sequential-structure rules to be ordered among the morphophonemic rules. Since MSRs look like ordinary phonological rules, and in some cases they also do the work of ordinary phonological rules, the question naturally arises, Why not consider *all* MSRs to be simply part of the set of phonological rules, applying not to the lexicon, but rather to syntactic representations where morphemes have been strung together to form words and phrases? We shall return to this question later when we examine the domain problem.

Let us now turn to an examination of the adequacy of the ordering solution to the duplication problem. This solution assumes that the redundant feature value supplied by the MSR will never have to be referred to by a phonological rule that must be ordered before that MSR. Although we have no clear counterexamples at the moment, we seriously doubt that this assumption can always be maintained. Let us briefly discuss a hypothetical counterexample to see what is involved. Suppose a language has a rule assimilating the voicing of an obstruent to a following obstruent and that this rule both describes alternations and at the same time expresses a constraint on lexical representations. According to the ordering solution, the noninitial members of an obstruent cluster will be 0 for voice and the voicing assimilation rule will simultaneously fill in 0's and alter distinctive plus and minus values. Now suppose this language has a rule lengthening vowels before voiced obstruents, but that this rule must be ordered before the voicing assimilation rule. Thus, we might find forms like the following: *pa, pa-ta,* but *pa:-da*; and *map, map-ta, mab-da,* but *ma:b, ma:p-ta, ma:b-da.* Now if we were to find a form like *ma:zg* (and *ma:sk-ta, ma:zg-da*), there would be no way in which the length rule could correctly assign [+long] to the *a*, since at the point where this rule applies (i.e., before voicing assimilation), the *z* will be [0 voice]. Although this is only a hypothetical example, we would not be at all surprised to find a language with similar properties.

Another argument we can offer against the ordering solution is based on the fact that its attendant double function rules (filling in zeros and changing pluses and minuses) will often fail to correctly state the constraints on underlying morpheme shapes. For example, in Klamath (Barker, 1963) phonetic representations aspirated stops (here as *p, t, č, k, q*) contrast with unaspirated ones (*b, d, ǰ, g, g̣*) prevocalically. Except before voiced nonglottalized sonorants, there is no phonetic contrast preconsonantally—a phonological rule makes all stops voiceless unaspirated (represented here as P, T, Č, K, Q) in this position. Now, stops may contrast in the underlying structure for aspiration preconsonantally as well as prevocalically. For example, consider the following alternation. *mboтy'-a* 'wrinkles', but *mbodi:-tk* 'wrinkled up'. The verb root here is evidently /mbody'/. We need to set up an underlying unaspirated stop /d/ to account for the fact that when /y'/ vocalizes to /i:/ in the environment C____C, a /d/ appears. In *mboтy'-a*, however, the /y'/ is not vocalized; consequently a voiceless unaspirated stop appears before the glottalized sound /y'/. Compare the following alternation: *lo:čw'-a* 'covets', but *lo:čo-t* 'can covet'. The verb root here is evidently /lo:čw'/. We must posit an underlying aspirated stop /č/ to account for the fact that when /w'/ vocalizes to /o:/ (ultimately /o/ by virtue of a rule not discussed here) in the environment C____C, a /č/ appears. In *lo:čw'-a*, however, the /w'/ is not vocalized and thus a voiceless unaspirated sound appears before it.

The following examples provide further evidence that an underlying contrast between aspirated and unaspirated stops in preconsonantal position exists. An underlying root /t'abk'/ 'mash up s.t. sticky' is motivated by the following alternation: *n-t'apk'-a* 'mashes up s.t. sticky with a round instrument', but *n-t'abaк-t-a* 'mashes up s.t. sticky with a round instrument against s.t.'. The root ends in the cluster /bk'/ in its underlying representation. If this cluster remains intact, the underlying /b/ is realized as /P/. But if an epenthetic schwa (represented here by the symbol /a/) separates this cluster, then the underlying /b/ surfaces. Compare, on the other hand, the root /t'apq/ 'leaf'. When unsuffixed, this root appears in the form *t'apaq*, with the epenthetic vowel separating the final consonant cluster. The underlying aspirated stop surfaces in this environment but is neutralized to /P/ in examples like *t'apq'-al-a* 'leafs out (as a tree in spring)'.

We have seen that while there is a morphophonemic rule in Klamath that neutralizes the aspirated/unaspirated contrast in preconsonantal position, it is nevertheless necessary to posit URs where both types of stops appear in preconsonantal position. There are, however, many morphemes containing an internal obstruent cluster that do not undergo any morphophonemic rule that would place the initial member of the cluster in an environment that would reveal whether it is aspirated or unaspirated in its underlying form: for example, *ǰigačg-is* 'grasshopper', *paᴘg-as* 'board', *k'oČč'a* 'bullhead', *m'oᴛč'oč'o: y'-a* 'grins'. If a vowel never breaks up the consonant cluster in these forms, it is impossible to determine whether the initial member is aspirated or unaspirated in the underlying structure. It would be quite reasonable, therefore, simply to leave these stops unspecified for aspiration in the lexicon and allow the morphophonemic rule to supply the correct phonetic specifications for the stops in question. This solution would accomplish three things: First, it would avoid having to choose arbitrarily between, for example, /p/ and /b/ as the underlying representations of /ᴘ/ in a form such as *paᴘg-as*; second, it would characterize the fact that the UR of such preconsonantal stops is indeterminate; and third, it would require fewer underlying feature specifications than if the stops were specified for the feature [aspiration].

The consequence of such an analysis is that there would be many stops unspecified for aspiration in underlying forms, and these stops would be assigned their correct phonetic shape by virtue of the morphophonemic rule neutralizing the aspirated/unaspirated contrast in preconsonantal position. This rule would thus count as one that has what we are calling a double function. Nevertheless, it would not be correct to claim that the language does not maintain a contrast between aspirated and unaspirated stops in preconsonantal position in the underlying structure. The language does maintain such a contrast. Clearly then, a rule that has a double function does not necessarily express a constraint on the shapes of morphemes in underlying structure. Given that a phonological rule both supplies unspecified feature values and also alters feature values, one can discover whether that rule expresses a constraint on underlying morpheme shapes only by examining each lexical representation to see whether there are any that violate the rule. Thus, according to the ordering solution discussed earlier the proper MS constraints would never be directly expressed.

Perhaps the strongest reason for rejecting the ordering solution to the duplication problem is that this problem is really just a special subcase of the more general problem of "conspiracies." It is reasonable to suppose that any adequate theory of conspiracies will naturally extend itself to the duplication problem as a special subcase. On the other hand, there is simply no way in which the ordering solution can be generalized to handle conspiracies.

Recall, for instance, that in Yawelmani a morphophonemic rule inserts *i* in the environment C___CC. In the UR at most two consonants may occur adjacently in a single morpheme. Clearly, there is an underlying constraint against a three-consonant cluster. As a consequence of this constraint it is

predictable that any segment before or after a cluster of two consonants will
be a vowel. The following MSR will formally express this constraint and at
the same time assign the redundant feature values that are the result

(12)   [+ segment] ⟶ [+ syll]/____[− syll]   [− syll]
                                    [− syll]   [− syll]____

The constraint on morpheme shapes expressed by (12) is closely related to the
morphophonemic rule that inserts *i* in the environment C____CC. The insertion of a vowel to break up a three-consonant cluster and a rule preventing
more than two consonants from appearing successively in the same morpheme
(in the UR) appear to be two instances of the same phenomenon. They seem
no less related than any of the examples discussed earlier where a MSR and a
morphophonemic rule seemed related to one another.

Notice, however, that the ordering solution provides no means of avoiding
the duplication, no means of relating the morpheme-structure rule to the *functionally identical* morphophonemic rule. (Vowel epenthesis is functionally identical to (12) in the sense that both play a role in guaranteeing that the language
will not have three-consonant clusters.) The ordering solution depends upon
the MSR performing exactly the same changes as the morphophonemic rule
that it duplicates. But (12) does not perform the same change as vowel epenthesis; it states that a segment standing next to a consonant cluster is necessarily syllabic. Vowel epenthesis *inserts* a vowel to break up an existing
three-consonant cluster (arising through affixation). The vowel-epenthesis rule
cannot do the work of (12); it cannot assign redundant feature values. Similarly,
(12) cannot do the work of vowel epenthesis; it can supply redundant feature
values, but it cannot *insert* the vowel *i*.

There are several other rules that conspire to prevent three-consonant clusters
from arising in Yawelmani PRs (Kisseberth, 1970). One deletes an initial ʔ or *h*
from certain suffixes when they follow a verb stem ending in a consonant cluster.
Yet another rule affects suffixes of the shape -ʔ/hC. . ., deleting the initial laryn-
geal if the preceding stem ends in a consonant. All three of the rules mentioned
so far eliminate the three-consonant clusters that arise from chaining morphemes together to form words. There is also a rule that deletes a short vowel
in the context VC____CV, which means that it deletes short vowels except
where a three-consonant cluster would arise. This represents a case where a
condition on a rule functions to preserve the MSR.

Perhaps a more striking example of the latter kind of relationship between
a MSR and a phonological rule is provided by Tonkawa. In Tonkawa there is
a rule eliding the first or second vowel of a verb stem. The first stem vowel is
lost when a CV- prefix precedes the stem, and the second when no such prefix
precedes. Further examination of Tonkawa reveals that if the first stem vowel
is long, it will shorten when a CV- prefix precedes; if it is short, it will simply
delete when a CV- prefix precedes.

(13) netle-n-o?   we-ntale-n-o?   'he is licking it/them'
      picna-n-o?   we-pcena-n-o?   'he is cutting it/them'
      na:t-o?   we-nat-o?   'he steps on it/them'
      ya:c-o?   ke-yac-o?   'he sees him/me'

Although elision is an extremely general rule in Tonkawa, there are many cases where it does not apply. But in each case an explanation for its failure to apply exists: Namely, if elision were to apply, the resulting structure would contain a sequence not permitted in the UR of morphemes. For example, there are no three-consonant clusters in the UR of Tonkawa morphemes, and we find that a root like /salke/ 'pull sinew from meat' does not delete its first vowel when a CV- prefix is attached: we-salk-o? 'he pulls sinews from meat'. If elision were to apply, *we-slk-o? would result, a structure that violates the constraint against the occurrence of three-consonant clusters that governs the UR of morphemes. Similarly, a root like /nepaxke/ 'smoke' does not delete its second vowel: We find nepaxke-n-o? 'he is smoking', not *nepxke-n-o?. The first vowel of this stem can of course delete if a CV- prefix precedes: we-npaxk-o? 'he smokes them'. No three-consonant cluster results in this case.

There is striking evidence that elision is blocked from affecting the first vowel of /salke/ due to the fact that a three-consonant cluster would result if it were to drop. Recall that elision does not delete a long vowel, but just shortens the vowel. Consequently, a root of the shape CV:CCV- could undergo elision and no three-consonant cluster would arise. And in fact, we find that a root like /c'a:pxe/ 'put up a bed' is subject to elision: we-c'apx-o? 'he puts up several beds'. The fact that /c'a:pxe/ is subject to elision while /salke/ is not strongly supports the proposition that elision blocks if it would create a three-consonant cluster. And this failure of elision to apply would seem to be closely related to the fact that three-consonant clusters are not permitted in the UR of morphemes.

In Tonkawa it is also the case that a glottalized consonant never occurs before another consonant in the UR of morphemes. Again, this constraint on morpheme shapes is clearly related to the fact that elision does not affect a short vowel in the environment C'____C. Consequently, the root /s'ako/ 'scrape' does not elide its first vowel after a CV- prefix: we-s'ak-o? 'he scrapes them'. The root /s'e:t.../ 'cut' shortens its long vowel after a CV- prefix: ke-s'et-o? 'he cuts me' (this root may have a final vowel, but in the data available to us there is no evidence for which vowel it is).

Once again, to say that there are MSR in Tonkawa barring CCC or C'C and that there is a condition on elision blocking it from deleting a short vowel if CCC or C'C would arise fails to bring out that a single phenomenon underlies both. Clearly, ordering the MSR among the phonological rules is of no use. Since examples like those from Yawelmani and Tonkawa are common, it seems that the duplication problem is not in fact limited to MSRs, but is rather more general. The term "conspiracy" (due to John Robert Ross) is often used to refer to a situation where several formally distinct rules or conditions on rules seem to work towards the same target structure (such as no vowel clusters, no three-consonant clusters). What we have been calling the duplication problem is thus simply one facet of the problem of conspiracies.

2 THE DOMAIN PROBLEM

According to our initial hypothesis a MSR applies to the lexical representations of morphemes *in the lexicon*. The rule-ordering solution to the duplication problem would have abandoned this position, but there is not much evidence in its favor. Consequently, as matters stand at present, the initial hypothesis can still be maintained. In this section we will sketch some of the problems arising out of the view that the DOMAIN of MSRs is the morpheme as it appears in the lexicon.

One difficulty is that there are instances of constraints where the domain is apparently the word rather than the morpheme. For example, every word in Tunica (Haas 1940) begins (phonetically) with a consonant followed by a vowel. Examining the underlying structures of root morphemes, one finds that they generally conform to this same constraint—that is, they are of the structure +CV. . . . This is natural, since root morphemes often function as words in Tunica. There are, however, roots in Tunica that *never* occur without a prefix (expressing inalienable possession). Roots of this type *do* sometimes begin with a consonant cluster or a vowel rather than a single consonant plus vowel. Such roots are the only ones in the language that are not of the structure +CV. . . . It would seem, then, that the appropriate constraint in Tunica is that a word must be CV- initial and not that a root must be CV-initial, since roots that are never word-initial may be CC-initial or V-initial.

Another Amerindian language, Odawa (Piggott 1974), provides an example quite parallel to Tunica, but with an interesting twist. Recall that in Tunica all words are phonetically CV-initial. One could thus reasonably ask whether the language does not actually have a *phonetic* constraint requiring words to be CV-initial which also happens to be satisfied by underlying structures as well. In the case of Odawa, one can argue that CC-initial words are not allowed in underlying representation, though such words do occur phonetically as the result of a process of vowel syncope: *nnipā* 'I sleep' from /ni-nipā/; *nkītkkonān* 'I held it' from /ni-kī=takkon-am-n/; *nškasīk* 'my nails/claws' from /ni-škansy-ak/. No CC-initial words occur that cannot be argued to be derived by rule rather than deriving from an underlying CC-initial representation. For the most part root morphemes in Odawa obey the principle that prohibits an initial-consonant cluster, but once again there is a small set of roots that must be represented as CC-initial. The root -*škansy* 'nail, claw' is in this category. However, all CC-initial roots belong to the class of "dependent" nouns—that is, they occur only with a prefix attached. In Odawa, then, the constraint against an initial-consonant cluster is neither a phonetic constraint nor a morpheme constraint, rather it is a constraint on words occurring in the UR.

One can legitimately ask: Is there any solid evidence that the absence of CC-initial words in underlying structure is due to a constraint that is part of the Odawa speaker's knowledge of his language? Is it a constraint that must be part of the grammar? Some evidence in favor of the existence of a constraint seems to exist. In Odawa voiceless consonants have the same pattern as consonant clusters and seem to be appropriately analyzed as geminate (fortis) consonants. Kaye (1974a) observes that when English words with an initial voiceless consonant are borrowed into Odawa, Odawa speakers reanalyze them as containing an initial vowel in their underlying structure. For example, the English word *pen* has been borrowed into Odawa and is pronounced exactly as in English. Yet there is evidence that Odawa speakers have assigned this word an initial underlying vowel that surfaces in prefixed forms of the noun: *ntappēn* 'my pen', from /ni-appēn/; and *kitappēn* 'your pen', from /ki-appēn/. Note that there is a rule in Odawa that inserts *t* between a personal prefix and a following vowel-initial stem.* That this rule has applied in the above forms clearly indicates that the root is vowel-initial /appēn/. Similarly, the proper name *Ken* is analyzed as /akkēn/; cf., *ntakkēn* 'my Ken', from /ni-akkēn/.

The preceding examples indicate that there are constraints that hold not for the morpheme as it appears in the lexicon, but rather for *words*. Examples have also been adduced illustrating that the domain of a constraint is often the syllable and not the morpheme. Since syllable structure is determinable only after morphemes have been juxtaposed to form words, such examples would indicate that the constraints in question apply not to the lexicon but after lexical insertion.

Hooper (1973) points out that in Spanish the progressive morpheme is represented as /ndo/ in the lexicon. /ndo/ is suffixed to a verb stem plus thematic vowel: *habl-a-ndo* 'speaking', *com-ie-ndo* 'eating', *viv-ie-ndo* 'living'. Because of the existence of a morpheme like -*ndo*, it is not possible to prohibit a sequence like /nd/ from appearing initially in Spanish morphemes. Nevertheless, the distribution of a sequence like /nd/ is heavily restricted. In particular, an /nd/ sequence appears only if the /n/ is syllable-final and the /d/ syllable-initial; /nd/ never occurs in syllable-initial position in Spanish. A morpheme like /ndo/ is permissible since this suffix occurs only after vowels, consequently the /n/ coheres with that preceding vowel to form one syllable, and /do/ forms a separate syllable. If the occurrence of /nd/ clusters is to be satisfactorily characterized, it seems that the morpheme is not the appropriate domain, but rather the syllable. If this is so, then the constraint must apply after /ndo/ has been suffixed to a verb stem plus thematic vowel, for it is only after this suffixation has taken place that the /n/ of /ndo/ can be grouped with a preceding

---

* Compare *či:ma:n*, *ni-či:ma:n* '(my) canoe'; *akkwe:*, *ni-t-akkwe:* '(my) wife'; *ni-ki:-iša:* 'I have gone', *ni-t-iša:* 'I go'.

vowel into a syllable. (We are assuming here that at some point, or points, in the grammar the representations of words and phrases are organized into syllables. Until recently generative phonology largely ignored syllabification, assuming that it was entirely a matter of the surface phonetic structure and not relevant to the operation of phonological rules. Vennemann (1972b) and Hooper (1972) dispute this assumption.)

Hooper (1974) cites another example from Spanish. She observes that the affricate /č/ (orthographic *ch*) has a restricted distribution, occurring in items such as those in (14):

(14) | *chico* | /čiko/ | 'small' |
|---|---|---|
| *ancho* | /ančo/ | 'wide' |
| *bolchevique* | /bolčebik/ | 'Bolshevik' |
| *marchar* | /marčar/ | 'to go, operate' |
| *macho* | /mačo/ | 'manly' |

When looked at in terms of its location within the morpheme, /č/ appears morpheme-initially before a vowel and morpheme-medially before a vowel if preceded by a nasal, liquid, or vowel. When looked at in terms of Spanish syllable structure, the location of /č/ is readily stated: /č/ occurs only in syllable-initial position. Assuming that syllable structure must be stated in any case, it appears that the constraints on the occurrence of particular sounds can often be stated in maximally simple form by making reference to the syllable.

We have discussed examples in this section purporting to show that the *word* is the relevant domain for some constraints on phonological representations. Other examples have suggested that the *syllable* may be the relevant domain. We might ask now whether there are clear cases where in fact it is the *morpheme* that is the relevant domain.

Kaye (1974b) presents a particularly strong example where the morpheme rather than the syllable or word is the appropriate domain for a constraint on phonological representations. In Desano the phonetic feature [nasal] is "suprasegmental" in the sense that the domain of nasality transcends a single segment: A given syllable is either wholly oral or wholly nasal. The term "oral" syllable indicates that the vowel is oral and the nasal consonants *m*, *n*, *ŋ* and *ñ* do not occur. In "nasal" syllables the vowel is nasalized and the oral consonants *b*, *d*, *g*, and *y* do not occur. However, voiceless sounds—*p*, *t*, *k*, *s*, *h*, and '—may occur in either nasal or oral syllables.

Although a given syllable is either nasal or oral, the same is not true of words. Words may contain both nasal and oral syllables: *pea-mĩ* 'he breaks', *bohse-nĩ* 'holiday', *kõmẽ-da* 'wire', *õmã-bɨ* 'I ran', *wa'a-nĩ-sa* 'go away'. There is, however, an important point to be made about words that include both nasal and oral syllables: a nasal and an oral syllable *never* belong to the same morpheme. In other words any given morpheme in Desano is composed either entirely of nasal syllables or entirely of oral syllables. (It should be pointed out that in Desano both syllables and morphemes end in a vowel; consequently, morpheme-final position always corresponds to syllable-final position.) The syllable is thus too small a domain for the condition on the distribution of the feature [nasal]. To say that the syllable is either wholly nasal or wholly oral is not sufficient to characterize the fact that *all* syllables within the same morpheme agree in nasality. The word is too large a domain, since it is not true that all syllables in a word agree in nasality. The condition imposed on the feature [nasal] is a condition on the morpheme.

This claim can be supported by observing the behavior of Spanish or Portuguese loanwords in Desano.

(15)   *barateru*   (Port. *martelo* 'hammer')
             kãmĩsã   (Span./Port. *camisa* 'shirt')
             sabo   (Port. *sabão* 'soap')
             ñũ   (Port. *João* 'John')

It will be seen from these examples that if a Spanish or Portuguese word contains a mixture of nasal and oral sounds, Desano modifies the pronunciation so that all syllables are either nasal or oral. Consequently, Desano speakers adjust *martelo* to the Desano phonological pattern by realizing all the syllables as oral, yielding *barateru*; but they adjust *camisa* by realizing all the syllables as nasal, yielding *kãmĩsã*. Words in Desano contain a mixture of nasal and oral syllables. Thus, a word like Portuguese *martelo* would not have to be wholly oral or wholly nasal to be an acceptable Desano word. Why, then, are these words changed so that all their syllables are oral or nasal? The answer would seem to be that these loanwords are (quite naturally) regarded as monomorphemic and thus subject to the constraint that all syllables within a morpheme must agree in nasality.

A few other examples can be mentioned. In Hindi (Narang and Becker, 1971; Bhatia and Kenstowicz, 1972), native morphemes conform to the constraint that a nasal must be homorganic with a following stop: *lamb-a:* 'tall', *tund* 'sharp', *paṇḍit* 'learned man', *gañj* 'marketplace', *uŋgli:* 'finger'. This constraint is, however, only effective at the level of the morpheme in the UR. It does not apply when morphemes are juxtaposed to form words: *dun-ka:* 'crumb', *an-ja:n* 'unknown', *an-bhal* 'misfortune', *kan-ṭop* 'helmet', *ka:m-da:r* 'manager', *cu:m-kar* 'having kissed'. Nor is it true at the phonetic level even within morphemes. A nasal that precedes a stop as the result of the syncopation of *a* (phonetically a schwa), does not assimilate: *sanak* 'craze', *sank-õ:* (pl.); *camak* 'to shine', *camk-a:* 'shined'; *ki:mat* 'price', *ki:mt-i:* (adj.).

There are also many instances of regularities involving the structure of root morphemes as opposed to affixes. For instance, we have already mentioned that in Lɔmóngɔ the contrast between *e* and *ɛ* and *o* and *ɔ* is operative only in roots, not affixes. Only *e* and *o* occur in the underlying forms of affixes. In Yawelmani the contrast between *i* and *u* and *a* and *o* is fully operative only in roots; affixes (with one exception) contain just *i* and *a* in their underlying structure. Furthermore, in many languages root morphemes may be highly restricted in shape. For example, roots may be restricted to a maximum of three syllables, or be required to begin or end in a consonant, or be required to have identical vowels in all syllables, and so on.

The preceding discussion suggests that constraints on phonological representations do not have a single domain. Although some constraints seem to refer to the morpheme as it appears in the lexicon, other constraints refer to the structure that exists after words have been formed. These constraints refer either to the word or to the syllables that comprise the word.

3 THE LEVEL PROBLEM

In the early development of generative phonology, Halle (1964) noted that *brick* is an actual morpheme of English, that *blick* is not a morpheme of English but could be, and that *bnick* not only does not occur but could not occur. As a general principle nasals do not occur after a stop in morpheme-initial position in English. Halle proposed to account for this systematic gap in the lexicon by postulating a MSR of roughly the following form.

(16)
$$[-\text{syll}] \longrightarrow [-\text{nasal}]/ + \begin{bmatrix} -\text{syll} \\ -\text{cont} \end{bmatrix} \underline{\quad\quad}$$

Give a MSR in the grammar of English such as (16), the morpheme *brick* would be entered in the lexicon with the *r* unspecified for the feature [nasal]. MSR (16) would supply the value [−nasal] automatically, and in doing so would rule out the possibility that a nasal could follow a stop morpheme-initially in underlying structure.

This analysis can be questioned, of course, on the following grounds: whether the limitation is really that *bn* is impossible morpheme-initially or that *bn* may not occur syllable-initially. That is, *bnick* could be ill-formed because it has a stop plus nasal in syllable-initial position; the fact that *bn* is also morpheme-initial in this example is simply a function of the fact that morpheme-initial position is the same as syllable-initial position when one is dealing with morphemes that can occur by themselves as words. This, clearly, is the problem of the domain of the constraint.

There are, however, other grounds on which the analysis of *bnick* might be questioned. Granting that speakers of English reject *bnick* as a possible English word (while accepting *blick* as possible), it is not obvious that this rejection is based upon the unacceptability of +*bn*... as an underlying structure. It could very well be that *bnick* is rejected because it is not an acceptable phonetic form in English. The question at issue here is: At what level are constraints on phonological representations relevant? Is it the underlying structure? Or is it the phonetic structure?

The fact that a given form is rejected as inappropriate does not tell us what sort of principle the form in question violates. For instance, a Yawelmani speaker might well reject a hypothetical verb of the form * ʔ*um-hin* as ill-formed. This reaction, however, would not tell us that this form violates a constraint on Yawelmani morphemes. There is a much more plausible explanation of why * ʔ*um-hin* might be regarded as unacceptable—namely, it violates the rigid principle of vowel harmony. To establish that a given form is unacceptable due to underlying constraints one must find examples where a form is phonetically possible in the language, in accordance with the phonological rules of the language, but is still unacceptable.

The Odawa example discussed earlier represents the kind of situation we need to establish firmly that a constraint is underlying. Recall that Odawa speakers analyze the English word *pen* as underlying /appēn/, even though they pronounce the word almost exactly as English speakers do. Even though *pen* is a possible phonetic realization in Odawa, it is *not* a possible underlying representation because the language does not allow underlying word-initial consonant clusters (and voiceless aspirated consonants are treated as geminates). The fact that Odawa speakers reanalyze *pen* as underlying /appēn/ strongly supports the view that an underlying, not a phonetic, constraint is at work.

If other examples parallel to the Odawa case can be found, we can assume that constraints on phonological representations may exist at the level of underlying structure. We can now turn to the following question: Is there any reason to believe that there are constraints that govern phonetic shapes, rather than underlying shapes, where the constraints in question are not properly expressed in the form of ordinary phonological rules?

In a typical example we might have a language where no words end in a voiced obstruent phonetically. This situation could be due to a constraint on words that they must end either in a vowel, a sonorant, or a voiceless obstruent in the underlying representation. On the other hand, it could also be that there are words that terminate in underlying voiced obstruents, but that a rule of word-final devoicing operates to yield phonetic structures where no voiced obstruents occur finally. Given the latter situation, one might well claim that by postulating a rule of word-final devoicing we express the constraint on phonetic representations that exists in the language. The constraint *is* just the rule of word-final devoicing. There is, however, another view of the matter, according to which a phonological rule does nothing more than express a constraint that is valid for the level of derivation at which the rule applies. A phonological rule is not in any direct way a statement about constraints on phonetic representations. Of course, there will be phonological rules that are "true" statements about phonetic representations, but such rules are not formally distinguishable from rules that are violated on the surface. We can determine whether a rule is a true statement about phonetic forms only by examining the phonetic representations. Furthermore, a phonological rule can be viewed as a means of implementing a constraint on phonetic representations. In other words, if a language disallows a particular phonetic shape, there must be underlying constraints or phonological rules that guarantee that the phonetic shape in question will not occur. The constraint and the rule or rules that implement the constraint can be distinguished.

In many instances making a distinction between a constraint and a rule that implements the constraint would seem to be pointless. Taking our example of word-final devoicing as a case in point, what point is there in saying that there is a phonetic constraint in the language barring word-final voiced obstruents and that there is also a phonological rule that implements this constraint by devoicing any underlying voiced obstruent that occurs in word-final position? The proposed "constraint" would not have any function in the derivation of phonetic representations from underlying representations; so what is the point of including it in the grammar of the language?

The proponent of phonetic constraints which are distinct from the phonological rules that implement them can justify this position by looking for "nonderivational" facts that such constraints might explain. By nonderivational facts we mean aspects of the behavior of speakers that go beyond the simple problem of deriving phonetic forms from underlying forms. For example, suppose that speakers of the language that we have been considering (where word-final obstruents are devoiced by a morphophonemic rule) make the following "mistake" when they attempt to pronounce a foreign language admitting word-final voiced obstruents: they add a schwa to the end of those words in the foreign language that have a word-final voiced obstruent. Behavior of this sort could be taken as evidence that these speakers are governed by a constraint that a word may not end phonetically in a voiced obstruent. This constraint is implemented in their own language by means of a morphophonemic rule of final devoicing. The same constraint is implemented in their foreign language learning by means of a rule inserting an epenthetic schwa after the offending voiced obstruent. Examples of this sort of mispronunciation might suggest that a constraint on phonetic representations must be distinguished from the phonological rules that adjust underlying representations so that they obey the constraint. Similar kinds of arguments might be adduced from the treatment of loanwards.

We can develop, however, another line of argument in support of the need for phonetic constraints independent of phonological rules proper. This argument makes use of the phenomena that we referred to as earlier as conspiracies. In Yawelmani, for instance, no three-consonant clusters exist phonetically. This represents a constraint on Yawelmani phonetic representations. There is not, however, one rule in Yawelmani that can be claimed to *be* the constraint in question. As was discussed earlier, several rules conspire to achieve the elimination of all three-consonant clusters from surface forms. Similarly, in Chi-Mwi:ni no vowel clusters occur phonetically, but there is no one phonological rule that is responsible for this distributional pattern. Three separate rules of vowel coalescence, glide formation, and glottal stop insertion all play a role in guaranteeing that the phonetic constraint against vowel clusters is upheld.

Functionally equivalent rules are generally just those groups of rules that modify phonological representations so that they conform to a particular surface constraint.

If we accept the existence of surface phonetic constraints as part of the grammar of a language, in addition to the phonological rules that implement these constraints, then we are admitting rules that neither fill in redundant features nor alter feature values. In other words these rules would not play a role in generating sentences. In the next section we will examine the question of whether morpheme-structure rules might not be better treated as "constraints" or "conditions" on representations rather than rules that assign feature values.

4   CONDITION OR RULE?

The term redundancy rule has sometimes been used to refer to the kinds of rules that we have been discussing under the label morpheme-structure rule. There is, of course, a close connection between the observation that certain features of pronunciation are redundant, being predictable from other features either within the same segment or in a neighboring segment, and the observation that there are limitations on the sounds and the sequences of sounds that may occur within a morpheme. Features of pronunciation are redundant (predictable) by virtue of such limitations. Therefore, the specification [−voice] will be redundant for stops in a language if that language does not have voiced stops in its repertoire of underlying sounds. The point of articulation of a nasal will be redundant when it precedes an obstruent if a language does not allow nonhomorganic clusters of nasal plus obstruent within the same morpheme. Given the intimate connection between redundancy and limitations on morphemes, it might be natural to propose that the postulation of rules that predict redundant feature values will *at the same time* express the limitations on morpheme shapes that occur in a language. This was in fact the position expressed in Halle (1964), where he argued that a morpheme-structure rule is motivated only if the postulation of such a rule would result in a simplification of the grammar (in particular, simplification of the lexicon as a consequence of eliminating feature specifications).

Significant problems arise as a result of the claim that the constraints on the shapes of morphemes in a language are to be expressed by means of rules assigning redundant features. The prediction of all the redundant features in a language will not necessarily lead to an expression of all the significant limitations on morpheme shapes in the language. A single example should make this point clear. Suppose that in some language all the morphemes of a particular grammatical class must exhibit a particular shape. For the sake of simplicity we will assume that the shape involved is simply -C-. (The same observations could be made if the limitation involved was that the morphemes had to be of the shape -CVC- or -CV- or -VCV- or anything else.) Given that all morphemes of the class in question must have the shape -C-, a morpheme-structure rule could be formulated to predict that the segment involved has the property [−syll].

(17)   [+segment] ⟶ [−syll]/+____ if the morpheme is a member of
                                    the grammatical class in question

Rule (17) predicts all the feature values that are redundant by virtue of the fact that morphemes of this class must be of the shape -C-. But notice that (17) does not itself express the generalization that all morphemes of the class are of the shape -C-. This rule in no way prevents the occurrence of morphemes of the shape -CV-, or -CC-, or -CVC-, and so on. To bar such morphemes from the lexicon would require a principle that states that no segment may follow the initial consonant. But a principle of this sort does not predict redundant feature values. Consequently, it is not true that the prediction of redundant features will automatically express the significant limitations on morpheme shapes.

We can make a distinction, therefore, between "if-then" and positive morpheme-structure rules. If-then rules state that if x occurs, then y also occurs. They do not, however, require that x occur; they simply express the fact that y always appears if x does. Since a rule that assigns redundant feature values also claims that if x occurs, then y also (predictably) occurs, it is clear that such rules will in general be able to express if-then constraints on morpheme shapes. Positive morpheme-structure rules, on the other hand, require that x appears. Morphemes not possessing the property x are simply disallowed. As we have seen, rules assigning redundant features do not succeed in expressing positive constraints on morpheme shapes.

Although redundancy rules can in general express if-then constraints, problems arise involving directionality. A rule that assigns redundant feature values assumes that certain feature values are specified in the lexicon and that other feature values are predictable on the basis of those already given. There is consequently a direction in which the prediction works: Given x, y can be predicted. It turns out that in many cases the direction of the prediction is ambiguous. That is, given x, y can be predicted, but given y, x can be predicted.

Consider the following example. In Alur (Tucker, 1969), an African language belonging to the Nilotic family, the alveolar stops t and d are mutually exclusive with the interdental stops, written th and dh, in CVC roots. Thus, words such as *tado* and *tato* are possible, as are words such as *dhetho* and *thedho*, but not words such as *dhato* or *detho*. In other words within a CVC root the constraint states that if one of the consonants is dental, the other cannot be interdental; and if one of the consonants is interdental, the other cannot be dental. By virtue of this constraint, if a CVC root occurs whose consonants are both stops specified [+anterior, +coronal], we can predict whether the first consonant is alveolar or interdental if we know what the second consonant is, and vice versa. But this means that it is necessary to posit one of the consonants as specified in the UR as dental or alveolar, while predicting the value of the other one. The choice of which consonant to posit as underlying in this kind of example appears to be an arbitrary one. Although we are dealing here with a kind of if-then constraint (if one of the consonants in a CVC root is alveolar, the other must be alveolar also, if it is marked [+anterior, +coronal]; if one of the consonants is interdental, the other must be interdental also, if it is [+anterior, +coronal]), it is not a directional one. Rules that assign redundant features are directional by nature, and so do not seem to be appropriate devices to characterize constraints such as that exhibited by Alur.

The Alur example cited above is by no means an isolated case. Recall our discussion of Desano earlier in this chapter, where morphemes are either entirely oral or entirely nasal. By virtue of this constraint on morpheme shapes one could claim that the feature [nasal] is predictable for all the sounds in the morpheme except one. One sound will have to be specified as either oral or nasal; the remaining sounds can be left unspecified, being predictable by a rule. (The discussion above is concerned only with the consonants and vowels that have both oral and nasal counterparts; there are consonants in Desano that cannot be nasalized and thus are allowed to occur in both oral and nasal morphemes.) But once again choosing the particular sound to specify as [±nasal] is arbitrary.

There is some evidence, then, that at least some of the limitations on morpheme shapes should be expressed by means of conditions imposed on underlying representations, rather than by rules that assign redundant feature values. Many linguists have accepted the view that *all* limitations on morpheme shapes should be expressed in the form of conditions rather than redundancy rules. This view implies that the constraints that define a possible morpheme are not involved in the generation of sentences—they are not processes at all, but instead static conditions. They are therefore similar to the surface-structure constraints discussed briefly in the preceding section of this chapter. Most of the criticism that has been leveled against the proponents of static conditions has been based on the claim that there are processes that seem to be reflections of the morpheme structure constraints (see the lengthy discussion of the duplication problem earlier in this chapter). We have seen in our discussion of conspiracies, however, that it sometimes makes sense to talk about a constraint and the processes that implement that constraint. It might well be the case that there are static constraints that must be formulated at the morpheme level, and that in addition there are processes that work to enforce these constraints in the course of derivations.

In the course of this chapter we have presented a number of problems that arise in connection with the morpheme-structure rules (conditions) of a language. We have not sought to propose definitive answers to these problems, but rather to clarify the issues as much as possible.

4

Natural Rule Interactions

Concepts such as marked and unmarked were not, of course, applied to the interaction of rules until the focus of phonological investigation turned from the inventory of sound units in a language to the rules that govern the combination of these sound units to form morphemes and words and that relate these underlying sound units to their phonetic manifestations. Thus, the investigation of problems of naturalness with respect to rule interaction is still, comparatively speaking, in its infancy, and can be dated back only to the early work of Kiparsky (1965, 1968b). Kiparsky's initial work on the subject focused on an analysis of the functional relationships that rules exhibit—in particular, on a rule's possible effect on the application of some other rule to a given phonological structure. He distinguished two basic functional relationships, which he referred to as feeding and bleeding.

Take two rules, A and B, and an input structure S. If S does not meet the structural description (SD) of B, but the structure that results from applying A to S does meet the conditions for the application of B, then A and B may be said to stand in a feeding relationship; A may be said to be a feeding rule with respect to B, and B may be said to be a fed rule.* Two rules in a feeding relationship may be applied in one of two sequences. If the feeding rule is applied

* It would be preferable to refer to potentially feeding rules and potentially fed rules, as will be seen from the discussion below, but to add this qualification would make the terminology too clumsy.

first, we have what may be called a feeding order of application. If the feeding rule is applied after the fed rule, we have what may be called a counterfeeding order of application. Some examples will clarify these remarks.

In Lɔmɔ́ngɔ (Hulstaert, 1957), a Bantu language, there is a rule whereby *t*, *d*, and *l* are affricated to *ts*, *j* ($=dz$), and *j* ($=dz$), respectively, when followed by a glide, *w* or *y*. The application of this rule of affrication is exemplified as follows.

(1)   *-bák-a*   *-bák-w-a*   *-bák-y-a*   'fasten'
        -kámb-a   *-kámb-w-a*   *-kámb-y-a*   'suffer'
        -sɛŋg-a   *-sɛŋg-w-a*   *-sɛŋg-y-a*   'sculpt'
        -mat-a   *-mats-w-a*   *-mats-a*   'tread'
        -kund-a   *-kunj-w-a*   *-kunj-a*   'bury'
        -ul-a   *-uj-w-a*   *-uj-a*   'be imprisoned'

These examples reveal not only the affrication of *t*, *d*, *l* before *w* or *y*, but also the absence of *y* in the final phonetic output. We assume that the deletion of *y* after *ts* or *j* is accomplished by a separate rule, operating on the output of affrication, but the appropriateness of this analysis is not relevant here. There is also a glide rule in the language whereby a nonlow vowel will be converted to the corresponding glide prevocalically (under somewhat varying morphological conditions). Examination of the paradigm of 'see' as opposed to 'work' in (2) reveals the application of glide formation.

(2)   *ŋ́-kamb-a*   'I work'   *nj-ɛ́n-a*   'I see'
        ó-kamb-a   'you work'   *w-ɛ́n-a*   'you see'
        á-kamb-a   'he, she works'   *ɛ́n-a*   'he, she sees'
        tó-kamb-a   'we work'   *tsw-ɛ́n-a*   'we see'
        ló-kamb-a   'you work'   *jw-ɛ́n-a*   'you see'
        bá-kamb-a   'they work'   *b-ɛ́n-a*   'they see'

From these paradigms it is evident that prefixal *o-* shifts to *w-* in prevocalic position, while prefixal *a-* does not (it simply elides). Thus, /ó-kamb-a/ remains, but /ó-ɛn-a/ shifts to /w-ɛn-a/.

Glide formation and affrication stand in a feeding relationship. This can be seen by considering a remote structure such as /lo-ɛn-a/. Notice that this structure does not satisfy the SD of affrication, since the *l* of the prefix is not followed by a glide. However, if we apply glide formation to /lo-ɛn-a/, the resulting structure /lw-ɛn-a/ now meets the conditions for the application of affrication. Thus, glide formation is what we have referred to as a feeding rule with respect to affrication. In (3) we show the two possible sequences in which these rules could apply to /lo-ɛn-a/.

(3)   (a)   /lo-ɛn-a/   (b)   /lo-ɛn-a/
              lw-ɛn-a   glide   inapplicable   affrication
              jw-ɛn-a   affrication   *lw-ɛn-a*   glide

Derivation (3a), which yields the correct PR, is an instance of a feeding order of application, since the feeding rule—glide formation—is applied before the fed rule. Observe that when rules are applied in a feeding order, the fed rule is able to apply, because of the previous application of the feeding rule. Derivation (3b) is an instance of counterfeeding order, since the feeding rule, glide formation, is applied after the fed rule, affrication. (Recall the earlier footnote, where we emphasized that the terms feeding rule and fed rule, to be more accurate, should read "potentially feeding" and "potentially fed." Only in the feeding order of application is this potentiality realized.) Observe that when two rules are applied in a counterfeeding order, the fed rule is not able to apply nonvacuously; at the point where it is applied, the input structure has not yet been modified by the feeding rule, and thus the correct conditions are not present for the fed rule to apply.

In the particular example from Lɔmɔ́ngɔ already discussed the two rules standing in a feeding relationship have to be applied in a feeding order in order to obtain the correct phonetic result. There are, however, many cases where rules must be applied in a counter-feeding order. For example, in the Bantu language Mwera (Harries, 1950) the singular and plural of a certain noun class are marked by the prefixes /lu-/ and /N-/, respectively, where /N-/ stands for a nasal homorganic with the root-initial consonant. A rule of cluster simplification optionally deletes a voiced stop after /N-/: *lu-juci, ñ-juci/ñ-uci* 'bee'; *lu-gomo, ŋ-gomo/ŋ-omo* 'lip'. Mwera also has the widespread rule voicing a stop after a nasal: *lu-pundo, m-bundo* 'piece of string'; *lu-kuya, ŋ-guya* 'cape bean'. Consideration of a remote structure like /m-pundo/ reveals that cluster simplification and voicing stand in a feeding relationship. This structure does not satisfy the SD of cluster simplification; but when voicing is applied, the resultant /m-bundo/ now satisfies the conditions for the application of cluster simplification. Thus, the two rules are in a feeding relationship: voicing is the feeding rule and cluster simplification the fed rule. In (4) we give the two possible sequences in which these rules could apply to /m-pundo/.

(4)   (a) /m-pundo/
             m-bundo   voicing
             m-undo   cluster simplification

        (b) /m-pundo/
             inapplicable   cluster simplification
             m-bundo   voicing

(4a) represents a feeding order of application: The feeding rule, voicing, applies before the fed rule, cluster simplification, thus making the application of the latter rule possible. In (4b), which represents the correct derivation in Mwera, we find a counterfeeding order—the fed rule is tried first, the feeding rule second—and as a consequence the fed rule does not apply.

We shall return later to a closer scrutiny of the notion of a feeding relationship. For now let us turn to the second fundamental relationship discussed by

Kiparsky—bleeding. Take two rules, A and B, and a phonological structure S. If S meets the SD of *both* A and B, and if the application of A to S would result in a structure that no longer meets the conditions for the application of B, we may say that A and B stand in a bleeding relationship. A is a bleeding rule with respect to B, and B is a bled rule. (Again, it would be better to qualify both these phrases by the term "potentially," but we will refrain from doing so for stylistic convenience.) If the bleeding rule is applied before the bled rule, we may say that the rules are applied in a bleeding order. If the bled rule is applied first, followed by the bleeding rule, we may say that the rules have applied in a counterbleeding order. Again, some examples will clarify these remarks.

The Yawelmani rules (Chapter 1) shortening a vowel before a consonant cluster and epenthesizing *i* between two consonants followed by a third stand in a bleeding relationship. Epenthesis is the bleeding rule and shortening the bled rule. Consider the remote structure /ʔa:ml-hin/, which is realized as *ʔa:mil-hin*. This structure satisfies the SD of both rules. Furthermore, if epenthesis were applied to this structure, the resultant /ʔa:mil-hin/would no longer meet the SD of shortening. Thus, the rules are in a bleeding relationship. The two possible derivations of /ʔa:ml-hin/ are shown in (5).

(5)　(a)　/ʔa:ml-hin/　　　　　　　　(b)　/ʔa:ml-hin/
　　　　ʔa:mil-hin　epenthesis　　　　*ʔaml-hin*　shortening
　　　　inapplicable　shortening　　　　*ʔamil-hin*　epenthesis

Derivation (5a), which yields the correct PR, is a bleeding order, since the bleeding rule applies before the bled rule. In a bleeding order the bled rule is prevented from applying because of the prior application of the bleeding rule. Derivation (5b) is a counterbleeding order, since the bled rule is applied before the bleeding rule. In a derivation where counterbleeding occurs, the (potentially) bled rule does in fact apply.

Although in the Yawelmani example it is the bleeding order that yields the correct phonetic output, there are many cases where counterbleeding achieves the correct PRs. Washo, an Amerindian language spoken near Lake Tahoe, Nevada, provides an interesting comparison with the Yawelmani example (Jacobsen, 1964). In Washo, a cluster of two consonants in stem-final position is separated by an epenthetic *i* in final position or if a consonant-initial suffix follows.

(6)　*t'-apš-a*　'on his body'　　　*t'-apiš*　'his body'

　　　m-ašg-a　'on your back'　　　*m-ašik*　'your back'
　　　m-ašik-le:we　'towards your back'

　　　l-ešm-i　'I'm singing'　　　*l-ešim-hi*　'I'll sing'　　　*g-ešim*　'sing!'

Now consider *l-emlu-leg-i* 'I ate' and *l-emeʔ-leg-i* 'I drank'. The morpheme *-leg-* is the recent past suffix. Combination of this suffix with a stem ending in *l* provides the context for application of a degemination rule in Washo. For example, the stem meaning 'give' is /išl-/: cf., *ʔ-išl-aša ʔ-i*, 'he'll give it to him'; *ʔl-išíl* 'give it to me!' Now in *ʔl-iší-leg-i*, 'he gave me one', epenthetic *i* appears even though no three-consonant cluster or final cluster exists on the surface. The UR /ʔl-išl-leg-i/ meets the conditions for both *i*-epenthesis and degemination. If degemination were to apply to this structure, /ʔl-iš-leg-i/ would result (we indicate the final consonant of the stem deleting rather than suffixal *l*, but this is an arbitrary decision that is of no importance here). This structure no longer meets the SD of *i*-epenthesis, since the relevant consonant cluster no longer exists. Thus, degemination and *i*-epenthesis are in a bleeding relationship: Degemination is the bleeding rule, and *i*-epenthesis is the bled rule. Given the remote structure /ʔl-išl-leg-i/, two possible derivations exist.

(7) (a) /ʔl-išl-leg-i/   (b) /ʔl-išl-leg-i/
       ʔl-iš-leg-i   degemination   ʔl-išíl-leg-i   *i*-epenthesis
       inapplicable   *i*-epenthesis   ʔl-iší-leg-i   degemination

Derivation (7a) exhibits the bleeding order of application, where the bleeding rule is applied before the bled rule and thus prevents the application of the latter. Derivation (7b), which yields the correct form, presents the counterbleeding order of application, where the (potentially) bled rule is in fact able to apply, since it applies before the bleeding rule has had a chance to destroy the context for its operation.

After this brief description of the concepts of feeding and bleeding, we can turn to the role these two functional relationships have played in the investigation of the relative naturalness of rule interactions. Kiparsky (1968b) noted that feeding and counterbleeding orders of application both serve to *maximize* the utilization of the rules of the grammar. For example, in (3) the (a) derivation represents a feeding order, and we see that both of the rules in question have applied, whereas in (b), the counterfeeding order results in the failure of affrication to apply. In (5) the (a) derivation involves a bleeding order of the rules, which prevents shortening from applying; the (b) derivation, where the rules are applied in a counterbleeding order, permits both rules to apply. Thus, feeding and counterbleeding allow both rules to apply, whereas counterfeeding and bleeding prevent one of the rules from applying.

It does not of course follow from the observation that feeding and counterbleeding maximize the utilization of rules that these particular orders of application are therefore relatively more natural than counterfeeding and bleeding. There is no a priori connection between maximal utilization of rules and naturalness—at least we know of no facts about the structure of the human vocal tract or of the human mind that would make it probable that the question of the extent to which a rule is utilized in a grammar would be a relevant consideration in determining the relative naturalness of particular rule interactions. The basis for the claim that there is a connection between maximization of rule use and naturalness was not a priori, but rather the consequence of Kiparsky's interpretation of certain linguistic changes.

Assuming that it is proper to view grammars as consisting of a series of rules applied in a particular order, it would seem that one way in which grammars might change is through the *reordering* of rules. That is, while rule A is applied before rule B at some stage in a language's history, at a later stage rule B is applied before rule A. Kiparsky (1968b) claimed to have identified a number of instances of this phenomenon, and noted furthermore that in each case the direction of reordering was from either a counterfeeding to a feeding or from a bleeding to a counterbleeding order of application. Thus, rule reordering was always in the direction of the maximization of the utilization of the rules. Kiparsky concluded from this that

> the order towards which rules gravitate in this way is linguistically simpler than its opposite. It is hard to see what other explanation there could be for such a consistent tendency towards a specific kind of order in linguistic change. As a convenient designation for the order types which are shunned and preferred . . . I suggest *marked* and *unmarked* order, respectively [p. 200].

We are not familiar enough with any of the languages that Kiparsky draws upon to illustrate this supposed asymmetry in the reordering of rules, in order to be able to reproduce a convincing example of the principle he claimed to have adduced. We shall therefore illustrate them with a couple of examples with which we are familiar. Although nobody has described these particular changes as rule reorderings to our knowledge, they are quite parallel to the examples Kiparsky discusses, and undoubtedly would have been described as reorderings by him.

As an example of the shift from a bleeding to a counterbleeding order, consider the following data from Slavic.

(8)

	Russian		Ukrainian	
singular				
1st	*pek-u*	*mog-u*	*peč-u*	*mož-u*
2nd	*peč-e-š*	*mož-e-š*	*peč-e-š*	*mož-e-š*
3rd	*peč-e-t*	*mož-e-t*	*peč-e*	*mož-e*
plural				
1st	*peč-e-m*	*mož-e-m*	*peč-e-mo*	*mož-e-mo*
2nd	*peč-e-te*	*mož-e-te*	*peč-e-te*	*mož-e-te*
3rd	*pek-ut*	*mog-ut*	*peč-ut'*	*mož-ut'*
past	*pek-la*	*mog-la*	*pek-la*	*mog-la*
stem	*pek-* 'bake'	*mog-* 'can'		

Russian verb stems ending in a velar exhibit a palatalization of that consonant in some, but not all, of the forms of the present tense. This is achieved by a palatalization rule shifting *k* and *g* to *č* and *ž* before suffixal *e*. According to the generally accepted analysis of these verbs, originally due to Jakobson (1948), the *e* appearing in the desinences is a present-tense thematic vowel that is posited in the UR of all the present tense verbal forms. In particular, the

URs of 'bake' in the 1st sg. and 3rd pl. would, according to this analysis, be /pek-e-u/ and /pek-e-ut/. A general truncation rule deletes the /e/ before vowel-initial suffixes. It is easy to see that in the derivation of *pek-u* and *pek-ut* truncation bleeds the palatalization rule. Turning now to the Ukrainian cognates, although in certain cases the inflectional endings are slightly different, in all relevant respects these verbs are parallel to the Russian ones, except that the allomorphs with a final palatal consonant occur throughout the present tense. Consequently, Ukrainian also has the URs /pek-e-u/ and /pek-e-ut'/ for the surface forms *peč-u* and *peč-ut'*. Likewise, these alternations would be analyzed as the result of the same two rules as in Russian, palatalization and truncation. The only difference is that in Ukrainian they apply in a counter-bleeding fashion, so that palatalization has a chance to apply before the *e* is deleted by truncation. We know that the bleeding order occurs earlier historically, since this is the order found in Old Church Slavic and all of the other modern-day Slavic languages except Colloquial Czech. Consequently, Ukrainian has innovated, and this innovation could be described as a switch from a bleeding to a counterbleeding order of application.

Ukrainian also provides an illustration of a linguistic change that could be described as a switch from a counterfeeding to a feeding order. Before discussing the specifics of this example, we must dispense with a few preliminaries. In Ukrainian there is a general rule that depalatalizes consonants before the vowels *e* and *y* (a slightly centralized vowel intermediate between *i* and *e*, not to be confused with the Russian *y*, which is a high, back unrounded vowel). This rule's effect may be seen in the following partial paradigms for the nouns *učytel'* 'teacher' and *l'ud'-* 'people', which end in underlying palatalized consonants:

(9)

nominative singular	*učytel'*	nominative plural	*l'ud-y*
genitive singular	*učytel'-a*	genitive plural	*l'ud-ej*
dative singular	*učytel'-u*	dative plural	*l'ud'-am*
instrumental singular	*učytel-em*	instrumental plural	*l'ud'-my*
nominative plural	*učytel'-i*		

On the other hand, with one exception to be discussed later, all consonants are palatalized before *i*, as evidenced by the following nominative and locative forms: *m'ist-o*, *m'ist'-i* 'place'; *ryb-a*, *ryb'-i* 'fish'. Before the remaining back vowels, palatalized consonants are opposed to nonpalatalized ones: *l'uk* 'trapdoor', *luk* 'bow'; *l'on* 'flax', *lon-o* 'lap'; *l'apas* 'slap in the face', *lap-a* 'paw'. Ukrainian thus possesses the rules of "sharping" (10) and "desharping" (11).

(10) $C \longrightarrow C' /\underline{\quad} i$ (11) $C' \longrightarrow C /\underline{\quad} [y, e]$

Ukrainian also has the interesting morphophonemic rule (see Chapter 2 for a discussion of the historical basis of this rule), traditionally called *itazimus*, which shifts *e* and *o* to *i* in a number of contexts, the most common being before one or more final consonants: Compare *m'id* 'honey' and *nis* 'nose' with their gen. sg. forms *med-u* and *nos-u* or the past masculine forms *n'is* 'carry' and *mig* 'can' with the corresponding feminine forms *nes-la* and *mog-la*. Note that consonants are palatalized before the *i* that is derived from *e* (*n'is*), but not before the *i* that derives from *o* (*nis*).

These alternations can be explained as follows. Consonants preceding an underlying *e* will be set up as palatalized in the UR. Hence, 'carry' will have the underlying shape /n'es/, while 'nose' will have /nos/. Palatalization will be preserved in such consonants only when the *e* is shifted to another vowel that permits palatalization before it (*i*, for example, in the case of 'carry'). If the *e* does not shift, the palatalization will be lost by the desharping rule. Thus, the *itazimus* rule is ordered before desharping in a bleeding order. On the other hand, to explain why there is no palatalization before an *i* that derives from *o*, it is necessary to order sharping before *itazimus*, a counterfeeding interaction. Thus, we have derivations like the following.

(12) $/\#n'es\#/$ $/\#n'es\text{-}la\#/$ $/\#nos\#/$ $/\#nos\text{-}u\#/$

——	——	——	——	, sharping
n'is	——	*nis*	——	itazimus
——	*nes-la*	——	——	desharping

The analysis in (12) describes the situation in Standard Ukrainian and essentially recapitulates the development and order of the rules from Proto-Slavic, except that the sharping rule also palatalized consonants before *e* as well as before *i*. We have chosen to restrict sharping to applying before *i*, but it could be generalized to apply before *e* as well, without materially affecting the point at issue.

Many dialects of Ukrainian (Pan'kevich, 1938) have deviated from the standard language by losing such contrasts as *nis* versus *n'is*. In these dialects consonants are palatalized before an *i* that derives from *o*, as well as before those that derive from *e* and underlying *i*. Consequently, in such dialects it is necessary to permit sharping to apply to the output of *itazimus*. Since we know that the ordering of the rules in Standard Ukrainian occurred earlier historically, this dialectal innovation can be described as a shift from a counterfeeding to a feeding order.

If rule reordering were in fact consistently directed toward the maximal utilization of rules, as Kiparsky has suggested, we would clearly be dealing with an extremely important situation that must be accounted for. There would have to be something about the state of affairs that results from applying rules in feeding and counterbleeding orders that could be considered linguistically natural. There is, however, some reason to doubt the validity of the correlation between maximal utilization of rules and naturalness.

One source of doubt is simply the lack of any obvious reason why a rule interaction should be more expected if it maximizes rule use than if it does not. Of course, the apparent lack of connection could simply be due to our ignorance of the relevant physical or psychological data that would make the connection clear. It is, however, possible to give a fairly straightforward account of why a feeding order might be natural, where the notion of 'use' is not directly resorted to. Observe that in cases of counterfeeding such as (3b) and (4b), surface forms contain sequences that superficially violate the fed rule. For instance, in the case of the hypothetical form *lw-ɛn-a in (3b) the rule of affrication that converts l to j before a glide seems to be violated. In the case of feeding orders of application, however, such as (3a) and (4a), the resulting surface forms do not contain apparent contradictions to the rules in question. One might say then that counterfeeding creates superficial exceptions, whereas feeding does not. (This is an oversimplification, as we will see later, but it does not render the discussion here totally irrelevant.) Since there is some evidence that exceptions are more difficult to learn than regular forms, it seems reasonable to conclude that apparently irregular forms would be more difficult to learn than regular forms. Thus, historical change from a counterfeeding to a feeding order can be explained in terms of a shift from a less regular to a more regular linguistic pattern. Hence, another, more plausible explanation is available for the Ukrainian dialectal change: a form such as *nis* is a superficial exception to the sharping rule. But by switching to a feeding order, *n'is* is produced—a form that is not a phonetic violation of the same rule.

The "maximal-utilization" principle also claims, as we have seen, that counterbleeding interactions are more favored than bleeding ones. In many cases, however, this claim is at odds with the characteristic interaction displayed by particular pairs of rules. For instance, many languages possess a rule which assimilates an obstruent to the voicing of a following obstruent, and in addition an epenthesis rule, which breaks up certain consonant clusters by the insertion of a vowel. If these rules are applied in a counterbleeding order, an obstruent will assimilate the voicing of a following obstruent even if these two consonants are phonetically separated by a vowel. If the rules are applied in a bleeding order, an obstruent will not assimilate the voicing of a following obstruent if, as a result of epenthesis, it becomes separated from that obstruent by a vowel. In a situation like this it seems to us that there is little reason to believe that a counterbleeding order is, in fact, unmarked, as maximal utilization claims. Examples of a bleeding order in such cases are easy to cite. For example, they occur in Lithuanian, Latvian, Hebrew, and most of the Slavic languages. But we know of no cases of a counterbleeding interaction between these rules. This example is by no means an isolated one. Other pairs of rules that characteristically interact in a bleeding fashion are discussed in Kenstowicz and Kisseberth (1971).

In addition to the fact that bleeding interactions are in fact expected for certain pairs of rules, Kiparsky has pointed out in a later publication (1971) that all of the examples of a shift from a bleeding to a counterbleeding order adduced in his (1968) paper as support for the maximal-utilization principle can be reinterpreted as being motivated by a tendency to regularize paradigms. That is, switching the order of the rules has the effect of reducing the phonetic variations in the shape of a particular morphological element in the paradigm in which it appears. It has been claimed that regular paradigms are more natural than irregular ones, and that rule orderings that achieve a more regular paradigm are more natural than those producing irregular ones (see Chapter 2). The Ukrainian example discussed earlier as an illustration of the shift from a bleeding to counterbleeding order of application clearly falls under this rubric, since the Ukrainian ordering of palatalization and truncation creates a constant stem shape throughout the present-tense paradigm. Thus, the historical evidence cited by Kiparsky (1968) as the only real support for maximal utilization can be (more satisfactorily) explained in a manner that does not appeal to the extent to which the rules are utilized in the grammar.

There are, however, further shortcomings of the maximal-utilization principle. Although accepting the proposition that the utilization of rules tends to be maximized, Kiparsky (1968b) nevertheless tacitly assumes a conception of the organization of the rules of grammar that inherently *restricts* the extent to which a rule may be utilized. If maximal utilization were in fact the unmarked case, it would seem to be somewhat surprising if the organizational principles of grammar were designed so as to bar such maximization of rule use. The restricting principles that are implicitly accepted in Kiparsky (1968b) can be summarized as follows: The rules of the grammar are applied in a prescribed sequence; each rule applies just once (on any given cycle); if two rules are applied in a given order for one UR, they are applied in that same order for all other URs. These principles limit the maximization of rule use since, first, rules would apply more times if they were permitted to apply more than once in a given derivation, and second, there are times when two rules can be maximally utilized, when they are applied in one order for certain underlying forms, but in the opposite order for others.

As an example of how limiting a rule to one application in a derivation results in preventing the full use of that rule, we can examine again the Lardil example discussed in Chapter 1. The relevant rules are summarized below.

(13)   apocope $V \longrightarrow \emptyset / VC_1 VC_1 \underline{\qquad} \#$

(14)   cluster simplification $C \longrightarrow \emptyset / C \underline{\qquad} \#$

(15)   nonapical deletion $C \longrightarrow \emptyset / \underline{\qquad} \#$
                                      $[-\text{apic}]$

The derivation of *muŋkumu* from /muŋkumuŋku/ (cf., *muŋkumuŋku-n*) follows.

(16)   /#*muŋkumuŋku*#/
           muŋkumuŋk   apocope
           muŋkumuŋ   cluster simplification
           muŋkumu   nonapical deletion

Within an approach requiring that rules apply just once in any derivation, there is no possibility that apocope might apply to /muŋkumu/ to derive /muŋkum/. To do so would involve a second application of the rule of apocope in the derivation. Thus, the limitation to a single application of a rule in a derivation bars full utilization of the rules.

The following paradigms from Karok (Bright, 1957) will illustrate how requiring a pair of rules to apply in the same order for all URs can prevent the maximal utilization of rules.

(17) *ʔišva:k* 'chin'   *ʔapsu:n* 'snake'
      mi-šva:k 'your chin'   *mi-pšu:n* 'your snake'
      mu-sva:k 'his chin'   *mu-psu:n* 'his snake'

The URs of the stems are /isva:k/ and /apsu:n/, while the 2nd and 3rd person are marked by the prefixes /mi-/ and /mu-/. The uninflected forms arise from the prothesis of a glottal stop to vowel-initial words. The initial vowel of the stem is lost in the prefixed forms by a general rule truncating the second of two successive vowels (18). Finally, s palatalizes to š after a front vowel (19).

(18) $V \longrightarrow \emptyset/V\_\_\_\_$ (19) $s \longrightarrow š/[i, e](C)\_\_\_\_$

The derivations for 'your snake' and 'his chin' follow.

(20)   /mi-apsu:n/   /mu-isva:k/
            mi-psu:n   *mu-sva:k*   truncation
            mi-pšu:n   inapplicable   palatalization

Truncation and palatalization are in a feeding relationship relative to /mi-apsu:n/, where the UR does not meet the SD of palatalization, but the structure resulting from truncation does. Since palatalization does apply, the rules are in feeding order. On the other hand, /mu-isva:k/ satisfies the SD of both rules, but if truncation applies to give /mu-sva:k/, the SD for palatalization is no longer satisfied. Since palatalization does not apply, the rules are in bleeding order.

This example demonstrates that two rules may stand in different functional relationships for different URs. And in this case the two rules apply in the same order for both URs, truncation before palatalization. This results in a feeding order for structures like /mi-apsu:n/, but a bleeding order for ones like /mu-isva:k/. If the rules had applied in the opposite order for both URs, /mi-apsu:n/ would surface as *mi-psu:n* and /mu-isva:k/ as *mu-šva:k*. The former would be an instance of counterfeeding and the latter of counterbleeding. Thus, either sequence results in an order that maximizes rule utilization for one class of URs but not for the other.

The assumption that rules apply in the same relative sequence for all URs thus means that such pairs of rules as truncation and palatalization cannot be applied in a fashion that maximizes the utilization of rules. Fully maximal utilization of the rules would involve having truncation precede palatalization for URs such as /mi-apsu:n/, but having palatalization precede truncation for such forms as /mu-isva:k/. Now, if the assumed limitation on rule interaction is correct (rules apply in the same relative order for all URs), we are placing a severe limitation on the claim that rules tend to apply in a fashion that maximizes rule utilization. This principle is contradicted by a requirement that rules apply in a fashion that does not maximize rule utilization. Perhaps such contradictory principles exist, but this exception to the claimed tendency for maximization of rule application should provoke some reconsideration of the issue.

We have seen that Kiparsky's original hypothesis was subject to important restrictions imposed by general constraints on how phonological rules may be applied. It should be noted that other linguists, particularly S. Anderson (1969, 1974), have claimed that the restrictions on rule application accepted by Kiparsky cannot be maintained. Anderson has suggested that rules can apply in different orders for different URs and can apply more than one time in a single derivation, when the consequence of such a mode of application is the maximal utilization of the rules. For example, in Anderson's theory it would be possible to have derivations in Karok such as (21), where the rules of truncation and palatalization apply in different orders, thus maximizing the application of rules.

(21)   /mi-apsu:n/   /mu-isva:k/
        mi-psu:n   truncation   *mu-išva:k*   palatalization
        mi-pšu:n   palatalization   *mu-šva:k*   truncation

It would not be possible to have derivations such as (22), however, where the two rules are applied in different orders, resulting in the minimization of rule application.

(22)   /mi-apsu:n/   /mu-isva:k/
        inapplicable   palatalization   *mu-sva:k*   truncation
        mi-psu:n   truncation   inapplicable   palatalization

Therefore, Anderson not only continues Kiparsky's original claim that the unmarked interaction is the one that maximizes rule use, he extends the claim by exempting it from the limitations imposed by the general restrictions that Kiparsky implicitly accepts. But Anderson's extension is fraught with difficulties. If the unmarked case were really to have derivations like those in (21), why is it that such cases are so marginally attested? Anderson attempts to present some examples of such interactions, but most of them are anything but clear-cut. On the other hand, examples of cases where the rules do not apply in different orders, even though to do so would maximize rule use, are readily available. We gave only one example above—the case from Karok—but many others could be cited.

For instance, recall from Chapter 1 the Yawelmani rule of vowel harmony that rounds *a* after underlying nonhigh rounded vowels and rounds *i* after underlying high rounded vowels, and epenthesis that inserts /i/ in the environment C____CC. The rules are applied in the order epenthesis before harmony, as the following derivations illustrate.

(23)   /#t'oyx-k'a#/   /#ʔugn-k'a#/
        t'oyix-k'a   ʔugin-k'a   epenthesis
        ____   ʔugun-k'a   harmony

In t'oyix-k'a 'give him medicine', epenthesis and harmony apply in a bleeding order, where as in ʔugun-k'a they apply in a feeding order. The principle of maximal utilization, however, predicts the derivations below to be the expected case, rather than those in (23).

(24) (a) /#t'oyx-k'a#/   (b) /#ʔugn-k'a#/
           t'oyx-k'o   harmony   ʔugin-k'a   epenthesis
           *t'oyix-k'o   epenthesis   ʔugun-k'a   harmony

Not only is the derivation in (24a) wrong for Yawelmani, it seems to represent a rather bizarre system of vowel harmony that is not at all expected. Vowel harmony does not typically apply as in (24a)*. Thus, whether or not such derivations as (21) and (24a) are possible, which is another issue, there are strong grounds for doubting that they are unmarked, as Anderson's principles would predict.

Another shortcoming of the maximal utilization principle is that it does not provide a totally general characterization of possible rule interactions. There are cases in which exactly the same kinds of judgments about natural interactions can be made, but where the question of the extent of the use of the rules is immaterial. Yokuts (Newman, 1944) provides a couple of examples. First, consider how the rule of penultimate stress interacts with epenthesis in the Yawelmani dialect. Given a UR like /ʔilk-hin/, 'sings', two possible derivations exist.

(25) (a) /#ʔilk-hin#/   (b) /#ʔilk-hin#/
           ʔilk-hin   stress   ʔilik-hin   epenthesis
           ʔilik-hin   epenthesis   ʔilík-hin   stress

Derivation (b) is the correct one. But notice that in both derivations the two rules are applied. Thus, the rules are maximally utilized, whatever the order in which they are applied.

To take another example, in the Chawchila dialect of Yokuts (Newman 1944, p. 26), a word-final vowel is optionally unvoiced. When this takes place, the vowel completely assimilates to the preceding vowel. Thus, cognate to Yawelmani ṭun-k'a 'close the door!', ʔoṭ-k'a 'steal!', and hiwet-k'a 'walk!' are Chawchila ṭun-k'U, ʔoṭ-k'O, and hiwet-k'E. The last example derives from the

---

* This point is further developed in the discussion of Turkish later in this chapter.

UR /hiwi:t-k'a/. In the Yawelmani dialect it is derived by an application of vowel lowering followed by shortening. In Chawchila the same derivation obtains, except that it is optionally completed by the devoicing process described above. Once again, two derivations are possible. In (26a) lowering precedes unvoicing, while in (26b) it follows.

(26) (a) /#hiwi:t-k'a#/   (b) /#hiwi:t-k'a#/
           hiwe:t-k'a   lowering   *hiwi:t-k'ı*   unvoicing
           hiwe:t-k'ɛ   unvoicing   *hiwe:t-k'ı*   lowering
           hiwet-k'ɛ   shortening   *hiwet-k'ı*   shortening

Note that in either derivation both lowering and unvoicing apply. Once again the rules are maximally utilized no matter in which order they are applied.

The principle of maximization of rule application makes no claim about which of the derivations in (26) constitute the unmarked interaction of the rules. As far as this principle is concerned, the contrast marked/unmarked is inapplicable in these cases. But we suspect that, for example, *hiwet-k'ɛ* represents a more expected surface form than *hiwet-k'ı* and that *ʔilik-hin* is somewhat more expected than *ʔilik-hin* (though it might be possible to consider *ʔilik-hin* somewhat more expected than *hiwet-k'ı*). If these intuitive judgments do have some basis in fact, then a theory of natural rule interaction that includes interactions of the preceding type within its domain will be preferable to the principle of maximization of rule application, which fails to extend to these cases.

In the preceding pages we have pointed out a number of difficulties with Kiparsky's (1968b) principle of maximal utilization. In a subsequent publication (1971) he abandoned this principle and replaced it by a new principle of opacity, which overcomes some of the problems mentioned above. Given a rule of the form A $\longrightarrow$ B/____C, it will be said to be opaque to the extent to which, first, there are phonetic counterexamples to it, or second, there are in phonetic representation Bs derived from A by the rule, which appear in an environment other than before C. According to Kiparsky the natural interaction of a pair of rules is for them to sequence in such a way as to minimize opacity. Some examples will help to clarify this notion.

Recall the Mwera example, discussed earlier as an illustration of counterfeeding, where there is a rule that voices a stop after a nasal and another rule that (optionally) deletes a voiced stop after a homorganic nasal. A form such as *m-bundo* 'piece of string' from /m-pundo/ renders the deletion rule opaque, since *m-bundo* is (superficially) a counterexample to the rule: *m-bundo* can never be converted to **m-undo*, even though the deletion rule says that voiced stops may delete after homorganic nasals. In general, counterfeeding orders of application will represent interactions that render rules opaque. In feeding orders of application, on the other hand, the rules are more transparent (less opaque). In the Lɔmɔ̀ngɔ example application of glide formation to a form such as /to-ɛ́n-a/ 'we see' creates an input to affrication, /tw-ɛ́n-a/, which in fact undergoes the rule to yield surface *tswéna*. Since the derivation does not terminate with a *t* standing before a glide, no phonetic counterexample to the affrication rule is created. Hence, the feeding interaction minimizes opacity. If the rules had applied in counterfeeding fashion to derive *twéna, the rule of glide formation would be rendered opaque. In general, then, feeding interactions minimize opacity and hence are claimed to be more natural than counterfeeding ones.

Turning to opacity of the second type, it is apparent that counterbleeding interactions in general create opacity whereas bleeding ones do not. Recall the Washo example, where /ʔl-išl-leg-i/ is converted to *ʔl-iš̵-leg-i* by epenthesis and degemination. The environment for the insertion of the *ɨ* is C____CC, but in *ʔl-iš̵-leg-i* we find an inserted *ɨ* in the context VC____CV, a context that does not normally trigger the insertion in Washo. The degemination rule has thus obscured the context that calls forth the epenthesis of *ɨ*. This interaction thus makes epenthesis opaque, since we find the rule applying to a form that does not meet the SD of the rule on the surface.

Bleeding interactions in general preserve the phonetic transparency of a rule's application. Two rules are applicable to the Yawelmani UR /ʔa:ml-hin/: epenthesis and vowel shortening. If both were to apply, we would derive surface * *ʔamilhin*, with a short vowel derived from a basic long vowel appearing in a phonetic context (an open syllable) different from that required by the shortening rule (a closed syllable). In the derivation of the correct surface form *ʔa:milhin* epenthesis bleeds vowel shortening, thereby helping to preserve the transparency of the latter rule.

Having illustrated briefly the notions of opacity and transparency, we can now turn to a discussion of their explanatory power. The proposal to view transparent interactions as more natural than opaque ones overcomes some of the difficulties noted earlier with the maximal utilization principle. First, it derives some independent a priori support from the psychology of language. As we have seen, an opaque interaction will create a superficial counterexample to a rule. Since there is some evidence to indicate that exceptions are more difficult to learn in first language acquisition, calling such interactions marked or unnatural seems reasonable. This would, of course, also explain why a language would tend to shift from a counterfeeding to a feeding order, rather than vice versa. Opacity of the second type can also be interpreted as making the application of a rule less accessible and hence more difficult to learn. Consider again Washo *ʔl-iš̵-leg-i* from /ʔl-išl-leg-i/. The surface form is in a sense misleading, since it suggests that the context for epenthesis is not C____CC after all, because an inserted *ɨ* appears in VC____CV. The language learner must go beneath the surface to the underlying form in order to see that C____CC is indeed the correct environment for the insertion of *ɨ* in the derivation of this word.

In addition to some possible psychological plausibility, which the principle of maximal utilization lacks, the principle of minimization of opacity is also more general, because it naturally extends to cases such as those from Yokuts discussed earlier, where the notions of feeding and bleeding do not apply. Recall the interaction of epenthesis and penultimate stress; these rules apply in this order to derive *ʔilíkhin* from /ʔilk-hin/. Applied in the opposite order, they would yield the incorrect * *ʔilikhin*. The latter is doubly opaque, since a stressed vowel appears in other than penultimate position and the penultimate vowel is not stressed. Similarly, the Chawchila derivation of *hiwetk'ᴇ* from /hiwi:t-k'a/ is transparent, while the incorrect *hiwetk'ɪ* would be opaque, because in the former the model for the copied vowel is present on the surface, while in the latter it is not. Insofar as evidence can be gathered to support the claim that derivations producing such forms as *ʔilíkhin* and *hiwetk'ᴇ* are in fact less marked than derivations producing forms such as *ʔilikhin* and *hiwetk'ɪ*, the principle of minimization of opacity will be supported: the unmarked derivations would in fact be the ones that yield more transparent rules. The fact that the minimization of opacity principle predicts that these derivations will be unmarked, whereas any principle based on the extent of utilization of rules does not, is likely to support the claim that opacity of rules rather than utilization of rules is the relevant consideration.

Although the minimization-of-opacity principle is certainly an advance over maximal utilization, there is still a great deal that remains to be explained. Most important, the proposed correlation between transparency = unmarked, opacity = marked fails to explain why marked interactions occur over and over again in the languages of the world. Why should this be so if marked means unfavored and a relatively unnatural state of affairs? Reflection on the basic assumption of the principle—natural interactions are those that make the conditions for the application of the rule accessible on the phonetic surface— reveals that it is phonetically biased and fails to take into account what Leopold (1930) has termed the fundamental *polarity* in language. In order for language to function as a communication system it must keep semantically contrasting forms distinct by phonetic means. In general this is accomplished by providing semantic concepts with distinct, and largely constant, phonetic shapes. It is based on the principle that if, on any given day in any given sentence, a particular phonetic form is associated with a particular meaning, then on any other day, in any other sentence, that same phonetic form will be associated with the same meaning. But although sounds are the means by which semantic contrasts are communicated in language, the sounds themselves are subject to inherent forces that are often detrimental to the very ends for which they are used. For when sounds are chained together, they are quite naturally liable to morphophonemic and phonetic mutations. From this broader perspective human language is in a state of tension between these two forces or "poles," as Leopold refers to them. The natural state of affairs, semantically speaking, is for there to be constant meaning-form relationship and for semantic contrasts to be conveyed by phonetic contrasts. The natural state of affairs, phonetically speaking, is for the inherent phonetic processes to regulate speech. Any language system is the product of the constant interplay of these forces, and its structure must be understood in terms of this overriding tension.

Looked at in this way, many of the rule interactions that would be considered marked by the minimization-of-opacity principle can be viewed as serving the semantic pole of language by preserving underlying semantic contrasts. Let us reconsider, for instance, the Mwera example introduced at the beginning of this chapter to illustrate a counterfeeding interaction. Recall that in this language a basic voiced stop is (optionally) deleted after a homorganic nasal, while a voiceless stop is voiced after a nasal: *lu-gomo, ŋ-gomo/ŋ-omo* 'lip'; *lu-kuya, ŋ-guya* 'cape bean'. Here the underlying contrast between stem-initial voiced and voiceless stops is preserved, although in a modified fashion, in a phonetic contrast between ϕ and a voiced stop. From the point of view of the "phonetic pole" *ŋguya* is opaque, since it contains a voiced stop after a homorganic nasal, and there is a rule deleting voiced stops in this position. But in terms of the "semantic pole" *ŋguya* is relatively transparent, since the voiced stop after a nasal signals that this form comes from an underlying stem with an initial voiceless stop. If the rules had applied in a phonetically transparent order (post-nasal voicing followed by voiced stop deletion, converting both /N-gomo/ and /N-kuya/ to *ŋomo* and *ŋuya*), there would be no way to tell from the forms alone which derived from an underlying voiced stop and which from a voiceless one. The phonetically opaque interaction of these rules thus preserves, in a displaced fashion, the underlying opposition between voiced versus voiceless initial stems, which presumably aids in the recovery of the underlying form and ultimately of the meaning of the sentence.

In addition to helping to maintain underlying semantic contrasts, phonetically opaque interactions may arise from the inherent nature of the phonological processes themselves. An example is provided by Nootka (Sapir and Swadesh, 1939). In Nootka there is an opposition between rounded versus unrounded velars and uvulars: *katak* 'proud', *kʷan'is* 'wild onion'; *qičin* 'louse', *qʷini:* 'seagull'. The language also possesses two rules neutralizing this opposition in certain positions. One delabializes the gutturals in preconsonantal and final position. For instance, the morpheme meaning 'turn about, twist' is underlying /mitxʷ-/. The underlying labialization surfaces in the durative form *mitxʷ-a:*, but is lost in the first half of the reduplicated repetitive *mi:tx-mi:txʷ-a*. The morpheme 'dead', which is underlying /qahakʷ-/, illustrates neutralization in final position. Its underlying rounded velar emerges to the surface in *qahak'ʷ-as* 'dead on the ground' (the suffix glottalizes the final stem consonant), but undergoes the effects of neutralization in *qahak* 'dead'. The other neutralization rule rounds gutturals after *o*. For instance, the morpheme meaning 'making' is set up as /ki:ł/ by Sapir and Swadesh. When the morpheme meaning 'many' is prefixed, the initial velar appears unrounded, though in a slightly disguised form in which the *k* has been shifted to *č: ʔaya:-či:ł* 'making many'.

The form *?o-k^wi:ɬ* 'making it', on the other hand, shows the effect of the labialization rule. Now consider a pair like *qo:x* 'ice', *qox^wa:* 'to freeze'. In the derivation of *qo:x* the two neutralization rules contradict one another, the application of one rendering the other opaque. This can be seen by comparing the following two possible derivations:*

(27)   (a) $/\#qo:x^w\#/$
                 qo:x   delabialization
                 qo:x^w   labialization

            (b) $/\#qo:x^w\#/$
                 inapplicable labialization
                 qo:x   delabialization

In (a) labialization undoes the effect of delabialization, making the latter phonetically opaque, since a rounded velar stands in final position. In (b), which happens to be the correct derivation for Nootka, delabialization undoes the effect of labialization, rendering the latter opaque, because an unrounded velar follows a rounded vowel. Here the phonetic opacity does not arise from an effort to preserve an underlying contrast, but rather from the contradictory nature of the phonological rules themselves.

In the preceding pages we have examined two different kinds of situations in which the phonetic opacity of a rule interaction can be considered motivated: either by serving to preserve underlying semantic contrasts or by the nature of the phonological rules themselves. In view of this we might propose the following hypothesis as a subject for future research.

(28) *Phonological rules will not (normally) interact in a fashion that creates phonetic opacity unless motivated to do so.*

The prima facie plausibility of this hypothesis can be illustrated by a consideration of examples where opaque interactions would be most bizarre and where their extreme unexpectedness is attributable to the lack of any motivation for opaque interactions in these cases.

The Yawelmani rules of epenthesis and vowel shortening discussed earlier provide a clear case. Given a UR such as /?a:ml-hin/ 'helps' and /?a:ml-al/ 'might help,' the correct surface forms are obtained by applying epenthesis before shortening.

(29)   /?a:ml-hin/   /?a:ml-al/
            ?a:mil-hin   inapplicable   epenthesis
            inapplicable   *?aml-al*   shortening

This order of application is the one that maximizes transparency. The reverse order of application yields the following derivations.

---

* We assume the underlying form to be /\#qo:x^w\#/, but it could also be argued to be /\#qo:x\#/. In either case, the same problem arises.

(30)   /ʔa:ml-hin/   /ʔa:ml-al/
         ʔaml-hin   ʔaml-al   vowel shortening
       * ʔamil-hin   inapplicable   vowel epenthesis

A form like * ʔamil-hin renders shortening opaque, since in * ʔamilhin the initial
vowel has undergone shortening but is not in the correct environment for
shortening on the surface (a case of Kiparsky's second type of opacity). This
ordering of the rules, however, not only results in opacity, but also eliminates
any surface evidence for the underlying contrast between roots of the form
CV:CC and roots of the form CVCC, like /ʔilk/ 'sing', cf., ʔilik-hin 'sings',
ʔilk-al 'might sing'. One might suggest that in a surface form like * ʔamil-hin
the fact that the underlying long vowel of the root is shortened provides a
surface clue that the following i is not underlying but inserted. But since
Yawelmani verb roots of the shape CVCiC- do not occur in the underlying
structure, there is no particular value to such a surface clue. All realizations of
i in the context CVC____C- are epenthetic.

Another example is provided by the rules of voicing assimilation and epenthesis in Modern Hebrew. The former rule's effects are evident in pairs like
taval 'he immersed', ti-dbol 'you will immerse'; šavor 'he broke', yi-žbor 'he
will break'; bicea 'he operated', mi-fca 'an operation', where an obstruent
assimilates in voicing to a following obstruent. Epenthesis results from the
juxtaposition of several suffixes beginning with t to imperfective verb stems
ending in t to d. Such stems may, optionally, be separated from the t-initial
suffixes by an epenthetic e (phonetically a schwa). Thus, /kišat-ti/ 'I decorated'
may be pronounced kišateti, and /yarad-ti/ 'I descended' may be rendered
yaradeti. If however, the optional epenthesis does not take place, the resulting
forms are kišatti and yaratti, with voicing assimilation in the latter case.
Clearly, optional epenthesis must be ordered before voicing assimilation,
otherwise /yarad-ti/ would become *yarateti. We contend that such an output
would be highly marked. Of the many languages with rules of voicing assimilation and epenthesis, we know of no cases where both rules apply in a derivation.
Epenthesis seems always to bleed voicing assimilation. The reason seems to be
that if voicing assimilation were to apply to yield an output like *yarateti, such
an output would result in an opaque assimilation rule, but the opacity would
not be offset by any gain in semantic transparency. In fact, instead of preserving
any underlying semantic contrast, this interaction would eliminate the distinction between stem-final t and d. The lack of any semantic motivation, along
with the phonetic opacity that would result, explains the rarity of such interactions as this.

Another interesting example illustrating the same point is provided by
Turkish, which has two rules affecting suffixal vowels (and, depending on the
analysis, noninitial root vowels as well): a backness harmony (BH) rule, which
assimilates the backness of suffixal vowels to the backness of the immediately
preceding vowel, and a rounding harmony (RH) rule, which makes high vowels

agree with the rounding of the immediately preceding vowel. In general, noninitial vowels are rounded only when they meet the conditions for the rounding harmony rule. Hence, round is not an independently selectable, distinctive feature in noninitial vowels.

Certain Istanbul dialects (Kumbaraci, 1966) exhibit a process called palatal umlaut (PU), which raises and unrounds vowels before the alveopalatals y, $\check{s}$, and $\check{\jmath}$. This rule produces alternations of the stem-final vowel in the following infinitive and imperative forms: *ye-mek, yi-yin* 'eat'; *üšü-mek, üsi-yin* 'be cold'; *oku-mak, okı-yın* 'read'; *sakla-mak, saklı-yın* 'hide'. The rules of RH and PU are formulated below.

(30)
$$\begin{bmatrix} V \\ +hi \end{bmatrix} \longrightarrow [\alpha round]/\begin{bmatrix} V \\ [\alpha round] \end{bmatrix} C_0 + \underline{\quad}$$

(31)
$$V \longrightarrow \begin{bmatrix} +high \\ -round \end{bmatrix}/\underline{\quad} + [y, \check{s}, \check{\jmath}]$$

Let us consider a form like *okıyın* in detail. Assuming for purposes of discussion the correctness of Kiparsky's (1968a) analysis of vowel harmony, in which harmony within a root is to be handled by a morpheme structure condition, the UR would be /oku-yın/, ignoring the question of the UR for the suffixal vowel, and RH would be limited to suffixal vowels.* Given these limitations, there are two possible derivations.

(32) (a) /oku-yın/   (b) /oku-yın/
     oku-yun   RH (and BH)   *okı-yın*   PU
     okı-yun   PU   *okı-yin*   RH (and BH)

The derivation in (a) represents an opaque interaction of the rules, since the rounded vowel that triggers the rounding of the suffixal vowel appears unrounded on the surface. We believe that such a derivation is highly unusual and unexpected. We know of no languages in which two rules interact in this fashion. The hypothesis in (28) explains the extreme unexpectedness of such an interaction, because the phonetic opacity that results has no semantic value whatsoever. The appearance of the *u* in the suffix preserves no underlying semantic contrast, since [±round] is a distinctive opposition only in initial position in Turkish.

The hypothesis sketched in (28) thus seems, initially at least, quite plausible. It limits the equation opaque = marked to cases where opaque interactions are truly unexpected, and consequently is consistent with the existence of so many opaque interactions that are found in the world's languages.

Nevertheless, many problems remain in the area of naturalness of rule interactions. To cite just one, recall our discussion of mutually contradicting rules

---

* If the rounding harmony rule is permitted to specify the roundness of noninitial root vowels as well as suffixal ones, an ordering paradox results. With the UR /okı-yın/, *okıyun* results if RH applies before PU, while the opposite order yields *okuyun*.

in the Nootka example. In the derivation of /#qo:xʷ#/ two rules are involved: labialization after a rounded vowel and delabialization in preconsonantal and final positions. In such derivations application of either rule will render the other opaque. The correct derivation for Nootka is the one that terminates in *qo:x*, where the delabialization process prevails. The question that arises, of course, is whether or not this particular interaction is expected. Given the rather diffuse and unrefined definition of opacity that we have been using, either order of the rules is equally opaque. We should therefore find no preference on the part of the world's languages for one interaction over the other in such mutually contradicting cases. Preliminary work on this question strongly suggests that, at least in one type of contradictory interaction, this expectation is incorrect.

Rules specifying vowel length often participate in such contradictory interactions. Many languages have both lengthening and shortening rules whose environments partially overlap. In such cases of overlapping environments a vowel segment will be subject to two contradictory instructions. One rule will require the vowel to be long, and the other will require it to be short. Application of one of the rules renders the other opaque. Recall, for example, our discussion of the lengthening and shortening rules in Chi-Mwi:ni (Chapter 2). In an example like /kuna ma:yi/ 'to drink water', word-final lengthening predicts that the final vowel of *kuna* should be long, but prelength shortening predicts that this same vowel should be short, since it is followed by a long vowel in the same phrase. The correct surface form is *kuna ma:yi*, with prelength shortening prevailing over word-final lengthening. The application of pre-length shortening in the phrase *kuna ma:yi* has the effect of rendering word-final lengthening opaque, since *kuna* is a surface counterexample to the principle that a phrase-medial word-final vowel is long. It is of course impossible for both word-final lengthening and prelength shortening to be transparent. Since they contradict one another, phonetic representations can conform to just one of the rules, not both.

Similarly, in an example such as /kaṇḍikiɬa xaɬamu/, 'to write with a pen', word-final lengthening predicts that the final vowel of *kaṇḍikiɬa* should be long; preantepenultimate shortening, however, predicts that this same vowel will be short, since it is earlier in the phrase than antepenultimate. Since the correct surface form is *kaṇḍikiɬa xaɬamu*, preantepenultimate shortening must be allowed to prevail over word-final lengthening. As a result word-final lengthening is opaque—forms like *kaṇḍikiɬa xaɬamu* represent surface counterexamples to the principle that phrase-medial word-final vowels are long.

All of the vowel shortening rules in Chi-Mwi:ni prevail over word-final lengthening, and in so doing render that rule opaque. In fact, all the vowel shortening rules take precedence over all the vowel lengthening rules. The vowel shortening rules are (generally) not opaque; the vowel lengthening rules are opaque. These observations raise the question; When vowel lengthening rules and vowel shortening rules are in conflict, is there a natural resolution in favor of the shortening rules? The Chi-Mwi:ni data would support such a contention.

There are many other examples from diverse languages to suggest that the Chi-Mwi:ni pattern is the expected one. To cite just one additional example, in Nootka (Campbell, 1973) there is a contraction rule that converts a V(glide)V sequence to a long vowel. Thus, /ʔo-atah/ becomes *ʔo:tah*, which by a number of reduplication rules may appear as *ʔoʔo:tah* 'whaling' or *ʔoʔoʔotah* 'whaling here and there'. The latter derives from /ʔoʔoʔo:tah/ and has lost its long vowel by a general rule that shortens vowels in the third syllable of a word. It is apparent that the shortening rule applies to the output of contraction, which creates a long vowel. Once again the shortening rule prevails.

If there is some validity to the claim that vowel shortening rules tend to prevail over vowel lengthening rules when they are in conflict, we must conclude that there are factors over and above opacity and the preservation of semantic and/or morphological contrasts at work in determining the relative naturalness of rule interactions. For instance, in the present example one might be led to claim that asymmetry exists between long and short vowels such that the latter can be considered in some sense unmarked and the former marked. Some evidence for this proposition might be claimed to exist by virtue of the observation that rules very often restrict long vowels so that they may not occur in particular syllables in a word, but the occurrence of short vowels is not normally so restricted. Thus a long vowel in Chi-Mwi:ni may not appear more forward in the word than the antepenultimate. It would be unusual to find a language where a short vowel was not allowed to appear in a preantepenultimate syllable. (A short vowel may of course be prevented from appearing in particular syllable *types*, such as open syllables.) If this asymmetry does exist, then one might propose that when two rules are contradictory, the natural interaction is the one that leads to the appearance of the unmarked sound in the phonetic representation. Much further research is necessary to determine whether any such principle is of general validity. In any case, the examples discussed do illustrate that principles beyond transparency/opacity and preservation of contrast may well be involved in determining unmarked rule interactions.

5

The Multiple Application Problem

In most discussions of the way in which phonological rules apply to convert a UR to a PR, three general positions are distinguished, which we shall label here the direct-mapping principle, the free-reapplication principle, and the rule-ordering principle (Postal, 1968; Chomsky and Halle, 1968: p. 342ff.). According to the direct mapping principle, all rules are defined to operate on the UR and must apply at each point in the UR where their structural description is met. The application of one rule may not materially affect the application of another. One rule may neither create nor destroy the conditions which make possible the application of another rule. The free-reapplication approach, on the other hand, states that any rule may apply to the output of any other rule. More specifically, each rule applies whenever its structural description is met in the UR to obtain a derived representation r_1. This derived representation is then resubmitted to the rules, which will apply wherever their SD is met to obtain another derived representation r_2. The process of reapplication continues until no more rules apply nonvacuously, at which point the derivation terminates in the PR. These hypotheses have in fact been proposed by various linguists at various times (e.g., direct mapping by the stratificational school, cf., Postal, 1968, and free reapplication by Vennemann, 1974, under the label of random-sequential order), but most generative phonologists have, correctly in our opinion, rejected these two principles as too restrictive. Phonological structure is such that the same two rules can lead to reapplication in one language (thus contradicting direct mapping) and no reapplication in another (contradicting free reapplication). In order to be consistent with this degree of diversity in the interaction between rules, most generative phonologists have employed the device of rule ordering, which permits one to control whether or not a given rule creates or destroys the conditions required for the application of another rule.

In this chapter we deal with a problem closely connected with the interaction of different rules in the course of the derivation of the PR from the UR, namely the interaction between different applications of the same rule. Not surprisingly, three positions have been discussed in the literature that closely parallel the direct-mapping, free-reapplication and rule-ordering principles. These are the simultaneous-application principle, the iterative-application principle, and the directionally-iterative principle, respectively. We will make the claims of each principle precise and critically evaluate them in light of a representative sample of data drawn from a diverse set of languages.

The standard approach to rule application in generative phonology is the position outlined in Chomsky and Halle (*SPE*, 1968):

(1)   To apply a rule, the entire string is first scanned for segments that satisfy the environ-
       mental constraints of the rule. After all such segments have been identified in the string,
       the changes required by the rule are applied simultaneously [p. 344].

The simultaneous-application principle (SA) claims that given an input string to a rule of the form A $\longrightarrow$ B/C____D, all As in the context C____D will be converted to B regardless of whether they remain in that context after the rule has been applied elsewhere in the string. It is the original input string that determines the application of the rule to any point in the string. Application of the rule at any one point in the string cannot prevent (bleed) the application of the rule at any other point in the string. In addition, SA claims that application at one point in the string may never create the conditions that make possible the application of the rule at another point in the string. A feeding interaction between applications is prohibited. Thus, SA is entirely analogous to the direct-mapping principle.

The counterfeeding corollary of SA is consistent with the input-output relations required by many phonological rules. For example, in Hidatsa (Harris, 1942) there is a rule apocopating the final mora of a word, as is evident from the following past tense and imperative verb forms: *cixi-c*, *cix* 'jump'; *ika:-c*, *ika* 'look'; *kikua-c*, *kiku* 'set a trap'. If long vowels are represented as geminates, these alternations can be described as the product of the following rule.

(2) $V \longrightarrow \emptyset /\_\_\_\_ \#$

Application of this rule to the URs for the imperative forms /#cixi#/, /#ikaa#/, and /#kikua#/, yields the correct surface forms *cix*, *ika*, and *kiku*. But the latter two forms also contain word-final vowels and hence meet the SD of (2). But it is only underlying final vowels that delete in Hidatsa; vowels that come to stand in final position as a result of a prior application of (2) do not. SA produces the correct results here, because it permits a rule to apply only to the original input string. The structure resulting from one application of the rule may not undergo a subsequent application of the same rule, even if the SD of the rule is satisfied as a result of a prior application of the rule.

The Tonkawa elision rule (Chapter 3) that shortens a long vowel and deletes a short vowel from the second syllable of a word (provided no CCC or C'C cluster arises) is of the same character. If long vowels are treated as geminates, this rule will not only convert /we-netale-n-o?/ to *we-ntale-n-o?*, but will also convert /we-naat-o?/ to *we-nat-o?*. Note, however, that after the application of elision to shorten the long vowel in the latter word, the resultant structure is of the same nature as a form like /we-netale-n-o?/, which is converted to *we-ntale-n-o?*. Thus, elision must be prevented from applying to its own output to ensure that *we-nat-o?* is not converted to *we-nt-o?*. SA guarantees this, since it requires all rules to be applied only to the original input string.

The simultaneous-application principle also requires multiple applications to interact in a counterbleeding fashion. That is, application of the rule at one point in the string may not inhibit application at another point, because all applications are defined on the original input string. The rhythmic law of Slovak (Kenstowicz, 1972) illustrates this pattern. According to this rule, a long vowel shortens following a syllable containing a long vowel.

(3) $V: \longrightarrow [-\text{long}]/V:C_0\underline{\hspace{2em}}$

This rule accounts for the fact that in the following data the conjugation vowels, underlying /e/, /i:/, and /a:/, are short when the preceding syllable is long.

(4)

	3rd singular	1st plural	2nd plural	gloss
	čes-e	*čes-e-me*	*čes-e-te*	'comb'
	pi:š-e	*pi:š-e-me*	*pi:š-e-te*	'write'
	rob-i:	*rob-i:-me*	*rob-i:-te*	'work'
	ku:p-i	*ku:p-i-me*	*ku:p-i-te*	'buy'
	vol-a:	*vol-a:-me*	*vol-a:-te*	'call'
	či:t-a	*či:t-a-me*	*či:t-a-te*	'read'

Examples with three underlying adjacent long vowels are limited to verbs formed with the derivational suffix /-a:v/, denoting frequent or repeated action. This suffix takes the /-a:/ conjugation vowel. The following examples show roots with underlying short (a) and long (b) vowels.

(5) (a) *čes-a:v-a*   *čes-a:v-a-me*   *čes-a:v-a-te*   'comb, freq.'
         vol-a:v-a   *vol-a:v-a-me*   *vol-a:v-a-te*   'call, freq.'

     (b) *pi:s-av-a*   *pi:s-av-a-me*   *pi:s-av-a-te*   'write, freq.'
         ku:p-av-a   *ku:p-av-a-me*   *ku:p-av-a-te*   'buy, freq.'
         či:t-av-a   *či:t-av-a-me*   *či:t-av-a-te*   'read, freq.'

In the verbs in (a), the conjugation vowel /-a:/ is preceded by long vowel and hence is shortened by the rhythmic law. But in the verbs of (b) the SD of the rule is met at two adjacent points in the original input string. For instance, the UR of *pi:s-av-a* is /pi:s-a:v-a:/. The long vowel of the derivational suffix is immediately preceded by the long vowel of the root, and the long vowel of the conjugation marker is preceded by the long vowel in the derivational suffix. Note that when the vowel of the derivational suffix shortens, the conjugation vowel is no longer preceded by a long vowel. We are thus dealing with a counterbleeding interaction. Shortening of the derivational suffix creates a structure in which the conjugation vowel is no longer preceded by a long vowel. The conjugation vowel would not shorten, if application of the rule to the latter were permitted only after an application of the rule to the derivational suffix. Thus, in this case the shortening of the conjugation vowel must be defined upon the original input string, in which there are three successive long vowels. This pattern of interaction between individual applications of the rhythmic law is guaranteed by the simultaneous-application principle, which requires that all applications take place simultaneously on the original input string.

To summarize briefly, we have seen that the simultaneous-application principle adopted by SPE requires all rule applications to be defined on the original input string. This principle of rule application is consistent with counterfeeding and counterbleeding interactions. We will now turn to a brief discussion of cases in which the multiple applications must interact in a feeding and bleeding fashion. It will be shown that if one maintains simultaneous application, one is forced into the same position as that which results from the acceptance of the direct-mapping hypothesis: the repetition of one rule inside another and the acceptance of highly unnatural and/or impossible phonological rules.

First, let us consider bleeding interactions. One interesting example is found in a description of the Australian language Gidabal by Brian and Helen Geytenbeek (1971). In fact, this language has a rule of exactly the same form as the Slovak rhythmic law, except that the application of shortening to one vowel bleeds the shortening of an adjacent vowel. Numerous examples attest to the existence of a rule in Gidabal that shortens a long vowel when preceded by a long vowel. Call this rule vowel shortening, to distinguish it from the Slovak rhythmic law, even though the rules are in fact the same. As our first example of the operation of vowel shortening (VS), consider the following data.

(6)   *badi-ya:*   'should hit'   *badi-ye*   'may hit'
       yaga:-ya   'should be fixing'   *yaga:-ye*   'may fix'
       ga:da-ya: 'should chase'   *ga:da-ye*   'may chase'

The potential suffix *-ye* is invariable after the verb roots *badi-*, *yaga:-*, and *ga:da-*; the subjunctive suffix is *-ya:* except when the preceding vowel is long, in which case it has the shape *-ya*. These data suggest that *-ye* has an underlying short vowel and -*ya:* an underlying long vowel that is shortened by VS when a long vowel appears in the immediately preceding syllable.

A comparison of the suffixes -*gali* 'typified by, fond of', and -*ya:gan* 'to get' provides a second example. The initial consonant of the latter assimilates to a homorganic stop after a nasal by a rule we can ignore here.

(7)

ŋagam-gali	'dog lover'	*mani-ya:gan*	'to get wallaby'
gunu:m-gali	'place with many stumps'	*gudim-ba:gan*	'to get wild game'
dalagař-gali	'muddy place'	*muřu:n-dagan*	'to get firewood'

The first vowel of /-ya:gan/ is long if the preceding vowel is short; it is short if the preceding vowel is long. Once again VS accounts for this variation, given that the suffix has an underlying long initial vowel.

In the course of suffixation, three or more successive long vowels may occur in Gidabal underlying structures. For example, the (present) locational suffix /-ya:/, and the intensifier suffixes /-da:ŋ/ and /-be:/, contain underlying long vowels.

(8)

bala-ya:	'is under'	*njule-da:ŋ*	'he' (emphatic)
ba:m-ba	'is halfway'	*nu:n-daŋ*	'too hot'
gila:-ya	'that'	*yu:-daŋ*	'much later'
djubunj-dja:	'is night'		
gadi-be:	'right here'		
bugal-be:	'very good'		
buřu:ř-be	'only two'		

Now consider some cases where these suffixes are combined with one another: *babař-a:-daŋ* 'straight above' from /babař-ya:-da:ŋ/ has two successive long vowels in the UR, the second of which shortens. In *djalum-ba:-daŋ-be:* 'is certainly right on the fish' from the UR /djalum-ba:-da:ŋ-be:/ where there are three successive underlying long vowels, only the middle vowel shortens. The simultaneous-application principle would predict the form **djalum-ba:-daŋ-be*, where the intensifier /-be:/ would also be shortened, since the vowel of this suffix is preceded by a long vowel in the UR. *gunu:m-ba-da:ŋ-be* 'is certainly right on the stump' is a case where there are four successive long vowels in the UR. Only the second and the fourth shorten. SA incorrectly predicts **gunu:m-ba-daŋ-be* with a shortening of all long vowels that appear after a long vowel in the underlying form.

In order for SA to be consistent with the data from Gidabal it is necessary to suppose that the rule of vowel shortening has a rather different character from that attributed to it in the preceding discussion. In order for this rule to shorten alternate long vowels it would have to have the following form, where V̆ is a cover symbol for a short vowel.

(9) $$\text{V:} \longrightarrow \text{V̆} / \left\{ \begin{matrix} \# \\ \text{V̆} \end{matrix} \right\} \text{C}_1\text{V:}(\text{C}_1\text{V:}\text{C}_1\text{V:})^*\text{C}_1\_\_$$

The material inside the braces is necessary in order to identify the following long vowel as the first in a sequence of long vowels. The remainder of the environment identifies the vowel that will undergo the rule as the second, fourth, sixth, and so on, in a sequence of long vowels. This rule has recourse to the "infinite schema" notation introduced in *SPE* (p. 344). The notation ( )* abbreviates an infinite set of rules. One of the rules contains no occurrence of the material inside the parentheses, thereby denoting a string of two successive long vowels. The next contains one occurrence of the material in parentheses, denoting a string of four consecutive long vowels. The next one contains two occurrences of the parenthesized material, identifying a string of six long vowels. And so on.

This formulation of vowel shortening, which one must assume in order to maintain SA, is objectionable for the very same reasons as the direct-mapping hypothesis. To apply two or more phonological rules simultaneously to the UR often leads to the repetition of the structural description of one rule (or its complement) in the structural description of another rule. Similarly, in order to apply vowel shortening in Gidabal simultaneously, the SD of the rule must be repeated in its own SD. The material in parentheses, with its reference to two successive long vowels, repeats the remainder of the SD, which also mentions two successive long vowels. With the infinite schema notation, this repetition of material is treated as entirely accidental. The material inside the parentheses could just as well have been totally different from the material outside. In fact, every case we know of in which phonologists have appealed to the infinite schema notation has involved mentioning material inside the parentheses that also occurs outside the parentheses. But this fact demonstrates that the relationship between the material inside and outside the parentheses is not at all accidental.

In addition, only one of the rules abbreviated by the infinite schema given above can be shown to be a real rule of grammar: namely, the subrule that results when there is no material inside the parentheses (and also when the material inside the braces is omitted, for this information is present merely to identify the first vowel in a sequence of long vowels, and is not really an integral part of the rule at all). We have seen, for example, that Slovak possesses this rule. The remaining rules abbreviated by the infinite schema, continuing to ignore the braces, are as follows.

(10) $V: \longrightarrow \check{V}/V:C_1V:C_1V:C_1\underline{\quad\quad}$

$V: \longrightarrow \check{V}/V:C_1V:C_1V:C_1V:C_1V:C_1\underline{\quad\quad}$

Clearly, none of these rules has independent justification, in the sense that there is probably no language where just one of these rules and not the other would have to be assumed operative. That is to say, there is no language that shortens the final vowel in a string of six successive long vowels unless that language also shortens the final member of a string of four, and of two. A similar objection can be made to many of the rules one is forced to write if one does not permit separate rules to apply in sequential fashion rather than simultaneously. Consequently, it appears that many of the same reasons that lead to a rejection of simultaneous application of *separate* rules also force the rejection of a principle that a *single* rule must be applied simultaneously to all points in the input string that satisfy the structural description of the rule.

A rather more complex, but quite instructive case is offered by the Macushi dialect of Carib (Hawkins, 1950). In Macushi there is a rule that sharply reduces odd-numbered vowels counting from the beginning of the word (or certain other definable points) and subject to a number of restrictions discussed later. For example, the morpheme /wanamari/ 'mirror' has the allomorph wənaməri in its unsuffixed form. The vowels underlying the reduced ə's surface in the utterance əwanəmararï 'my mirror' from the UR /u-wanamari-rï/, where the prefix and suffix indicate 1st person sg., alienable possession.

Hawkins describes the above reduction process as complete: that is, loss of the underlying vowel. Thus, he cites wnamrï 'mirror' and wanmarrï 'my mirror'. From the information contained in the article, however, it appears that a case can be made for the alternative interpretation of a sharp reduction to a schwalike vowel. There are several reasons for this. First, consonant clusters that arise from a "deletion" of an intervening vowel have a phonetically open transition, while similar underlying clusters do not. Second, for some informants this open transition is longer, "tending to a stressless neutral vowel /ə/" (p. 87). Finally, phrase-initial vowels can optionally be pronounced instead of deleted. But such vowels are described as always being stressless, in marked contrast to other vowels: rawtá or àrawtá from /arawta/ 'baboon'. Here the grave accent marks the stressless vowel; acute, the stressed vowel. Since a loud stress regularly occurs on the phrase-final vowel, and since all other vowels except a vowel in phrase-initial position are described as having a "more or less even stress", it would appear possible to represent the phrase-initial vowel that alternates with ∅ as a reduced vowel. In any case, whether the process is described as a reduction or a deletion makes little difference to the present discussion.

Considering just the two URs /wanamari/ and /u-wanamari-rï/, what sort of rule is required to obtain the correct phonetic forms wənaməri and əwanə-mararï? If we adopted SA, the reduction rule would have to be formulated so as to select every other vowel beginning from the left. Using the infinite-schema notation, this rule could be written as follows.

(11) $\qquad V \longrightarrow ə /\, \# (C_1 V C_1 V)^* C_1 \underline{\qquad}$

Suppose, however, that we were to adopt a position that permits one application of a rule to bleed another application. We might then formulate the rule as follows.

(12) $\qquad V \longrightarrow ə / \left\{ \begin{array}{c} \# \\ V \\ [-\text{reduced}] \end{array} \right\} C_1 \underline{\qquad}$

In this rule the specification [−reduced] characterizes any vowel other than ə. This rule says that a vowel is reduced if it is either in word-initial position or preceded by a nonreduced vowel. Observe that in the UR /wanamari/ every vowel meets the SD of this rule. Since only the first and third vowels reduce, we must assume that application of the rule to the first vowel bleeds application to the second. It does this by changing the first vowel to a reduced vowel, thus causing the second vowel to be in an inappropriate environment for reduction. Similarly, application of the rule to the third vowel must bleed application to the fourth. In the case of a UR like /u-wanamari-rï/ application of the rule to the first, third, and fifth vowels is responsible for the lack of reduction of the second, fourth, and sixth vowels.

These two examples represent the simplest cases. The reduction rule must be modified to accommodate certain "disturbances" in the pattern of reduction, three of which are cited by Hawkins. The significant point for the present discussion is that "following the point of disturbance, the pattern of loss [or reduction] begins over again so that the first following vowel is number one in the sequence of vowels remaining in the word" (p. 88).

The first disturbing factor is that a vowel never reduces if it is followed by two or more consonants. Thus, in *ši ʔmərikəpé* 'little now', from /ši ʔ-miri-ki-pe/, the first vowel does not reduce, since a cluster follows. The count begins again, and the second and fourth vowels of the word now count as the first and third for purposes of the reduction rule. A second disturbing factor is that a vowel will reduce following a consonant cluster only if that cluster contains at most two elements, the first of which must be a sonorant. Note *pakrayəmïn ʔ* 'bush hogs' from the UR /pakra-yamïn ʔ/, where the first vowel fails to reduce because it is followed by a consonant cluster and the second vowel fails to reduce because it is preceded by a consonant cluster whose first element is an obstruent. Similarly, *kratəpé* 'alligator now' from /kratu-pe/. Contrast *kəraywəpé* 'Brazilian now' from /karaywa-pe/, where the third vowel reduces because it is preceded by a consonant cluster whose first member is a sonorant. The final disturbance that needs to be noted is that the last vowel of the phrase fails to reduce. Since this vowel is regularly stressed, however, this restriction is quite expected: *pəripí* 'spindle' from /piripi/, and *əmanərirí* 'my cassava grater' from /umanari-rï/.

Attempting to incorporate such constraints into an infinite schema version of vowel reduction presents gross difficulties. We leave this point for the reader to verify for himself. The version of the reduction process that assumes the possibility of a bleeding interaction among the various applications of a single rule may be formulated as follows.

(13)
$$
\begin{array}{c} V \\ [-\text{stress}] \end{array} \longrightarrow \text{ə} / \left\{ \begin{array}{c} \# \\ V \\ [-\text{reduced}] \end{array} \right\} ([+\text{son}]) \, C\underline{\hspace{1cm}}CV
$$

Consider an input like /ši ʔ-miri-ki-pé/; the first vowel cannot reduce, since it is not followed by a CV structure; since the first vowel is not reduced, application of the rule to the second vowel is not bled. Reduction of the first vowel of /miri/ bleeds application of the rule to the second vowel of the morpheme, which then allows the vowel of /ki/ to reduce. The last vowel cannot reduce, being stressed and also preceded by a reduced vowel. The ultimate form is thus *ši ʔ-məri-kəpé*.

Consider now /pakra-yamïn ʔ/. The first vowel cannot reduce, since a cluster follows. The second vowel cannot reduce either; (13) permits only a sonorant-initial cluster to precede. The third vowel is able to reduce, however, since the preceding vowel remains unreduced and the other conditions are satisfied as well. The last vowel cannot reduce, being stressed and also preceded by a reduced vowel.

The revised version of vowel reduction will thus correctly predict vowel reduction in Macushi, provided it works so that application of the rule to certain vowels will bleed application to certain adjacent vowels. We have not yet discussed how to obtain this effect. What is important is that this effect is required to deal with the Macushi data. Reduction affects only alternate vowels. In order to know whether a vowel is to be reduced, it is necessary to know whether the preceding vowel is reduced.

This point is driven home forcefully when we consider the fact that there appear to be exceptions to reduction. For example, in *pakəpi ʔpï* 'cow-hide' from /paka-pi ʔpï/, the first vowel should reduce but does not. Notice that since the first vowel exceptionally fails to reduce, the second one may. And the third one cannot, since it is preceded by a reduced vowel. These facts follow automatically from the rule of reduction we have formulated, as long as the first vowel is marked as an exception. Such a form is difficult for the infinite-schema version of reduction to handle, because this approach attempts to determine from the original input string alone whether a rule applies at any point in the string. Given an input /paka-pi ʔpï/, the third vowel should reduce and the second one should not. It is only the failure of the first vowel to be affected that permits the second to reduce, which in turn prevents reduction of the third.

In our opinion these examples from Macushi argue strongly against the simultaneous-application principle, for they indicate that whether or not any given vowel in a Macushi word is reduced depends upon whether the preceding vowel has been reduced. If this observation is correct, the decision as to whether to reduce a vowel must be able to take into account other applications of the same rule. But this is precisely what the simultaneous-application principle denies.

Let us now turn to the counterfeeding corollary of the simultaneous-application principle. If all rule applications operate on the original input string, a feeding relationship between individual applications of the same rule is prohibited. Surely the most important phenomenon calling this into question is vowel harmony. For example, in Yakut, a Turkic language of Siberia, all the vowels of a word agree in the feature [back] (Krueger, 1962). Suffixes show different allomorphs, depending upon the vocalism of the preceding root. For instance, the morphemes *aɣa* 'father' and *bie* 'mare' exhibit the following paradigms.

(14)

		singular	plural	singular	plural
nominative	*aɣa*	*aɣalar*	*bie*	*bieler*
dative	*aɣaɣa*	*aɣalarga*	*bieɣe*	*bielerge*
comparative	*aɣataaɣar*	*aɣalardaaɣar*	*bieteeɣer*	*bielerdeeɣer*

Since certain foreign words that fail to induce harmony take back vowel suffixes, we will assume the suffixes /lar/, /ga/ and /taagar/ to be underlying. Underlying *g* is spirantized between vowels, and *t* is voiced to *d* between sonorants. This decision concerning the underlying vocalism of the suffixes is essentially independent of the point under consideration. To account for the front vowel variants of the plural and dative suffixes in *bieler* and *bieɣe*, we require a rule fronting *a* to *e* if the preceding syllable contains a front vowel.

(15) $V \longrightarrow [-back]/ \quad V \quad C_0$_____
            $[-back]$

Now consider cases where there is more than one suffixal vowel. The UR of the dative pl. of 'mare' is /bie-lar-ga/; application of (15) yields /bie-ler-ga/. This fronting of the vowel of the plural suffix to agree with the frontness of the root vowels produces a situation in which the vowel of the dative suffix is eligible for harmony, since it is now preceded by a front vowel. Since the correct output is one where the vowel of the dative suffix is fronted, it is possible to claim that vowel harmony is applied a second time, yielding *bie-ler-ge*. If this is true, one application of the rule must be able to feed another application, contrary to simultaneous application. Inspection of an example like *bie-ler-deeɣer* from /bie-lar-taagar/ reveals that harmony in Yakut extends to the end of the word, however many vowels there may be. Each time a front vowel is created, the next vowel is also fronted.

SPE recognizes the existence of such examples. However, in order to maintain that the input string alone determines a rule's applicability—and thus that rules do not apply to their own output—*SPE* requires an analysis that will simultaneously front all suffix vowels if the root contains front vowels. Once again it is the infinite-schema approach that is appealed to. *SPE* claims that a separate rule fronts each suffixal vowel by virtue of the presence of a front vowel in the root. These rules all collapse into a rule schema of the following form.

(16) $V \longrightarrow [-back]/ \quad V \quad (C_0 V)^* C_0$_____
            $[-back]$

Thus, *SPE* relies upon the infinite schema notation to deal with apparent instances of the feeding of one application by another, just as it is forced to rely on this same notation to deal with apparent instances where one application of a rule bleeds another. But this use of the infinite-schema notation does not seem to us to be any better motivated than the uses examined earlier. Most of the "rules" abbreviated by the infinite schema version of vowel harmony are not in fact possible rules, in the sense that they could occur as independent phonological processes. For example, we trust that there is no language with a rule that fronts a vowel just in case it is preceded by a front vowel three syllables earlier in the word.

That the infinite-schema formulation of vowel harmony formulated above also repeats significant information is perhaps less obvious. There are two crucial facts to note relative to the vowel mentioned inside the parentheses: First, it meets the conditions imposed on the segment that undergoes the rule (in the present instance the only condition is that the segment be a vowel); second, it will acquire, by virtue of one of the rules abbreviated by the infinite schema, the property of the vowel conditioning the harmony process (in the present case, frontness). Given the infinite-schema approach, these are purely accidental facts. But when we look at other cases where the infinite-schema approach would be used, we find the same thing.

Recall the harmony process in Yawelmani (Chapter 1). There we saw that the language has an underlying system of eight vowels: i, u, a, and o ($=$ low back vowel), each of which can be long or short. In words containing two syllables (a root and a suffix) the harmony process is observed whereby suffixal i becomes u if the preceding root contains u, and suffixal a becomes o if the preceding root contains o.

(17)	$xilit$	$xilhin$	$xilal$	$xilk'a$	'tangle'
	$gopit$	$gophin$	$gopol$	$gopk'o$	'care for an infant'
	$dubut$	$dubhun$	$dubal$	$dubk'a$	'lead by the hand'
	$maxit$	$maxhin$	$maxal$	$maxk'a$	'procure'

The suffixal alternations in these data can be accounted for by the following rule, which states that a vowel becomes rounded (and back) if the preceding vowel is rounded and of the same tongue height.

$$(18) \quad \begin{bmatrix} +\text{syll} \\ \alpha\text{high} \end{bmatrix} \longrightarrow \begin{bmatrix} +\text{round} \\ +\text{back} \end{bmatrix} / \begin{bmatrix} +\text{syll} \\ +\text{round} \\ \alpha\text{high} \end{bmatrix} C_0 \underline{\hspace{1cm}}$$

Now let us consider verbal roots with the basic shape CVCC-. When a consonant-initial suffix follows, these roots are subject to the rule of epenthesis that inserts i in the context C____CC.

(19)	$?ilkit$	$?ilikhin$	$?ilkal$	$?ilikk'a$	'sing'
	$logwit$	$logiwhin$	$logwol$	$logiwk'a$	'pulverize'
	$?utyut$	$?utuyhun$	$?utyal$	$?utuyk'a$	'fall'
	$pa?tit$	$pa?ithin$	$pa?tal$	$pa?itk'a$	'fight'

Let us focus on the derivation of $?utuyhun$ from /$?uty$-hin/. After epenthesis we will have the structure /$?utiy$-hin/. Since the inserted i is preceded by u,

roundness harmony is applicable and would yield /ʔutuy-hin/. But now the
suffixal i is in the proper context for the rule to operate. If one application of a
rule can feed another application, we will be able to obtain the correct output
ʔutuyhun simply by reapplying the rule. But if the simultaneous-application
principle is accepted, we must revise the rule by making it an infinite schema.
It could not, however, simply be the following.

(20)
$$\begin{bmatrix} +\text{syll} \\ \alpha\text{high} \end{bmatrix} \longrightarrow \begin{bmatrix} +\text{round} \\ +\text{back} \end{bmatrix} / \begin{bmatrix} +\text{syll} \\ +\text{round} \\ \alpha\text{high} \end{bmatrix} (C_0V)^*C_0\underline{\quad}$$

To see why such a rule would not work, consider *logiwk'a* from /logw-k'a/.
Application of epenthesis yields /logiw-k'a/. If harmony were formulated as
in (20), the suffixal vowel in /logiw-k'a/ would round, since it meets the SD of
the rule. It is separated from a rounded vowel of the same height by one vowel,
and the infinite schema permits any number of vowels to intervene. Given
the harmony rule in its original formulation, however, the suffixal vowel could
not be affected, since the presence of the epenthetic vowel means that the
suffixal vowel is not immediately preceded by a rounded vowel of the same
height. In order for the infinite schema approach to achieve the same results
it would have to be reformulated as follows.

(21)
$$\begin{bmatrix} +\text{syll} \\ \alpha\text{high} \end{bmatrix} \longrightarrow \begin{bmatrix} +\text{round} \\ +\text{back} \end{bmatrix} / \begin{bmatrix} +\text{syll} \\ +\text{round} \\ \alpha\text{high} \end{bmatrix} \left(C_0 \begin{bmatrix} +\text{syll} \\ \alpha\text{high} \end{bmatrix} \right)^* C_0\underline{\quad}$$

The rule formulated above requires that between the vowel being harmonized
and the conditioning vowel there may occur only vowels that are themselves
eligible to undergo harmony and would, once affected by the SC of the rule,
be able to condition harmony. This requirement means that whether or not
any vowel in the word is subject to harmony depends upon whether or not the
preceding vowel itself harmonizes. Actually, the rule does not require that the
intervening vowel undergo harmony, only that it be eligible to do so. In all
cases that we know of, however, the intervening vowel does in fact undergo
the rule. We know of no cases where harmony hops over a vowel and continues
to operate even though the vowel that is skipped could not itself condition
harmony.

In the face of the examples discussed above, it appears that the simultaneous-
application principle formulated in *SPE* cannot be maintained. A rule must
be permitted to apply to its own output. This effect could be achieved by
modifying the principle in the following fashion.

(22) ITERATIVE-APPLICATION PRINCIPLE: *To apply a rule to a string, identify
all segments in the string that meet the SD of the rule. Carry out the SC
of the rule simultaneously for all segments so identified to obtain a derived
string S_1. Then identify all segments in S_1 that meet the SD of the rule*

and carry out the SC for these segments to obtain a derived string S_2. Repeat this process until a derived string S_n has been obtained to which the rule can no longer apply nonvacuously. When such a string has been obtained, the derivation moves on to the next rule in the ordered set.

The iterative principle is analogous to the free-reapplication principle discussed at the beginning of this chapter. It permits a feeding interaction between applications of a rule and hence is able to overcome the objections raised against simultaneous application with respect to the Yakut and Yawelmani examples discussed earlier. The iterative-application principle permits the most optimal formulation of roundness harmony in Yawelmani. A form like *ʔutuyhun* from /ʔuty-hin/ will now be derived as follows. Epenthesis yields /ʔutiy-hin/. This structure is now submitted to the harmony rule. Only the inserted *i* meets the SD of the rule, since only it is immediately preceded by an *u*. Application of the rule produces the derived string /ʔutuy-hin/. The suffixal *i* now meets the SD of the rule, because the immediately preceding syllable now contains an *u*. Consequently, the harmony rule must be applied again, producing the correct surface form *ʔutuyhun*. A form like *logiwkʼa* from /logw-kʼa/ causes no problem. After epenthesis of the *i* suffixal *a* is not immediately preceded by a low rounded vowel. Hence, it will not round.

The iterative principle is consistent with counterbleeding interactions as well. In a Slovak word like *piːs-av-a* from /piːs-aːv-aː/ both long *aː*'s in the UR meet the SD of the rhythmic law. This rule is then applied simultaneously to both of these vowels, shortening each to produce the correct surface form. The iterative principle always produces a counterbleeding as opposed to a bleeding interaction, because it is exactly like simultaneous application as far as the original input string is concerned.

But it is for exactly this reason that the iterative-application principle must be rejected. It cannot produce the bleeding multiple applications required by the Gidabal and Carib examples. A Gidabal form containing more than two successive long vowels will always be converted into the wrong output by shortening all vowels but the first. The correct output, in which only the second, fourth, and succeeding even-numbered vowels in a string of successive long vowels are shortened, can be obtained only if the SD of the rule makes use of the infinite schema notation. Hence, all the arguments against simultaneous application in examples like this apply to the iterative principle as well.

In addition, the iterative principle cannot deal effectively with the counterfeeding interactions found in languages like Hidatsa and Tonkawa. If the Hidatsa apocope rule is applied iteratively, /#kikua#/ will be converted to /#kiku#/ by one application of the rule. This derived string also meets the SD of the apocope rule. According to the iterative principle the rule must be applied a second time. But this produces the incorrect *kik*.

In permitting a rule to apply to its own output the iterative principle is a step in the right direction. However, like free reapplication, it is too strong in its claim that a rule must always be reapplied whenever its SD is met.

Evidently, then, some device must be developed that will permit control over when reapplication will occur. A number of generative phonologists (Anderson 1969; Johnson, 1971; Morin and Friedman, 1971) have suggested the following kind of principle to control the reapplication of a rule.

(23)   DIRECTIONAL-ITERATIVE APPLICATION: *A rule may be applied to a string in one of two ways: iteratively left-to-right or iteratively right-to-left. In left-to-right iterative application the leftmost segment in the string is examined first to see if it meets the SD of the rule. If it does, the rule is applied to obtain a derived string S_1. One then moves on to examine the next segment in the string (the derived string S_1 if the rule has applied, or the original string S_0 if it has not) and applies the rule to this segment if it meets the SD of the rule. This procedure is repeated segment by segment until the rightmost segment in the string has been processed. At this point the derivation moves on to the next rule in the ordered set.*

In right-to-left iterative application, the same procedure obtains except that the rightmost segment is the one checked first, and the application of the rule to the string ceases after the leftmost segment has been processed.

Under this mode of application the reapplication of a rule is possible. However, reapplication can (always?) be prevented by reversing the direction of iteration. This is made possible by the fact that once a segment x has been checked (and modified by the rule if the SD has been satisfied), one may not go back and reapply the rule to x even though subsequent applications of the rule may have modified the string so that x does come to meet the SD of the rule. For example, consider Hidatsa. If a left-to-right application is imposed on the rule of apopcope, a form like / # kikua # / will be derived as follows. The first, second, third, and fourth segments of the string will be checked successively. The rule will not apply to any of them, since they are not in final position. When the fifth segment is examined, it will be deleted since it satisfies the SD of the rule, deriving the string / # kiku # /. Since the apocopated *a* was the final segment of the string, we must move on to the next rule in the ordered set. In particular, apocope cannot apply to the *u* in / # kiku # / even though it meets the SD of the rule because the *u* has already been checked. Under the directional-iterative mode of application, once a segment has been checked we cannot return and reapply the rule to that segment.

The counterfeeding interaction found in the Tonkawa example can be handled by employing a directional-iterative application. In this case the direction must be right-to-left. In the derivation of *wenato?* from / # we-naat-o? # /, if we proceed from right-to-left, the second mora of the long vowel will not elide because it is not the second vowel in the word. Passing to the first mora, elision will drop the vowel, since it is the second vowel of the word. The correct output is insured because we cannot return and delete the second mora, which has already been checked. If the direction of iteration were from left-to-right, both moras would be deleted, since elision of the first *a* produces a derived string /#we-nate-o$^{\gamma}$#/, in which the remaining *a* is now the second vowel of the word and hence would delete.

In the Yakut and Yawelmani examples the required feeding-application pattern can be achieved by employing a left-to-right direction of iteration. For instance, Yawelmani /$^{\gamma}$utiy-hin/ will be converted into /$^{\gamma}$utuy-hin/ when the first *i* is checked. And when the suffixal vowel is checked, it will also be rounded because in the derived string it is immediately preceded by a high rounded vowel.

Turning to bleeding and counterbleeding multiple applications, we argued earlier that both Slovak and Gidabal have essentially the same rule that shortens a vowel in the context $V:C_0$——. In Slovak the rule must shorten all but the first vowel in a string of consecutive long vowels: V:CV:CV:CV:, etc. ——→ V:CVCVCV. We can obtain this pattern by imposing a right-to-left direction on the application of the rule. On the other hand, Gidabal requires an alternating pattern: V:CV:CV:CV: ——→ V:CVCV:CV. If the same shortening rule is applied in a left-to-right direction, this pattern is readily achieved. Finally, we can account for all the data in the Carib example if the reduction rule is applied left-to-right. Such a direction of application produces the appropriate alternating pattern of reduced and nonreduced vowels.

The directionally-iterative principle explains all the data considered so far and has been accepted by many phonologists. To our knowledge, only one serious alternative has been proposed in the literature—by Anderson (1974). According to Anderson, instead of marking each rule for its direction of iteration, each rule is idiosyncratically specified for whether or not it can apply to its own output. A feeding pattern of application like that in Yakut or Yawelmani is thus insured by marking the vowel harmony rules as applying to their own outputs (the application terminating when the rule can no longer apply nonvacuously). The counterfeeding pattern exemplified by the Hidatsa apocope rule would be handled by specifying the rule as not applying to its own output.

The interesting features of Anderson's principle arise in the case of bleeding and counterbleeding patterns, i.e., when the SD of the rule is met at more than a single point in the input string. Here a rather complex algorithm is developed to generate two patterns of application. For obligatory rules the algorithm has three steps.

(24) (*1*) *Circle each segment meeting the SD of the rule and underline the segments in the string serving as the context for each application.*

　　　(*2*) *If any circled segment appears in the context of another application of the rule, eliminate the minimal number of circled segments and associated contexts from consideration so as to remove all cases of overlap.*

　　　(*3*) *Apply the rule simultaneously to all remaining circled segments.*

(2) is the crucial step in this algorithm, defining the notion of overlap, which will occur when a segment eligible to undergo a rule also appears in the context serving for the application of the rule to another segment. If such overlap occurs, (2) resolves it by eliminating the minimal number of cases so that there is no longer any overlap.

To see what is involved here, consider a language having the Slovak or Gidabal rule shortening a vowel after a long vowel. Step (1) of the algorithm would give the following analysis to various strings:

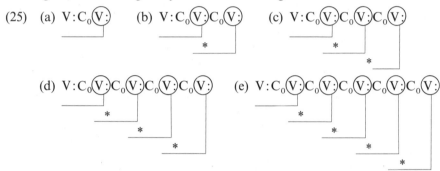

(25)   (a) $V:C_0\underline{(V:)}$ (b) $V:C_0\underline{(V:)C_0(V:)}$ (c) $V:C_0(V:)C_0(V:)C_0(V:)$

(d) $V:C_0(V:)C_0(V:)C_0(V:)C_0(V:)$ (e) $V:C_0(V:)C_0(V:)C_0(V:)C_0(V:)C_0(V:)$

In (a) there is no overlap, so step (2) is skipped and (3) yields $V:C_0V$. In (c) there are two cases of overlap, indicated by the asterisks; step (2) will remove the circle and underlining from the third long vowel (removal of just the second or fourth would still result in overlap) and (3) will give $V:C_0VC_0V:C_0V$. Similarly, in (e) there are four cases of overlap and the minimal elimination involves erasure of the circles and underlining associated with the third and fifth vowels, producing the resultant string $V:C_0VC_0V:C_0VC_0V:C_0V$. It is easy to see that when the input string contains an even number of successive long vowels, the algorithm will produce an alternating pattern of application. But when there is an odd number of adjacent long vowels, step (2) fails to yield a unique answer. Thus, in (b) overlap can be eliminated by disregarding either the first or the second circled vowel, and in (d) by disregarding either the second and fourth or the first and third circled vowels. Anderson resolves this choice in one of two ways. If the rule is marked as not applying to its own output, the segments disregarded are those that produce a transparent (bleeding) pattern. Thus, according to this principle, the shortening rule in Gidabal would be marked as not applying to its own output. In cases of three successive long vowels, the third would be eliminated from eligibility to undergo the rule, and in cases of five long vowels, the third and the fifth would lose their circles by step (2) and hence remain long.

On the other hand, if the rule is marked as applying to its output, a rather different pattern emerges. In such cases, according to Anderson, the indeterminancy of step (2) is resolved in favor of a counterbleeding pattern. For (b) this means that the first circled vowel is disregarded; step (3) then applies yielding $V:C_0V:C_0V$. Reapplication of the rule gives $V:C_0VC_0V$. For (d) resolution at step (2) eliminates the circles around the second and fourth long vowels in the string, with shortening of the third and the fifth. The derived string is then resubmitted to the rule to yield as its final output $V:C_0VC_0VC_0V:C_0V$, a rather unexpected outcome.

The algorithm in (24) thus produces the alternating pattern of Gidabal plus one other rather bizarre pattern. Note, in particular, that it cannot generate the nonalternating pattern of Slovak where all long vowels but the first are shortened. We return to this point momentarily.

Anderson posits the algorithm of (24) in order to describe the multiple application pattern of a rule in the Southwestern Amerindian language Acoma. This language has a very complex accentual system containing three basic accents: high pitch (acute), falling (circumflex), and glottalized falling (marked by a glottal stop). There are approximately a dozen suffixes that trigger an accent "ablaut" rule that places a high tone on all vowels of the word, except the final in certain cases.

(26) | *tâ:m'a* | 'five' | *tá:m'a-wá* | 'five times' |
hâ:	'east'	*há:-námí*	'the east'
rû:niši	'Monday'	*rú:níší:-zé*	'on Monday'
suwagôni	'I got dressed'	*súwágô-ní*	'when I got dressed'

Under certain circumstances short vowels will lose the high tone assigned by the ablaut rule: adjacent to a glottalized sonorant (cf., *tá:m'a-wá*) and in the context defined by rule (27): *kubáni* 'at sunset', *siukʌčáni* 'when I saw him'.

(27) $\acute{V} \longrightarrow V/[+\text{obstr}]\underline{\quad}[+\text{obstr}] C_0 \acute{V}$

If two adjacent syllables meet the conditions of (27) both undergo the rule, while if there are three in a row, only the first and third do. These multiple-application patterns are evident in (28).

(28) | *k'ʌpɪšú-m'a* | 'every night' (cf., *k'ápišu* 'it is night') |
s'ɪpəká:wá-ní	'when I chopped wood'
k'ʌçəkán'i	'his cigarettes'
kəẓáçəkáni	'your cigarettes'
suc'ítistá:-ní	'when I was thinking'

Taking a form like *suc'ítistá:-ní* from /súc'ítistá:-ní/ first, we have three successive vowels meeting the SD of (27) and two cases of overlap: the first /í/ forms the context for application of the rule to the /ú/, and the second /í/ forms the context for application to the first /í/. Here step (2) of the algorithm applies unambiguously: the circle around the first /í/ is removed and the high tone is removed from the /ú/ and the second /í/ to produce the correct PR. On the other hand, in a form like *k'ʌpišú-m'a* from /k'ápíšú-m'a/ the /á/ and /í/ overlap. Elimination of either one would remove the overlap. Now, if it is assumed that rule (27) applies to its own output, then the correct pattern can be obtained. The circle is removed maximalizing application of the rule in a counterbleeding fashion.

Thus, the circle around the /í/ is erased and step (3) yields /k'apíšŭ-m'a/. After the next application of the rule, the correct PR is obtained.

Anderson's algorithm is thus able to describe correctly the complex and unusual application pattern of the Acoma tone-loss rule. A directionally-iterative approach fails because it would require a left to right direction for a form like *k'ʌpišŭ-m'a* and a right to left direction for forms like *suč'itistá:-ni*. But this would be inconsistent with the whole idea underlying the directionally-iterative principle: namely, that the pattern of application in larger domains is predictable from the direction of iteration in smaller domains.

Nevertheless, we believe that it would be rash to reject the directionally-iterative principle in favor of an algorithm like (24). First, the one example which distinguishes them, the Acoma tone-loss rule, is anything but clearcut. One legitimately wonders whether this example would remain a counter-example once the complex tone system of the entire language is worked out. More importantly, Anderson's algorithm claims that there are no bona fide examples of counterbleeding multiple-application patterns. Realizing this, he attempts to provide reanalyses for the four or five examples of this kind of applicational pattern that have been reported in the literature. However, these analyses are hardly straightforward. Here we shall confine ourselves to Anderson's reinterpretation of the Slovak data discussed earlier. We have seen from the Acoma case that the algorithm permits a counterbleeding pattern for strings that contain just two adjacent overlapping inputs to the rule. Thus, a form like *či:t-av-a* can be derived from /či:t-a:v-a:/ by merely specifying the rhythmic law as applying to its own output. However, the algorithm cannot derive *či:t-av-av-a* 'he reads and reads' from /či:t-a:v-a:v-a:/. Since this form contains an even number of successive long vowels, step (2) of the algorithm uniquely defines an alternating pattern, which would yield **či:t-av-a:v-a*. Anderson points out that it is only though repetitions of the frequentative morpheme /-a:v/ that strings of four or more successive long vowels can be generated in Slovak. He then claims that there is a tendency in such constructions for the iterated element to exhibit a constant phonetic shape, citing as support the observation of Wayles Browne that English verbs with alternant past tense forms in free variation like *leaped* and *lept* cannot be freely combined in the iterative construction: cf., **He leaped and lept and leaped....** Anderson attempts to capitalize on this property of iterated constructions by claiming that the UR of *či:t-av-av-a* is not /či:t-a:v-a:v-a:/ but rather /či:t-a:v-a:/. At this point the rhythmic law applies yielding /či:t-av-a/. It is only after the rhythmic law has applied that iteration of the frequentative morpheme takes place, thus guaranteeing that it will have a constant phonetic shape. If it is assumed that this is the source for *či:t-av-av-a* and all longer constructions, then the counterbleeding pattern these words

---

* A similar observation has been developed by Wilbur (1973) to explain many peculiarities exhibited by reduplicated words.

exhibit has an alternative explanation and does not constitute a counterexample to the algorithm.

This reanalysis does not hold however, for it fails to correctly describe forms with a short root vowel such as 'call': cf., *vol-a:v-a*, *vol-a:v-av-a*, and so on. In the latter form, the rhythmic law would have to apply to the output of the iteration process, in a counterbleeding pattern, in order to shorten all but the first occurrence of the frequentative morpheme. It thus appears that counterbleeding is a genuine multiple-application pattern and that any theory which fails to accommodate it must be rejected.

There is nevertheless a sense in which Anderson's theory provides a step in the right direction as compared to the directionally-iterative theory. He attempts to relate the principles governing the interaction between applications of the same rule to those principles that control the interaction between applications of different rules (i.e., the notions of opacity and transparency, discussed in Chapter 4). This is something the directionally-iterative approach fails to do. It claims that interactions between applications of the same rule are determined by the direction of scansion, while interactions between applications of different rules are controlled by some other device, e.g., rule ordering. But why should there be two theoretical devices for what appears to be the same descriptive problem? Surely it would be preferable to have just one. We shall return to this question briefly at the end of the next chapter after we have re-examined the problem of interactions between separate rules.

6

The Role of Derivational
History in Phonology

In Chapter 4 it was suggested that, at least from the phonetic point of view, the natural order of application of a pair of rules is the order that minimizes opacity. Given that such a sequencing of the rules is natural, we might assume that rules are applied in this fashion without requiring any language-specific statement to obtain the desired result. In other words, there is a universal convention specifying that rules are to be applied in an order that minimizes opacity. Thus, in the grammar of Lɔmóngɔ (see Chapter 4), for example, no statement would be required to guarantee that the rule of affrication would apply after glide formation in the derivation of *tsw-ɛ́n-a* from /to-ɛ́n-a/. The universal convention would guarantee the correct derivation. The question would then become: How are those interactions that create opacity to be described? Similarly, how are those interactions where opacity appears to be irrelevant to be described? One means of describing these cases is to postulate a language-specific rule-ordering statement that will require a particular sequencing of the rules. For example, in Mwera (see Chapter 4) there will be a statement that requires the optional rule of cluster simplification to apply before the rule of voicing, thus accounting for why *ŋguya* 'cape bean' from underlying /N-kuya/ does not undergo cluster simplification, whereas *ŋgomo ~ ŋomo* 'lip' from underlying /N-gomo/ does. Note that a general convention would have to be invoked that says that a language-specific ordering statement overrides the sequencing of rules that would be imposed by the universal convention that requires that sequencing of rules that minimizes opacity.

Although the device of rule-ordering statements as a means for guaranteeing opaque interactions of rules has been heavily exploited in the course of this work, the arguments usually put forth supporting the necessity of this device rest on one critical but often implicit assumption, which we will refer to here as the "localist assumption." We attempt in this chapter to render the localist assumption explicit and to see what alternatives there are to rule-ordering statements if we abandon the localist assumption.

It is generally assumed that a surface phonetic representation is the consequence of the application of a set of phonological rules to the underlying representation of the utterance in question. A rule applies when the structural description (SD) of the rule is satisfied. The localist assumption represents a limitation on the possible configuration of a SD. Specifically, the localist assumption claims, first, that the SD of a rule refers to properties that co-occur in *one* phonological representation, and, second, the representation in question is the structure that is the input to the rule. In other words, whether or not a rule applies to a particular input structure is entirely a matter of whether that input structure contains the phonological and/or grammatical properties specified in the SD of the rule.

The following example from Chi-Mwi:ni will clarify the preceding statements. In most cases the perfective suffix has the shape -*i:ɬ*-(-*e:ɬ*- if preceded by a mid-vowel). But when the stem ends in *s*, *z*, *sh*, or *ñ* (there is no voiced counterpart to *sh* in the language), the lateral in the perfective suffix changes to *z*.

(1)   *ɬum-i:ɬ-e*   'he bit'   *bus-i:z-e*   'he kissed'
       reb-e:ɬ-e   'he stopped'   *was-i:z-e*   'he made a will'
       kun-i:ɬ-e   'he scratched'   *uz-i:z-e*   'he sold'
       had-i:ɬ-e   'he said'   *yez-e:z-e*   'he filled'
       tov-e:ɬ-e   'he dipped'   *ush-i:z-e*   'he hid (it)'
       ɬew-e:ɬ-e   'he got drunk'   *fañ-i:z-e*   'he did'
       i-vuy-i:ɬ-e   'it trickled'   *oñ-e:z-e*   'he showed'

Since it is difficult to incorporate the sounds triggering this rule into a natural class, while excluding *f*, *v*, *θ*, *j*, *n*, and so on, we simply list the relevant sounds in the following schematic rule.

(2)   ɬ ⟶ z/[s, z, sh, ñ] V____
                       perf

This rule interacts with another rule which we shall call mutation. Mutation applies to the final consonants of verb stems when these stems precede the perfective suffix; in particular, mutation (i) converts stem-final anterior voiceless stops to *s* and converts *k* to *sh*, (ii) changes stem-final voiced stops to *z* (but only if a nasal immediately precedes the voiced stop), and (iii) shifts stem-final *ɬ* to *z*.

(3)

perfective	infinitive	gloss
ɬis-iɬ-e	ku-ɬip-a	'pay'
kus-iɬ-e	x-kuṭ-a	'fold'
ɬo:s-eɬ-e	ku-ɬo:t-a	'dream'
shi:sh-iɬ-e	x-shi:k-a	'seize'
ɬo:nz-eɬ-e	ku-ɬo:mb-a	'beg'
pe:nz-eɬ-e	x-pe:nḍ-a	'like'
shi:nz-iɬ-e	x-shi:nd-a	'win'
fu:nz-iɬ-e	x-fu:ŋg-a	'close'
mo:z-eɬ-e	ku-mo:ɬ-a	'shave'

As was noted above, mutation applies only before the perfective suffix. It does not apply before the so-called "applied" (or prepositional) suffix -iɬ-, which is phonologically identical to the perfective suffix (except that it does not have any surface allomorphs displaying a long vowel, whereas the perfective suffix does—cf., reb-e:ɬ-e 'he stopped' versus ku-re:b-eɬ-a 'to stop for'). Thus we find ku-gi:ṭ-iɬ-a 'to pull with', not *ku-gi:s-iɬ-a.

Comparison of a perfective form like bus-i:z-e 'he kissed' from (1) with one like kus-iɬ-e 'he folded' from (2) reveals that only stems ending in s, z, sh, and ñ in the UR trigger the ɬ-to-z rule. Stems that terminate in one of these consonants as a result of mutation do not. The question now arises as to how these data are to be described in an explicit theory of phonology. One logically possible description would proceed as follows. The rule of mutation states that stem-final p, ṭ, and t mutate to s preceding the perfective suffix; stem-final k mutates to sh in the same environment; stem-final voiced stops mutate to z, but only when a nasal precedes; and stem-final ɬ mutates to z. The rule of ɬ-to-z would be formulated as in (4).

(4)   ɬ of the perfect suffix changes to z following a stem whose basic phonological representation ends in s, z, sh, or ñ.

(4) says that in order to determine whether the ɬ-to-z rule is applicable, one simply examines the underlying representation of the stem. It would apply to a structure like /bus-i:ɬ-e/, changing it to bus-i:z-e 'he kissed', since the UR of the stem is /bus/, with a final s. Rule (4) would not apply to kus-iɬ-e 'he folded', since the UR /kuṭ/ does not end in one of the consonants that triggers the ɬ-to-z rule. Note that according to this sort of analysis the relative order of application of mutation and ɬ-to-z is immaterial. What determines the applicability of (4) is the underlying structure of the verb stem. Mutation assigns underlying /kuṭ/ the surface shape /kus/ when it occurs before the perfect suffix, but doing so does not alter the fact that the UR of the stem ends in /ṭ/.

The localist assumption does not permit the preceding account of the Chi-Mwi:ni data. Rule (4) violates the localist assumption because it says: change the ɬ of the perfect suffix to z if the preceding stem ends in s, z, sh, or ñ in the underlying structure. The last four words are the crucial ones. Rule (4) applies to a structure not on the basis of phonological and/or morphological properties of the structure that is the input to the rule, but rather on the basis of a phonological property of the UR of the input structure. The localist assumption requires that the SD of a rule refer only to properties present in the input structure itself.

If we adopt the localist assumption, we are led to formulate the rule as in (2): change the *l* of the perfect suffix to *z* when preceded by a stem ending in *s*, *z*, *sh*, or *ñ*. But in order to prevent this rule from incorrectly applying to /kus-il-e/, yielding **kus-iz-e*, we must find a way to guarantee that the input structures to the l-to-z rule are the structures that exist prior to mutation. Structures on which mutation has operated must be excluded as inputs to the l-to-z rule. It is, of course, the device of rule ordering that has been relied on in such cases. One would order *l*-to-*z* before mutation. The derivation of *bus-i:z-e* 'he kissed' as opposed to *kus-il-e* 'he folded' would then be as in (5).

(5)

/bus-i:l-e/	/kuṭ-i:l-e/	
bus-i:z-e	inapplicable	*l*-to-*z*
inapplicable	*kus-i:l-e*	mutation
inapplicable	*kus-il-e*	other rules

By applying *l*-to-*z* before mutation, the former rule will apply only in examples where the stem ends in underlying *s*, *z*, *sh*, or *ñ*. The *s*, *z*, and *sh* sounds that arise from mutation do not yet exist and cannot therefore trigger the *l*-to-*z* rule. As a consequence the latter rule will not apply in the derivation of *kus-il-e* even though this form, on the surface, satisfies its structural description.

Notice that this use of rule ordering (which represents one very important use of the device, but is not by any means the only use to which rule ordering has been put) seeks to distinguish those instances of *s*, *z*, *sh*, and *ñ* that are underlying from those that are the result of mutation. This distinction is absolutely crucial to the correct application of the *l*-to-*z* rule, which is triggered only by underlying *s*, *z*, *sh*, and *ñ*, not by phonetically identical consonants that are the result of mutation. The origin of a sound—that is, whether the sound is part of the underlying structure or derived by a particular rule—is clearly pertinent to the applicability of a given rule to a given structure. The device of rule ordering is one way of allowing the derivational history of a sound to be taken into account. Given the localist assumption, the rule ordering approach to describing the role of derivational history in limiting the applicability of rules seems fairly attractive. But what if the localist assumption is abandoned?

By abandoning the localist assumption we mean relinquishing the restriction that a SD must refer only to properties contained in the input structure itself. We do not necessarily mean that there would be *no* restrictions on what a SD may refer to. Rather, we wish to consider the possibility of relaxing the localist assumption to permit reference specifically to certain additional kinds of information. Consider first of all the possibility that a rule might be formulated so that it applies to a given structure just in case the UR of that structure satisfies certain conditions. In doing this, we would then permit the formulation of *ɬ*-to-*z* in Chi-Mwi:ni given in (4). Recall that given this formulation, *ɬ*-to-*z* will (correctly) fail to apply to a representation such as /kus-iɬ-e/ since the stem preceding the perfect suffix does not end in an underlying *s*, *z*, *sh*, or *ñ*. Consequently, there is no need to prevent this representation from being an input to *ɬ*-to-*z*. And if there is no need to prevent this, then there is no need to require that *ɬ*-to-*z* be applied before mutation. The formulation of *ɬ*-to-*z* in (4) thus renders a rule ordering statement superfluous.

If a SD is permitted to make reference to the UR as well as to the input structure, then many cases where rule ordering is purportedly required would no longer constitute evidence for such a device. Recall, for example, the Lardil facts discussed in Chapter 1. There it was pointed out that a rule is required in Lardil that lowers word-final high vowels. In particular, /u/ is lowered to /a/ and /i/ is lowered to /e/. Examples such as those in (b) provide support for this rule.

(6)

uninflected	nonfuture	future	gloss
ŋuka	ŋuku-n	ŋuku-r̪	'water'
kaṭa	kaṭu-n	kaṭu-r	'child (of a woman)'
muṇa	muṇu-n	muṇu-r	'elbow'
kela	kela-n	kela-r	'beach'
pape	papi-n	papi-wur̪	'father's mother'
ŋiṇe	ŋiṇi-n	ŋiṇi-wur	'skin'
tjimpe	tjimpi-n	tjimpi-wur̪	'tail'

In the inflected forms of the above nouns the final vowel preserves its underlying shape, but in the uninflected form where the final vowel of the noun stem occurs in word-final position, lowering occurs. Thus underlying /kaṭu/ is retained in *kaṭu-n*, but has its final vowel lowered in *kaṭa*. Compare /kela/ 'beach', which ends in an underlying /a/, retaining this vowel in both the uninflected and the inflected forms as well.

There are, however, numerous apparent counterexamples to the rule of lowering.

(7)

puṭu	puṭuka-n	puṭuka-r	'short'
ṭipiṭi	ṭipiṭipi-n	ṭipiṭipi-wur	'rock-cod sp.'
tulnhu	tulnhuka-n	tulnhuka-r̪	'month fish'
murkuni	murkunima-n	murkunima-r̪	'nullah'
thapu	thaputji-n	thaputji-wur	'older brother'

All of the uninflected forms in (7) end in a final high vowel—apparently in violation of the rule that lowers word-final high vowels. It will be noted, however, that the final vowel in the uninflected form is *not* an underlying stem-final vowel. In Chapter 1 we indicated that the inflected form reveals the UR of Lardil noun stems, because various rules of vowel and consonant deletion shorten the noun stem when not protected by a suffix. Consequently, /puṭuka/

is the UR of the stem meaning 'short'; in its uninflected form this stem undergoes rules that delete its final vowel and also its final consonant; /puṭuka/ is shortened to *puṭu*. Since the final vowel of *puṭu* is not subject to the rule of lowering, within a rule ordering framework it would be necessary to order lowering before the rule that generates the shortened form /puṭu/. This ordering is required in order to bar lowering from having /puṭu/ as an input. If /puṭu/ were an input to lowering, the incorrect **puṭa* would be derived.

If, however, rules can make reference to underlying structure as well as to the input structure itself, then lowering could be formulated as in (8).

(8)   *Lower a vowel that occurs in word-final position if that vowel is stem-final in the underlying structure.*

Given this formulation, (8) will not apply to a structure /puṭu/, from underlying /puṭuka/, since in UR /u/ is not stem-final. Given (8), there would be no need to order lowering with respect to any of the rules that derive *puṭu* from /puṭuka/. No ordering is required because it is no longer necessary to bar /puṭu/ from being an input to lowering. Even if /puṭu/ is an input to (8), that rule will not affect /puṭu/ in any way, since this structure does not end in a vowel that is stem-final in the UR.

Let us refer to rules whose SD refers to some level of structure besides the input structure itself as "global rules." The type of global rule that we are presently considering is one where the other level of structure mentioned is the UR itself. So far we have considered two examples where by permitting global rules an ordering statement would be rendered superfluous. In both of these cases the localist assumption would require a rule ordering statement. Furthermore, in both cases the reason that the localist assumption would require an ordering statement is exactly the same: It would be necessary to exclude certain structures as inputs to a particular rule. If the structures were not excluded, they would incorrectly undergo the rule. The ordering involved here is, of course, just what we referred to earlier as a counterfeeding order of application. What we have seen, then, is that while a counterfeeding rule ordering is one means of describing situations such as those discussed above in Chi-Mwi:ni and Lardil, global rules offer an alternative.

The same thing is true for counterbleeding interactions. Recall from Chapter 3 the rule of nasal-cluster lengthening in Ki-Rundi which lengthens a vowel before a nasal plus consonant cluster. This rule was motivated in part by the behavior of the first person object prefix /-N-/, which, when prefixed to a consonant-initial root, assimilates in point of articulation and also invokes a lengthening of the preceding vowel, as seen in (9).

(9)   *ku-ror-a*   'to look at'   *n-tabáar-e*   'that I help'
       ku-ba-ror-a   'to look at them'   *ba-tabáar-e*   'that they help'
       kuu-n-dor-a   'to look at me'   *baa-n-tabáar-e*   'that they help me'

We have seen that the first person object marker is a nasal homorganic with a following consonant. If the following consonant is itself a nasal, the result is not a geminate nasal but simply a single nasal of the same quality as the stem-initial consonant. Consider, for example, the verb roots *meñ-* 'know' and *ñag-* 'rob'.

(10)   *ku-meñ-a*   'to know'   *ku-ñag-a*   'to rob'
        ku-ba-meñ-a   'to know them'   *ku-ba-ñag-a*   'to rob them'
        kuu-meñ-a   'to know me'   *kuu-ñag-a*   'to rob me'

From these examples we see that the first person object prefix has no overt realization before a stem beginning with a nasal consonant. This fact can be attributed to the nasal assimilation rule and a rule of degemination. Note that in forms such as *kuu-meñ-a* and *kuu-ñag-a* the infinitive prefix occurs with a lengthened vowel in contrast to *ku-meñ-a* and *ku-ñag-a*. This can be attributed to nasal-cluster lengthening (NCL), even though on the surface there is no nasal cluster following the vowel of the prefix. Within a rule-ordering framework this phenomenon would be described by ordering NCL before degemination. The derivation of *kuu-meñ-a* would then be as in (11).

(11)   /ku-N-meñ-a/
                kuu-N-meñ-a   nasal cluster lengthening
                kuu-m-meñ-a   nasal assimilation
                kuu-meñ-a   degemination

(The relative ordering of NCL and nasal assimilation in this derivation is not critical. Since the precise nature of the UR of the first person prefix is not relevant to the present discussion, we have simply represented it by the symbol N-that is, a nasal consonant.)

The ordering of NCL before degemination is motivated by the need to guarantee that the input to NCL will be the structure that exists prior to degemination. For if the input to NCL were the structure resulting from degemination, then NCL would incorrectly fail to apply. In other words the function of rule ordering in this case is to guarantee that a structure that meets the conditions for a rule does in fact get a chance to act as input to the rule. (Recall that in the earlier Chi-Mwi:ni and Lardil examples the function of rule ordering was to prevent a structure that met the conditions for a rule from actually being an input to that rule.)

It is clear that the reason NCL applies in the derivation of *kuu-meñ-a* 'to know me', but not in the derivation of *ku-meñ-a* 'to know', is that in the derivational history of the former, the infinitive prefix /ku/ is followed by a cluster of nasal plus consonant, whereas in the derivational history of the latter form, no such cluster exists. The localist assumption requires that this fact concerning the derivational history of *kuu-meñ-a* be overt in the input to NCL: That is, the nasal cluster must actually be present in the input itself, thus necessitating ordering NCL before degemination. If global rules are permitted, however, the following formulation of NCL will suffice (without any need for a rule ordering statement).

(12)   *Lengthen a vowel if in UR that vowel occurs in the environment_____NC.*

Given a formulation such as (12), NCL will apply correctly to either the structure /ku-N-meñ-a/ (the structure prior to the application of degemination) or to the structure /ku-meñ-a/ (the representation resulting from the application of degemination); for the vowel in the infinitive /ku/ is underlyingly in the environment ____NC. As long as it is this information that is crucial to whether or not NCL applies, it is immaterial whether the actual input to NCL is /ku-N-meñ-a/ or /ku-meñ-a/. According to the global-rule approach information about the UR of a given form is available in determining whether that form is subject to a given rule. Thus, a rule R_i (such as NCL) does not have to be crucially ordered to apply before some rule R_j merely because R_j destroys the conditions that trigger R_i's application.

Another example parallel to Rundi is provided by the rules of degemination and *i*-epenthesis in Washo (discussed earlier in Chapter 4). Recall that in Washo the vowel *i* is inserted between two consonants followed by a third. Within a rule-ordering framework it is necessary to apply *i*-epenthesis before degemination in order to account for an item like *ʔlišilegi* from underlying /ʔl-išl-leg-i/. This ordering is justified on the grounds that if degemination were applied first, it would reduce the sequence . . .*šl-l*. . . to . . .*šl*. . . and thus eliminate the three-consonant cluster that is required for the application of *i*-epenthesis. To prevent this bleeding of *i*-epenthesis by degemination the former must be applied before the latter (in a counterbleeding order of application). Assuming global conditions, however, it would be possible to account for these data without recourse to an ordering statement. All that is required is that *i*-epenthesis be formulated as below.

(13)   *Insert i between two successive consonants if in underlying structure these consonants were the initial part of a three-consonant cluster.*

i-epenthesis will then apply correctly whether it has the underlying structure /ʔl-išl-leg-i/ as input or the structure resulting from degemination, /ʔl-iš-leg-i/. It will apply to /ʔl-iš-leg-i/, since this form contains two successive consonants that in the UR were part of a three-consonant cluster. (We have arbitrarily assumed the final *l* of /išl/ 'give' to be the one deleted by degemination; although we have no justification for doing so, the problem of deciding which consonant is deleted by degemination seems to us to be a separate question that bears on the details of the global-rule description, but is irrelevant to the basic point.) Global conditions will in this case provide an alternative to a counterbleeding order as a means of characterizing the fact that a phonological rule may apply in the derivation of a given form on the basis of properties that the form in question contained at some remote (in the present examples, underlying) level of representation, but not phonetically.

We have now presented two examples each of counterfeeding and counterbleeding orders of application. In all these examples global conditions provide an alternative to rule ordering as a means for describing the data. Both counterfeeding and counterbleeding orders lead to opacity, and have been characterized as representing a marked interaction of rules (from the phonetic point of view); global conditions—which restrict a rule's application not on the basis of a form's superficial structure, but rather on the basis of the deeper structure from which the superficial structure derives represent (from a phonetic point of view) a relatively unnatural limitation. In a sense, global conditions make explicit what is implicit in the counterfeeding and counterbleeding orders of application: These orders are marked because more remote rather than more superficial levels of structure are determining whether a rule applies or not. Recall that within an ordering framework a shift from a counterfeeding to a feeding order of application is interpreted as a natural change, since it represents a shift into an order of rules that minimizes opacity. For example, if in Mwera (Chapter 4) forms like *ŋguya* from /N-kuya/ were to ultimately have the optional pronunciation *ŋuya*, just as *ŋgomo* from /N-gomo/ has the optional pronunciation *ŋomo*, one would say according to rule ordering that the ordering of cluster simplification and voicing has changed into an unmarked, feeding order of application. In a global-rule framework, however, one would say that cluster simplification has lost its global conditions. That is, the rule of cluster simplification operative in Mwera would have the following form in a global-rule framework: An underlying voiced consonant deletes optionally after a homorganic nasal. This rule would not affect *ŋguya*, since the /g/ here is an underlying voiceless consonant; *ŋgomo* would be optionally changed to *ŋomo*, since the /g/ here is voiced in its underlying form. Now, if in Mwera's future history *ŋguya* came to be pronounced optionally as *ŋuya*, we would simply say that the rule of cluster simplification simplified: It would no longer require that the consonant that deletes be voiced in the underlying structure. All that would be required would be that the postnasal consonant be voiced. The loss of a global condition represents a natural change (from the phonetic point of view), since it is a change in the direction of a rule that is determined more by the superficial (phonetic) form of an utterance than its deeper (morphophonemic) form.

In summary, we suggested at the beginning of this chapter that rules (by convention) apply in a sequence that minimizes opacity. To account for opaque situations—for example, the fact that an epenthetic *i* occurs in the Washo form *ʔl-iši-leg-i* or that *ŋguya* in Mwera does not have an alternative pronunciation **ŋuya*—we could conceivably invoke a language-specific ordering statement, which would override the general universal convention for applying rules. But an alternative is available, if we abandon the localist assumption: placing a global condition on the *i*-epenthesis rule in Washo and the cluster-simplification rule in Mwera. Given that we have two alternative descriptions of these opaque situations, the question naturally must be asked: Is there a basis for preferring one solution over the other?

Many linguists have expressed a preference for rule ordering over the global-condition solution on the grounds that the latter is an unnecessarily more powerful device than the former. By "more powerful," what is generally meant is that the global-condition approach permits certain general principles or rules to be formulated that are not possible within a rule-ordering approach and that are not in fact really possible phonological rules. In other words the argument is that although in many cases a global condition may be equivalent to a rule-ordering statement, the two descriptive devices are not in fact equivalent; there are principles formalizable within a global-rule framework that are not formalizable within a rule-ordering framework; furthermore, these principles are not linguistically possible generalizations.

This excessive power argument is somewhat overvalued, in our opinion. If one examines any descriptive device currently in use in generative phonology, one will immediately observe that it is too powerful in the sense that it permits the formulation of principles that may in fact be impossible rules of grammar. For example, permitting rules to alter the feature values of a segment in a particular phonological environment permits such "crazy" rules as p $\longrightarrow$ l/____VCV. The problem of distinguishing between possible and impossible rules is not just a formal problem, but also a problem of the phonetic, morphological, and other functions of the rules. If a particular descriptive device allows an appropriate account of the data (in the sense that it makes explicit the essential nature of the phenomena being described) that is not otherwise available, that device must be permitted even though it has excessive power. While formal limitations should certainly be actively sought, functional constraints on rules are also a key area of study.

Global conditions on rules are doubtless excessively powerful. But the major question is whether they provide appropriate descriptions of linguistic data that are not possible within the rule-ordering framework. Some examples will help to illustrate some differences in the relative power of global rules and rule-ordering statements. Let us begin with an hypothetical example.

Suppose a language has a rule that raises word-final mid-vowels *e* and *o* to *i* and *u*, respectively. Furthermore, suppose that if these high vowels are preceded by a dental stop, that stop is affricated. For example, a root such as /lute/ would be unchanged if followed by a suffix, but in final position it would appear as *luci*. Similarly, /kado/ would be retained in unaltered form before a suffix, but would be pronounced *kadzu* in final position. One description of such data would be to posit the two rules of raising and affrication.

(14)   [e, o] $\longrightarrow$ [i, u]/____ #   [t, d] $\longrightarrow$ [c, dz]/____[i, u]

Affrication would be ordered after raising. But now suppose that there are underlying morphemes like /kiti/ and /padu/ that are unaffected by affrication. Within a rule-ordering approach there is no way to limit affrication so as to apply to a *t* or *d* followed by an *i* or *u* that has arisen by rule and is not underlying. To prevent affrication from affecting underlying /kiti/ and /padu/ it would be necessary to treat these items as exceptions to affrication. But if all morphemes containing underlying sequences of a dental stop and a high vowel fail to undergo affrication, it would be difficult to accept that they are simply exceptions. Some regularity would appear to be present.

If global conditions are allowed, this situation could be described in one of two ways. If a "positive" condition were employed, the rule might take the form of (15a).

(15a)   *A dental stop becomes an affricate before a high vowel, provided this vowel is an underlying nonhigh vowel.*

Using a "negative" condition, the rule would look like (15b).

(15b)   *A dental stop becomes an affricate before a high vowel, provided this vowel is not an underlying high vowel.*

Given either of these versions of affrication, the rule will fail to apply to /kiti/ and /padu/: (15a) will not apply to these forms, since the high vowel following the dental stop is not an underlying nonhigh vowel; (15b) will not apply because the high vowel following the dental stop is high in the underlying structure, and thus violates the negative condition. Affrication will apply, however, to /luti/ (from /lute/) and /kadu/ (from /kado/), deriving *luci* and *kadzu*, respectively. Rule (15a) would apply to these structures, since the high vowel following the dental stop is nonhigh in the UR. (15b) would apply, since the high vowels in question are not underlying, and thus do not violate the negative condition.

This hypothetical example shows that there are logically possible regularities that are readily describable by means of global conditions, though they are not appropriately describable in a rule-ordering framework. (The rule-ordering framework would require *kiti* and *padu* to be exceptions, but since all underlying high vowels behave in this fashion, it seems inappropriate to treat them as exceptions.) The next question is whether such data occur in natural languages. In recent years a number of purported examples have been presented. We begin with an example from Chi-Mwi:ni.

In Chapter 2 we provided ample justification for a rule in Chi-Mwi:ni that shortened a long vowel followed by another long vowel in the same phrase. However, there are certain complications that we can now take into consideration. First, two successive long vowels occur in many loanwords: *la:lu:shi* 'a bribe', *fa:nu:si* 'lamp', *ba:ko:ra* 'walking stick', *ka:ba:ṭi* 'cupboard'. One might claim that these words are simply exceptions to prelength shortening (PLS). But there are grounds for doubting this. First, there is no tendency to nativize such words by eliminating the offending occurrence of successive long vowels. Furthermore, PLS does affect these words in such cases as the following, where another rule has lengthened the final vowel: *kabaṭi:-ni* 'in the cupboard', *fanusi:-ni* 'in the lamp', *bakora:nde* 'a long walking stick'. If forms like *la:lu:shi* are not exceptions, one might propose to account for them by revising PLS so that it applies just across morpheme boundaries and not within a morpheme. Since there is no morpheme break between the successive long vowels in *la:lu:shi*, this revised form of PLS will not apply. But this reformulation will not account for forms like *mi-ṭana:-ni* 'in the rooms' from /mi-ṭa:na-ni/ (cf. *mi-ṭa:na* 'rooms'). When the rule lengthening a vowel before the locative suffix /-ni/ is applied, two successive long vowels within a single morpheme arise (/mi-ṭa:na:-ni/), the first of which must be shortened by PLS. Thus, PLS does apply within a morpheme, but in such cases the second long vowel is derived by a rule. It is not an underlying long vowel. This suggests that PLS must be formulated in global fashion, as in (16).

(16)   V: ⟶ [−long]/___XV:

   Condition: (positive version) One of the vowels is short in UR
                 (negative version) The vowels may not both be long in UR

This formulation is not correct as it stands, however, for PLS does apply to two underlying long vowels, provided they belong to different morphemes. Thus, when a root such as /so:m/ 'read' is followed by the passive suffix /o:w/, PLS affects the root vowel: *x-som-o:w-a* 'to be read by'. The global condition (either version) in (16) must be modified by adding the condition: "if the two vowels are in the same morpheme."

In Kiparsky (1973) it is suggested that the two cases where PLS does apply— across morpheme boundaries and within morphemes when the conditions for the rule's application arise as a consequence of phonological rules—represent a typical conjunction, and that both can be labeled as derived environments. In fact, he claims that for rules of a certain type (which he refers to as nonauto- matic neutralization rules), their application is predictably restricted to derived contexts; furthermore, only such rules are restricted to derived contexts. We shall return to this claim in some detail, but first let us sketch briefly an addi- tional putative example where underlying elements or sequences of elements do not undergo the same rules as derived ones do.

Kiparsky (1973) has argued that Finnish possesses a rule changing *t* to *s* before *i*, which must be limited to derived contexts. This rule applies across morpheme boundaries, as evidenced by the fact that the past tense suffix /-i/ triggers the change of a final /t/ of a preceding verb stem: *halut-a* 'want', *halus-i* 'wanted'. On the other hand, there are many examples of *ti* sequences contained entirely within morphemes: *tila* 'room', *äiti* 'mother', *neiti* 'Miss'. It might appear that the difference between a form like *halus-i* (from /halut-i/), where the *t*-to-*s* rule applies, and a form like *äiti*, where it does not, could be accounted for by limiting the rule to apply only across morpheme boundaries. But this limitation will not explain why the rule applies in forms like the following.

(17)

nominative singular	essive singular	gloss
vesi	vete-nä	'water'
käsi	käte-nä	'hand'
rupi	rupe-na	'scab'
joki	joke-na	'river'
äiti	äiti-nä	'mother'

The data in (17) indicate that Finnish has a rule that raises /e/ to /i/ in final position. Before an /i/ derived from /e/, a preceding /t/ will change to /s/, even though the /ti/ sequence is contained wholly within a morpheme. A form like *käsi* must therefore receive a derivation such as the following.

(18)   /#käte#/
                   käti   raising
                   käsi   *t*-to-*s*

It is clear that in order for the *t*-to-*s* rule to apply in *käsi*, but be prevented from applying to a form like *äiti*, the SD of the rule must be stated in such a way that the rule applies only in derived contexts.

   If examples such as these do occur in natural languages, the localist assumption is—to some extent—incorrect. To prevent rules like prelength shortening in Chi-Mwi:ni and *t*-to-*s* in Finnish from incorrectly applying to nonderived structures, some means of distinguishing such sequences from phonetically identical derived structures must be found. Rule ordering is of no avail. Some form of a global condition is required. The main question is whether examples such as these require that language-specific structural descriptions be global, or if the global conditions required in examples such as the preceding can be predicted by a general principle. Kiparsky (1973) suggests that there is a general principle. His proposal makes use of two critical terms: NEUTRALIZATION RULE and AUTOMATIC RULE. Kiparsky defines these terms as follows.

(19) *Suppose we have a phonological process P:*
     (P) A ⟶ B/XC____DY
     where C, D represent a (phonological and/or morphological) context, and X, Y are arbitrary strings. Then:

     (a)—*P is **nonautomatic** iff there are strings of the form CAD in the immediate output of P*
        —*otherwise P is **automatic**,*

     (b)—*P is neutralizing iff there are strings of the form CBD in the immediate input of P*
        —*otherwise P is nonneutralizing.* (p. 68)

Roughly speaking, a rule will be nonautomatic if there are input structures that satisfy the phonological and/or morphological conditions of the rule, but nevertheless fail to undergo the rule; a rule will be neutralizing if it creates structures identical to structures that existed prior to the rule's application.

   Kiparsky claims that it is precisely the rules that are both nonautomatic and neutralizing that are limited to derived environments, and that no other type of rule can be so limited. This claim is based, first of all, on the fact that all of the rules that Kiparsky had observed to be limited to derived contexts were in fact nonautomatic neutralization rules. Furthermore, evidence is available that other types of rules must be allowed to apply in nonderived environments; consequently, such rules cannot be restricted to apply only in derived environments.

Let us consider each type of rule. First, automatic nonneutralization rules are exceptionless phonetic rules that supply nondistinctive feature values—for example, the rule lengthening a vowel before a voiced consonant in English. It is obvious that rules of this sort must be allowed to apply in nonderived contexts. Otherwise, the rule could not affect such words as *cab*, *bid*, and *bed*, where the sequence of vowel plus voiced consonant is part of the UR of a single morpheme and thus constitutes a nonderived environment. Automatic nonneutralization rules must be allowed to apply freely to derived and nonderived environments alike.

Consider next automatic-neutralization rules. They merge morphophonemic contrasts, but they are characterized by being totally general rules that apply without exception. Kiparsky concludes that such rules must be permitted to apply in nonderived environments if various examples of abstract analyses, such as that given for Yawelmani in Chapter 1, are to be permitted. Recall that in Yawelmani a rule was postulated that lowers a long high vowel in all contexts. This rule neutralizes the contrast between underlying /u:/ and /o:/ (the contrast is not, of course, totally lost, since it is reflected in different patterns of vowel harmony). This rule is automatic, since there are no exceptions to it. If the analysis presented in Chapter 1 is correct, then this automatic neutralization rule must be applied in nonderived environments.

It is not, however, only abstract analyses that lead to the conclusion that automatic neutralization rules must apply in nonderived as well as derived contexts. Klamath provides a typical example. Recall from Chapter 3 the rule neutralizing the opposition between aspirated/unaspirated/glottalized stop consonants before obstruents and all glottalized consonants. A voiceless, unaspirated nonglottalized consonant, which we represent by a capital letter, appears in these positions: *skod-a* 'puts on a blanket', but *skoᴛ-bli* 'puts a blanket back on'; *nqot'-o-* 'scorches', but *nqoᴛ-di:l-a* 'scorches underneath'. Klamath also has a rule vocalizing the glides *y* and *w* (plain or glottalized) to *i:* and *o:*, respectively, between consonants or in final postconsonantal position: *čonw-a* 'vomits', *čono:-n'apg-a* 'feels like vomiting'; *m'olw'-a* 'is ready', *m'olo:-wapk* 'will be ready'; *qbat'y-a* 'wraps the legs around', *qbat'i:-wapk* 'will wrap the legs around'; *gego:* 'tries', *gegw-at* 'pl. try!'. Given the existence of these two rules, an example like *mboᴛy'-a* 'wrinkles', but *mbodi:-tk* 'wrinkled up' has a perfectly straightforward explanation if the UR of the root is /mbody'/. The correct derivations are obtained if vocalization is allowed to bleed the neutralization rule in *mbodi:-tk*; in the case of *mboᴛy'-a* vocalization is inapplicable, and neutralization is able to apply.

(20)   /mbody'-tk   /mbody'-a/
        mbodi:-tk   inapplicable   vocalization
        inapplicable   *mboᴛy'-a*   neutralization

This explanation of the forms requires, however, that neutralization apply to an underlying morpheme-internal sequence . . . dy' . . . .

Thus, if this explanation of the forms is appropriate, at least some neutralization rules must be allowed to apply in nonderived contexts. Since the Klamath neutralization rule is apparently an automatic rule (in the published data a couple of forms may be found violating the rule, but these may be typographical errors), one could, following Kiparsky, assume that it is only automatic neutralization rules that can apply to nonderived contexts. Nonautomatic neutralization rules could still be excluded from applying in nonderived contexts.

Nonautomatic nonneutralization rules do not merge a phonological opposition and do not apply exceptionlessly. Chi-Mwi:ni provides an example of this sort. There is no contrast in Chi-Mwi:ni between aspirated and unaspirated consonants; aspirated consonants occur only following a nasal consonant. Furthermore, it is only voiceless stops that may be aspirated in this environment. Given the limited occurrence of aspirated consonants, it is natural to seek to account for aspiration by a rule that will aspirate a voiceless stop after a nasal consonant. Within morphemes this rule will correctly account for the general fact that in postnasal position only aspirated voiceless stops (and *not* unaspirated voiceless stops) tend to occur. The rule is not without exceptions, however. In particular, there are a number of loanwords that violate the rule: *bonṭa* 'bridge', *sanṭu:ri* 'gramophone', *sṭanṭi:vo* 'badge'. The aspiration rule in Chi-Mwi:ni counts then as a nonautomatic nonneutralization rule. The rule must be applied in nonderived environments, however, in order to account for the voiceless aspirated consonants in examples like *ku-nu:ŋkʰ-a* 'to smell', *x-ku:nṭʰ-a* 'to be in (financial) difficulty', *x-pepe:nṭʰ-a* 'to separate husks from grain', where the nasal and following voiceless stop occur morpheme-internally in underlying structure.

Karok provides another example of this sort. Recall from Chapter 4 that in this language there is no *s/š* contrast—*s* occurs generally, except that it is replaced by *š* when preceded by a front vowel. It seems clear that *s* should be regarded as underlying and that we can postulate a rule of palatalization that palatalizes *s* to *š* under the influence of a preceding front vowel. This rule of palatalization is not a neutralization rule. It is also not automatic, for it fails to apply to certain items (some of them obvious loanwords): *síkspič* 'six bits', *ké:ks* 'cake', *símsi:m* 'knife, metal', *ʔutasinsir* 'he brushed it repeatedly' (Bright 1957, p. 17). Palatalization is thus a nonautomatic nonneutralization rule and must not be restricted to just derived environments, otherwise we would be unable to account for such alternations as *ʔišva:k* 'chin' from /isva:k/, but *mu-sva:k* 'his chin' from /mu-isva:k/. Palatalization applies in a nonderived environment in the case of *ʔišvak*, where the sequence . . . *is* . . . occurs morpheme-internally in underlying structure. In the case of *mu-sva:k* the vowel of the prefix induces the truncation of the stem-initial vowel, and the rule of palatalization is bled.

We have cited some evidence that three types of rules—automatic nonneutralization rules, automatic neutralization rules, and nonautomatic nonneutralization rules—cannot be restricted only to derived contexts. Kiparsky's proposal is that the fourth type—nonautomatic neutralization rules—is limited only to derived contexts. But this claim seems to us dubious. Why should automatic neutralization rules apply in both derived and nonderived contexts, but nonautomatic neutralization rules just in derived contexts? Take the Klamath case again as an example. Suppose that there are one or two items that are exceptions to the rule of neutralization (which eliminates the contrast between aspirated, unaspirated, and glottalized consonants). Why should the existence of such random exceptions have the consequence that an alternation like *mbo*ᴛy'*-a* versus *mbodi꞉-tk* cannot be accounted for in terms of an underlying representation /mbody̓/?

Even if a psychologically plausible answer to the above question is forth-coming, there are other problems with Kiparsky's proposal. In particular, there are examples where it appears that a nonautomatic neutralization rule must be permitted to apply in nonderived contexts. The Yawelmani rules of epenthesis and shortening provide an excellent example. The rule of shortening is clearly a neutralizing one, eliminating the underlying contrast between long and short vowels in the environment preceding a consonant cluster. The rule is a highly productive one in Yawelmani, but it is not fully automatic: There is one suffix with an initial consonant cluster before which a long vowel fails to shorten. Thus, we have *nine꞉-lsa꞉-hin* 'gets to keep still several times', *da'e꞉-lsa-'* 'will bring to life often', *'ope꞉t-sa꞉-nit* 'will be made to get up repeatedly'. (The causative-repetitive suffix *-lsa꞉* has the property of changing the final vowel of a preceding stem to /e꞉/; these examples are taken from Newman, 1944, p. 95.

But if shortening is in fact a nonautomatic neutralization rule, Kiparsky's principle would then predict that it could not affect a nonderived sequence V꞉CC. There is reason to believe, however, that shortening does in fact affect such structures. Recall that in Yawelmani there are roots that exhibit mor-phophonemic alternations of the following sort: *'a꞉mil-hin* 'helps', but *'aml-al* 'might help'. This alternation pattern appears to reflect the effects of epenthesis in the case of *'a꞉mil-hin*, and of shortening in the case of *'aml-al*. To account for this alternation pattern in terms of these independently motivated rules requires assuming that the UR of the verb root is /'a꞉ml/. In the case of *'a꞉mil-hin* the insertion of the epenthetic vowel prevents shortening from ap-plying. But in the case of *'aml-al* there is no epenthetic vowel; consequently shortening applies to the root vowel. If shortening does apply in the derivation of *'aml-al*, it affects a long vowel followed by a consonant cluster where this sequence occurs in the UR of a single morpheme and thus constitutes a non-derived environment. Kiparsky's principle predicts that one should derive **'a꞉ml-al* rather than *'aml-al*, but this is incorrect.

Another example of a nonautomatic neutralization rule applying in a non-derived environment is provided by Byron W. Bender's (1970) analysis of a process of vowel dissimilation in Marshallese. Consider the following alternations.*

---

* The *&* represents a vowel intermediate between /i/ and /e/.

(21)   *w&b*   'chest'   *wibe-n*   'his chest'
         k&l   'technique'   *kile-n*   'his technique'
         b&q   'bladder'   *beqi-n*   'his bladder'
         l&p   'egg'   *lepi-n*   'its egg'
         jeneq 'footprint'   *jeneqa-n*   'his footprint'
         kinej 'wound'   *kineja-n*   'wound'

Bender analyzes the 3rd sg. possessive forms as consisting of a noun root plus an ending *-n*. The final vowel of the noun root is deleted when it occurs word-finally, as in the unpossessed noun forms listed in the left-hand column. In some cases deletion of the final vowel is accompanied by certain morpho-phonemic changes: Thus, /wibe/ becomes /w&b/, and /lepi/ becomes /l&p/. In other cases no morphophonemic variation occurs: Thus, /jeneqa/ simply drops its final vowel, resulting in /jeneq/. (An alternative description would postulate that the final vowel of the root, instead of deleting, metathesizes into the root. The resulting vowel cluster is reduced in various ways. Thus, /wibe/ would become /wieb/ by metathesis and ultimately /w&b/ by the vowel-cluster rules. Whether a deletion or a metathesis approach is adopted is immaterial to the present discussion.)

Now consider alternations of the following sort.

(22)   *bar*   'head'   *bera-n*   'his head'
         yat   'name'   *yeta-n*   'his name'
         maj   'eye'   *meja-n*   'his eye'
         dam'   'forehead'   *dem'a-n*   'his forehead'

Bender proposes that this alternation involves a process of vowel dissimilation. In particular, he postulates that the roots involved are /bara/, /yata/, /maja/, and /dam'a/. The addition of *-n* preserves the root-final vowel. But a rule that says (roughly) that /a/ becomes /e/ when followed by /a/ in the next syllable converts /bara/ to /bera/, /yata/ to /yeta/, and so on. In the unpossessed form, however, the rule that deletes the final vowel (or metathesizes it into the root, with a subsequent reduction of the resulting vowel cluster) eliminates the environment for the *a*-dissimilation rule.

If /bera/ rather than /bara/ were assumed to be the root, it would be necessary somehow to convert /bera/ to /bar/. Examples like /jeneq/ from /jeneqa/ would provide some difficulty for such a rule, since one would have expected /jeneqa/ to become */jenaq/. Even if examples like /jeneqa/ could be circumvented, there is additional support for the *a*-dissimilation rule. For example, roots with an initial geminate such as /lliw/ 'angry', /bbej/ 'swell', /m'm'an/ 'good' appear unaltered when prefixed. As a result, we find *yi-lliw* 'I am angry', *ye-bbej* 'he is swelling', *ye-m'm'an* 'he is good'. When these stems occur in an unprefixed form, however, a vowel that is identical with the root vowel is inserted between the initial geminate cluster (in the Eastern dialect of Marshallese), resulting in *liliw*, *bebej*, and (crucially) *m'em'an*. We see that although the vowel insertion rule predicts /m'am'an/, the actual result is *m'em'an*—which is of course the form predicted, provided that we accept the rule of *a*-dissimilation in the language.

Additional evidence is provided by Bender; he notes that the causative prefix generally has the shape /ka/ (*ka-q&y&t* 'catch octopuses') but appears as /ke/ when a stem with /a/ as its first vowel follows (*ke-łapłap* 'exaggerate'). Similarly, the negative prefix is ordinarily /ja/ (*ja-rreğreğ* 'deaf'), but is /je/ if the following stem has /a/ as its initial vowel (*je-wwan* 'lazy').

The rule of *a*-dissimilation that Bender proposes is apparently not automatic, however. There are a few exceptions; for example loadwords from Japanese (*tam'ah* 'light bulb', *kam'ah* 'tea kettle'). *a*-dissimilation is a neutralization rule, since both /a/ and /e/ are underlying elements in the language. Thus, if Bender's analysis is correct, and items like *bera-n* 'his head' derive from /bara-n/, we have another case where a nonautomatic neutralization rule applies in a nonderived environment (since /bara/ itself contains the successive /a/ vowels that trigger *a*-dissimilation).

Examples such as these suggest that Kiparsky's principle may be too strong in that some rules of nonautomatic neutralization apply in nonderived contexts. If so, it is not immediately clear that there is a way to predict which rules will apply only in derived contexts and which will apply in nonderived contexts as well. If no general principle is at work, the structural descriptions of particular rules would have to be permitted to be global in nature.

At this point let us turn to Kiparsky's claim (1973) that only rules of nonautomatic neutralization may be restricted to derived contexts. This claim is ultimately not quite as strong as it appears at first sight; the present theory of generative phonology admits a particular descriptive device that allows numerous putative counterexamples to be avoided. The device in question is the so-called TRANSFORMATIONAL rule, which basically allows two separate structural changes to be carried out on two separate phonological elements by a single phonological rule. Particularly relevant to the present discussion is that the rule permits one of the structural changes to occur just in case the other does. A hypothetical example illustrates how the transformational rule approach offers a way to limit a phonological rule to a derived context, excluding its application to a nonderived environment.

Suppose that a language has a rule that inserts the vowel /i/ in the environment C___C#, and that if /u/ precedes, that /u/ changes to /i/. Suppose, however, that an underlying sequence *uCi* remains unchanged. Although one means of describing this phenomenon would be to limit the /u/-to-/i/ rule to derived contexts, another alternative is a transformational rule that simultaneously inserts /i/ and changes a preceding /u/ to /i/. The rule would take the approximate form of (23).

(23) $\langle u \rangle$ C   C   #
                $\langle 1 \rangle$ 2   3   4 $\longrightarrow$ $\langle i \rangle$ 2i34

Clearly, then, transformational rules provide considerable possibilities for restricting the domain of phonological rules.

Transformational rules are of course fairly well motivated as devices for describing a process like metathesis or perhaps vowel contraction and other cases of fusion of separate phonological elements. On the other hand, it is not so clear that transformational rules provide the best way of describing a phenomenon of the type described above. The epenthesis of a vowel to break up a word-final consonant cluster is a natural phonological process. Vowel assimilation of the sort where /u/ shifts to /i/ when followed by /i/ is also a natural process. They are, however, two separate processes. A transformational approach melds them into a single rule. But the motivation for doing so lies in the fact that it is the /i/ that results from epenthesis, and not an underlying /i/, that triggers the /u/-to-/i/ rule. This is of course just the problem of guaranteeing that only structures of a certain derivational origin are inputs to a particular rule. The problem is, then, the one that originally led to rule ordering and that we are suggesting here might lead to global conditions on rules.

Let us now turn to a case where an automatic neutralization rule might be argued to be restricted to derived contexts, but which could be described in transformational terms also. In the morphophonemic alternations involved in the construction of the perfective verbal form in Chi-Mwi:ni two principal rules were adduced: the *l*-to-*z* rule, which changes the *l* of the perfect suffix to *z* after stems ending in underlying *s*, *z*, *sh*, or *ñ*, and mutation, which effects a variety of changes in a stem-final consonant in position before the perfect suffix. The vowel of the perfect suffix is long under certain conditions, short under others. The suffix vowel is long if preceded by one of the stem-final consonants that does not undergo mutation.

(24)   *łum-i:ł-e*   'he bit'   (cf., *ku-łum-a*)
          reb-e:ł-e   'he stopped'   (cf., *ku-re:b-a*)
          xof-e:ł-e   'he feared'   (cf., *xo:f-a*)
          kun-i:ł-e   'he scratched'   (cf., *x-kun-a*)
          bus-i:z-e   'he kissed'   (cf., *ku-bu:s-a*)
          haḍ-i:ł-e   'he said'   (cf., *ku-haḍ-a*)
          ṭez-e:z-e   'he played'   (cf., *x-ṭez-a*)
          i-jaj-i:ł-e   'it itched'   (cf., *ku-ja:j-a*)
          i-vuy-i:ł-e   'it trickled'   (cf., *ku-vu:y-a*)
          fañ-i:z-e   'he did'   (cf., *x-fa:ñ-a*)
          rag-i:ł-e   'he was late'   (cf., *ku-ra:g-a*)

Notice that it does not matter whether the vowel of the root is long or short in the underlying structure: The suffixal vowel is long in either case. The fact that an underlying long vowel of a root is shortened before the perfective suffix in these examples can of course be accounted for by pre-length shortening.

The vowel of the perfective suffix is short when it is preceded by a stem-final consonant that has arisen as a result of mutation. The following examples illustrate this point

(25)   *łas-ił-e*   'he swore (an oath)'   (cf., *ku-łap-a*)

          ło:nz-eł-e   'he begged'   (cf., *ku-ło:mb-a*)

          vu:s-ił-e   'he pulled'   (cf., *ku-vu:t-a*)

          pis-ił-e   'he passed'   (cf., *x-pit-a*)

          tu:nz-ił-e   'he picked off (fruit)'   (cf., *x-tu:nd-a*)

          vu:nz-ił-e   'he broke'   (cf., *ku-vu:ṇḍ-a*)

          pish-ił-e   'he cooked'   (cf., *x-pik-a*)

          we:sh-eł-e   'he put'   (cf., *ku-we:k-a*)

          fu:nz-ił-e   'he opened'   (cf., *x-fu:ŋg-a*)

Notice once again that the length of the root vowel is irrelevant in these examples: Whether the root vowel is long or short, the vowel of the perfective suffix remains short.

Let us assume that the vowel of the perfective is an underlying long vowel. It is then necessary to formulate a principle that will shorten this vowel in (25). The principle clearly cannot be: Shorten the vowel of the perfective after stems ending in *s*, *z*, or *sh*, since every stem ending in an underlying *s*, *z*, or *sh* would be an exception to such a principle. One couldn't modify the rule to say: Shorten the vowel of the perfective vowel after a stem ending in *s*, *z*, or *sh*, provided the perfective vowel is followed by *ł*. Such a principle would correctly exclude *bus-i:z-e*, *ṭez-e:z-e*, *ush-i:z-e*, and so on, provided it applied to the output of the *ł*-to-*z* rule (which accounts for the fact that the *ł* of the perfective suffix is changed to *z* in these examples). The revised form of the rule would fail, however, in all those cases where the *ł*-to-*z* rule exceptionally fails to apply—for example, *jasus-i:ł-e* 'he spied', *asis-i:ł-e* 'he founded (an organization)'. In these cases the vowel of the perfective suffix is long even though it occurs after a stem ending in *s*, *z*, or *sh* and followed by *ł*.

We have seen that the vowel of the perfective cannot be shortened on the basis of its being preceded by stem-final *s*, *z*, or *sh*, simply because shortening occurs only after the stem-final *s*, *z*, or *sh* that has originated via mutation. Given this observation, one might attempt to account for the shortening by a rule that would say: Shorten the vowel of the perfective suffix when it follows a stem-final voiceless stop or a stem-final voiced stop (if that stop is preceded by a nasal) or a stem-final *ł*. This rule would of course precede mutation; the latter rule will effect the conversion of all the consonants mentioned above to *s*, *z*, or *sh*. An analysis of this type would attempt to distinguish between *łas-ił-e* 'he swore' and *bus-i:z-e* 'he kissed' on the basis of the difference in their underlying representations: The /s/ in the former case is an underlying voiceless stop, /p/, whereas the /s/ of the latter form is derived from an underlying /s/. Such an analysis fails, however, to make the correct predictions. This can be seen by examining cases where a stem-final voiceless stop, or voiced stop (preceded by a nasal), or *ł* exceptionally fails to undergo mutation. In such cases the vowel of the perfective suffix remains long: *ṭap-i:ł-e* 'he tossed around', *pamb-i:ł-e* 'he decorated', *sajił-i:ł-e* 'he recorded', *onḍ-e:ł-e* 'he tasted'. These data are clear counterexamples to the claim that the vowel of the perfect suffix shortens after a stem-final voiceless stop, or a voiced stop after a nasal, or *ł*. This shortening takes place only when such consonants are in fact shifted to *s*, *z*, or *sh* by mutation.

We have seen that rule ordering cannot characterize the fact that the vowel of the perfective suffix is shortened only after a *s*, *z*, or *sh* arising from mutation and not after an underlying *s*, *z*, or *sh*. This situation could be described globally by shortening the vowel of the perfective suffix following an *s*, *z*, or *sh*, which is not present in underlying structure. (It should be pointed out that this formulation would predict that an *s*, *z*, or *sh* arising from a source other than mutation would also trigger a shortening of the vowel of the perfective suffix; we doubt that this would be an appropriate claim, but there are no other sources of *s*, *z*, or *sh* that can be used to test this prediction. We will return to this point.)

Transformational rules provide an alternative to this global condition by allowing a single rule to be written, which would simultaneously mutate certain stem-final consonants before the perfective suffix and shorten the vowel of the perfective suffix. Such a rule would convert, for example, /łap-i:ł-e/ directly to /łas-ił-e/, rather than going through a two-step process whereby /łap-i:ł-e/ is first changed to /łas-i:ł-e/ by mutation and then to /łas-ił-e/ by the global rule that shortens the vowel of the perfective suffix. The one-step approach, requiring a rule that performs two structural changes simultaneously, does not require a global condition. But it does much of the same work and has much of the same power as a global rule, for it permits one structural change to occur whenever a second structural change also occurs.

The rule that shortens the vowel of the perfective suffix after an *s*, *z*, or *sh* that has arisen from mutation is without exceptions. Since vowel length is contrastive in Chi-Mwi:ni, the rule is a neutralizing one. Thus, we have an automatic neutralization rule that is restricted to just derived contexts (in particular, contexts resulting from mutation). But this would constitute a counterexample to Kiparsky's claim only in the event that the transformational rule approach were not possible (or could be shown to be incorrect).

The global-rule approach and the transformational-rule approach do differ in significant ways. In particular, the transformational approach permits one structural change to be limited to just those cases where another structural change also occurs. It cannot generalize to the case where two or more separate rules trigger a particular additional change. For example, if a rule that had to be treated as separate from mutation also created *s*, *z*, or *sh*, and if the perfective suffix's vowel were also shortened following these occurrences of *s*, *z*, or *sh*, then the transformational rule could not provide an appropriate description of the data. Second, the transformational-rule approach works just in case the two structural changes can be collapsed into a single rule; if this collapsing is not possible, the connection between the two structural changes cannot be stated. Consequently, the transformational approach is (in at least some ways) more restrictive than the global-rule approach—that is, it is unable to describe situations that the global-rule approach is able to describe. The questions that must eventually be answered are: Is the added power of the global-rule approach necessary in any case? Does the global-rule approach provide a more appropriate characterization of the processes involved?

We have already seen that global conditions may be required to account for the limitation of certain rules to nonderived environments. Notice that in cases such as the Finnish example discussed earlier, the t-to-s rule could be collapsed together with the e-raising rule, so that we would have a transformational rule that raised final /e/ to /i/ and simultaneously changed a preceding /t/ to /s/. This transformational rule would not, however, account for the change of /t/ to /s/ before an /i/ in the following morpheme. Thus, the transformational rule would have as a consequence the postulating of two t-to-s rules. Of course, the global-rule approach allows the formulation of a single rule. Insofar as a single rule appears to be involved, the global-rule approach is to be preferred.

Similarly, the transformational approach is of no avail in the case of prelength shortening in Chi-Mwi:ni. It should be pointed out that this rule has no exceptions when applying in derived contexts, and thus represents an automatic neutralization rule. Since it is restricted to derived contexts (as shown earlier), it is a counterexample to Kiparsky's claim that only nonautomatic neutralization rules are restricted to derived environments. Furthermore, it represents a case where a transformational analysis is not possible. There is no *one* rule with which PLS can be combined so as to limit its domain to derived environments. Several lengthening rules are involved in creating the sequences of long vowels that undergo PLS. And, of course, underlying long vowels in separate morphemes undergo the rule. We must have a global condition in this case; transformational rules are of no avail. Examples of this sort, if correct, mean that the choice between global rules and transformational rules cannot be made on the basis of the relative power of the two approaches, since the global power is required in any case. If so, the question boils down to one of appropriateness to the particular data being described. Much work will be required to bring evidence to bear on this particular issue.

We have offered some evidence so far to suggest that neutralization rules (whether nonautomatic or automatic) may be restricted to derived environments, and thus may have global conditions placed on them to effect this limitation to derived environments. The question of whether nonneutralization (phonetic) rules can be restricted to derived contexts will be dealt with only briefly here. First, it is clear that phonetic rules may be so restricted. For example, it is not unusual for a language that has both underlying nasalized vowels as well as vowels that are nasalized next to a nasal consonant to distinguish the two types phonetically: The underlying nasalized vowels are more heavily nasalized than the rule-derived nasalized vowels. The consequence of such examples, with respect to the issue of global rules, is not so clear. It is certainly possible to claim that the rule of vowel nasalization, formulated as (26), introduces the degree of nasality directly, while underlying nasal vowels are assigned their value by a rule like (27), ordered before (26).

(26)   V ⟶ [3 nasal]/in the context   (27)   V   ⟶ [1 nasal]
                     of a nasal   [+nasal]

The global rule approach offers an alternative to this description, since it would allow the rule of nasalization to simply specify a vowel as [+nasal] in the context of a nasal. The phonetic detail would be assinged by a rule of the following form.

(28)   V   ⟶ [1 nasal]   if present in the UR
                      [+nasal]   [3 nasal]   if not present in the UR

This approach has one possible merit: It allows the language-specific aspect of the process of vowel nasalization (the degree of nasality) to be factored from the more universal aspects. But in any case it is clear that by permitting phonological rules to introduce degrees of a phonetic property directly without going through the step of specifying a plus or minus value first, certain phonetic principles can be restricted to the output of a particular rule. Of course, it would not permit a generalization like that implied by (28), where it is claimed that all derived nasalized vowels would have the third degree of nasality. Thus, crucial examples would be ones where, say, more than one phonetic process specifies vowels as nasalized: If all such vowels were [3 nasal] and only underlying nasalized vowels were [1 nasal], the only alternative to the global approach would be to specify as part of the structural change of each vowel-nasalization rule that the resulting vowel is [3 nasal]. We have no relevant examples of this form at the present time, and thus must leave the matter open.

We have spent some time reviewing Kiparsky's claim that global conditions on rules could be predicted. It should be noted that Kiparsky's proposal assumed the availability of rule-ordering statements as a means for describing cases where a given rule does not apply to a particular derived environment. Thus, his proposal that nonautomatic rules apply in derived contexts did not mean that such rules applied in all derived contexts.

Our discussion in this chapter so far has dealt with two broad questions. First, does abandoning the localist assumption permit us to do without rule ordering statements in describing opaque rules? Second, is there any evidence that the localist assumption must be abandoned? We have seen that the answer to the first question is affirmative (at least in the various cases so far discussed). The answer to the second question is doubtless much more controversial. Our view is that there is some evidence to support the view that the localist assumption does not in fact permit appropriate descriptions of linguistic data. Furthermore, we have presented some reasons for doubting the validity of Kiparsky's claim that all deviations from the localist assumption are in fact predictable.

Up to this point we have considered global conditions of only one sort: namely, conditions that make reference to both the input structure and the underlying structure from which that input structure is derived. One could put a fairly heavy constraint on the use of global conditions if rules were permitted to refer to just these two levels of structure. However, a limitation of this sort would render global rules incapable of providing an appropriate description of situations that seem to exist (situations that rule ordering is also able to describe). If global conditions are to be allowed the same power as rule ordering, they cannot be restricted so as to allow reference only to underlying structure and the input structure.

The palatalization of /s/ to /š/ after front vowels in Karok will allow us to make the above point clear. It will be recalled that in Karok there is a rule of truncation that deletes a vowel when another vowel precedes. Truncation must be applied before palatalization, so that a UR like /mu-isva:k/ will be pronounced *mu-sva:k* rather than **mu-šva:k*. Consequently, it cannot be said that palatalization applies to an /s/ preceded by a front vowel in UR. If that were the condition on palatalization, we would get **mu-šva:k*. There is another rule in Karok that optionally elides a short unaccented vowel followed by two consonants in phrase-initial position. Thus, /akva:t/ 'racoon' may be pronounced as /kva:t/ or as /ʔakva:t/ at the beginning of a phrase. (Karok has another rule that inserts a glottal stop at the beginning of a word if the word would otherwise begin with a vowel.) A root with the underlying shape /isC. . ./ has the optional surface form /šC. . ./ in phrase-initial position: Thus, /ispuk/ 'money' appears as /špuk/ or /ʔišpuk/. Let us call the rule that elides the initial vowel in these examples elision. The rule of elision fails to bleed palatalization. In a rule ordering framework elision must be applied after palatalization. In a global-rule approach some condition must be placed on palatalization that will allow it to apply in the derivation of an example like *špuk* on the basis of the fact that prior to elision the sequence . . . *is* . . . occurred. But we have already seen that one cannot formulate the rule as (29).

(29)   s ⟶ š/*if preceded by a front vowel either in the input structure or in underlying structure.*

The formulation in (29) is not possible because it would predict that /mu-isva:k/ would become **mušva:k*.

In order to block palatalization in the derivation of **mušva:k*, but allow it in *mi-pšu:n* (from /mi-apsu:n/) and *škak* (from /iskak/), it would be necessary to formulate the following rule.

(30)   s ⟶ š/*if preceded by a front vowel (in the input structure) or preceded by a phrase-initial front vowel in underlying structure.*

But this formulation requires that we repeat (in part at least) the conditions for elision (phrase-initial position) as part of the environment for palatalization.

This repetition of environments can be avoided if we reformulate the rule as follows.

(31)   s ⟶ š/*if preceded by a front vowel in the input string or if the rule of elision has effected the dropping of a preceding front vowel earlier in the derivation.*

This formulation of the rule specifies that palatalization will be applicable if /s/ is preceded by a front vowel in the input structure itself or if it is the rule of elision that has dropped a front vowel that formerly stood before the /s/. By referring directly to the rule of elision, we do not need to repeat the conditions that trigger elision in the rule of palatalization itself.

Permitting global conditions like (31) gives a rule access, in essence, to each step in the derivation. A global condition of this sort allows global rules to do the kind of things that rule ordering can do. It also allows things that rule ordering cannot do. In particular, it would allow a global rule like (32).

(32)   s ⟶ š/*if preceded by a front vowel in the input structure provided that front vowel is not underlying and has not been derived by rule X (where rule X is, say, an i-epenthesis rule).*

This kind of rule would permit palatalization to be triggered by front vowels created by any phonological rule except rule X, but not by underlying front vowels. Rule ordering could not describe such a situation, since rule ordering could not prevent underlying front vowels from triggering palatalization; it could of course prevent the output of *i*-epenthesis from triggering palatalization by ordering palatalization before *i*-epenthesis.

The Chi-Mwi:ni rule of prelength shortening actually represents a case of this sort. Recall that this rule does not affect a long vowel followed by another long vowel when both vowels are underlying and within the same morpheme. The rule typically applies in derived environments, however. Furthermore, there is one class of cases where PLS fails to apply in a derived context—namely, a long vowel resulting from a particular type of contraction does not shorten. For instance, an expression such as *mara ya ka:nda* 'the first time (lit. time of first)' has a contracted form *mara: ka:nda*, which is not affected by PLS. Thus, it is not correct to say that PLS applies in all derived contexts. If a long vowel is the result of contraction, it is exempt from the rule. If rule ordering is not a viable device to describe PLS in Chi-Mwi:ni, then a global rule is required that exempts from PLS certain nonderived vowels and also vowels derived by a particular rule (contraction).

We have considered so far just those cases where a rule would make reference to prior steps in the derivation of the input structure. Call this "looking back." One might ask whether there is any motivation for allowing rules to "look ahead"—that is, for there to be a condition on a rule that makes reference to subsequent steps in the derivation. "Look-ahead" rules have often been invoked in informal linguistic descriptions of the following sort: Delete an unstressed vowel unless an impermissible cluster (in the language in question) would result. A rule of this form is a look-ahead rule in the sense that you cannot tell whether to apply the rule to an input structure until you determine what the result of applying the rule (a subsequent step in the derivation) is. If the result is a permissible consonant cluster, the derivation is well-formed. If the result is an impermissible consonant cluster, the rule must not be applied.

The motivation for look-ahead rules of this type is fairly obvious. If independent rules are required to specify what is and what is not a permissible consonant cluster in the language, and if a rule of vowel deletion is sensitive to these independently motivated conditions, it is natural to seek to invoke these conditions in delimiting the scope of application of the vowel deletion rule. To build the conditions directly into the rule of vowel deletion entails repeating information. For example, in Tonkawa (Chapter 3) two-consonant clusters are not permitted if one of the consonants is glottalized. The rule of vowel elision in Tonkawa fails to apply to a vowel if either of the adjacent consonants is glottalized. To specify the environment for vowel elision as being (in part)

$$\begin{matrix} C & \underline{\quad\quad} & C \\ [-\text{glottal}] & & [-\text{glottal}] \end{matrix}$$ is to repeat (in an indirect manner) that clusters containing a glottalized consonant are not permissible.

Examples such as the one from Tonkawa are extremely common. But whether look-ahead rules must be allowed on the basis of such examples can been questioned. For instance, it might be said that since it is common for languages to avoid creating sequences by rule that are not allowed in the language, any condition on a rule that accomplishes this end is a natural condition. In the Tonkawa example, for instance, requiring that both consonants adjacent to the vowel must be nonglottalized prevents the rule from deriving clusters containing a glottalized consonant. Thus, this condition is a natural condition. The argument that we are repeating information is not pertinent, since these are natural conditions by virtue of the existence of a constraint barring clusters that contain a glottalized consonant.

If the only argument in favor of look-ahead rules is that they allow a generalization to be captured—that they avoid repeating information in different parts of the grammar—then there seems no particularly compelling reason to accept them, provided we have some other way of revealing the conditions on vowel elision in Tonkawa, for example, as motivated, not idiosyncratic conditions unrelated to any other fact about the structure of the language.

A second category of cases where look-ahead rules might find some support would be if a rule could be shown to apply to a given structure only by virtue of the fact that having done so, certain additional changes ensue. In other words one phonological change is directly correlated with some subsequent change. Klamath provides one possible example (see Kisseberth, 1973, for details). In this language there are distributive verb forms like the following.

(33)

	nondistributive	distributive	gloss
a.	*pe:w-a*	*pe-pe:w-a*	'bathe'
b.	*s²a:²-a*	*s²a-s²a:²-a*	'make someone cry'
c.	*p'et'-a*	*p'e-pt'-a*	'a hole becomes larger'
d.	*qniy'-a*	*qni-qny'-a*	'has an erection'
e.	*beqs-a*	*be-baqs-a*	'grinds'
f.	*čonw-a*	*čo-čanw-a*	'vomits'

As can be seen, distributives are formed by reduplicating the initial consonant
(cluster) of the stem and a short version of the initial vowel of the stem. If the
stem vowel is long, it remains (as in a. and b.). If it is short, it appears as *a*
(phonetically a schwa) before a consonant cluster (as in e. and f.), and as zero
before a single consonant plus vowel (as in c. and d.). We will assume here that
a rule of vowel reduction changes all short stem vowels to /a/ in distributives
and that another rule of vowel drop deletes the /a/ in the context _____ CV.
According to this analysis a form like *qni-qny'-a* receives the following derivation.

(34)   /qniy'-a/
              qni-qniy'-a   reduplication
              qni-qnay'-a   reduction
              qni-qny'-a   vowel drop

Recall from earlier discussion in this chapter the vocalization rule that vocalizes
y and *w* (plain and glottalized) to *i:* and *o:* between two consonants. This rule
appears to be active in the derivation of distributives like *si-so:g-a* (*siwg-a* 'kills')
and *nǰo-nǰi:lg-a* (*nǰoylg-a* 'is numb'). These forms could be accounted for if the
following derivations obtain.

(35)   /siwg-a/   /njoylg-a/
              si-siwg-a   *nǰo-nǰoylg-a*   reduplication
              si-sawg-a   *nǰo-nǰaylg-a*   reduction
              si-swg-a   *nǰo-nǰylg-a*   vowel drop
              si-so:g-a   *nǰo-nǰi:lg-a*   vocalization

But these derivations violate the principle of reduction according to which /a/
deletes only in the context _____CV. For in /si-sawg-a/, for example, it must
delete before the consonant cluster /wg/ and in /nǰo-nǰaylg-a/ before the cluster
/ylg/. But the striking thing to note is that these consonant clusters do not remain
consonant clusters. The first consonant in the cluster becomes a vowel. This
situation comes about, of course, as a consequence of the rule of vocalization,
which applies to the output of vowel drop.

These facts (as well as certain additional data that cannot be discussed here)
suggest a formulation of vowel drop along the following lines.

(36) *Delete the reduced vowel /a/, provided that the immediately following consonant does not appear in the ultimate phonetic representation followed by another consonant.*

In other words, /a/ deletes unless a (phonetic) consonant cluster occurs to its right in the string of sounds.

A representation like /so-sam'alw'-a/ (where the reduced vowel is underlined) will be converted to *sosm'alw'a*, since in this phonetic representation no consonant cluster occurs to the right of the reduced vowel (at any point in the derivation). Similarly, the representation /si-sawg-a/ will be converted to /si-swg-a/ and ultimately to *siso:ga*; the reduced vowel deletes in this example because the consonant cluster that occurs to its right in the UR is eliminated in the PR due to the application of vocalization. Note that given a verb like *čonwa* 'vomits', the distributive is *čočanwa*. The reduced vowel /a/ in this form cannot delete. If it were deleted, the phonetic result would be *čočnwa* (with the *n* syllabic as a consequence of a general rule in the language); *čočnwa* contains the cluster *nw* and thus violates the look-ahead condition on vowel drop stated in (36)— namely, the reduced vowel deletes only if the immediately following consonant (*n* in the present example) is *not* followed by another consonant in the phonetic representation.

If the description of Klamath we have sketched is basically correct (we believe it is, but the morphophonemics of the language are sufficiently complex so as to lead other investigators to pursue differing analyses), then the look-ahead rule would permit an appropriate derivation of examples like *siso:ga* and *nǰonǰi:lga*. (There are numerous examples of this type, incidentally.) The alternative to a look-ahead rule would be to complicate the environment for vowel drop to say either ___CV or

$$ \text{---} \left\{ \begin{matrix} y \\ w \end{matrix} \right\} \left\{ \begin{matrix} C \\ \# \end{matrix} \right\}. $$

This second environment recapitulates the environment for vocalization, of course, and fails to explain the essential unity of the conditions under which the reduced vowel /a/ may delete.

It might be pointed out that there would be nothing unnatural about not allowing the reduced vowel to drop in examples like /si-sawga/. The resulting structure is phonetically permissible in the language. Therefore, the situation is different from the Tonkawa example discussed earlier, where the result would be impermissible clusters containing a glottalized consonant, if the added condition on the vowel-elision rule were dropped. Thus, whereas the added condition in Tonkawa could be claimed necessary to avoid impermissible sequences, the same rationale is not possible for the additional context in the Klamath case. Nevertheless, the added context is not in fact something idiosyncratic, but rather a special instance of the generalization that the reduced vowel deletes if there is not a consonant cluster to its right. If additional examples similar to the

Klamath one can be adduced, then the claim that look-ahead global conditions are necessary will have a stronger basis than just the observation that rules often fail to apply if their application would yield unacceptable sound sequences in the language.

If we assume a general convention that rules are applied in the sequence that minimizes opacity, then we require either rule ordering or global conditions to describe phenomena such as counterfeeding and counterbleeding interactions of rules. We have shown how global conditions not only do much of the work of rule ordering, but also can describe situations not (apparently) describable in an appropriate manner by the device of rule ordering. We must now ask whether there are situations that global conditions cannot appropriately describe and that cannot be accounted for by a general principle (such as the one that requires rules to be sequenced in the manner that minimizes opacity).

A phenomenon that we can refer to as "mutual bleeding" poses a problem for global conditions. Some rules of Klamath illustrate mutual bleeding nicely. Recall the rule of vocalization that changes the glides y and y' to $i:$ and the glides w and w' to $o:$ in the environment

$$C\underline{\hspace{1cm}} \begin{Bmatrix} \# \\ C \end{Bmatrix}.$$

Another rule of n-drop deletes a morpheme-final n in the environment $C\underline{\hspace{1cm}}V\#$ (hence the forms, $yebn\text{-}o\text{:}l\text{-}a$ 'finishes digging', but $yeb\text{-}a$ 'digs'; $sge\text{:}n\text{-}at$ 'buy! (pl.)', but $sge\,?\text{-}a$ 'buys').* Now consider the following derivation for $swi\text{-}sw\text{-}a$, which is the distributive form of the verb $swin\text{-}a$ 'sings'.

(37)   /swin-a/
          $swi\text{-}swin\text{-}a$ reduplication
          $swi\text{-}swan\text{-}a$ vowel reduction
          $swi\text{-}swn\text{-}a$ vowel drop
          $swi\text{-}sw\text{-}a$ $n\text{-}$ drop
          inapplicable   vocalization

It will be noted that at the point where we have the form /swi-swn-a/, both n-drop and vocalization would be applicable. In this derivation n-drop has applied and derived /swi-sw-a/, a form to which vocalization is now inapplicable. In other words n-drop bleeds vocalization. If vocalization is instead applied to the structure /swi-swn-a/, the result would be /swi-so:n-a/, a structure to which n-drop would then be inapplicable. Thus, vocalization would bleed n-drop. The bleeding relationship that exists between n-drop and vocalization is two-directional. The bleeding relationships that we dealt with earlier in this chapter were all unidirectional. For example, vowel epenthesis in Yawelmani can (and

---

* The URs of the roots here are /yebn-/ and /sge?n-/. For the latter there is a rule applying after n-drop that deletes a preconsonantal glottal stop and compensatorily lengthens the preceding vowel.

does) bleed vowel shortening (given an underlying representation like /ʔa:ml-hin/), but vowel shortening can never bleed vowel epenthesis (since the latter rule is insensitive to vowel length).

According to a rule-ordering framework the Klamath example can be described by ordering n-drop before vocalization. Can a global condition provide an appropriate alternative? It is difficult to see how global conditions could be of any use in this situation. Given /swi-swn-a/, we must guarantee that n-drop and not vocalization applies. There is nothing about the prior steps in the derivation relevant to selecting the rule that is to apply. For example, it is not the case that the rule of vowel drop, which converts /swi-swan-a/ to /swi-swn-a/, *never* derives structures that undergo vocalization.

(38)   /hV-swin-e:ʔ-a/   'sings in competition with one another'
        hi-swin-e:ʔ-a   vowel copy
        hi-swan-e:ʔ-a   vowel reduction
        hi-swn-e:ʔ-a   vowel drop
        hi-so:n-e:ʔ-a   vocalization

The derivation in (38) requires that vocalization apply to structures arising from vowel drop. Thus, prior steps that result in the input structure /swi-swn-a/ seem to be irrelevant to determining whether n-drop or vocalization applies.

Furthermore, the result of applying vocalization to /swi-swn-a/ is /swi-so:n-a/, and there is nothing about this form that makes it an unacceptable output as compared with /swi-sw-a/—that is, nothing other than the fact that in /swi-so:n-a/ vocalization has applied whereas in /swi-sw-a/ it is n-drop that has applied. We must conclude, then, that there is no global property that can be used to guarantee that n-drop applies to /swi-swn-a/ and not vocalization.

To account for examples like this we must either find some general principle that will predict that n-drop and not vocalization applies, or admit into the theory of grammar some device that will produce this effect. Note that if vocalization applies, we derive /swi-so:n-a/; if n-drop applies, we derive /swi-sw-a/. There is no basis for claiming that one of these outputs results in less opacity than the other. In neither case is there a surface structure that contains structures violating a rule of the language. Furthermore, the conditions that triggered vocalization in the former case and n-drop in the latter are still present on the surface. There is no opacity either of Kiparsky's first or second type.

If there is no principle that says that /swi-so:n-a/ is an impossible output, given a grammar with the two rules of n-drop and vocalization and an input structure like /swi-swn-a/, then a language-specific device to guarantee that /swi-sw-a/ is derived must be postulated. Any device that one postulates would be somewhat akin to an ordering statement. It might be restricted in its usage so that it could be invoked just in cases of mutual bleeding—nevertheless, it would have to have the property of requiring that n-drop rather than vocalization be allowed to apply to a structure that simultaneously satisfies the conditions for both rules. Thus, even if global rules are accepted as an appropriate device for describing limitations on the applicability of phonological rules, there is a small class of cases—mutual bleeding—where something similar to an ordering statement is required.

Interestingly enough, the same thing seems true with respect to the interaction between applications of the same rule, which we dealt with in Chapter 5. Recall that we objected to the directionally-iterative theory on the grounds that it fails to relate the principles governing the interaction between applications of the same rule to those controlling the interaction between separate rules. It is relatively easy to see how this gap could be bridged in terms of the theory of rule interaction developed in this chapter. First, we might assume that, at least from the phonetic point of view, the natural multiple-application pattern is a transparent one (i.e., a feeding or bleeding pattern) and that a rule will apply to a string to produce this kind of pattern unless otherwise indicated. Secondly, we might also assume that opaque multiple-application patterns are to be handled by global conditions on the rule. For example, the counterbleeding pattern displayed by the Slovak rhythmic law could be described in terms of a global condition which would say that a vowel shortens after another vowel if that vowel was long in the original input string. The Hidatsa apocope rule would be formulated to drop a vowel that is word-final in the original input string. According to this analysis, *kiku* from /kikua/ would not have to be prevented from being an input to the apocope rule by virtue of a linear direction in the scansion of the rule. The global condition would ensure that the rule could not apply to *kiku* since the *u* is not word-final in the original input string. Although we know of no examples in which a global condition rather than a linear scansion is *required* in order to describe a multiple application pattern, this may simply be due to the fact that there are relatively few rules whose multiple-application properties have so far been studied. A hypothetical example requiring global information would be something like the following. Suppose a language has a rule raising *e* to *i* if the following syllable contains *i*. Suppose that this rule is initiated across morpheme boundaries, so that we have *tete* 'dog', but *titi-si* 'dogs' from /tete-si/. But suppose we also find *sesi* 'cat', and *sesi-si* 'cats'. That is, within morphemes, *e* is raised to *i* only if the following *i* originates from *e* via the raising rule. In particular, an *i* in the original input string does not trigger the rule within morphemes. If such examples could be shown to exist, they would add additional strength to the contention that the multiple-application problem and the interaction of separate rules are aspects of the same problem.

We noted above that if global rules are added to the theory of phonology and accorded the same power as rule ordering, there is still one type of interaction that they cannot appropriately describe—mutual bleeding. This same gap seems to occur in the multiple-application problem.

Recall the rule of high-vowel drop (HVD) of Chi-Mwi:ni (Chapter 2). This rule has two subcases. Prefixes consisting of an obstruent plus high vowel delete their vowel when a voiceless obstruent follows, whereas prefixes consisting of a sonorant plus high vowel will drop their vowel regardless of the nature of the following consonant. Both subcases of HVD share the significant limitations that deletion does not occur when these prefixes precede an object prefix or appear in the context ____CV#.

Let us consider how these two subcases interact with one another. Consider first the verbal form *wa-sh-paɬ-a* 'if they scrape', which derives from /wa-chi-paɬ-a/, where /wa/ is the 3rd pl. subject prefix and /chi/ is a conditional prefix. It is readily apparent that the conditional prefix drops its high vowel before the voiceless obstruent /p/. Compare *nchipaɬa* 'if you (pl.) scrape', from /ni-chi-paɬ-a/. The sonorant prefix /ni/ drops its vowel, but the /chi/ retains its vowel. A plausible explanation of why /chi/ retains its vowel is that once the vowel of /ni/ is dropped, a consonant cluster arises preceding the vowel of /chi/. The language does not tolerate three-consonant clusters; consequently, the consonant cluster before /chi/ could be interpreted as blocking HVD. In order to make this proposal work we would need to constrain HVD so that it does not affect a prefix vowel if a three-consonant cluster arises. Furthermore, we would have to guarantee that HVD applies to /ni/ before it applies to the conditional prefix /chi/. Application of HVD to /ni/ clearly has the effect of preventing the application of the rule to /chi/. Consequently, we have an instance of a bleeding interaction.

Since the dropping of the vowel of a sonorant prefix like /ni/ is a different subcase of HVD vis à vis the dropping of the vowel of an obstruent prefix like /chi/, it might be questioned whether a form like *nchipaɬa* illustrates that one application of a rule bleeds a second possible application of the same rule. Therefore, let us turn to an unambiguous example: *sh-chi-paɬ-a* 'if we scrape', from /chi-chi-paɬ-a/. The first prefix in this example is the 1st pl. subject prefix and the second is the conditional prefix. These two prefixes are both obstruent prefixes. Note that the subject prefix /chi/ drops its vowel, since that vowel is followed by a voiceless obstruent, namely the /ch/ at the beginning of the conditional prefix. The vowel of the conditional prefix is not, however, affected by HVD. Once again this can be explained by virtue of the proposed constraint that HVD does not affect a vowel if a three-consonant cluster would result. Implementing this analysis, however, requires that HVD apply first to the subject prefix /chi/ before any attempt at applying it to the conditional prefix. Application of the rule to the first prefix in the item inhibits application of the rule to the second prefix.

Chi-Mwi:ni provides strong evidence that the failure of HVD to apply to the *second* /chi/ prefix in *shchipaɬa* is attributable to the fact that the rule does apply to the first /chi/. Notice the following example: *chishpishiɬe* 'we cooked it' from /chi-chi-pik-i:ɬ-e/. The first /chi/ in this example is the 1st pl. subject prefix again, while the second one is an object prefix (agreeing with nouns of the /chi/ class such as *chi-su* 'knife'; *ch-a:kuja* 'food'; *sh-kapu* 'basket'). The first /chi/ prefix in *chishpishiɬe* does not undergo HVD, because of the limitation on the rule that prevents it from applying if an object prefix follows. As a result of the fact that the first /chi/ retains its vowel, the second /chi/ will be able to drop its high vowel without a three-consonant cluster arising. The fact that the second /chi/ undergoes HVD wherever the first /chi/ does not clearly establishes the bleeding interaction involved here.

One additional example will be given here to illustrate the fact that one application of HVD bleeds another application of the same rule. Consider the verbal form *nt^ha-wa-ku-gaf-a* 'they didn't make a mistake', where /nt^ha/ is a prefix used to indicate a negative perfective verbal form, /wa/ is the 3rd pl. subject prefix, /ku/ is the infinitive prefix (which is used in Chi-Mwi:ni in certain finite verbal forms as well as the infinitive). Compare *nt^ha-wa-x-kas-a* 'they didn't hear', where we see that the prefix /ku/ has undergone HVD as a conse-quence of appearing before a verb root with an initial voiceless obstruent. Now compare *nt^ha-sh-ku-kas-a* 'we didn't hear', from /nt^ha-chi-ku-kas-a/. In this example the 1st pl. subject prefix /chi/ precedes the infinitive marker. Since the infinitive marker begins with a voiceless obstruent, it triggers the deletion of the vowel of /chi/. HVD does not, however, affect the /ku/ in this example, even though /ku/ precedes a root with an initial voiceless obstruent. Once again the explanation for this phenomenon seems to clearly be the fact that application of HVD to /chi/ creates a consonant cluster that inhibits application of the rule to /ku/.

Note that in terms of the theory we sketched above, there is no way to ensure that it is the vowel of /chi/ rather than the vowel of /ku/ that is dropped in /nt^ha-chi-ku-kas-a/. Dropping of the vowel of /chi/ would bleed dropping of the vowel in /ku/ and vice versa. Thus, the general convention to select the applicational pattern that results in transparency would not determine which of the two vowels to drop. Similarly, there is nothing in the derivational history of /chi/ that would explain why its vowel should be lost as opposed to the vowel in /ku/. Hence, a global condition on the rule is of no use. It appears, therefore, that we require some kind of ad hoc statement analogous to a direction of iteration in order to explain why the first vowel deletes but not the second. It is striking that mutual bleeding interactions lead to this result in both the interaction between separate rules, as shown by the Klamath example discussed earlier, and in the interaction between applications of the same rule. This fact lends further support to the contention that these two problems are merely different aspects of the same general problem.

The question of how rule applications interact with one another, and how best to describe these interactions, remains a subject of much discussion. We have not attempted to discuss here all of the positions that have been taken on this subject. Rather, we have attempted to explore certain aspects of the problem that we find particularly interesting.

References

ALLEN, W. S. (1956). Structure and system in the Abaza verbal complex. *Transactions of the Philological Society*, 127–176.

ANDERSON, STEPHEN (1969). *West Scandinavian vowel systems and the ordering of phonological rules.* Bloomington, Indiana: Indiana University Linguistics Club.

ANDERSON, STEPHEN (1974). *The organization of phonology.* New York: Academic Press.

BARKAI, MALACHI (1972). *Problems in the phonology of Israeli Hebrew.* Unpublished University of Illinois Ph.D. thesis.

BARKER, M. A. R. (1963). *Klamath dictionary.* University of California Publications in Linguistics **31**. Berkeley and Los Angeles: University of California Press.

BEACH, D. M. (1938). *The phonetics of the Hotentot language.* Cambridge.

BECKER, LEE (1974). A rule inversion in Polish. Unpublished ms., University of Illinois.

BENDER, BYRON (1968). Marshallese phonology. *Oceanic Linguistics* **8**, 16–35.

BENDER, BYRON (1969). *Spoken Marshallese.* Honolulu: University of Hawaii Press.

BENDER, BYRON (1970). Vowel dissimilation in Marshallese. *University of Hawaii Working Papers in Linguistics* **1:1**, 88–96.

BEVER, THOMAS (1967). *Leonard Bloomfield and the phonology of the Menomini language.* Unpublished Massachusetts Institute of Technology Ph.D. thesis.

BHATIA, TEJ & MICHAEL KENSTOWICZ (1972). Nasalization in Hindi: a reconsideration. *Papers in Linguistics* **5**, 202–212.

BLOOMFIELD, LEONARD (1939). Menomini morphophonemics. *Travaux du Cercle Linguistique de Prague* **8**, 105–115.

BOAS, FRANZ & ELLA DELORIA (1939). *Dakota grammar. National Academy of Sciences Memoirs* **23**.

BRIGHT, WILLIAM (1957). *The Karok language. University of California Publications in Linguistics* **13**. Berkeley and Los Angeles: University of California Press.

BURROW, T. (1970). *The Pengo language*. Oxford: The Clarendon Press.

CAMPBELL, LYLE (1973). *Extrinsic ordering lives*. Bloomington, Indiana: Indiana University Linguistics Club.

CHOMSKY, NOAM & MORRIS HALLE (1968). *The sound pattern of English*. New York: Harper and Row.

COOK, T. L. (1969). *The Efik consonant system*. Unpublished ms., University of Ibadan.

DELL, FRANÇOIS (1973). Two cases of exceptional ordering. In M. Bierwisch et al. (Eds.), *Generative grammar in Europe*. Dortrecht: Reidel.

FOSTER, MARY & GEORGE (1947). *Sierra Popoluca speech*. Smithsonian Institution, Institute of Social Anthropology, Publication **8**. Washington, D.C.

FROMKIN, VICTORIA (1971). The non-anomalous nature of anomalous utterances. *Language* **47**, 27–54.

FROMKIN, VICTORIA (1975). When does a test test a hypothesis, or, What counts as evidence? In D. Cohen and J. Wirth (Eds.), *Testing linguistic hypotheses*. New York: Wiley.

GEYTENBEEK, BRIAN & HELEN (1971). *Gidabal grammar and dictionary*. Australian Institute of Aboriginal Studies **43**. Canberra.

HAAS, MARY (1940). Tunica. *Handbook of American Indian languages* **4**. Smithsonian Institution, Bureau of American Ethnography, Washington, D.C.

HALE, KENNETH (1973). *Deep-surface canonical disparities in relation to analysis and change: an Australian example Current Trends in Linguistics* **11**, 401–458.

HALLE, MORRIS (1964). Phonology in generative grammar. In Jerry Fodor and Jerrold Katz (Eds.), *The structure of language*, Englewood Cliffs, New Jersey: Prentice-Hall.

HALLE, MORRIS (1973). The accentuation of Russian words. *Language* **49**, 312–348.

HARRIES, LYNDON (1950). *A grammar of Mwera*. Johannesburg: University of Witwatersrand Press.

HARRIS, ZELLIG (1942). Morpheme alternants in linguistic analysis. *Language* **18**, 169–180.

HAWKINS, W. (1950). Patterns of vowel loss in Macushi (Carib). *International Journal of American Linguistics* **16**, 87–90.

HOIJER, HARRY (1933). Tonkawa: an Indian language of Texas. *Handbook of American Indian languages* **3**. New York.

HOMBERT, JEAN (1973). Speaking backwards in Bakwiri. *Studies in African Linguistics* **4**, 227–236.

HOOPER, JOAN (1972). The syllable in generative phonology. *Language* **48**, 525–540.

HOOPER, JOAN (1973). *Aspects of natural generative phonology*. Bloomington Indiana: Indiana University Linguistics Club.

HOOPER, JOAN (1974). Rule morphologization in natural generative grammar. In A. Bruck et al. (Eds.), *Papers from the parasession on natural phonology*. Chicago: Chicago Linguistics Society.

HULSTAERT, G. (1957). *Dictionnaire Lɔmɔ́ngɔ-français*. Annales du Musée Royal du Congo Belge. Tervuren. Linguistique **16**.

ISAČENKO, A. V. (1970). East Slavic morphophonemics and the treatment of the jers in Russian: a revision of Havlik's Law. *International Journal of Slavic Linguistics and Poetics* **13**, 73–124.

JACOBSEN, W. (1964). *A grammar of the Washo language*. Unpublished University of California, Berkeley Ph.D. thesis.

JAKOBSON, ROMAN (1948). Russian conjugation. *Word* **4**, 155–167.

JAKOBSON, ROMAN (1949). The phonemic and grammatical aspects of language in their interrelations. In R. Jakobson, *Selected writings*. Vol. II. The Hague: Mouton.

JAKOBSON, ROMAN (1965). Stroj ukrainskogo imperativa. In R. Jakobson, *Selected Writings*. Vol. II. The Hague: Mouton.

JOHNSON, C. D. (1971). Unbounded expressions in rules of stress and accent. *Glossa* **4:2**, 185–196.

KAYE, JOHNATHAN (1974a). Constraintes profondes en phonologie: les emprunts. Unpublished ms.

KAYE, JOHNATHAN (1974b). Morpheme structure constraints live! *Montreal Working Papers in Linguistics* **3**, 55–62.

KENSTOWICZ, MICHAEL (1972a). Lithuanian phonology. *Studies in the Linguistic Sciences* **2:2**, 1–85. Urbana, Illinois: Dept. of Linguistics, University of Illinois.

KENSTOWICZ, MICHAEL (1972b). The morphophonemics of the Slovak noun. *Papers in Linguistics* **5**, 556–567.

KENSTOWICZ, MICHAEL & CHARLES KISSEBERTH (1971). Unmarked bleeding orders. In Charles Kisseberth (Ed.), *Studies in generative phonology*. Edmonton, Alberta: Linguistic Research, Inc.

KIPARSKY, PAUL (1965). *Phonological change*. Bloomington, Indiana: Indiana University Linguistics Club.

KIPARSKY, PAUL (1968a). How abstract is phonology? Bloomington, Indiana: Indiana University Linguistics Club. Also in O. Fujimura (Ed.), *Three dimensions of linguistic theory*. Tokyo: TEC.

KIPARSKY, PAUL (1968b). Linguistic universals and linguistic change. In E. Bach and R. Harms (Eds.), *Universals in linguistic theory*. New York: Holt.

KIPARSKY, PAUL (1971). Historical linguistics. In W. Dingwall (Ed.), *A survey of linguistic science*. College Park: University of Maryland.

KIPARSKY, PAUL (1973). Abstractness, opacity, and global rules. Bloomington, Indiana: Indiana University Linguistics Club. Also in O. Fujimura (ed.). *Three dimensions of linguistic theory*. Tokyo: TEC.

KIPARSKY, V. (1963). *Russische historische grammatik*. Heidelberg.

KISSEBERTH, CHARLES (1970). On the functional unity of phonological rules. *Linguistic Inquiry* **1**, 291–306.

KISSEBERTH, CHARLES (1973). On the alternation of vowel length in Klamath: a global rule. In Michael Kenstowicz and Charles Kisseberth (Eds.), *Issue in phonological theory*. The Hague: Mouton.

KNUDSON, LYLE (1975). A natural phonology and morphophonemics of Chimalapa Zoque. *Papers in Linguistics* **8**, 283–346.

KRUEGER, J. (1962). *Yakut manual*. Uralic and Altaic series **21**. Bloomington Indiana: Indiana University.

KUMBARACI, T. (1966). Consonantally conditioned alternation of vocalic morphophonemes in Turkish. *Anthropological Linguistics* **8**, 11–24.

LAKOFF, GEORGE (1965). *On the nature of syntactic irregularity*. Harvard Computational Laboratory Progress Report no. NSF-16.

LANGDON, MARGARET (1975). Boundaries and lenition in Yuman languages. *International Journal of American Linguistics* **41**, 218–233.

LEBEN, WILLIAM & DAUDA M. BAGARI (1975). A note on the base forms of the Hausa verb. *Studies in African Linguistics* **6**. 239–248.

LEES, ROBERT B (1961). *The phonology of modern standard Turkish*. Uralic and Altaic series **6**. Bloomington Indiana: Indiana University.

LEOPOLD, WERNER (1930). Polarity in language. *Language* **7**, 102–109.

LIGHTNER, THEODORE (1968). On the use of minor rules in Russian phonology. *Journal of Linguistics* **4**, 69–72.

LIGHTNER, THEODORE (1969). On the alternation $e \sim o$ in modern Russian. *Linguistics* **54**, 44–69.

LIGHTNER, THEODORE (1972). *Problems in the theory of phonology: Russian phonology and Turkish phonology*. Edmonton, Alberta: Linguistic Research, Inc.

LIGHTNER, THEODORE (1974). A problem in the analysis of some vowel $\sim$ zero alternations in modern Russian. In Michael Flier (Ed.), *Slavic Forum*. The Hague: Mouton.

MATTESON, ESTER (1965). *The Piro (Arawakan) language. University of California Publications in Linguistics* **42**. Berkeley and Los Angeles: University of California Press.

MCCAWLEY, JAMES D. (1967). Sapir's phonological representation. *International Journal of American Linguistics* **33**, 106–111.

MCCLENDON, SALLY (1975). *A grammar of Eastern Pomo*. Berkeley and Los Angeles: University of California Press.

MEEUSEN, A. E. (1959). *Essai de grammaire rundi*. Tervuren. Musée Royal du Congo Belge.

MORIN, YVES (1970). Syntax and phonology meets at more than one point. *University of Michigan Phonetics Laboratory Notes* **6**, 6–11. Ann Arbor, Michigan.

MORIN, YVES & JOYCE FRIEDMAN (1971). *Phonological grammar tester. Underlying theory. Natural Language Studies* **10**. Ann Arbor, Michigan: University of Michigan Phonetics Laboratory.

NARANG, G. C. & D. A. BECKER (1971). Aspiration and nasalization in the generative phonology of Hindi-Urdu. *Language* 47, 646–667.

NEWMAN, PAUL (1973). Grades, vowel tone classes and extensions in the Hausa verbal system. *Studies in African Linguistics* 4, 297–346.

NEWMAN, STANLEY (1944). *Yokuts language of California. Viking Fund Publications in Anthropology* 2. New York.

ORR, CAROLYN (1962). Ecuador Quichua phonology. In B. Elson (Ed.), *Studies in Ecuadorian Indian languages* 1. Norman, Oklahoma: Summer Institute of Linguistics.

OSBORN, HENRY (1966). Warao I: phonology and morphophonemics. *International Journal of American Linguistics* 32, 108–123.

PAN'KEVICH, I. (1938). *Ukrain'ski hovory pidkarpac'koji rusi i sumežnyx oblastej*. Prague.

PIGGOTT, G. (1971). *Some implications of Algonquian palatalization*. Odawa Language Project, First Report. University of Toronto, Dept. of Anthropology, Anthropological Series no. 9.

PIGGOTT, G. (1974). *Aspects of Odawa morphophonemics*. Unpublished University of Toronto Ph.D. thesis.

PIKE, KENNETH (1948). *Tone languages*. Ann Arbor: University of Michigan Press.

POSTAL, PAUL (1968). *Aspects of phonological theory*. New York: Harper and Row.

PYLE, CHARLES (1972). On eliminating BM's. *Proceedings from the 8th regional meeting*, 516–532. Chicago: Chicago Linguistics Society.

RODEGEM, F. M. (1970). *Dictionnaire Rundi-français*. Tervuren, Musée Royal de l'Afrique Central.

SAPIR, EDWARD (1925). Sound patterns in language. *Language* 1, 37–51.

SAPIR, EDWARD & MORRIS SWADESH (1939). *Nootka Texts*. Baltimore: Linguistics Society of America.

SAPORTA, SOL (1965). Ordered rules, dialect differences and historical processes. *Language* 41, 218–224.

SCHANE, SANFORD, 1972. Some diachronic deletion processes and their synchronic consequences in French. In Mario Saltarelli and Dieter Wanner (Eds.), *Diachronic Studies in Romance Linguistics*. The Hague: Mouton, 1975.

SCHENKER, ALEXANDER (1966). *Beginning Polish*, Vol. 1. New Haven: Yale University Press.

SCHUH, RUSSELL (1972). Rule inversion in Chadic. *Studies in African Linguistics* 3, 379–397.

SHERZER, JOEL (1970). Talking backwards in Cuna. *Southwestern Journal of Anthropology* 26, 343–353.

SELKIRK, ELISABETH & JEAN-ROGER VERGNAUD (1973). How abstract is French phonology? *Foundations of Language* 10, 249–254.

TERSIS, NICOLE (1972). Le Zarma (République du Niger): Etude du parler djerma de Dosso. *Société d'études linguistiques et anthropologiques de France* 33-34. Paris.

TOPPING, DONALD (1968). Chamorro vowel harmony. *Oceanic Linguistics* 7, 67–79.

TUCKER, A. N. (1969). Review of Amaat Burssens, Problemen en inventarisatie van de verbale struckturen in het dho alur (Nordoost-Kongo). *Journal of African Languages* 8, 125–126.

VENNEMANN, THEO (1972a). Rule inversion. *Lingua* 29, 209–242.

VENNEMANN, THEO (1972b). On the theory of syllabic phonology. *Linguistische Berichte* 18, 1–18.

VENNEMANN, THEO (1974). Phonological concreteness in natural generative grammar. In Roger Shuy and C. -J. Bailey (Eds.), *Towards tomorrow's linguistics*. Washington, D.C.: Georgetown University Press.

WANG, WILLIAM S-Y. (1968). Vowel features, paired variables, and the English vowel shift. *Language* 44, 695–708.

WATERHOUSE, VIOLA (1949). Learning a second language first. *International Journal of American Linguistics* 15, 106–109.

WELMERS, WILLIAM (1968). *Efik*. Institute of African Studies, Occasional Publications 16. University of Ibadan.

WELMERS, WILLIAM (1973). *African language structures*. Berkeley and Los Angeles: University of California Press.

WELMERS, WILLIAM & BEATRICE WELMERS (1969). Noun modifiers in Igbo. *International Journal of American Linguistics* **35**, 315–322.

WILBUR, RONNIE (1973). *The phonology of reduplication*. Bloomington, Indiana. Indiana University Linguistics Club.

ZIMMER, KARL (1975). Some thoughts on likely phonologies for non-ideal speakers. In R. Grossman et al. (Eds.), *Papers from the parasession on functionalism*. Chicago: Chicago Linguistics Society.

Language Index

Subject Index